Electoral Politics and Africa's Urban Transition

Two aspects of contemporary urban life in Africa are often described as sources of political change: the emergence of a large urban middle class, and high levels of ethnic diversity and interethnic social contact. Many expected that these factors would help spark a transition away from ethnic competition and clientelism toward more programmatic elections. Focusing on urban Ghana, this book shows that the growing middle class and high levels of ethnic diversity are not having the anticipated political effects. Instead, urban Ghana is stuck in a trap: clientelism and ethnic voting persist in many urban neighborhoods despite changes to the socioeconomic characteristics and policy preferences of voters. Through a unique examination of intra-urban variation in patterns of electoral competition, Nathan explains why this trap exists, demonstrates its effects on political behavior, and explores how new democracies such as Ghana can move past it.

Noah L. Nathan is Assistant Professor of Political Science at the University of Michigan.

Cambridge Studies in Comparative Politics

General Editors

Kathleen Thelen *Massachusetts Institute of Technology*
Erik Wibbels *Duke University*

Associate Editors

Catherine Boone *London School of Economics*
Thad Dunning *University of California, Berkeley*
Anna Grzymala-Busse *Stanford University*
Torben Iversen *Harvard University*
Stathis Kalyvas *Yale University*
Margaret Levi *Stanford University*
Helen Milner *Princeton University*
Frances Rosenbluth *Yale University*
Susan Stokes *Yale University*
Tariq Thachil *Vanderbilt University*

Series Founder

Peter Lange *Duke University*

Other Books in the Series

Christopher Adolph, *Bankers, Bureaucrats, and Central Bank Politics: The Myth of Neutrality*
Michael Albertus, *Autocracy and Redistribution: The Politics of Land Reform*
Santiago Anria, *When Movements Become Parties: The Bolivian MAS in Comparative Perspective*
Ben W. Ansell, *From the Ballot to the Blackboard: The Redistributive Political Economy of Education*
Ben W. Ansell and David J. Samuels, *Inequality and Democratization: An Elite-Competition Approach*
Ana Arjona, *Rebelocracy: Social Order in the Colombian Civil War*
Leonardo R. Arriola, *Multi-Ethnic Coalitions in Africa: Business Financing of Opposition Election Campaigns*
David Austen-Smith, Jeffry A. Frieden, Miriam A. Golden, Karl Ove Moene, and Adam Przeworski, eds., *Selected Works of Michael Wallerstein: The Political Economy of Inequality, Unions, and Social Democracy*
S. Erdem Aytaç and Susan C. Stokes *Why Bother? Rethinking Participation in Elections and Protests*
Andy Baker, *The Market and the Masses in Latin America: Policy Reform and Consumption in Liberalizing Economies*

Continued after the index

Electoral Politics and Africa's Urban Transition

Class and Ethnicity in Ghana

NOAH L. NATHAN
University of Michigan

CAMBRIDGE
UNIVERSITY PRESS

CAMBRIDGE
UNIVERSITY PRESS

University Printing House, Cambridge CB2 8BS, United Kingdom

One Liberty Plaza, 20th Floor, New York, NY 10006, USA

477 Williamstown Road, Port Melbourne, VIC 3207, Australia

314-321, 3rd Floor, Plot 3, Splendor Forum, Jasola District Centre, New Delhi - 110025, India

79 Anson Road, #06-04/06, Singapore 079906

Cambridge University Press is part of the University of Cambridge.

It furthers the University's mission by disseminating knowledge in the pursuit of education, learning and research at the highest international levels of excellence.

www.cambridge.org
Information on this title: www.cambridge.org/9781108468183
DOI: 10.1017/9781108594820

© Noah L. Nathan 2019

This publication is in copyright. Subject to statutory exception and to the provisions of relevant collective licensing agreements, no reproduction of any part may take place without the written permission of Cambridge University Press.

First published 2019
First paperback edition 2020

A catalogue record for this publication is available from the British Library

ISBN 978-1-108-47495-5 Hardback
ISBN 978-1-108-46818-3 Paperback

Cambridge University Press has no responsibility for the persistence or accuracy of URLs for external or third-party internet websites referred to in this publication, and does not guarantee that any content on such websites is, or will remain, accurate or appropriate.

Contents

Figures	*page* viii
Tables	ix
Acknowledgments	xi

I INTRODUCTION

1 Urban Politics in a Trap — 3
   1.1 The Puzzle — 7
   1.2 The Argument — 19
   1.3 Contributions — 29
   1.4 The Case and Empirical Strategy — 35
   1.5 Plan of the Book — 38

2 Urban Ghana in Context — 40
   2.1 The Growth of Greater Accra — 40
   2.2 The Explanatory Variables — 44
   2.3 Spatial Geography of Greater Accra — 54
   2.4 Comparison to Urban Growth Elsewhere in Africa — 65
   2.5 Ghana's Political System — 73
   2.6 Extensions to Other Political Systems — 82
   2.7 Summary — 85

II THE MIDDLE CLASS AND PROGRAMMATIC POLITICS

3 Class and Preferences — 89
   3.1 Particularistic versus Universalistic Preferences — 91
   3.2 Effects of Class on Preferences — 93
   3.3 The Survey Data — 94
   3.4 Measuring Demands — 96

	3.5	Differences by Class and Location	100
	3.6	Summary	104
4	**Credibility, Patronage, and Participation**	105
	4.1	The Credibility Problem	107
	4.2	Data Sources	117
	4.3	Evidence	118
	4.4	Summary	144

III   NEIGHBORHOODS AND ETHNIC COMPETITION

5	**Ethnic Competition across Neighborhoods**	149
	5.1	A Puzzle: Neighborhood-level Variation in Greater Accra	152
	5.2	Where Is There Ethnic Favoritism in Cities?	157
	5.3	Patterns of Ethnic Voting	168
	5.4	Extensions	173
	5.5	Summary	178
6	**Distributive Politics in Urban Areas**	180
	6.1	Mixed Targeting of Particularistic Goods	181
	6.2	The Roots of Favoritism	188
	6.3	Neighborhood Characteristics and Particularistic goods Distribution	193
	6.4	Comparison to Rural Areas	203
	6.5	Summary	209
7	**Neighborhood Context, Expectations of Favoritism, and Voting**	210
	7.1	Vote Choice in Presidential Elections	213
	7.2	The Mechanism: Favoritism Expectations	226
	7.3	Alternative Explanations	230
	7.4	The Ga: An Exception that Proves the Rule?	236
	7.5	Summary	241

IV   IMPLICATIONS FOR URBAN GOVERNANCE

8	**Turnout Inequality and Capture in Municipal Elections**	245
	8.1	Ghana's Local Government System	247
	8.2	Low Turnout and Its Consequences	251
	8.3	Favoritism in District Assemblies	255
	8.4	Quantitative Data Sources	258
	8.5	Analysis	259
	8.6	Summary	275
9	**Paths out of the Trap?**	277
	9.1	External Cases: The US and Latin America	280

	9.2	What Could Break the Trap in Urban Ghana? The Cases Applied	290
	9.3	Conclusion	304
A	**Data Appendix**		306
	A.1	Urban Survey Sampling Procedure	306
	A.2	Rural Survey Sampling Procedure	307
	A.3	Calculation of Neighborhood Characteristics	308
	A.4	Calculation of the Neighborhood Wealth Index	308
	A.5	Summary Statistics for the Urban Survey	309
	A.6	Interviews and Focus Groups in Greater Accra	310
	A.7	Coding Rules for Manifestos	310
	A.8	Survey Experiment Prompts and Conditions	312
	A.9	Coding Ethnicity of Assembly Candidates	317
	A.10	Polling Station Survey Sample	317

Bibliography 320
Index 338

Figures

1.1	The trap	page 5
1.2	Proportion middle or upper class in urban Ghana	10
1.3	Ethnic diversity in Ghana by census enumeration area	14
1.4	Chapter organization	39
2.1	Map of Ghana	42
2.2	Greater Accra metropolitan area	44
2.3	Urban Greater Accra at different scales	55
2.4	Distribution of middle-class residents in Greater Accra	58
2.5	Majority ethnic groups in Greater Accra	63
2.6	Comparison in size of urban middle class from DHS surveys	71
2.7	Levels of competitiveness within Greater Accra	81
4.1	The ideological muddle	123
4.2	Overlapping promises	124
5.1	Ethnic voting in four neighborhoods of Greater Accra	154
6.1	Reported goods delivery by survey sampling cluster	196
7.1	First differences in the probability of voting for the co-ethnic party	219
7.2	Change in the probability of voting for the NDC	223
7.3	First differences for the co-ethnic party treatment effect	228
8.1	Example of spatial segregation of Ga residents by electoral area	269
A.1	Balance for survey experiment treatment conditions	318

Tables

1.1	Neighborhood-level variation in ethnic voting	page 26
2.1	Middle class size and ethnic composition by parliamentary constituency	61
2.2	Class status by ethnicity in urban Greater Accra	65
2.3	Urban population in sub-Saharan Africa's democratic or hybrid regimes	67
2.4	Twenty-five largest cities in African countries with competitive elections	69
3.1	Typical voter demands by category and topic	98
3.2	Universalistic preferences, by socioeconomic status and local need	101
4.1	Overlapping manifestos: NDC and NPP 2012 campaign pledges	121
4.2	Survey experiment: credibility of MPs' campaign promises	132
4.3	Campaign mobilization, by neighborhood wealth and socioeconomic status	136
4.4	Turnout and participation, by universalistic preferences	140
5.1	Ethnic favoritism from the perspective of a Group A voter	166
5.2	Vote choice for a Group A voter	171
6.1	Typical goods delivered by local politicians	195
6.2	Respondent reports of goods distribution (urban sample)	199
6.3	Respondent reports of private goods distribution (rural sample)	207
7.1	Vote choice for a Group A voter	215

7.2	Support for ethnically aligned party in the 2012 presidential election	218
8.1	Turnout in 2010 and 2015 district assembly elections in Greater Accra	262
8.2	Reported helpfulness of assembly members	267
8.3	Distribution of roads, schools, and streetlights in Greater Accra	273
A.1	Summary statistics for the urban survey	309
A.2	Treatment permutations in the survey experiment in Chapter 4	312
A.3	Differences in means, co-ethnic name treatment	315
A.4	Balance after treatment assignment for survey experiment (from Chapter 7)	316

Acknowledgments

Many people helped make this book possible. At Harvard, I am thankful for the guidance of my dissertation committee: Robert Bates, Steven Levitsky, and Nahomi Ichino. They were all instrumental in shaping this project from its earliest stages. Nahomi Ichino in particular has been a supportive mentor, collaborator, and now colleague throughout the research on this book. I am also grateful to Julie Faller, Robert Schub, and Ariel White for their friendship and insights from the very first brainstorming to the final drafts.

At Michigan, I thank Allen Hicken, Pauline Jones, Ken Kollman, Brian Min, and Anne Pitcher for their feedback and advice. Karen Ferree and Rachel Beatty Riedl provided incredible suggestions for improving the manuscript at my book workshop. At other points, elements of the argument and analysis benefited from the comments of Adam Auerbach, Adam Glynn, Shelby Grossman, Alisha Holland, Kathleen Klaus, Horacio Larreguy, John Marshall, Jeffrey Paller, Jonathan Phillips, Amanda Pinkston, Daniel Posner, Amanda Robinson, and Benjamin Schneer, as well as the helpful comments of the anonymous reviewers.

Data collection was supported financially by a National Science Foundation Graduate Research Fellowship, the Weatherhead Center for International Affairs at Harvard, and the Institute for Quantitative Social Science at Harvard. I am indebted to Dr. Franklin Oduro and the staff of the Ghana Center for Democratic Development for hosting me during my time in Ghana. At CDD, the friendship and advice of Adu Kakra Duayeden made much of the initial fieldwork possible. Primary research assistance in the field was provided by Alhassan Ibn Abdallah,

Francis Addo, Mahmuda Ainoo, and Maame Gyesiwa Sam. I also thank Dr. Philomena Nyarko and Rosalind Quartey of the Ghana Statistical Service and Anthony Amedzakey and Alex Poku Akubia of the Electoral Commission of Ghana for assistance in securing key data sources.

Finally, I thank my family for their support: my parents, for pushing me to explore the world and for supporting me as my life has run off in a direction they probably never expected; and, most importantly, Mai Hassan. No one has given more feedback on this book than she has. I can't imagine having written this without her along for the ride.

PART I

INTRODUCTION

1

Urban Politics in a Trap

Cities across the developing world are growing rapidly. The urban population in sub-Saharan Africa has increased by 250 million people since 1990.[1] Many African countries are now approaching – or have already passed – a critical threshold: a demographic transition to becoming majority urban societies. Scholars and policymakers often expect several features of contemporary urban areas to be conducive to an additional, political transition – a move away from the ethnic competition and clientelism that are thought to hinder democratic accountability in many of these countries. But broad political transformations should not be expected to follow from the demographic transformations underway across urban Africa.

Two aspects of urban life in particular are held up as potential sources of political change: the emergence of a large urban middle class; and high levels of ethnic diversity and interethnic social contact. Decades of economic growth have created a burgeoning middle class in Africa, concentrated in urban areas. The middle class is now estimated to include 120 million people in sub-Saharan Africa, comprising a potentially pivotal share of the electorate in the continent's more developed cities.[2] Higher incomes and higher levels of education are thought to change the demands that voters place on politicians, reducing voters' susceptibility to clientelism and creating a constituency for policy-based elections. Middle-class voters in cities are also expected to place less emphasis on

---

[1] United Nations (2014).
[2] African Development Bank (2011). In Chapter 2, I discuss different conceptualizations of the urban middle class and competing approaches to estimating its size.

ethnicity. In addition, contemporary African cities can be incredibly ethnically diverse, to a far greater extent than most rural areas. Sustained contact with other groups is thought to reduce the salience of ethnicity. Living in ethnically diverse areas has also been argued to reduce voters' instrumental incentives to support co-ethnic parties and politicians.

I examine the electoral effects of the growth of the middle class and high levels of ethnic diversity on political behavior in cities using the case of urban Ghana. I focus on the country's largest metropolitan area, Greater Accra, an economically booming, diverse, politically competitive metropolis of four million people. Ghana is a majority urban country at the leading edge of recent trends in urban growth across Africa and provides structural conditions – well-institutionalized parties, a peaceful history, and a relatively well-educated population – that should be among the most conducive of any in Africa to the emergence of programmatic, policy-based electoral competition.

At first glance, I find some evidence consistent with these expected transformations: many middle class voters in Greater Accra have different preferences and place different demands on politicians than poor voters; clientelism is virtually nonexistent in most of the city's middle- and upper-class areas; ethnicity is not a significant determinant of vote choice in diverse, middle- and upper-class neighborhoods of the city, in contrast to much of the rest of Ghana.

But evidence from other neighborhoods in the same city suggests that the expected transformations are not happening. Instead, ethnic competition and clientelism are thriving. Voters, even those in the middle class, still expect the government resources they receive to depend on ethnicity. Ethnicity strongly predicts vote choice in most of the city – including in middle and upper class neighborhoods when they are ethnically segregated. Wealthier and better educated voters are no less likely overall to support ethnically aligned parties than poor voters. In urban slums, individual-level clientelistic relationships between parties and voters appear even more extensive than in most rural areas.

No transition to programmatic politics appears to be occurring. Electoral competition is not becoming more programmatic as the middle class grows, with Ghana's major parties instead converging on effectively identical platforms that often bear little correspondence to how they govern. Politicians are differentially ignoring policy-motivated voters on the campaign trail while concentrating on nonprogrammatic forms of mobilization. Urban middle-class voters who demand programmatic policies

Urban Politics in a Trap 5

```
┌──────────────────────────────┐      ┌──────────────────────────────┐
│ Demand for particularistic   │      │ Credibility problem:         │
│ goods:                       │      │ cannot commit to             │
│ vulnerability to clientelism │      │ programmatic policies        │
└──────────────────────────────┘      └──────────────────────────────┘
                    ↘                    ↙
                    ┌──────────────────────────────┐
                    │ Turnout inequality:          │
                    │ policy-demanding voters      │
                    │ differentially exit          │
                    └──────────────────────────────┘
                    ↙                    ↙
            ┌──────────────────────────────┐
            │ Nonprogrammatic appeals:     │
            │ particularistic goods        │
            │ distributed as patronage     │
            └──────────────────────────────┘
                        ↘
                        ┌──────────────────────────────┐
                        │ Ethnic competition:          │
                        │ in many, but not all,        │
                        │ neighborhoods                │
                        └──────────────────────────────┘
                    ↙                    ↙
            ┌──────────────────────────────┐
            │ Low-quality governance:      │
            │ favoritism and capture       │
            └──────────────────────────────┘
```

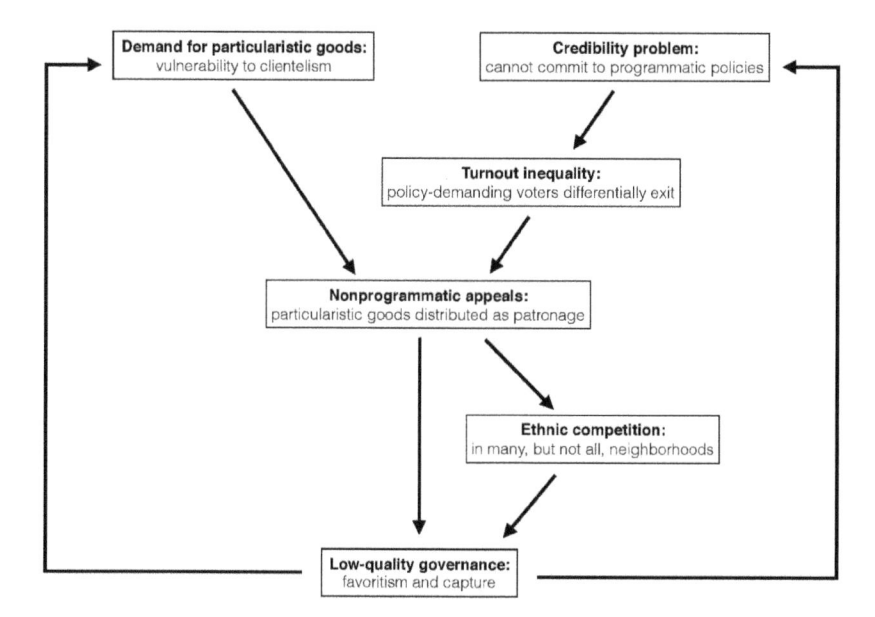

FIGURE 1.1: *The trap.*

are disproportionately opting out of participation, rather than changing underlying patterns of electoral politics.

Rather than being pulled in a new direction by demographic and socioeconomic change, electoral competition in urban Ghana appears to be *caught in a trap*. The trap is outlined in Figure 1.1. Voter demands for particularistic goods that can be exchanged as patronage are rooted in the state's inability to meet many of the service-delivery challenges created by urbanization. These demands sustain the viability of nonprogrammatic appeals that target scarce resources selectively. At the same time, low state capacity hampers politicians' ability to credibly commit to deliver programmatic policies. In the face of this credibility problem, voters who demand policy rather than patronage – most of whom are in the growing urban middle class – differentially refrain from political participation because they do not believe politicians will ever address their preferences. This reinforces politicians' incentives to concentrate on non-programmatic appeals. As patronage distribution dominates elections, voters expect politicians to primarily benefit favored ethnic groups, continuing to polarize voting along ethnic lines in much of the city. In the last step, ethnic voting and the differential abstention of policy-demanding voters allows narrow interest groups to capture city governments, producing inefficient allocations of already limited state resources. This only reinforces voter demand for scarce particularistic goods that can be targeted as patronage, forestalls investments in building local state capacity, and deepens beliefs that urban politicians cannot commit to delivering programmatic policies.

This book explains why this trap exists, shows its effects on political behavior, and explores how societies such as Ghana can move past it. My argument explores the interplay of voters' demands for different goods and policies and politicians' incentives to supply goods and policies in return. The trap in Figure 1.1 has emerged because urban politicians' incentives to supply nonprogrammatic electoral appeals remain fixed despite changes in voters' demands. My central analytic focus is on *intra-urban variation*, exploiting the fact that there are places *within the city at the same time* where clientelism or ethnic competition are prevalent and where they are largely absent. Explaining these within-city differences demonstrates the forces underlying Figure 1.1 and shows that the main constraints on a further shift away from nonprogrammatic and ethnic politics are on the *supply side*, rooted in the structural incentives of politicians to offer new appeals, not in further changes to the underlying socioeconomic characteristics of urban voters.[3]

Exploring the roots of this trap makes several contributions. It helps undercut common assumptions about urban Africa and explain how political competition operates in the continent's contemporary cities, a subject that has received little systematic study. It also provides an opportunity to refine general theories of political behavior, especially those focusing on the effects of neighborhood context on voters, the political salience of ethnicity, and the causes of class-based differences in participation. But perhaps most importantly, explaining the roots of this trap helps better understand what it takes to move away from nonprogrammatic politics in new democracies writ large. Many developing countries appear stuck in similar self-reinforcing cycles in which current clientelism and other forms of nonprogrammatic politics strengthen incentives for nonprogrammatic politics into the future.[4] Recent research suggests that countries can fall deeper into these traps as they undergo

---

[3] This echoes literature on the historical erosion of clientelism in advanced democracies (e.g., Shefter 1977, Shefter 1994), a connection I describe below and explore in depth in Chapter 9.

[4] For example, see Keefer (2007) and Keefer and Vlaicu (2008).

further socioeconomic development and enter middle-income status[5] – in contrast to common expectations that greater wealth leads societies away from clientelism – and that the process of extracting themselves can be "glacially slow," lagging decades behind socioeconomic conditions (Kitschelt et al. 2010, 4). Identifying the dimensions along which these traps might be overcome has implications for our ability to diagnose reforms that can improve the quality of governance in new democracies.

1.1 THE PUZZLE

This book addresses a central empirical puzzle: why are key features of urban life – the growth of the urban middle class and high levels of ethnic diversity – not producing the political changes that many existing theories expect? Answering this requires answering a second, closely related question: why is there so much variation across neighborhoods within cities in political behavior and the electoral strategies of politicians?

1.1.1 Existing Expectations: Effects of the Middle Class and Ethnic Diversity

I focus on two distinctions between forms of electoral competition. The first distinction is between *programmatic*, policy-based electoral competition and *nonprogrammatic*, patronage-based competition.[6] I follow Kitschelt et al. (2010) and define programmatic politics as when competing politicians or parties offer voters "alternative packages of policies that they commit to enact" (16), with benefits that are not contingent on political support, and voters are able to make vote choices based upon these policy proposals.[7] Under this definition, the mere existence of policy rhetoric is not evidence of programmatic politics; voters must have reasonable expectations that politicians' proposals at least partially reflect what they plan to do in office. The programs offered by competing

---

[5] Kitschelt and Kselman (2013).

[6] Electoral competition could also be personalistic. But because in practice personalistic appeals that are fully divorced from voters' expectations about policy or the distribution of particularistic goods are rare, I simplify the exposition by not considering personalistic appeals.

[7] Stokes et al. (2013) define programmatic politics more narrowly, as when benefits of government policies are distributed based on public, well-defined criteria. The noncontingent distribution of state resources is a central element of Kitschelt et al. (2010)'s definition, but their definition goes further in also emphasizing the importance of policy appeals in voter decision making.

politicians must also be sufficiently distinct that they provide voters a basis for choosing among options on the ballot.[8] I contrast programmatic competition with nonprogrammatic competition. While nonprogrammatic competition takes many forms, I focus in particular on the broad category of linkages between politicians and voters in which particularistic benefits are targeted selectively based on political criteria as a form of patronage.[9] Clientelism – the contingent, iterated exchange of benefits in return for support – is one type of nonprogrammatic linkage;[10] I also examine unmonitored pre-election gift-giving and various forms of "pork barrel" politics that do not involve contingent exchanges with voters.[11] At the core of each form of nonprogrammatic appeal is the targeted delivery of excludable benefits to specific individuals or to narrow, often geographically concentrated, groups of voters, such as those in rural villages or urban neighborhoods.

The second distinction is whether or not there is ethnic competition in elections. I identify the presence of ethnic competition based on whether the ethnicity of voters strongly predicts how they vote. This means examining whether or not members of the same ethnic group cluster their support for a party that is seen as associated with the interests of their group (if such a party exists).[12] When ethnic competition is absent, ethnicity provides little or no information about vote choice.

Studies of electoral politics in rural Africa often begin with two stylized facts: first, voters are susceptible to clientelistic appeals and other forms of nonprogrammatic politics; and second, ethnicity is a central

---

[8] Policy rhetoric and manifestos on their own can be cheap talk. Many benefits distributed in clientelistic exchanges come via policies that politicians claim are formally programmatic in campaign messaging. Moreover, it is common even in the world's most clearly nonprogrammatic political systems for parties to make campaign appeals about valence policy issues (growing the economy, fighting corruption) about which there is no actual differentiation in their substantive proposals or behavior (Bleck and van de Walle 2012).

[9] I use "patronage" broadly, as in Kitschelt and Wilkinson (2007), to describe general politicized distribution of state resources, not only the allocation of public jobs.

[10] I follow Hicken (2011) and Kitschelt and Wilkinson (2007) in using "clientelism" to refer specifically to contingent exchanges between politicians and voters in which targeted benefits are given in expectation that voters reciprocate with support.

[11] For example, see Golden and Min (2013) and Kramon (2016), or the typology in Stokes et al. (2013).

[12] I justify this bloc-voting-based definition of ethnic voting in Chapter 2 amid a more extensive discussion of the nature of ethnic cleavages in Ghana's party system. Defining ethnic voting more narrowly, as only a direct match in ethnicity between a specific candidate and voter, risks understating the role of ethnicity in elections.

feature of distributive politics and voting behavior in most countries. These stylized facts are explained by common features of rural life in many countries, including poverty, the concentration of ethnic groups in distinct regions competing for government resources, and the political power of traditional ethnic elites.[13]

But African cities differ from rural areas on several dimensions that appear to undermine these stylized facts. Two are particularly important: levels of wealth, and ethnic composition. Existing narratives about politics in urban Africa often expect the growth of the urban middle class and high levels of ethnic diversity in cities to lead electoral competition away from the clientelism and ethnic politics that are so often assumed to characterize rural areas. The evidence in support of these expectations remains sparse, and earlier scholarship on independence-era urban Africa often showed the exact opposite patterns.[14] Nonetheless, these expectations are increasingly becoming their own stylized facts about urban areas.

I outline the expected impacts of each of these two characteristics in turn. Among the most widely discussed transformations in urban Africa in the past decade has been the many millions of people pulled out of poverty into the middle class. There is considerable debate about how this middle class should be classified, leading to conflicting estimates of its size.[15] In Chapter 2, I justify categorizing middle-class status in Africa based on measures of formal sector employment, secondary education, and literacy, in the absence of reliable measures of income, and show that there is now a sizable urban middle class in many of Africa's new democracies. As of 2010, up to one-quarter of the adult population in Greater Accra, Ghana had achieved middle- or upper-class status.[16] Demographic and Health Surveys (DHS) suggest that this urban middle class has *tripled* in size since Ghana democratized in 1992; Figure 1.2 plots growth in the size of the middle class in Ghana's four largest metropolitan areas using

---

[13] For example, Bates (1983), Wantchekon (2003), Posner (2005). This is meant as a general characterization. There are of course also studies showing internal variation in clientelism and ethnic competition across rural regions within the same country, including Ichino and Nathan (2013a), and also some African countries where these features are not present (Koter 2016).

[14] For example, Epstein (1958), Cohen (1969), Scott (1969), Melson (1971), Baker (1974), Bates (1974), Wolpe (1974), and Gugler and Flanagan (1978). The implications and limits of this literature are discussed in more detail in Section 1.3.1.

[15] For example, see Banerjee and Duflo (2008), Ravallion (2009), Mitlin and Satterthwaite (2013), and Thurlow et al. (2015).

[16] This figure is based on individual-level 2010 census data.

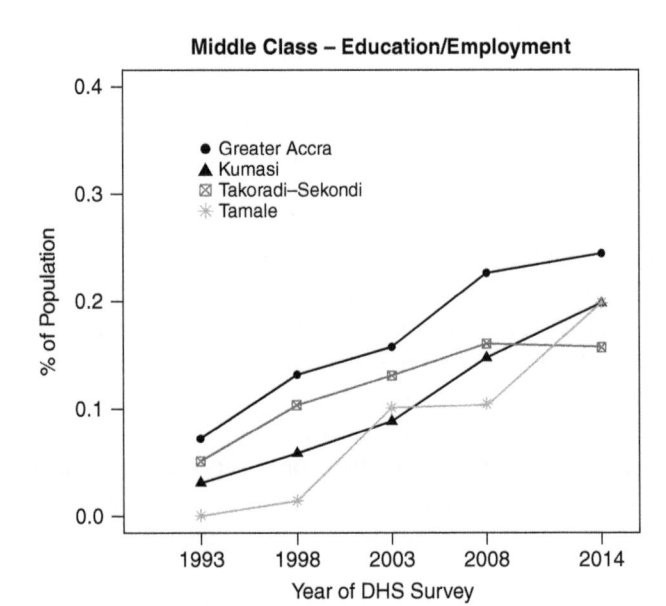

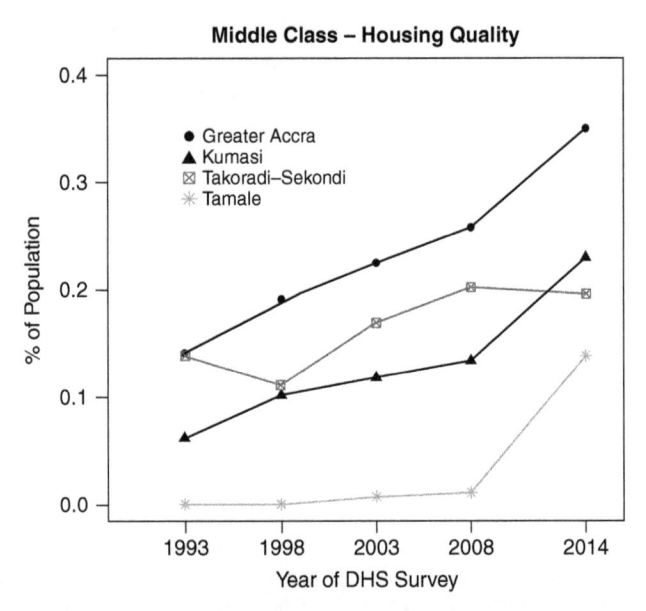

FIGURE 1.2: *Proportion middle or upper class in urban Ghana*: The top panel is the proportion of DHS respondents with secondary education, English literacy, and formal sector employment in each of Ghana's four largest metropolitan areas; the bottom panel adapts an alternative measure from Thurlow et al. (2015) to show the proportion of DHS respondents with electricity, clean drinking water, flush toilets, and at least two of the three education and employment characteristics.

two possible definitions of middle-class status.[17] Cross-national comparisons in Chapter 2 show that Ghana is on the high end of the spectrum in Africa in the size of its urban middle class. If the emergence of a large urban middle class induces political change, Ghana should be one of the first places in Africa that we see it.

Rising incomes and the growth of the middle class have long been argued to help explain transitions away from clientelism and other forms of nonprogrammatic appeal, primarily through changes to the demands voters place on politicians.[18] Wealthier and middle-class voters are less susceptible to clientelism because they often do not value the types of patronage goods politicians can provide, the marginal cost of buying their votes becomes prohibitively high, or their time horizons are longer, allowing them to place greater emphasis on major public policies and long-term performance.[19] Similarly, to the extent that urban voters have better access to basic public services than rural voters, they may place less demand on politicians to satisfy basic economic needs and instead have more space to develop "higher order" preferences about policy issues.[20] One might think an expectation that middle-class voters make fewer demands than the poor for patronage resources is unreasonable if the middle class remains largely dependent on the state for its economic position. But, with some exceptions,[21] most growth of the new African middle class has come via the private sector.[22]

---

[17] An adaptation of the definition in Thurlow et al. (2015) is provided in the bottom panel of Figure 1.2 for reference to my own preferred definition, which is in the top panel.

[18] There are clear exceptions to this pattern – wealthy countries in which forms of clientelism have persisted, such as Italy and Japan late into the twentieth century. But even in these cases, patronage-based political competition was most prevalent in less urbanized or less economically developed regions (Chubb 1982, Scheiner 2006, Scheiner 2007). Kitschelt (2007) argues that clientelism is most likely to persist despite high levels of wealth in settings where the state exerts significant control over economic planning and a hegemonic party dominates, with low levels of electoral competition. Weitz-Shapiro (2014) makes a similar argument at the local level, arguing that clientelism can persist in wealthier areas in the absence of real electoral competition. Neither of Kitschelt's conditions holds in Ghana, however; political competition is high – including within most districts of Greater Accra – and the economy is largely privatized.

[19] Among many variants of these arguments, see Kitschelt (2000), Hicken (2011), and Weitz-Shapiro (2014).

[20] Inglehart (1997).

[21] See Southall (2014) on the black middle class in South Africa.

[22] Kessides (2006). In Chapter 2, I show that the large majority of middle class residents in urban Ghana are not public sector employees directly dependent on the state.

Politicians should face electoral incentives to begin placing more emphasis on programmatic, policy-based appeals where fewer voters demand the types of particularistic goods typically targeted as patronage. The choice between employing programmatic and nonprogrammatic appeals is not mutually exclusive. Although some policy appeals and nonprogrammatic strategies can trade off against each other, various forms of "dual appeal" are common throughout Latin America, for example, with politicians engaging with the middle class and wealthy on the basis of policy while simultaneously building support among the poor with clientelism and other forms of patronage.[23] Even if the urban middle class is small as an overall share of the electorate, politicians stand to gain by adopting a dual appeal and catering to policy demands of middle-class voters as long as doing so is not prohibitively costly or actively counterproductive to maintaining support from poorer voters.

Catering to the preferences of the urban middle class should become especially likely where the middle class is electorally pivotal. At approximately one-quarter of the voting age population, the middle class is now a potential "king maker" in elections in Greater Accra. This may not appear to be the case if elections are viewed in a median voter framework in which income is the main dimension along which voters differ, as in Meltzer and Richard (1981). In such a model, the median voter is still poor in Greater Accra and, essentially, all African cities. But this is not a useful model of how elections work in Ghana, or in most other new democracies where class-based contestation over redistribution is not salient. Electoral competition is multidimensional and a key additional dimension is ethnicity. In a competitive electoral environment where ethnic voting remains extensive among the poor and the major parties have similar-sized ethnic coalitions – as I will show is the case in urban Ghana – a middle class of one-quarter of the electorate is by far large enough to swing election outcomes if middle-class voters disproportionately favor a particular party.[24]

The middle class becomes even more pivotal if they are less likely than the poor to engage in ethnic voting. Wealthier African voters have been

---

[23] For example, see Levitsky (2003) on Argentina, Luna (2014) on Chile and Uruguay, and Thachil (2014) on India.

[24] Moreover, in Chapters 4 and 9 I examine local elections in the specific parliamentary constituencies and wards of Greater Accra where middle-class voters explicitly are the median as defined in the Meltzer and Richard (1981) framework. I still find similar patterns of politician and voter behavior as in the city overall, suggesting that the median voter not being middle class is not a sufficient explanation for my results.

shown to identify less with ethnicity relative to national or class-based identities.[25] Under "expressive" theories of ethnic politics that tie support for ethnically affiliated politicians to voters' social identification,[26] the rise of the urban middle class in Africa should mean less emphasis is placed on ethnicity in voting behavior.[27] If this is true, the urban middle class should be an easier bloc of voters than most others among which politicians could add additional support to extend beyond their ethnic bases.

Empirical research on the political effects of the emerging middle class in Africa has been limited,[28] but many in the policy and journalism communities are already taking a programmatic transition induced by the new middle class as a given – to the point of claiming that this transition is already underway. *Reuters* describes Africa's middle class as "enlightened voters" and "drivers of democracy," who are "more likely to vote according to policies and issues rather than automatic or traditional allegiances to any party or ethnic group."[29] Now that they can have "preoccupations beyond where the next meal is coming from," *The Guardian* argues that Africa's urban middle class is "an agent of change" that is improving democratic governance.[30] *Foreign Policy* describes the middle class as "a massive boon to political growth," unwilling to "to put up with business as usual."[31] Similar examples are common in the policy world. Birdsall (2010), of the Center for Global Development, expects the growth of the middle class in developing countries to "play [a] positive political role in the provision of accountable government" (8), triggering a series of changes to politics and policy. In the introduction to a prominent volume on the African middle class, Ncube (2015), of the African Development Bank, states as an untested assumption that "as people gain middle class status, they use their greater economic clout to demand more accountability and transparency from their governments" (3).

---

[25] See Green (2014) and Robinson (2014), which are consistent with the expectations of classical modernization theorists about the possible effects of rising wealth and education on kin-based social ties (Lerner 1958, Lipset 1960).
[26] Horowitz (1985); see Ferree (2006) for an explanation of this theory of ethnic voting.
[27] Cross-national survey evidence in Conroy-Krutz (2009) appears to conform to this expectation.
[28] However, see, Southall (2014), Mattes (2015), Resnick (2015a), and Resnick (2015b).
[29] Fletcher (2013).
[30] Smith and Lamble (2011).
[31] Dickinson (2011).

Ethnic diversity is the second characteristic of African cities expected to produce new patterns of electoral competition. Buoyed by decades of rural–urban migration, there are now significantly higher levels of ethnic diversity in African cities relative to most rural areas. This can be seen clearly for the Ghanaian case in Figure 1.3. The top panel is the distribution of ethnic fractionalization in each enumeration area (EA) in all rural areas on the country's 2010 census.[32] These are highly localized units – each of the country's 37,000 census enumeration areas contains less than 1,000 people on average. The median rural census enumeration

Ethnic Diversity by Enumeration Area

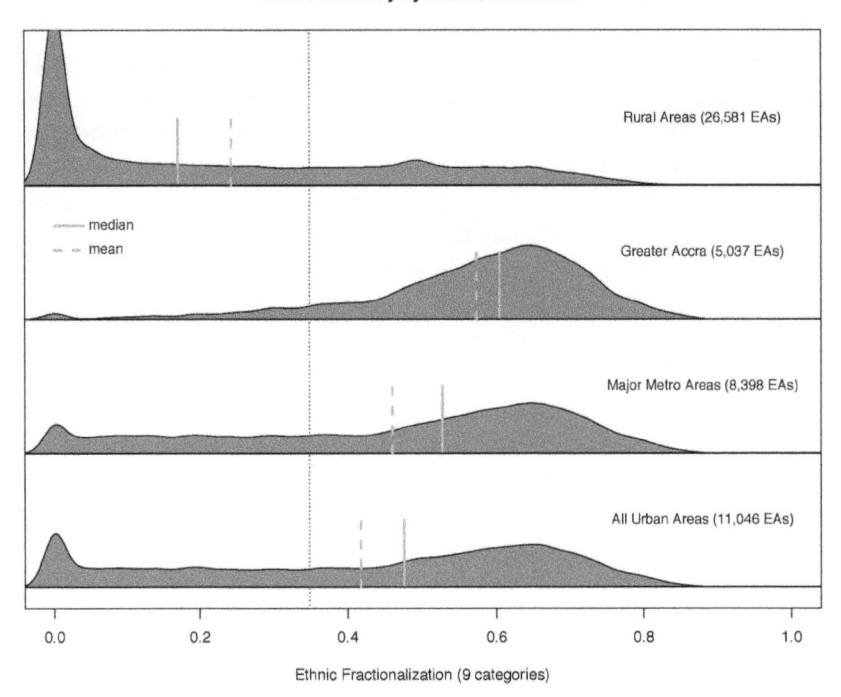

FIGURE 1.3: *Ethnic diversity in Ghana by census enumeration area*: Density distributions of ethnic fractionalization for each 2010 census enumeration area (tract) for: (a) all rural areas of Ghana; (b) Greater Accra metropolitan area; (c) Ghana's four major metropolitan areas (Greater Accra, Kumasi, Tamale, Takoradi-Sekondi); and (d) all Ghanaian cities. The dotted vertical line is the nationwide mean.

---

[32] Ethnic fractionalization is defined throughout the book as 1 minus the Herfindahl concentration index (e.g., Posner 2004). When defined in this way, ethnic fractionalization measures the probability that two randomly selected people are from different groups.

area in Ghana has ethnic fractionalization of 0.17. The distribution of ethnic fractionalization in the Greater Accra metropolitan area is in the second panel. Here, the median enumeration area has ethnic fractionalization of 0.60. In each panel of Figure 1.3, ethnic diversity within cities is dramatically higher than in rural areas.[33]

There are two reasons why high levels of ethnic diversity could change the political role of ethnicity. First, social contact theory suggests that residents of diverse communities will develop stronger cross-cutting social ties with other ethnic groups, increasing trust and reducing the emphasis placed on ethnic division in both daily and political life.[34] Contact theories are popular outside the academy. For example, Severino and Ray (2011), of the World Bank and *Agence Francaise de Developpement*, predict the "end of ethnicity" as a relevant political identity in urban Africa, arguing that ethnic identities are losing salience in cities through interethnic assimilation. In one of the most prominent examples from the recent press, *The New York Times*' David Brooks describes contemporary Africa's "main story" as an "impressive surge of growth, urbanization, and modernization," defined by a "cosmopolitan trend," including a "greater mixing of tribal groupings" in urban areas that is reducing the political importance of ethnicity and improving the quality of governance.[35] Second, when politicians are expected to allocate local public, or club, goods to local areas where more of their co-ethnic voters live, theories of instrumental ethnic politics suggest that voters' incentives to support ethnically aligned parties and candidates should be weaker in more diverse areas.[36] Either approach suggests that higher degrees of diversity in cities should reduce the political importance of ethnicity relative to rural areas.[37]

Ethnic diversity also has implications for clientelism. Forms of social organization evolve as ethnic groups mix together in cities. Chiefs and

---

[33] While similar micro-level census data is not available to reproduce Figure 1.3 for other countries, the distribution of ethnic fractionalization between urban and rural areas is very similar throughout most of sub-Saharan Africa. Ghana's postcolonial history of rural–urban migration into major magnet cities such as Greater Accra is common across the region, and in the developing world in general (Gugler and Flanagan 1978, Ades and Glaeser 1995).

[34] For example, see Allport (1954), Lerner (1958), and more recently Kasara (2013).

[35] Brooks (2014).

[36] This argument is made most directly in Ichino and Nathan (2013a).

[37] By contrast, theories of "group threat" predict the opposite: that ethnic competition will be heightened as new groups come into close contact with each other (Key 1949, Bobo and Hutchings 1996, Enos 2017). I examine the implications of a threat hypothesis in Chapters 7 and 8.

other traditional village elites play significant roles in rural politics in much of Africa, especially when residents live in homogeneous regions under the authority of traditional leaders from the locally dominant ethnic group. Traditional elites serve as intermediaries between citizens and the state and sometimes become clientelistic brokers who provide blocs of votes to allied candidates.[38] Urban residents have long been less connected to traditional authorities than people in rural areas,[39] and this is especially the case in ethnically mixed areas, where leaders of no particular group are dominant.[40] Where traditional elites are weak or absent and cannot serve as intermediaries, common clientelistic electoral strategies are believed to become more difficult. Koter (2016) argues, for example, that urban voters in Senegal are less likely to support the incumbent party because clientelism is less viable in cities, given the weakness of traditional elites, which renders urban votes harder for the ruling party to buy off. In more general terms, scholars such as Magaloni (2006) and Stokes et al. (2013) assume that the costs of clientelism are inherently higher in urban areas in developing countries because monitoring is more difficult in the absence of ties to rural brokers.

1.1.2 Unmet Expectations

In sum, there is a collective expectation that these two characteristics of cities – a large middle class and high levels of ethnic diversity – should induce a shift toward more programmatic and nonethnic competition. In the subsequent chapters, however, I show empirically that *neither of these two main expectations holds in most of urban Ghana*. Instead, the trap outlined in Figure 1.1 appears to prevail. Despite being a large segment of the population, urban middle-class voters are not serving as the "drivers of democracy," "agent[s] of change," and "boon to political growth" that fawning press coverage assumes. No programmatic transition aimed at addressing their preferences is underway. Individual-level clientelism is still pervasive in some neighborhoods of the city. And despite high levels of diversity, ethnicity still strongly predicts vote choice for many urban

---

[38] For example, see Acemoglu et al. (2014), Koter (2016), and de Kadt and Larreguy (2018); see Baldwin (2015), however, for a contrasting view of the role of rural chiefs.
[39] Gugler and Flanagan (1978).
[40] An important exception to this pattern is indigenous urban ethnic groups, among whom traditional leaders can still be active in cities. The Ga ethnic group in Greater Accra is one such example. I explore the different patterns of behavior that emerge among Ga voters as an extension of my main argument in Chapter 7.

voters, including those in the middle class. The "end of ethnicity" is not upon us.

There is neighborhood-level variation within Greater Accra in the prevalence of clientelism and ethnic voting, however. This includes variation between areas where individual-level clientelism is extensive and areas where it is absent; between areas where politicians distribute pre-election gifts widely during campaigns and areas within the same electoral constituencies that they largely ignore; and between areas where ethnicity and vote choice are almost perfectly correlated and areas where they are barely correlated at all.

Recent research on urban Africa largely ignores this intra-urban variation, implicitly viewing cities as uniform spaces and discussing "urban areas" or "urban voters" as single analytic categories. This can be seen, for example, in claims that urban voters in Africa, as a general category, are more likely to support opposition parties[41] or are more sophisticated and less susceptible to clientelistic appeals than rural voters,[42] or in claims that that clientelism is inherently more difficult in urban areas[43] or that politicians rely less on ethnic appeals in urban than rural areas.[44] This rarely grows from an explicit theoretical argument about the internal uniformity of cities, but instead from the imperatives of chosen levels of analysis: cross-national studies, those using nationally representative survey data, or those that primarily engage in rural–urban comparisons cannot explore the possibility of variation within cities because their data usually does not provide locally representative samples or the statistical power needed to examine intra-urban variation; others zoom in to study a single type of urban voter or neighborhood only.[45] This is not unique to studies of urban Africa[46] and is not necessarily a problem – if intra-urban variation is noise, or can be explained by standard

---

[41] Harding (2010), Resnick (2011), and Wahman and Boone (2018).
[42] Lindberg (2010).
[43] Koter (2016).
[44] Resnick (2014).
[45] For example, Resnick's (2014) core findings in Lusaka and Dakar are drawn from non-representative survey samples of poor people who work as traders in several informal markets in each city, not from representative cross-sections of the urban population.
[46] For example, Magaloni (2006) makes a common – almost always untested – assumption that clientelistic transactions are easier to enforce in rural areas than urban areas in developing countries because monitoring should be more difficult in cities. The possibility that monitoring costs might vary within urban areas is not considered because intra-urban comparisons fall beneath the chosen scale of analysis.

demographic variables, ignoring it has little significance.[47] But it is also possible that scholars would have reached fundamentally different conclusions about the nature of urban politics if they had better explored intra-urban variation.

Urban Ghana demonstrates the pitfalls of studying cities without examining intra-urban variation. Existing theories of voting behavior and distributive politics do not offer good explanations for why political competition differs so dramatically within a single city. More importantly, many of the theoretical mechanisms underlying existing expectations about the effects of the growth of the middle class and ethnic diversity fall apart when confronted with this intra-urban variation.

Rather than being uniformly more difficult in cities than in rural areas, clientelism varies significantly across neighborhoods even when holding fixed the absence of the typical types of brokers that parties can rely on in rural areas. In the poorest urban neighborhoods clientelism actually appears more extensive than in rural areas, even though it is rarely used to build support among similarly poor voters living elsewhere in the same city. And while the overall percentage of voters who support ethnically aligned parties is lower than in rural areas in Ghana, variation in support for ethnically affiliated parties within cities is not explained by voters' wealth, class, education, interethnic contact and cross-cutting social ties, ethnic social identification, or relationships with traditional leaders – the main list of factors pointed to by existing theories to explain why there should be less ethnic competition in urban areas. Instead, voters with the same socioeconomic characteristics behave differently when living in different neighborhoods of the same districts of the same city, even as many of the broader macroeconomic, policy-based, or institutional factors that might affect their behavior are held constant. These voters are choosing among the same candidates, in the same election, under the same rules.[48]

Understanding why this intra-urban variation exists is key to explaining the book's main puzzle. Cross-sectional variation in the presence of clientelism and ethnic competition provides empirical leverage to

---

[47] Moreover, if the explicit subject of interest is about some subset of urban life – for example, the politics of slums, as in Paller (2018) – then studying only that subset is appropriate.

[48] In Chapter 7, I examine in detail and rule out plausible alternative explanations for how this variation could instead be due to the endogenous sorting of voters into neighborhoods or other sources of confounding between neighborhood characteristics and behavior.

explore which potential constraints on these forms of electoral politics are actually binding and which are not.

1.2 THE ARGUMENT

I explain the limited effects of the growth of the middle class and high levels of ethnic diversity by considering, first, the benefits and costs to politicians of changing the appeals they supply in response to demographic and socioeconomic changes that alter voters' demands, and, second, how the appeals politicians supply affect voters' incentives to participate in politics and support different candidates and parties.

Three contextual features of African cities shape politicians' and voters' incentives. First is the low state capacity that characterizes most developing countries and defines the range of policies that politicians can credibly promise to supply voters. Second, scarcity created by the rapid pace of urban growth generates voter demands for state resources. Third, African cities are often internally heterogeneous, with neighborhoods that differ widely in their wealth and diversity coexisting in close proximity, even within the same electoral district. These neighborhood characteristics alter the effectiveness of different electoral strategies. In this section, I introduce these contextual features and lay out the main steps of my argument for why the interaction of supply-side and demand-side forces produces the trap in Figure 1.1.

While this argument is primarily developed within the context of African cities, the core claims have broader relevance for urban politics across the developing world. Low state capacity, scarcity, and stark intra-urban variation in neighborhood characteristics are common in urban areas in many new democracies and may have similar effects. Section 1.4 and Chapter 2 both identify scope conditions for extending the argument to other cases.

1.2.1 Contextual Features: State Capacity, Scarcity, and Neighborhood Variation

The first contextual feature that shapes the decision environment of politicians and urban voters is the level of *state capacity*. By state capacity, I mean the ability of the government to act on its stated policy goals.[49] Campaign promises to supply new programmatic policies in response to

---

[49] Evans et al. (1985).

voter preferences are often seen as noncredible where governments have limited resources, where there are few constraints on the politicization of bureaucratic service delivery, and where corruption, rent-seeking, and coordination problems within the organs of the state impede the successful implementation of major policies.[50] While there is variation in the capacity of states across the developing world,[51] each of these constraints is prevalent in most new democracies in Africa. Building policy credibility requires long-term investments in successful implementation that many politicians either cannot afford or are not capable of on their own.

Second, urban growth occurs in a context of scarcity. Governments cannot possibly respond to many service delivery challenges created by urbanization, even where urban economies are booming. In the words of one media account, the growth of contemporary African cities is "outstripping the ability of weak and plodding central governments to manage."[52] Most urbanization in Africa is unplanned and unregulated, occurring in spite of whatever government policies are in place to control it.[53] In recent decades, entire urban neighborhoods have emerged as if out of nothing despite lacking basic government goods provision – without paved roads, running water, sewers, trash collection, or public schools. Population growth is overwhelming pre-existing infrastructure in older neighborhoods. Even wealthier areas within cities face significant shortcomings in service delivery.

This generates demand on politicians for particularistic goods, even among many middle-class voters. Middle-class residents sometimes privately provide services to themselves, substituting for the state. Elsewhere, some communities organize on their own to provide basic local public goods.[54] But these are imperfect, expensive, and temporary solutions. Demands for new infrastructure and employment opportunities in cities exceed what most governments could ever satisfy. Scarcity means that governments have to pick, addressing the demands of some voters and some urban neighborhoods, but not others. Precisely because politicians cannot address all of these demands, scarcity helps incentivize nonprogrammatic electoral appeals. Politicians in urban Africa

---

[50] Keefer and Vlaicu (2008).
[51] For example, see Lieberman (2003).
[52] French (2013).
[53] UN-Habitat (2014).
[54] Bodea and LeBas (2016).

often have discretionary control over the allocation of many of the most valuable and scarce resources in the urban economy – the ability to decide who gets goods such as new roads, running water, or public sector employment, and, importantly, who does not. Many of the services urban voters demand – new schools, new water pipes, jobs, loans – are fundamentally targetable, with benefits that reach specific voters or neighborhoods rather than the entire city. This gives politicians significant political leverage and, in combination with low state implementation capacity, creates variation within cities in *state presence* – that is, the extent to which the state effectively governs and provides services in different areas of its territory.

The third contextual feature that shapes the decision environment of politicians is the range of demographic conditions across neighborhoods within a city. The emergence of an urban middle class has coincided with the simultaneous expansion of slum settlements in most African cities, with more than half of the urban population living in slums in many cities.[55] In contrast to arguments that clientelism is less viable in cities, conditions in urban slums may enhance the viability of individual-level clientelistic relationships between parties and voters. Due to a combination of concentrated poverty, scarcity fueled by the minimal presence of the state, and certain features of neighborhood social structure, including shared housing arrangements, slum conditions facilitate the ability of party agents to bind voters in sustained clientelistic relationships in a way that is not possible in the more anonymized, wealthier neighborhoods of cities – even among poorer residents who live in otherwise wealthier areas. In the absence of strong traditional leaders in urban areas, new forms of brokers and political intermediaries can also emerge in slums, building patron–client ties with residents.[56]

Moreover, even if cities as a whole are more diverse than rural areas, individual neighborhoods can still be ethnically segregated. Many African cities contain a mix of diverse neighborhoods and segregated ethnic enclaves. Similar to the emergence of immigrant enclaves in many American cities, migrants from an ethnic group can gain a foothold in a

---

[55] UN-Habitat (2010).
[56] For example, see Paller (2014) on the political roles of informal leaders in Accra's slums. Among many others, Auyero (2000) describes a similar phenomenon in Latin American slums, and Auerbach (2016) and Auerbach and Thachil (2016) do so for Indian slums. LeBas (2013) also documents how neighborhood vigilante groups fill leadership vacuums in the slums of Nairobi and Lagos and help enforce voter loyalties to local political party machines.

neighborhood that subsequent generations use as an entry point, creating a clustering that persists for decades.[57] These homogenous neighborhoods are not always slums; wealthier urban neighborhoods can also be dominated by specific ethnic groups. Indigenous urban ethnic groups can also maintain segregated neighborhoods in the locations of their original settlements, even as larger cities gradually envelop them. The resulting variation in the extent of neighborhood-level ethnic diversity can produce variation in politicians' incentives to engage in ethnic favoritism from neighborhood to neighborhood.

1.2.2 Origins of the Trap

These features interact to shape the incentives of politicians and voters, producing the trap in Figure 1.1. While the argument could conceivably begin at any step, I begin by explaining the trap from the top-left of Figure 1.1. Scarcity rooted in the state's failure to address the public service needs of a booming urban population produces widespread demands for particularistic resources, from private goods such as jobs and housing to local public, or club, goods such as pipe-borne water, paved roads, and government schools. These demands are especially acute among the poor. The politicians most successful in this environment are those who specialize in nonprogrammatic, patronage-based linkage strategies that selectively target particularistic goods.

What changes when a significant percentage of urban voters are markedly wealthier and better-educated and enter the middle class? In line with existing theory, I expect many middle-class voters to make different demands on politicians – with less emphasis on narrow particularistic benefits, especially private goods, and more on broader policy changes and public goods.[58] Politicians have two options for how to respond: (1) they could begin addressing these new demands, making investments in policy appeals designed to woo middle class voters even as they may also continue to mobilize other voters through more

---

[57] Examples include concentrations of ethnic Somalis in Nairobi's Eastleigh neighborhood and the segregated "Zongo" communities of Hausa-speaking Muslim migrants found across much of urban West Africa. See Cohen (1969), Schildkrout (1976), Gugler and Flanagan (1978), Pellow (2002), and Ntewusu (2012).

[58] This book does not examine the process by which becoming wealthier or better educated changes an individual's preferences over time. I predict only that there will be aggregate differences when the population is wealthier and better-educated. I also do not examine the potentially distinct preferences and behavior of the wealthiest urban elite for empirical reasons discussed in Chapter 2.

particularistic means; (2) politicians could instead double down on existing nonprogrammatic appeals and ignore new policy demands.

The first option can be substantially more costly than the second, even where the new middle class forms a potentially pivotal share of the electorate, for several reasons. First, and most importantly, politicians face a credibility problem when attempting to win support based on policy proposals. Much of this credibility problem emerges from low state capacity. Even if a particular politician is committed to delivering on a policy platform, her ability to do so is constrained where bureaucratic weakness means that programmatic policies are likely to be mired in corruption, rent-seeking, and ethnic and partisan favoritism when implemented. Many voters will not believe that such a politician is able to follow through on these proposals. Additional elements of the credibility problem are separate from state capacity. In overly centralized political systems – common in many of Africa's new democracies[59] – it is difficult for individual politicians to commit to implementing policy proposals because of coordination problems. Changes to at least some of the policies that middle-class voters demand require coordination with national-level leaders or rural legislators,[60] who may not have the same incentives to address middle-class preferences as local politicians from urban areas.[61] Overcoming this credibility problem requires long-term investments – whether via reforming bureaucracies, creating a record of implementation, or building cross-regional political coalitions – that are more expensive than most re-election-focused politicians with short time horizons can afford.

Second, the risks of the second option – not changing appeals – are diminished by neighborhood-level variation in the demands of the urban middle class. Because state presence remains low even in some wealthier neighborhoods, there are local areas where basic government services are

---

[59] For example, see van de Walle (2003), Olowu and Wunsch (2004), and Grossman and Lewis (2014).

[60] African legislatures, like those in many developing countries, usually have significant rural bias, with increasingly disproportionate districts that have not been adequately adjusted to keep pace with urbanization (Boone and Wahman 2015). Urban areas are typically not underrepresented in presidential elections, however, as most presidential elections are conducted in a single national constituency.

[61] This differs from more decentralized countries, such as in Latin America, where powerful local mayors are able to experiment with different types of linkages with voters based on the characteristics of their districts. I discuss the implications of greater substantive decentralization for the potential credibility of policy-based campaigns in more detail in Chapter 9.

sufficiently absent that the middle class voters living there still demand club (local public) goods from politicians that can be targeted to neighborhoods as patronage. Politicians who selectively target state resources to meet these demands can still win the support of many middle-class voters without offering new policy proposals.

The second option in the choice above becomes less costly than the first. Urban politicians avoid meaningful efforts to address policy preferences, under-investing in mobilizing the support of middle class voters whom they expect to be most difficult to convince. This does not mean that policy rhetoric is entirely absent from campaigns. In the absence of any credible commitments, making sweeping policy promises becomes essentially costless. But the policy promises that are made are heavily discounted by voters, and politicians know that their promises are not significant determinants of behavior. Politicians instead concentrate their effort on nonprogrammatic forms of voter mobilization.

This has effects on political participation and the composition of the electorate. Turnout inequality emerges, with policy-demanding members of the urban middle class participating less than the poor, in the opposite pattern of most advanced democracies.[62] These voters differentially exit the political arena both because they have no options on the ballot whom they trust to address their preferences and because they are less likely to be mobilized to participate by politicians. But the differential abstention of voters who demand programmatic policy reinforces politicians' incentives to select the second option above by reducing the weight of policy-demanding voters in the electorate and allowing political party organizations to remain dominated by poorer voters most susceptible to nonprogrammatic appeals, even as the middle class grows.

In turn, the continued nonprogrammatic distribution of state resources reinforces incentives for ethnic competition. The distribution of scarce state resources as patronage creates expectations among voters that they will benefit more if ethnically aligned politicians are in office. This occurs in many, but not all, urban neighborhoods, however, because the nonprogrammatic strategies that politicians employ vary across cities in two key ways. The first intra-urban difference is in the distribution of private goods through clientelism in poor versus middle- and upper-class neighborhoods. The social structures of slums lend themselves to sustained penetration by party networks. Dense concentrations of poor

---

[62] For example, Verba et al. (1995).

voters demanding private goods and opportunities for monitoring created by close social contact allow clientelism to thrive. Similar clientelistic relationships are costlier to maintain in more socially atomized middle- and upper-class neighborhoods, even among the poor voters who live there and still demand private goods.

The second difference in distributive strategies across neighborhoods is in the use of ethnic favoritism. Studies of patronage politics in Africa often assume that a government's core co-ethnic supporters are the prime beneficiaries of state spending on club (local public) and private goods.[63] But considering the different costs and benefits of a strategy of ethnic favoritism across urban neighborhoods suggests that a party's core ethnic groups are only likely to be beneficiaries of ethnic favoritism in some, but not all, areas of a city. Favoritism in the allocation of private goods is especially likely in poor neighborhoods where clientelism is prevalent and direct exchanges with voters are more enforceable. Ethnicity structures the grassroots partisan networks that carry out clientelistic transactions, reducing costs to targeting and monitoring members of core ethnic groups relative to other voters. Parties also have incentives to predominately target clientelistic benefits to aligned groups to keep their base from defecting.[64]

By contrast, the ethnic diversity of urban neighborhoods affects where politicians can most effectively target club goods to core ethnic groups in return for support.[65] By delivering club goods to relatively homogeneous neighborhoods within their districts where politically aligned ethnic groups are clustered, politicians can target benefits to specific groups while withholding benefits from supporters of opposing parties. Ethnic favoritism in spending on club goods remains common in segregated areas. But club goods delivered to more diverse neighborhoods will benefit voters from many ethnic groups who live there and cannot be targeted selectively. Club goods are still distributed in diverse neighborhoods, especially as part of pre-election spending aimed at building

---

[63] For example, see Bates (1983), Kimenyi (2006), and Franck and Rainer (2012), among many others.

[64] In Chapter 5, I engage the theoretical literature on core versus swing targeting (e.g., Dixit and Londregan 1996, Stokes 2005) and justify an assumption of core favoritism in the allocation of clientelistic benefits by extending the argument from Diaz-Cayeros et al. (2016). I still expect ethnically unaligned voters to also benefit from other, nonclientelistic forms of private goods distribution, such as unmonitored pre-election handouts (e.g., Kramon 2016).

[65] See Ichino and Nathan (2013a) and Ejdemyr et al. (2017).

TABLE 1.1: *Neighborhood-level variation in ethnic voting.*

	Ethnically Diverse or Integrated Neighborhood	Ethnically Homogenous or Segregated Neighborhood
Middle- or Upper-Class Neighborhood	Less ethnic voting	More ethnic voting
Poor or Slum Neighborhood	More ethnic voting	More ethnic voting

broader reputations of good performance. But voters from core ethnic groups are not systematically favored in access to public spending on club goods when they live in diverse neighborhoods.

These differences in distributive strategies combine to inform voters' *relative expectations of favoritism* – their beliefs about which party or candidate is more likely to benefit them in the distribution of state resources after an election. Neighborhood-level variation in distributive strategies produces neighborhood-level variation in expectations of favoritism for otherwise similar voters, depending on where they live within a city.

This leads to neighborhood-level variation in the extent to which ethnicity determines vote choice. Expectations of favoritism become significant determinants of voting behavior in settings of scarcity, where voters' access to government spending is in some sense figuratively on the ballot.[66] Table 1.1 summarizes predictions about voting behavior in four types of neighborhoods defined by their ethnic composition and wealth.[67] In both types of poor neighborhoods in Table 1.1 – including ethnically diverse poor neighborhoods – clientelism is extensive. Voters have strong incentives to continue supporting ethnically aligned candidates and parties to benefit from favoritism in the allocation of private goods. In middle- and upper-class neighborhoods, where clientelism and the selective distribution of private goods are rare, expectations about the delivery of club goods become more important for vote choice. In

---

[66] This argument extends existing instrumental theories of ethnic voting, such as Bates (1983), Chandra (2004), Posner (2005), Ferree (2006), Ichino and Nathan (2013a), and Carlson (2015). I do not argue that these expectations of favoritism are the *only* determinant of vote choice. As I show in Chapter 7, voters are also sensitive to other considerations also noted in the literature, including macroeconomic performance evaluations of parties and candidates (e.g., Bratton et al. 2011).

[67] Chapter 5 develops the underlying logic for these predictions in more detail.

segregated neighborhoods likely to be favored by one party and ignored by another in distribution of club goods, incentives to support ethnically aligned parties remain strong. But when middle- and upper-class neighborhoods are ethnically diverse, incentives to vote along ethnic lines diminish – to the point that there may be little ethnic voting at all. Voters in these areas are unlikely to receive systematically different private or club goods from politicians with different ethnic profiles – there is both little individual-level clientelism and little ethnic favoritism in the distribution of club goods.

As a result, Table 1.1 indicates that *neither* ethnic diversity nor neighborhood wealth lead to lower rates of support for ethnically aligned parties on their own. Instead, voters only face incentives against voting along ethnic lines when they live in neighborhoods that are both wealthy and ethnically diverse – where individual-level clientelism is absent and club goods also cannot be targeted as ethnic favoritism. Voters in poor, diverse neighborhoods still vote along ethnic lines at high rates, as do voters from local majority ethnic groups living in wealthy neighborhoods that remain segregated.[68]

Overall class-based differences in support for ethnically aligned parties do not emerge. The middle-class voters who demand policy over patronage and are least likely to be sensitive to this type of instrumental logic for vote choice are those most likely to have abstained from voting to begin with. Among most of the middle-class voters who remain in the electorate, expectations about club goods are important factors in voting decisions, and expectations of ethnic favoritism still help determine behavior.

In the final stage of the argument, I suggest that urban governments are prone to capture by narrow interest groups when nonprogrammatic appeals remain the norm and policy-demanding voters broadly abstain from participation. Capture is particularly likely in local elections for municipal governments where turnout can be especially low. Groups that have lower costs of mobilization relative to others have significant advantages in these elections, even if they represent only a minority of the population. In cases with significant ethnic competition, this can lead to ethnic capture, with, for example, specific ethnic groups that have

---

[68] In Chapter 5, I extend this argument further to consider the incentives of voters living as local ethnic minorities in segregated neighborhoods surrounded by a locally dominant ethnic group aligned with another party. I examine circumstances under which these voters will vote across ethnic lines, building on Ichino and Nathan (2013a).

turnout advantages relative to other groups dominating urban elections, not unlike what occurred in the "machine era" in the United States. In other contexts, other forms of capture may emerge, with different types of interest groups gaining disproportionate power in urban areas.[69]

Once in power, local politicians from minority interests have little incentive to deviate from in-group favoritism when allocating state resources or implementing national government policies, even those that are de jure programmatic. This reduces the quality of urban governance. Government spending targets narrow groups of voters rather than the needs of the city at large, creating more scarcity. As needs go unmet, demands for particularistic goods that can be targeted as patronage persist. Capture also helps reinforce voters' beliefs that the government is incapable of implementing programmatic policies. This is in part because local government actors who have captured power through nonprogrammatic appeals and are only accountable to narrow interest groups are free to forego the programmatic implementation of national government policies that would make national politicians' policy appeals more credible. Together, these outcomes help complete the loop in Figure 1.1, feeding back into voters' demands for patronage and worsening the credibility problem.

This argument explains the empirical puzzle mentioned earlier. Clientelism thrives both because many voters continue to demand patronage benefits and because there are still many poor neighborhoods with social structures highly conducive to clientelistic appeals. A programmatic transition is not underway because the costs of investing in policy appeals remain high in the face of significant credibility constraints. Ethnicity remains politically salient because the nonprogrammatic strategies that politicians use encourage voters in many neighborhoods to continue selecting ethnically aligned parties in expectation of better access to scarce government resources.

1.2.3 Ways Out?

I do not expect the cycle in Figure 1.1 to persist indefinitely. A political entrepreneur could emerge to better represent the interests of policy-demanding voters in the urban middle class, although I explain in Chapter 4 that there are considerable forces pushing back against this

---

[69] See Anzia (2014) on interest-group capture in low-turnout local elections in the United States.

possibility.[70] There could be a major economic crisis that leads to a political realignment, or policy demands in the electorate may eventually grow so large that politicians no longer have any choice but to change the way they appeal to voters in order to build viable winning coalitions. But for the medium term, I suggest that the features of electoral competition in Figure 1.1 feed into each other to create stable patterns that can persist in the face of underlying socioeconomic and demographic changes occurring in urban areas.

My argument thus suggests that the answer to the puzzle presented earlier is *not* simply to wait a few years longer for more socioeconomic change to happen. Instead, nearer-term departures from the patterns in Figure 1.1 are only likely to emerge if politicians' supply-side incentives to keep picking the second option in the choice noted earlier change. The insight that supply-side incentives are a more binding constraint on transitions to programmatic politics echoes the literature on historical political development in Western democracies, dating back at least to Shefter (1977). In particular, this suggests that African cities may share close parallels with nineteenth- and early twentieth-century American cities, where urban governments were bastions of clientelism and ethnic politics in a similar fashion to what I document for the Ghanaian case. These practices persisted in some US cities for decades, long after the emergence of large middle classes and despite significant interethnic social interaction and assimilation. The American urban "machine era" ended more because of institutional constraints imposed to restrict the ability of politicians to target government resources selectively, such as civil service reforms that professionalized bureaucracies and New Deal welfare state programs, than because of any socioeconomic transformations.[71] Chapter 9 draws on these historical cases, as well as more recent examples from Latin America, to consider nearer-term reforms that could be made in African cities to change politicians' supply-side incentives.

1.3 CONTRIBUTIONS

The book makes three core contributions. First, I return the study of electoral politics in sub-Saharan Africa to a focus on urban areas

---

[70] These include collective action problems inherent in coordinating middle class support behind a new movement, and that the credibility constraints faced by a political newcomer are potentially even more extreme than those faced by existing parties.

[71] For example, see Erie (1988), Shefter (1994), Trounstine (2008), and Kuo (2018).

after decades of scholarship have focused predominately on rural areas. Second, I contribute to broader theoretical debates in the study of comparative political behavior, expanding theories about the influence of local geographic context on voters, the nature of ethnic voting, and the relationship between class and political participation. Third, I contribute to a growing literature considering the conditions under which developing democracies shift away from nonprogrammatic electoral competition.

1.3.1 Urban Politics in Africa

Despite decades of urban growth, most recent research examining electoral competition in Africa still draws predominately, or exclusively, on rural data.[72] A disproportionate focus on rural politics is problematic. Many African voters have now never lived in a village. Assumptions about the political landscape based on observations of rural life will often be unsuitable to explain electoral outcomes in cities, both because voters' preferences and social pressures can differ and because politicians face new constraints and opportunities in cities that shape their distributive strategies.

Political competition in urban Africa received considerable attention during the independence era of the 1950s through 1970s.[73] But this earlier generation of scholarship offers limited guidance about electoral competition in the contemporary democratic period. This was an era before real multiparty electoral competition took hold in most countries; this earlier literature focused extensively on the rural–urban migration experience, but most urban voters in Africa are no longer first-generation rural–urban migrants;[74] and the middle and upper classes remained tiny relative to contemporary urban areas, with far less potential to impact elections. A smaller recent literature has begun examining individual

---

[72] For example, the main findings in recent work on voting behavior, ethnicity, and distributive politics, such as Wantchekon (2003), Posner (2004), Posner (2005), Ichino and Nathan (2013a), Koter (2013), Carlson (2015), Baldwin (2015), and Harding (2015), are based on rural areas only. Other recent work includes data from both urban and rural areas but does not examine in detail how the outcome under study differs between urban and rural locations. See, for example, Bratton et al. (2011), Lieberman and McClendon (2013), Weghorst and Lindberg (2013), Burgess et al. (2015), Casey (2015), and Horowitz (2016).

[73] For example, see Epstein (1958), Cohen (1969), Melson (1971), Baker (1974), Bates (1974), Wolpe (1974), and Gugler and Flanagan (1978).

[74] See Chapter 2; Kessides (2006).

facets of contemporary urban politics in Africa.[75] But these studies often either examine single-outcome variables, rather than tracing out the mutual interactions of voters and politicians, or focus on specific subsets of the electorate, rather than exploring outcomes across multiple socioeconomic classes and types of neighborhoods.

I expand this literature by exploring the mutually reinforcing behavior of politicians and voters across a wide range of types of voters and urban neighborhoods, offering a more complete picture of urban electoral politics. Doing so allows me to better explain how features of the contemporary urban context affect political behavior and better identify the conditions under which urban electoral competition does – and does not – differ from competition in rural areas.

1.3.2 Theories of Political Behavior and Electoral Politics

The book also uses urban Africa as a lens through which to examine more general debates in the study of political behavior and electoral politics. First, I help demonstrate the role local geographic contexts can play in shaping voter behavior in the developing world. Studies of advanced democracies, especially the US, have considered how voter attitudes and preferences are shaped by the local environments and neighborhoods in which voters live.[76] But neighborhood effects on behavior have received limited study in the developing world, where the impact of local context may be quite different.[77] In particular, I show that in developing democracies where political competition is more patronage based, it is not sufficient to consider the potential psychological effects of local context, as is the primary focus in the American politics literature, but also necessary to consider the more instrumental incentives neighborhood conditions can create for voters through explicit location-based distributive struggles over access to scarce state resources.

Second, I extend instrumental theories of ethnic politics to better account for voter incentives in urban areas. I show that even if social

---

[75] This includes studies of political competition among the urban poor (Resnick 2014, Paller 2018), attitudes and participation of the urban middle class (Cheeseman 2015, Resnick 2015a), and studies of aggregate rural–urban differences in ethnic identification (Green 2014, Robinson 2014) and voting behavior (Conroy-Krutz 2009, Harding 2010, Koter 2016, Wahman and Boone 2018).

[76] For example, see Key (1949), Gay (2004), Cho and Rudolph (2008), and Enos (2017).

[77] See Ichino and Nathan (2013a), Kasara (2013), and de Kadt and Sands (2017), however.

attachments to ethnic groups change, instrumental incentives to support ethnically aligned parties can persist if voters still expect ethnic favoritism in the distribution of state resources. While there are many reasons why ethnicity can become politically salient in different contexts, I suggest that changes to distributive politics are a more important margin along which ethnic competition can be reduced than changes in the social importance of ethnicity.

This demonstrates a key flaw in how many studies model the relationship between ethnicity and distributive politics. Formal theoretical approaches rooted in canonical probabilistic voting models, such as Lindbeck and Weibull (1987) and Dixit and Londregan (1996), often assume ethnicity has an inherent, fixed effect on voters – similar to ideology or partisanship – that is separate from any utility voters gain from distributive transfers from politicians.[78] Such an assumption lends itself to viewing ethnicity as a competing explanation for vote choice in contrast to clientelism or voter perceptions of politicians' performance.[79] But I join Chandra (2004), Posner (2005), Ferree (2006), and Carlson (2015) in reinforcing that ethnicity, clientelism, and performance expectations form a more unified explanation of behavior: ethnicity often matters specifically because of what it signals about access to distributive resources and the likely performance of politicians. In this view, ethnic voting is not an intrinsically negative behavior, incompatible with democratic accountability. Instead, voters support ethnically aligned parties because they are seeking politicians most likely to govern in their best interest.

Third, I build on a growing literature that demonstrates that the nonprogrammatic appeals that parties in new democracies employ can be highly variegated within the same context, with differences across places and across the electoral cycle in the use of clientelism and the types of voters who benefit from distributive politics.[80] In doing so, I contribute to the study of brokered politics in new democracies by providing new descriptive evidence about the roles different types of electoral intermediaries – whether grassroots party activists or traditional chiefs and other

---

[78] Modeling ethnicity as serving the same role as partisanship in the Dixit and Londregan (1996) framework is common in the political economy literature. For example, see Wantchekon (2003) and Casey (2015).

[79] For example, see Wantchekon (2003), Bratton et al. (2011), Hoffman and Long (2013), and Weghorst and Lindberg (2013).

[80] See, for example, Albertus (2013), Kramon and Posner (2013), Weitz-Shapiro (2014), and Diaz-Cayeros et al. (2016).

societal elites – play in shaping politicians' strategic decisions about the use of clientelism across both urban and rural settings.

Fourth, I expand existing theories on political participation by providing a new explanation for an empirical puzzle seen in many developing countries: that wealthier voters participate less than poorer voters, in the opposite pattern of advanced democracies. Kasara and Suryanarayan (2015) explain this as a function of wealthier voters' indifference: in countries with low tax capacity and no major class cleavages between parties, wealthier voters do not need to participate to protect their wealth because they are not threatened by the prospect of redistributive taxation. I instead show that any class-based turnout differences may be more a function of voters' preferences, not their wealth directly, in contexts of nonprogrammatic competition, which is likely to be closely correlated with the tax capacity of states.[81] Although their tax burden is comparatively low, middle-class voters in urban Ghana complain regularly about taxes and are by no means otherwise indifferent about government policy. The relative abstention of voters who demand programmatic policy is more a function of their (lack of) options: when living in a nonprogrammatic political equilibrium in which no party is credibly promising to act on their preferences, exit becomes a least-worse response.

1.3.3 Demand versus Supply-side Theories of Political Change

The third main contribution comes from examining how overarching modes of political competition evolve in contemporary new democracies. Existing research has established a clear, cross-national negative correlation between the wealth of the electorate and the presence of clientelism. A similar correlation holds within many countries, with more clientelism in poorer regions or municipalities.[82] Two broad streams of literature have attempted to explain these correlations: those focusing on "demand-side" and those focusing on "supply-side" factors.[83] The expectations about the effects of the middle class summarized above represent a common demand-side argument: the underlying assumption is that changes in voter preferences and social identities, rooted in socioeconomic development, lead to changes in how politicians behave.

---

[81] Amat and Beramendi (2016) provide another variant of clientelism-based argument to explain turnout inequality.

[82] For example, see Banfield and Wilson (1963), Chubb (1982), Kitschelt (2007), Luna (2014), Magaloni et al. (2007), Scheiner (2006), and Weitz-Shapiro (2014).

[83] Kitschelt and Wilkinson (2007) and Hicken (2011) summarize these two literatures.

In this way, demand-side theories are a form of modernization hypothesis.[84] Assumptions about the decline of ethnic politics and identification in cities are also rooted in a modernization framework.[85]

There are reasons to be skeptical of such arguments. Despite the correlations between clientelism and levels of development, little research has examined the process by which contemporary developing countries actually transition toward policy-based political competition as wealth and other societal conditions change.[86] Kitschelt and Kselman (2013) suggest that marginal increases in wealth in contemporary developing democracies may not actually translate into reductions in the use of clientelism, finding no strong correlation between societal levels of wealth and clientelism among poor and middle income countries. They argue that clientelism appears much more difficult to dislodge than demand-side and modernization theories assume.

By studying a new democracy in flux, undergoing rapid socioeconomic change, I zoom in on this potential transition and provide new empirical evidence in support of supply-side arguments. I show that changing demographic conditions alone do not mean that politicians face incentives to change their behavior in response. Some empirical patterns that I document – such as overarching rural–urban differences in the extent to which ethnicity predicts vote choice, or the low levels of clientelism in wealthier urban neighborhoods – appear consistent with broader predictions of demand-side or modernization theories. But I demonstrate that the mechanisms underlying these patterns are quite different than these theories often imply, and are based more in politicians' incentives to supply different types of appeals in different places than in the demands of voters: differences in the political importance of ethnicity emerge from patterns of distributive politics, not from changes to the wealth, ethnic identification, or social ties of voters; the presence of clientelism is not simply a function of voter wealth, but is also explained by costs

---

[84] Kitschelt (2000). Weitz-Shapiro (2014) also explicitly describes her theory about municipal-level variation in clientelism in Argentina as an extension of modernization theories.

[85] For example, Conroy-Krutz (2009), Robinson (2014), and Green (2014) each explain rural–urban differences in either ethnic voting or ethnic social identification by directly referencing classical modernization theories. For statements of classical modernization theories about the erosion of traditional kin-based ties, see Lerner (1958), Lipset (1960), Deutsch (1961), and Inkeles (1966).

[86] See Hagopian et al. (2009), Kitschelt et al. (2010), and Grindle (2012), however. A much larger literature – examined in Chapter 9 – explores historical transitions away from patronage-based politics in the US and Europe (e.g., Wolfinger 1972, Erie 1988, Trounstine 2008, Stokes et al. 2013, Mares 2015, Kuo 2018).

politicians face in engaging with voters with similar levels of wealth but different housing arrangements and degrees of embeddedness in their communities.

1.4 THE CASE AND EMPIRICAL STRATEGY

The remaining chapters develop the argument in the context of electoral competition in Ghana, focusing in particular on Ghana's largest metropolitan area – Greater Accra. Greater Accra's population has more than doubled since Ghana democratized in 1992, reaching approximately four million people. It is now the ninth-largest city in sub-Saharan Africa and a major regional economic hub.

The empirical analysis primarily comes from a single snapshot in time, examining variation in behavior across a representative cross-section of this city and comparing electoral competition in Greater Accra to rural areas of Ghana. This limits the extent to which I can test a dynamic argument. But I analyze electoral competition in Greater Accra *after* major demographic transitions – the growth of the middle class and the rise of ethnic diversity – have already reached a point at which the existing literature expects them to begin producing political change: ethnic diversity is already extensive; the middle class already forms a potentially pivotal section of the electorate. Moreover, to the extent that I can analyze trends – such as in the programmatic content of each party's campaign appeals – I show over time variation consistent with my argument: the major parties' platforms are becoming less programmatic over time despite the growth of the middle class, for example.

I examine original representative survey data alongside fine-grained, geocoded, enumeration area-level census data, which is rarely available in developing countries. The survey also includes embedded survey experiments that explore the underlying mechanisms in my argument. In addition, I analyze qualitative evidence collected during extended field research between 2012 and 2014, including interviews with nearly 50 local political candidates and party leaders and 13 focus groups conducted with voters in a cross-section of the city's neighborhoods. The main data collection focuses on Ghana's 2012 presidential and parliamentary elections. In Chapter 8, I also examine Ghana's 2010 and 2015 local government elections.[87]

---

[87] Ghana held a subsequent presidential and parliamentary election in December 2016, in which the opposition party during the period of data collection (the New Patriotic Party; NPP) won power for the first time since 2008. It is too soon to determine whether the actions of the new NPP government will change patterns of electoral competition, but I

Methodologically, the book furthers the trend toward subnational analyses in comparative politics.[88] But rather than comparing subnational administrative units, I zoom in even further, down to the level of individual neighborhoods within districts. A long tradition of scholarship in sociology, political science, and other disciplines has seen socioeconomic conditions at the neighborhood level as especially important for understanding how urban contexts operate.[89] At this scale of analysis, I am able to hold many important contextual factors fixed – political institutions, the nature of the party system, broader economic conditions, and candidate characteristics – to compare voters facing the same options in the same elections.

Ghana provides a good case for three reasons. First, urban Ghana exemplifies core patterns of urbanization occurring across sub-Saharan Africa. Ghana's political system also shares key features with other African democracies: a low-capacity state; a powerful president, with minimal political and fiscal decentralization; ethnic diversity and politicized ethnic cleavages; and little prior history of ideological or programmatic competition.

Second, on the dimensions along which it is not typical, Ghana provides a *harder case* for my argument. It is perhaps the sub-Saharan African country in which the conditions for programmatic politics are most favorable, other than the middle income states of Southern Africa (South Africa, Botswana, and Namibia). As of 2010, Ghana has become a majority urban country; there is no way to win national power without significant support in urban areas. Ghana has had one of the fastest rates of GDP growth in the world over the last two decades, is among a small set of African countries to have recently reached "lower middle income" status, and has one of the largest urban middle classes in sub-Saharan Africa. Ghana differs most from other African countries in its sustained success with democracy. Ghana's politics are often held up as a model to which other African countries should aspire. Elections are highly competitive and relatively free and fair, with competition between two well-institutionalized parties that have peacefully traded power. High

---

expect significant continuity given the highly similar nature of Ghana's parties and the many parallels in styles of governance between the previous NPP administration (2001–2008) and the National Democratic Congress (NDC) government in power from 2009 to 2016.

[88] Snyder (2001).
[89] For example, see Sampson (2012) and Enos (2017).

levels of competition should make Ghana's parties even more sensitive to the costs of clientelism, encouraging political change when facing a wealthier population.[90] An institutionalized party system should make it easier for parties to establish credible brands rooted in policy appeals. That this still does not happen is thus all the more puzzling. Showing that urban politics is stuck in a nonprogrammatic trap *even in Ghana* can help demonstrate how unlikely cities in other new democracies on the continent, with even less favorable conditions, are to break out of their own versions of the trap.

Third, the availability of detailed micro-level data on demographic conditions in urban Ghana allows for an analysis of intra-urban variation in neighborhood context, distributive politics, and political behavior that would simply not be possible in most developing countries. Census data disaggregated to the tract level has only been examined in a small handful of African countries.[91] Existing cross-national data sources, such as the Afrobarometer surveys, do not provide representative samples of specific urban areas within countries and, especially, of neighborhoods within cities that would allow for detailed comparative analyses of the main findings in this book.

While data limitations thus exclude the possibility of a broader comparative study, there are risks to external validity from analysis of a single overarching case. In Chapter 2, I place urban Ghana in comparative perspective and identify scope conditions for the argument. Four are particularly important. First, where state capacity is higher, credibility problems will serve as less of a constraint on politicians' ability to engage with middle-class voters. But in Chapter 2 I show that Ghana ranks among the highest capacity states in sub-Saharan Africa on standard indices; the credibility problem I describe in Ghana is likely even worse elsewhere. Second, in settings with more inchoate party systems, parties may not have the grassroots organizational capacity to sustain clientelistic relationships with individual voters in urban slums. But there are also reasons to doubt whether this is the case – nonparty substitutes in other developing countries emerge in slums to serve similar roles as Ghana's party organizations – and an inchoate party system should only exacerbate the credibility problems parties face in making programmatic appeals. Third, ethnic political competition has never been significant

---

[90] Kitschelt (2007) and Weitz-Shapiro (2014).
[91] I am aware only of studies using similarly disaggregated census data in Malawi (Ejdemyr et al. 2017) and Uganda.

to begin with – even in rural areas – in some African countries.[92] The elements of the argument relating to ethnicity will not be applicable in these countries. Fourth, some African cities are more internally homogeneous than Accra, with smaller middle classes and less ethnic diversity. This is especially common in smaller provincial cities rather than the main magnet cities that dominate each country's economy. Where there is less variation in the internal characteristics of cities, my argument would predict less intra-urban variation in patterns of electoral competition.

1.5 PLAN OF THE BOOK

The remainder of the book proceeds as follows. Chapter 2 introduces the Ghanaian case and the Greater Accra metropolitan area. It documents recent socioeconomic transformations in the city, places Ghana in the context of broader patterns of urbanization in sub-Saharan Africa, and discusses scope conditions for the main argument.

The subsequent chapters move step-by-step through Figure 1.1. Figure 1.4 lays out how each chapter corresponds to an element of Figure 1.1. Part II begins by considering why politicians continue to have incentives to engage exclusively in nonprogrammatic appeals despite the growth of the urban middle class. Chapter 3 shows that many middle-class residents of Greater Accra have different preferences than the poor, in line with existing theories. But Chapter 4 demonstrates that politicians do not respond to these new preferences because of a credibility problem in engaging with voters who demand programmatic politics. The chapter shows that policy-oriented voters differentially abstain from political participation in the face of entrenched patronage-based appeals, and documents that politicians under-invest in mobilizing middle-class voters.

Part III shows how the continued use of nonprogrammatic appeals leads directly to the persistence of ethnic competition and ethnic voting in urban areas. Chapter 5 begins by presenting the theoretical argument for why politicians engage in different patronage-based strategies across different neighborhoods within African cities. The chapter connects politicians' behavior to the expectations and behavior of voters, making predictions about how urban voters will value the election of ethnically aligned parties differently in different places within the same city. Chapters 6 and 7 provide evidence in support of this argument.

---

[92] For example, see Posner (2004), Dunning and Harrison (2010), and Koter (2016).

1.5 Plan of the Book

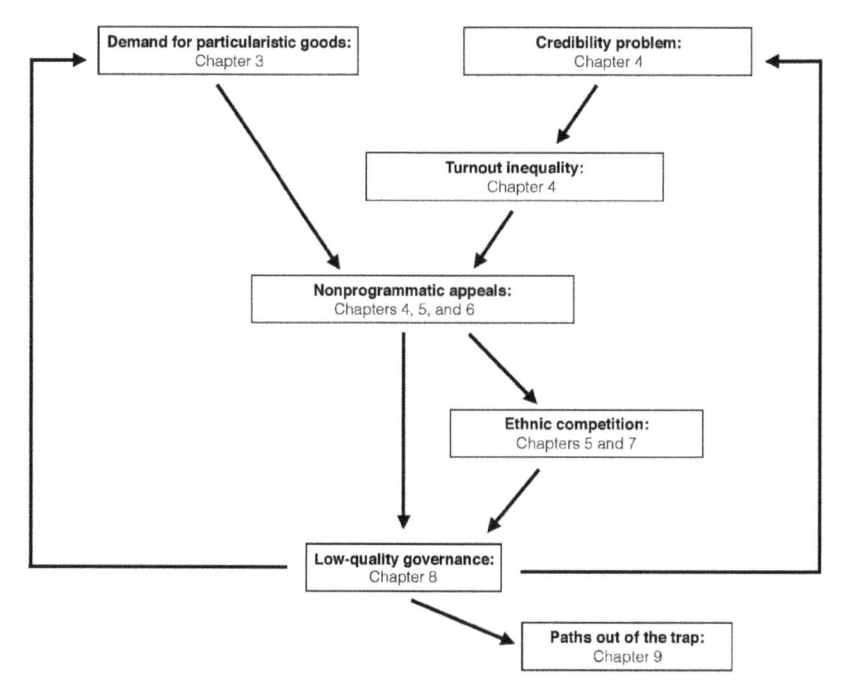

FIGURE 1.4: *Chapter organization.*

Chapter 6 documents spatially varied electoral appeals across urban neighborhoods and compares distributive strategies between urban and rural areas. In particular, it focuses on the role of local party organizations in implementing different clientelistic strategies across the city. Chapter 7 then examines the behavior of urban voters, showing that the political importance of ethnicity varies at the neighborhood level within cities in response to variation in the implementation of nonprogrammatic appeals.

Part IV considers the downstream impacts of these patterns of political competition on the quality of urban governance. Chapter 8 focuses on how entrenched patronage practices, the broad abstention of the urban middle class from local elections, and ethnic voting allow an ethnic minority to capture disproportionate local power in Greater Accra's municipal governments and govern narrowly in its own interest. Chapter 9 concludes, drawing parallels to cases beyond Africa – the historical United States and contemporary Latin America – to consider potential paths out of the trap.

2

Urban Ghana in Context

This chapter introduces characteristics of Greater Accra that underlie the argument and analysis in the subsequent chapters. In the first half of the chapter, I describe the main socioeconomic changes occurring in the city, including the rise of the urban middle class and city's evolving ethnic composition, and show how these changes are taking place in a context of scarcity in the provision of basic services. I define the scale at which I will examine intra-urban variation in these characteristics, and document that the size of the middle class and levels of ethnic diversity vary significantly across local areas. I then compare Greater Accra to other African cities, laying out scope conditions for the argument and describing how the Ghanaian case speaks to similar dynamics in other countries.

The second half pivots to Ghana's political system, introducing central features of the electoral environment that shape the analysis throughout the book. I again compare Ghana to other cases, describing additional reasons why Ghana provides a hard case for evaluating the argument in Chapter 1 about the effects of the middle class and ethnic diversity on electoral competition in urban Africa.

2.1 THE GROWTH OF GREATER ACCRA

In the mid-1980s, Accra already had more than one million residents. You did not need to drive far from the city center to find rural life, however. Seven miles from downtown Accra, for example, was Gbawe, a farming community nestled in the hills ringing the city's northern edge. The 1984 census counted 837 residents in the village. The 1970 census had recorded only 608. Almost all were Ga, the indigenous ethnic group of the Accra area. Many worked on small farms. A chief's palace sat at the center of the village, surrounded by traditional compound houses belonging to the community's original Ga families.[1]

But Gbawe changed in the 1990s. As Accra became increasingly overcrowded, housing shortages drove residents to seek new land on the outskirts of the city. The city soon spilled far beyond its official boundaries, producing a series of new urban neighborhoods in rapid succession. By 2000, Gbawe's population had mushroomed to 29,000. By 2010, Gbawe reached a total of 68,000 people, more than 80 times the 1984 population. Only 25% of Gbawe's residents were still Ga, the ethnic group of the village's original inhabitants. Their number were dwarfed by Akan residents, an ethnic group originally from elsewhere in Ghana that makes up nearly 60% of the current community.[2]

You can see vestiges of the village's past when visiting Gbawe today. The chief's palace still sits in the center of the community. The compound houses ringing it still belong to the original Ga families. The chief and his "stool elders" (traditional family heads) retain influence among the Ga who remain, but the new residents who now form the majority in the community have little relationship with Gbawe's chief and Ga elders. But walk past the palace in either direction and you find yourself in a diverse lower-class neighborhood that looks indistinguishable from others throughout Accra. Less than a mile up the main road north of the chief's palace you come to quiet suburban streets of single-family homes for Accra's growing middle class, built on what was farm land just two decades ago. These middle-class residents have built new homes in Gbawe despite significant shortcomings in access to basic public services; the neighborhood emerged faster than the local government could respond. The main road through the middle-class neighborhood north of Gbawe is unpaved and deeply rutted, flooding regularly. Most homes are not connected to regular running water. Residents complain about poor security and the need for a new police post.

The transformation of Gbawe from a small, poor, homogenous village to a dense, ethnically and economically diverse set of neighborhoods in the middle of a major metropolitan area is indicative of broader changes occurring across Ghana. Less than a quarter of Ghana's population lived in cities at independence in 1957. Today, more than 54% of Ghana's 25 million people live in urban areas.[3] Ghana now has four

---

[1] See Gough and Yankson (2006).
[2] Figures are from Ghana's 2010 Population and Housing Census.
[3] United Nations (2014) and World Bank (2015).

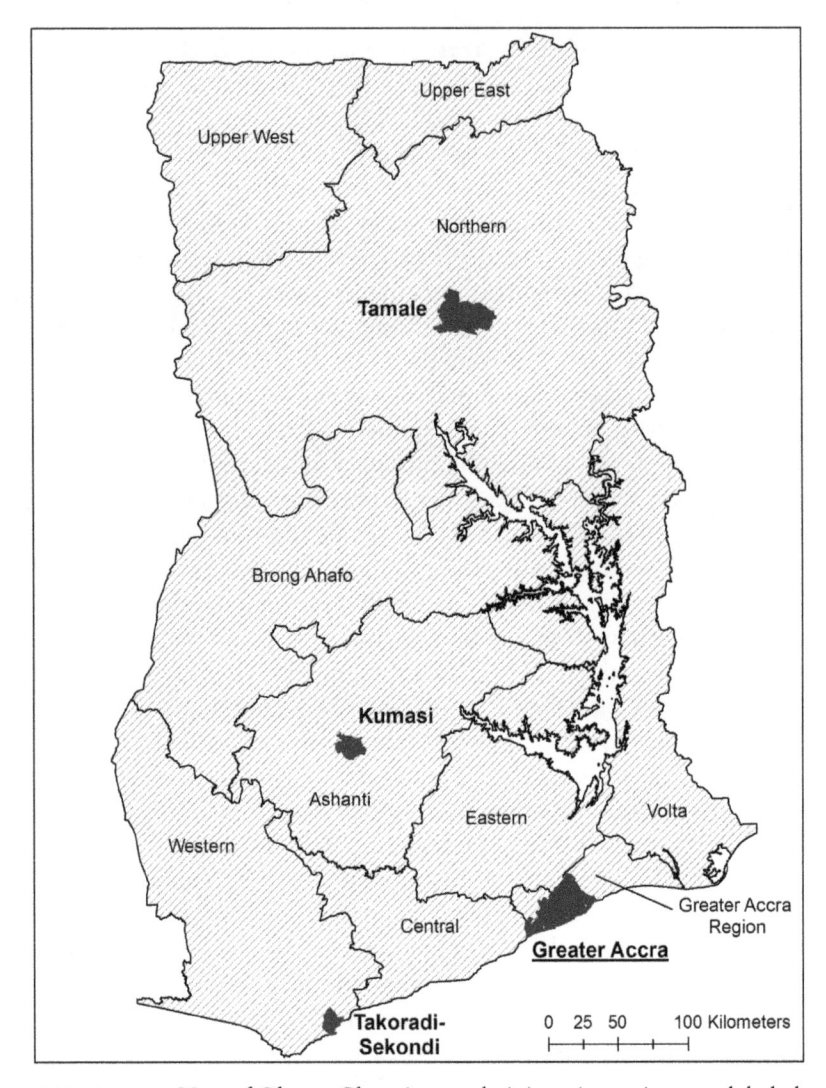

FIGURE 2.1: *Map of Ghana:* Ghana's ten administrative regions are labeled along with the country's four major urban areas.

large metropolitan areas, shown in Figure 2.1: Greater Accra (combining Accra, Tema, and surrounding districts), Kumasi, Tamale, and Takoradi-Sekondi; Greater Accra is the largest and holds a dominant position in the national economy.

The Accra area was originally composed of small fishing and farming villages inhabited by the Ga-Dangme ethnic groups. Ghana's Atlantic

2.1 The Growth of Greater Accra

Coast became home to a series of European forts and trading installations beginning in the second half of the fifteenth century. These outposts were central export points for gold and the Atlantic slave trade and gradually turned Accra into a commercial hub, linking the Ashanti kingdom in central Ghana to European markets. The city grew further after becoming the capital of the British Gold Coast colony in the late 1870s, and especially after the British built a railway in the 1920s linking Accra to the gold- and cocoa-producing regions of the interior.[4] But most of Accra's transformation into a large, multi-ethnic city occurred after independence in 1957. Initially, large streams of rural–urban migrants poured into the capital, similar to the pattern in most developing countries.[5] In recent decades, growth has been driven more by higher rates of natural increase in urban than rural areas than by migration. Although rural–urban migration still occurs, the majority of Greater Accra's residents have now always lived in urban areas.[6]

By the beginning of the twenty-first century, Accra had consumed its surrounding districts, including the area around Gbawe, and become contiguous with the nearby city of Tema. Figure 2.2 shows the 12 administrative districts – akin to municipalities – that now make up the urban reaches of the Greater Accra metropolitan area. The official city of Accra is only one district, known as the Accra Metropolitan Assembly (AMA).[7] As of the 2012 election, these 12 districts contained 30 parliamentary constituencies, of which 28 had become predominately urban. Throughout this book, "Greater Accra" refers to all of these 28 urban parliamentary constituencies within the Greater Accra Region.[8] The current population of the Accra Metropolitan Assembly (AMA) is approximately 1.9 million, while Greater Accra's full population is now approximately 4 million, up from 2.8 million in 2000 and only 1.4 million in 1984.[9]

---

[4] The European settler presence in Accra always remained small, unlike in many cities in East and Southern Africa.
[5] For example, see Ades and Glaeser (1995).
[6] Ghana Statistical Service (2008), World Bank (2015).
[7] As this book went to press, the government announced that it was creating six new municipalities out of the AMA, further splitting the official city of Accra into seven separate administrative districts.
[8] This excludes four parliamentary constituencies in the official Greater Accra administrative region that remain predominately rural – Ada, Ningo-Prampram, Shai Osudoku, and Sege – as well as two constituencies – Domeabra-Obom and Amasaman – that remain mostly rural but are in otherwise urban districts.
[9] Many sources, such as United Nations (2014), calculate Accra's population while excluding many of these outlying urban districts or not adjusting for changes to Accra's

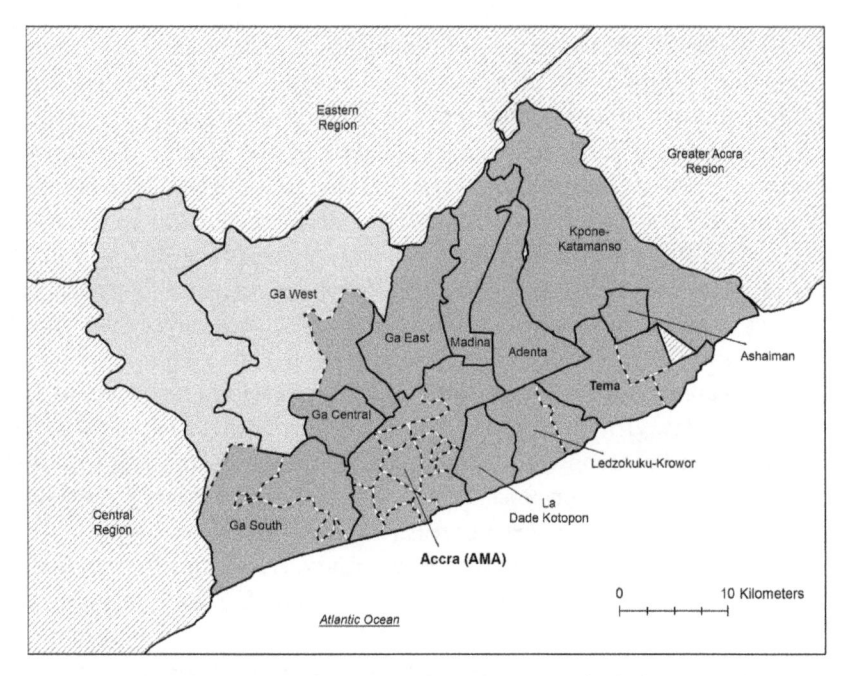

FIGURE 2.2: *Greater Accra metropolitan area:* The shaded areas and solid boundary lines demarcate the 12 urban administrative districts (local municipal governments) that comprise the metropolitan area. The official city of Accra is the Accra Metropolitan Assembly (AMA). The dashed lines demarcate the boundaries of the parliamentary constituencies nested within the larger districts. Two parliamentary constituencies – Domeabra-Obom and Amasaman, shaded in the lighter gray – fall within otherwise urban districts but are themselves still predominately rural.

2.2 THE EXPLANATORY VARIABLES

As it has grown, Greater Accra has taken on several characteristics of large African cities that serve as the main explanatory variables in this book. Each is typified by the example of Gbawe. A large middle class has emerged, even as slums have continued to grow. The city has become increasingly ethnically diverse, even as some neighborhoods

boundaries, leading to an understatement of the size of the metropolitan area. The AMA – the official city boundary – has actually shrunk in land area over time, with two large portions splitting off into their own municipalities in the last two decades. Irrespective of these boundaries, the Greater Accra metropolis now stretches as an uninterrupted urban agglomeration from Kasoa at the border of Ghana's Central Region, 15 miles west of central Accra, to Kpone, on the outer rim of Tema, 20 miles east of central Accra.

remain segregated. In addition, there is now wide variation in levels of state service provision – even within middle class and wealthy areas of the city – as the government struggles to catch up to the demands created by rapid urbanization.

2.2.1 Defining the "Middle Class"

I begin with the middle class. It is not possible to document the growth of the middle class in urban Ghana without first defining what the middle class actually is. Although recent growth of the middle class has been widely discussed in Africa and the developing world more broadly,[10] definitions have been wildly inconsistent.[11] I discuss the strengths and limitations of existing approaches for classifying middle-class status in developing countries and justify the use of a measure based on education and employment characteristics in the absence of high-quality data on income.

The most common approach to estimating the size of the middle class involves a daily-income threshold. But this approach is subject to significant disagreement about what the threshold should be. The African Development Bank (2011), the source of the most widely cited recent report estimating the size of the African middle class, defines the middle class as people with incomes in excess of US$4 per day, while Banerjee and Duflo (2008) define it as those with incomes of between US$2 and US$10 per day, and Birdsall (2010) defines it as incomes above US$10 per day. Others define the middle class as the literal middle of the nationwide income distribution, for example as incomes between 75% and 125% of a country's median.

Income-based definitions of the middle class have more substantive shortcomings besides lacking an agreed-upon threshold. Deaton (2010) argues that these measures usually fail to account for substantial variation in the goods and services that US$1 buys, both across countries and especially across regions within countries. The quality of life that US$4 per day or US$10 per day affords can be extremely different from what Western observers typically think of as a "middle-class" lifestyle, suggesting the need for different thresholds in different types of economies.[12]

---

[10] See Banerjee and Duflo (2008), Ravallion (2009), Lofchie (2015), Ncube (2015), and Resnick (2015b).
[11] Birdsall (2010), Mitlin and Satterthwaite (2013), and Thurlow et al. (2015).
[12] Ravallion (2009).

Problems of comparability also arise when comparing urban and rural areas of the same country. Costs of living in urban areas are often significantly higher, such that income-based measures can understate the extent of urban poverty by not accounting for the additional expenses required of urban dwellers.[13] There are also measurement limitations to defining class via an income threshold. Incomes are difficult to measure reliably on censuses and surveys in developing-country settings where much of the economy remains informal.[14]

A more tractable definition of the middle-class status in settings such as urban Ghana moves beyond daily incomes to account for the dimensions of middle-class status that are most important to theories linking the growth of the middle class to changes in political behavior. Conceptually, scholars who have tied rising prosperity and the emergence of a middle class to political change have often theorized socioeconomic classes less in terms of specific income levels or locations in an income distribution than as sociological categories (or even identity groups) that represent particular positions in a broader economic system.[15] Whether to Marxists or to classical modernization theorists, class status represents a structural position in the economy and civic community. To Lipset (1960) and Deutsch (1961), for example, the individual-level modernization that was expected to trigger political change encompassed a bundle of social characteristics – literacy, higher education, nonagricultural employment – that go beyond income alone. In this view, the middle class will not always be synonymous with a specific income level or the median zone of a national income distribution. It is instead "middle" in that it is an intermediate level of socioeconomic status between the poor and the economic elite.

More in line with this conceptual definition, Thurlow et al. (2015) propose identifying the African middle class based on indicators for the probability that someone has escaped basic poverty and can compete in the modern formal-sector economy. In lieu of reliable income data, they use survey data to code class status based on whether someone lives in a home that meets minimum standards – reliable electricity, running water, and a flush toilet – and by whether someone has secondary education and is employed in the formal sector economy. Measures of housing assets or of educational attainment have the benefit of being fairly stable

---

[13] Mitlin and Satterthwaite (2013).
[14] For example, see Filmer and Pritchett (2001) and Thurlow et al. (2015).
[15] Birdsall (2010), Thurlow et al. (2015).

indicators of long-term wealth accumulation that do not change rapidly with short-term fluctuations in macroeconomic conditions, unlike daily income measures. Others, such as Filmer and Pritchett (2001), have used more extensive asset indices to measure socioeconomic status, finding that asset measures correlate significantly with income in developing country settings. But there are downsides to measuring socioeconomic status based on housing quality or other basic household assets. These measures can conflate variation in government spending – political decisions about investments in public services, such as in the provision of electricity and water – with actual variation in private wealth.[16]

For this reason, I primarily measure socioeconomic class using a measure focused on educational attainment, English literacy (language of official business), and formal-sector employment. This is meant to capture the sociological nature of middle-class status: the probability that someone has reached at least a middle tier in the structure of the economy and has the skills necessary for nonmanual forms of employment.[17] I operationalize educational attainment as whether someone has attended at least some secondary schooling. Secondary school, or senior high school (SHS) attendance is a particularly important separator of class in Ghana because public education is free through middle school (junior high school; JHS). Many poor students attend public school through JHS and then exit; only those who can afford tuition continue to SHS.

Importantly, both my measure of education and employment and the measure from Thurlow et al. (2015) have the limitation that they primarily distinguish the poor from the nonpoor rather than the middle class from both the poor and upper-class elite.[18] Without detailed data on income it is difficult to differentiate the middle class and elite on the basis of education or formal-sector employment alone. But given high levels of income inequality, the truly wealthy elite remain a tiny proportion of the population and electorate in most developing countries, including in Ghana, and are not well represented in standard survey data. I set aside theoretical consideration of the potentially separate behaviors and attitudes of the small minority of wealthy elites and focus on comparisons of the middle class and poor.

---

[16] For example, see Mitlin and Satterthwaite (2013).
[17] Alongside this measure, I control separately for an index of basic household assets in all individual-level analyses.
[18] Cheeseman (2015) discusses similar limitations of education-based measures of class status.

2.2.2 Greater Accra's Middle Class

Using this definition, I estimate the size of the urban middle class in Greater Accra with two data sources: census data and Demographic and Health Surveys (DHS). The census allows for more accurate estimates of the size of the middle class, but cannot show variation over time.[19] The DHS provides a noisier measure of the size of the middle class, but allows for comparisons over time. Both sources suggest that just under one quarter of working-age adults in Greater Accra now meet the definition of middle-class status proposed above. As discussed in Chapter 1, this is a large enough group of residents to play a potentially pivotal role in the city's elections.

According to the 2010 census, 22% of working-age adults in metropolitan Greater Accra were employed in the formal sector (private or public), were literate in English (the language of official business), and had at least some secondary education.[20] The DHS provides measures of growth of the middle class over time. It collected nationally and regionally representative samples of Ghana at five different points between 1993 and 2014, which can be geolocated.[21] Figure 1.2 plots growth in the middle-class population in Greater Accra and the other three large metropolitan areas in Ghana from 1993 to 2014 using the DHS data.[22] The 2008 and 2014 middle-class proportions for each city

---

[19] The main census data analyzed throughout the book is from 2010, Ghana's most recent census. I only have access to the 2000 census data at a more aggregated level, which prevents direct comparisons with 2010 of the number of people with multiple characteristics, such as both literacy and formal-sector employment. Beyond population totals, the 1984 census data disaggregated to the local level is also not available.

[20] This is based on a 10% random sample of residents in each census enumeration area, selected by the Ghana Statistical Service. The figure is calculated for residents of the city age 18 and above, but excludes from the dominator those who report being retired or too old to work. Formal sector employment as calculated here includes full-time university students age 18 and above.

[21] The DHS does not directly measure formal sector employment in the manner of Ghana's census. I code a proxy for formal sector employment as respondents working in the "service," "clerical," "professional/technical/managerial," and "sales" sectors, as opposed to respondents working in "agricultural," "manual," or "unskilled" sectors. Some respondents in each sector, especially in "sales," will be in the informal sector economy, such that the measures from the DHS may over-count the true size of the middle class under my definition. Nonetheless, I find very similar estimates of middle-class size from the DHS and census, suggesting that the measurement error induced by this coding decision is small.

[22] Figure 1.2 also presents the same trends using an adapted form of the alternative definition of middle-class status from Thurlow et al. (2015) as a comparison. These quantities are calculated after geolocating DHS survey clusters and subsetting to those that fall

as measured on the DHS closely match the estimate of middle-class size from the 2010 census. Under my definition, the DHS records that 24.5% of Greater Accra's population had reached middle-class status in 2014, compared to 22.7% in 2008. This represents a dramatic rise from only 7.1% of the city's population in 1993. The growth of the middle class has been similarly dramatic in Ghana's other major cities. In Kumasi, for example, the percentage rose from 3.1% in 1993 to 19.9% in 2014.

Importantly, Greater Accra's emerging middle class is largely *not* dependent on ties to the state for its economic position, unlike in some democracies where extensive state intervention in the economy allows clientelism to persist despite rising wealth.[23] The emergence of a large urban middle class throughout sub-Saharan Africa, including in Ghana, has occurred primarily after structural-adjustment programs led to significant privatization of the urban economy.[24] The 2010 census data splits out formal sector employment by whether residents work in the private, public (or parastatal), or nonprofit sectors. Among residents of Greater Accra who meet the definition of middle-class status outlined earlier and are not full-time university students, 33% are employed as civil servants or work for state-owned companies. The large majority – 63% – work in the private sector.[25] As a result, most middle-class voters are not reliant on the ruling party to continue in their jobs.[26]

The middle class in Ghana – and in most of the rest of urban Africa – also differs from that in other settings in not having emerged through an industrialization process, the historical pattern of many Western democracies. Rapid urbanization in Africa is occurring in spite of low levels of industrialization; industrial employment has actually fallen as a share of

---

within the boundaries of the parliamentary constituencies that comprise each of the four metropolitan areas. The DHS sample is representative to the administrative region level, not the city level, such that some variation over time could be due to sampling variability. But this is the only individual-level data source that allows for clear subnational trends over time, and there are large samples of respondents in each city.

[23] Kitschelt (2007). This also differs, for example, from the black middle class in South Africa, many of whom Southall (2014) argues have achieved their position through state policy and intervention in the economy.

[24] See Herbst (1993) and Aryeetey (1996) on the history of structural adjustment in Ghana.

[25] The small remainder are employed by NGOs and various international organizations.

[26] Moreover, rank-and-file civil servants are typically not locked in ongoing clientelist relationships with politicians, with continued employment contingent on political support, even though there is politicization of initial hiring into entry-level civil service jobs (Brierley 2017) (also see Chapter 6). Luna (2016) and Brierley (2016) describe how civil servants may be put in less desirable posts because of political connections, but there are not mass purges of civil servants when a new party takes power.

the urban work force over time.[27] With the middle class more likely to be employed in the service sector than in factories, key institutions that historically provided a mechanism to advocate for class-based political interests in Western democracies – such as trade unions – are not major forces in Ghanaian politics or in most other African countries. There is a small union movement in Ghana and there are periodic strikes, especially among civil servants. But union members form a distinct minority of the middle class. In the representative survey data from Greater Accra analyzed in the subsequent chapters, 80% of the respondents who are formal-sector workers are not union members. Union members comprise only 6% of the overall sample of respondents.[28]

2.2.3 Changing Ethnic Composition of Greater Accra

The ethnic composition of Greater Accra has also changed considerably in the past half century. The area is the homeland of the Ga-Dangme ethno-linguistic groups. Accra itself is the historical capital of the largest Ga-Dangme ethnic group, the Ga. Throughout the colonial and early post-independence periods, the Ga remained the large majority in the city and dominated local politics.[29] But the Ga lost their numeric advantage as the city grew. As of 2010, the 28 urban parliamentary constituencies of Greater Accra had become 40% Akan, 23% Ga, and 20% Ewe, with 11% from northern ethnic groups and the remainder from various smaller ethnic groups as well as expatriate populations. The official city of Accra (AMA), which covers many of the original precolonial Ga settlements, was only 23% Ga in the 2010 census. Given recent trends, the Ga likely comprise an even smaller percentage of the city's population today.

Among the first non-Gas to develop a large population in Accra were the various ethnic groups from northern Ghana. Segregated northern-majority neighborhoods – known colloquially by the Hausa word *Zongo* for "foreigner's quarters" – are common throughout the city. The largest Zongos date to the colonial period. The first large group of Muslim migrants in Accra were Hausa traders from outside Ghana.[30] Over time, migrants from the various ethnic groups of northern Ghana emigrated

---

[27] Kessides (2006) and World Bank (2015).
[28] Half (49%) of the union members in the survey sample are informal sector workers. There are active trade associations in urban Ghana whose members are often not employed by a formal sector business. Union membership is not measured on the census or DHS.
[29] Parker (2000) describes the colonial history of Ga politics in Accra.
[30] Cohen (1969).

into the city's original Zongo neighborhoods, such as Sabon Zongo, Tudu, and Nima.[31] Since the colonial period, additional northern-dominated neighborhoods have emerged at Old Fadama (Agbogbloshie) and Madina Zongo, with other smaller Zongo communities sprinkled elsewhere throughout the metropolitan area.

But the largest ethnic group to migrate into Accra and overtake the indigenous Ga population has been the Akan, Ghana's largest ethnolinguistic group, with approximately 47% of the national population. By the mid-1990s, the Akan Twi language had replaced Ga as the primary *lingua franca* of Accra, alongside English.[32] Akans now live throughout Greater Accra, but are especially concentrated in neighborhoods along the northwestern edge of the original city, forming the clear majority in areas such as Dansoman, Awoshie, Kwashieman, Taifa, and Dome.

Despite these changes in ethnic composition, Greater Accra still has segregated Ga enclaves in the locations of the original Ga villages that predate urbanization. This includes the city's colonial-era central business district, which abuts the core communities of the Ga kingdom – Ga Mashie. Central Accra is ringed by these predominately Ga neighborhoods, such as Jamestown, Ushertown, and Chorkor. Many of these Ga communities have become economically marginalized, with some of the most concentrated poverty in the city.[33] But under Ghana's traditional land-tenure system, most land across the metropolitan area is still owned by Ga chiefs and clan (family) heads. Ga land rights in Greater Accra are irregularly enforced and frequently contested in court.[34] In Chapters 7 and 8, I discuss how grievances within the Ga community related to their weakened economic position despite titular land ownership shape the political behavior of many Ga voters.

A major consequence of the city's changing ethnic composition has been the variation it has produced in the importance of traditional leaders. Ga chiefs remain quite active in local politics in Greater Accra, both because the city is their traditional homeland and, especially, because of their land rights. Residents from other ethnic backgrounds lack similarly powerful traditional leaders and ethnic social institutions in Greater Accra, however. Chiefs from other groups are powerful in their own

---

[31] For the history of Accra's Zongos, see Pellow (2002), Kobo (2010), and Ntewusu (2012). Schildkrout (1976) describes the formation of similar Zongo neighborhoods in Kumasi.

[32] Kropp Dakubu (1997).

[33] Weeks et al. (2006) and Ardayfio-Schandorf et al. (2012).

[34] Yeboah (2008), Firmin-Sellers (1996), and Onoma (2010) describe the historical evolution of Ga land rights in Greater Accra.

home regions, but their formal authority does not extend to Accra. Some northern ethnic groups have appointed chiefs within the Zongo neighborhoods, but these chiefs do not own land and have much less political and social influence than they would have in the rural north.[35] In addition, ethnic migrant associations – often known as "youth associations" – historically emerged in African cities, shaping the political activities of new urban migrants around shared ties to rural ethnic homelands.[36] These associations have long since faded away in urban Ghana, however. In the representative survey data examined in the subsequent chapters, I find that less than 5% of non-Ga respondents report any connection to an ethnic association.[37] As a result, while chiefs remain active among one minority group in the city, the large majority of urban residents have little day-to-day connection with the main traditional institutions that help structure rural life.

2.2.4 Service Delivery Challenges

Much of Greater Accra's growth has been unplanned, with Ghana's government often unable to effectively enforce land-use regulations or keep up with the provision of infrastructure in new neighborhoods. In Chapter 3, I demonstrate how this inability to meet demands for new state services results in persistent demands on politicians for particularistic goods that can be targeted as patronage.

Despite the city's incredible recent gains in wealth, both the national government and the city's 12 municipal governments face service-delivery challenges on essentially every front: in the provision of roads, electricity, running water, education, healthcare, and housing. Large sections of the city's road network, primarily in newer neighborhoods, remain unpaved. Roads continually incur serious damage due to flooding. Where they exist, the city's sewers and storm drains are almost all open to the air, continually collecting debris; annual flooding ensues.[38] While the

---

[35] In my interviews, politicians in Greater Accra did not describe "Zongo chiefs" as playing any similar political role to Ga chiefs or as serving as electoral intermediaries. With much less power, their roles appear to be largely ceremonial.
[36] See Wallerstein (1964), Little (1964), Wolpe (1974).
[37] I also find in Chapter 7 that membership in these associations does not predict voting behavior.
[38] Recent floods in central Accra have caused hundreds of deaths, as well as recurring cholera outbreaks. For example, see: "Accra Floods: More than 100 Feared Dead After Explosion" (2015); Dery (2014).

electricity grid covers the entire metropolitan area, generating capacity cannot meet demand, leading to extended periods of rolling blackouts. Running water availability is also problematic. The city center has a pipe network, but large swaths of the outlying districts do not. In many areas where the pipe network exists, the supply is irregular, delivering water to homes once a week or less. Overcrowding in public primary schools in central Accra has forced education officials to resort at times to a shift system. Budget shortfalls in the public health system have led to recurring strikes by public sector doctors and nurses.[39] Finally, the city also has a housing shortage.[40] There has been significant recent construction of high-end housing by private developers, but these units rent at rates comparable to those in many American cities, far beyond the budget of most residents.[41] Construction of nonluxury housing has not kept pace, and the government abandoned most efforts at providing public housing decades ago.[42]

While cities everywhere – including in much of the developed world – face challenges in meeting the service delivery demands of all of their residents, Greater Accra's shortfalls are exacerbated by limited budgets and weak bureaucratic capacity – both hallmarks of a weak state. The municipal budgets for the city's districts are far too small to address all needs for new public services. Districts have limited ability to raise their internally generated funds and primarily rely on annual transfers from the national government. The Ghanaian government has made some major improvements in public services in Greater Accra in recent years – for example, by expanding major highways and extending piped water access into some of the more recently settled districts north of the city center. But each of these major projects was supported primarily by outside donor funding, secured on a case-by-case basis. In day-to-day management of the city, politicians in Greater Accra must continually decide how to allocate very scarce public resources across an urban area with numerous pressing demands. In doing so, they direct an underfunded bureaucracy susceptible to political pressure and control.[43] This provides politicians with

---

[39] For example, see: "Doctors in Ghana continue to strike over salary dispute" (2013); "Junior Doctors On Strike Over Unpaid Salaries" (2015); "35,000 Nurses, Midwives Declare Strike" (2014).
[40] This applies in all of urban Ghana, which is estimated to be approaching a two-million-unit housing deficit (World Bank 2015).
[41] Grant (2009) describes the changing housing market of Greater Accra.
[42] Arku (2009).
[43] Brierley (2016) and Luna (2016).

significant leverage to selectively target and withhold spending through nonprogrammatic electoral appeals.

2.3 SPATIAL GEOGRAPHY OF GREATER ACCRA

There is wide variation within Greater Accra in wealth, ethnic diversity, and the presence of the state. The subsequent chapters focus most attention on variation at the *neighborhood level*. In this section, I describe how neighborhoods nest within the city's official administrative and electoral units and introduce the strategy for measuring the demographic characteristics of neighborhoods employed throughout the book.

I then show how wealth, diversity, and existing levels of state service provision are spatially distributed across Greater Accra. Wealth differs starkly both between slums and middle- and upper-class neighborhoods, and also within middle- and upper-class areas, which still contain some poor residents. The city has a mix of both diverse and segregated neighborhoods. There is variation in state presence, with some neighborhoods where the challenges outlined in the previous section are extensive, but others where service delivery is much better. The subsequent chapters will show that these forms of intra-urban variation shape the costs and benefits of different strategies politicians employ to win elections, with implications for how voters behave.

2.3.1 Defining Neighborhoods

Variation in demographic characteristics can be examined at multiple scales, as outlined in Figure 2.3. At the most aggregated level, the city is divided into the 12 administrative districts, equivalent to municipalities, as depicted in Figure 2.2. As will be explained, each district is led by its own presidentially appointed Mayor (District Chief Executive) and also has a locally elected city council, called a District Assembly. Nested within each district are parliamentary constituencies, exclusively electoral units that serve as the single-member districts in elections to the national parliament. Constituencies fit within districts with a one-to-one or two-to-one match in most cases, but a many-to-one correspondence in the city of Accra itself (the AMA), which contained 13 parliamentary constituencies as of the 2012 election.[44] Within the AMA,

---

[44] In total, Ghana has 275 parliamentary constituencies nested within its 216 administrative districts.

2.3 Spatial Geography of Greater Accra

```
┌─────────────────────────────┐
│   Districts (Municipalities) │
│             12              │
└─────────────────────────────┘
              │
              ▼
┌─────────────────────────────────────┐
│     Parliamentary Constituencies    │
│  30 (28 urban), nested within districts │
└─────────────────────────────────────┘
              │
              ▼
┌─────────────────────────────────────┐
│        Electoral Areas (Wards)      │
│   255, nested within constituencies │
└─────────────────────────────────────┘
              │
              ▼
┌─────────────────────────────────────┐
│            Neighborhoods            │
│  Many hundreds, nested within wards │
└─────────────────────────────────────┘
              │
              ▼
┌─────────────────────────────┐
│   Census Enumeration Areas  │
│           2,701*            │
└─────────────────────────────┘
```

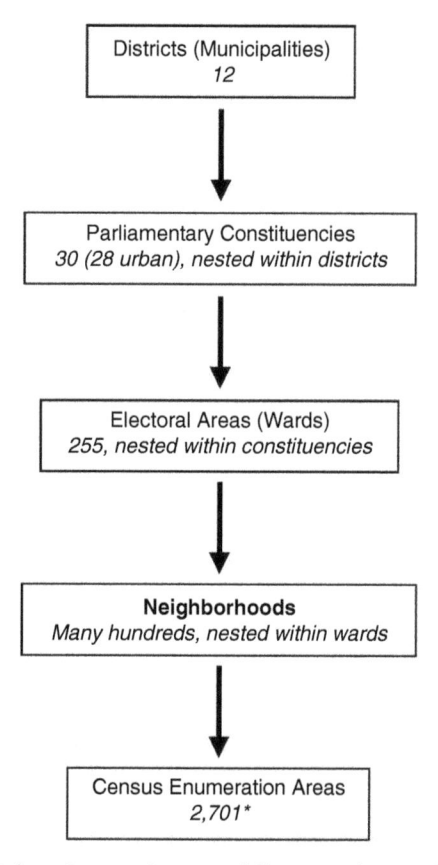

FIGURE 2.3: *Urban Greater Accra at different scales:* neighborhoods nest within Electoral Areas, Constituencies, and Districts.

Note: *I list the number of enumeration areas for which geocoded data is available for analysis. Tema and Ashaiman districts are excluded because of missing data.

parliamentary constituencies also largely overlap with an extra tier of subdistrict local government, the "submetropolitan assembly." Nested within constituencies are Electoral Areas, equivalent to wards, which serve as the single-member districts for city council (District Assembly) elections, examined in Chapter 8. There are 255 Electoral Areas across the metropolitan area's 12 urban districts. Most importantly, beneath Electoral Areas are the city's neighborhoods, the socially meaningful communities in which people live and interact. There are often multiple distinct neighborhoods within a single Electoral Area, and there can be a dozen or more within a parliamentary constituency. Finally, at a scale even lower than the neighborhood level are thousands of census Enumeration Areas, or tracts, each containing several hundred people. This is the most granular level at which the demographic data analyzed throughout the book can be geolocated. However, Enumeration Areas are a purely clerical demarcation of the census bureau and have no social or political significance.

Neighborhoods are the key focus of the subsequent analysis. But unlike officially demarcated administrative and electoral units, neighborhoods are more nebulous social constructs; people living in the same place in a city often disagree about their neighborhood's boundaries.[45] While Greater Accra has many distinct neighborhoods, a map of agreed-upon neighborhood boundaries does not exist and the other pre-existing administrative or electoral demarcations provide inappropriate means for defining them. In the absence of agreed-upon demarcations of neighborhood boundaries, it is impossible to define a single set of neighborhoods across the entire city. I approximate the characteristics of local neighborhoods by aggregating information across census enumeration areas to construct measures of the demographic characteristics in the immediate vicinity of survey respondents.[46]

This approach finds a workable middle ground between other possible definitions based on the other types of units in Figure 2.3. At the smallest extreme, census enumeration areas are themselves socially and politically irrelevant units with arbitrarily discrete boundaries.[47] Using these boundaries to define neighborhoods can also suffer from the "modifiable areal unit problem," in which imposing discrete boundaries on continuous geographic data can bias a study's results.[48] It is similarly problematic to define neighborhoods as existing units much larger than enumeration areas, such as administrative districts or parliamentary constituencies. This would use a level of aggregation so high that localized variation in demographic characteristics is no longer observable and requires examining areas far larger than any meaningful sociological definition of a neighborhood. For example, the average parliamentary

---

[45] Wong et al. (2012).
[46] The survey data itself is introduced in Chapter 3.
[47] For example, because enumeration area boundaries in Greater Accra largely follow the major street grid, people living directly across the street from each other would be counted as living in separate neighborhoods.
[48] Openshaw (1983) and Lee et al. (2008).

2.3 Spatial Geography of Greater Accra

constituency in Greater Accra is 29.8 sq. km (11.5 sq. miles), an area larger than Cambridge and Somerville, Massachusetts put together.

I overcome these problems by defining neighborhood boundaries in a systematic way *across survey respondents* that smooths the census data over enumeration area boundaries to mitigate the modifiable areal unit problem while still capturing the demography around each respondent's home at an appropriately localized scale. Following Reardon and O'Sullivan (2004) and Lee et al. (2008), as well as the approach used in Ichino and Nathan (2013a), I calculate weighted averages of the census characteristics from enumeration areas around each survey respondent, with data from enumeration areas closer to the respondent weighted higher, data further away weighted lower, and data outside a given radius weighted as 0. This means that neighborhoods are measured throughout the book *relative to each respondent's own location*. The main radius used is 500 meters around each respondent.[49]

I use such a small radius for several reasons. First, given the structure of the Ghanaian state described below, much of the opportunity for favoritism in the allocation of state resources occurs *within* districts and constituencies. Second, any variation in neighborhood characteristics becomes increasingly unobservable as the size of the radius used increases.[50] For example, what in reality may be a series of adjacent but highly segregated communities would inappropriately appear to be a single very ethnically diverse community if examined at too high a scale of aggregation.

Third, and most importantly for the theoretical argument in later chapters, many state services that function as club (local public) goods – such as primary schools, paved streets, sewers, and water mains – target benefits on a small scale due to high population density, reaching narrower areas than districts, constituencies, or even Electoral Areas. Population density is as high as 90,000 people per sq. km. in Greater Accra's densest slums. In such a setting, a new public toilet – one example of a club good commonly distributed as patronage before elections – may benefit everyone living in the same few city blocks around it within the same neighborhood, but may only benefit a minority of the residents of the Electoral Area, and at best only affects a very tiny fraction of residents of the entire parliamentary constituency or district.

---

[49] This weighting formula is described in the Appendix. The weights take into account the population density within the radius.

[50] Note that because the weights decline in distance, small changes to the maximum radius (e.g., to 400 or 600m) do not produce significantly different scores for most respondents.

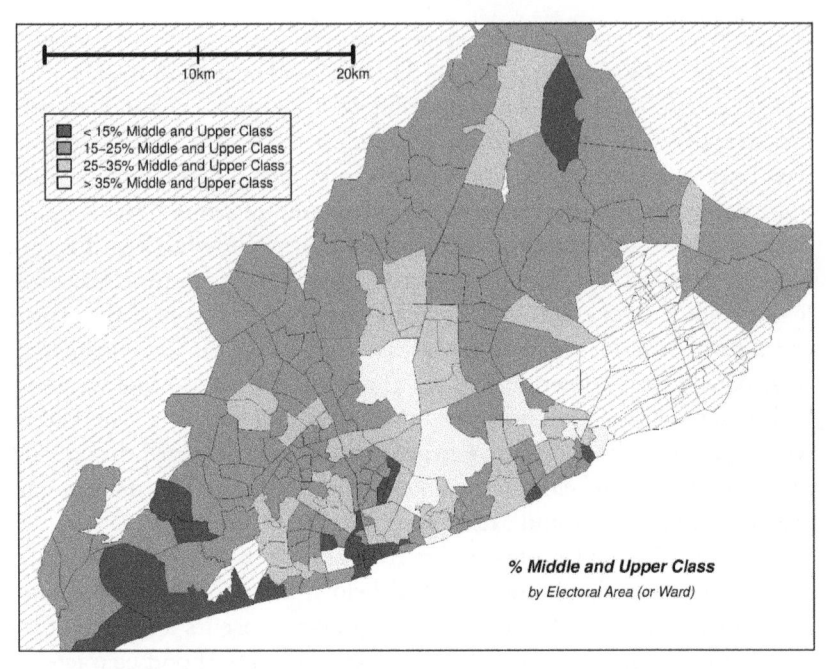

FIGURE 2.4: *Distribution of middle-class residents in Greater Accra:* urban Electoral Areas, or wards, shaded by the proportion of adults on the 2010 census who have formal sector employment, some secondary education, and fluent English literacy. Geocoded census data is missing in Tema and Ashaiman.

2.3.2 Intra-urban Variation

Using these measures, I document intra-urban variation in the main explanatory variables at different scales. I begin with the size of the urban middle class. Greater Accra is marked by considerable variation in levels of wealth within constituencies, at the Electoral Area level, and especially at the neighborhood level. There is also important variation in wealth at the individual level within most neighborhoods.

To give a sense of the breadth of variation within the larger districts and constituencies, Figure 2.4 shades each urban Electoral Area by the proportion of adults on the 2010 census who meet the definition of middle class status given earlier, with formal sector employment, literacy, and at least some secondary education. Several Electoral Areas in Figure 2.4 have large middle- and upper-class populations, while there are also some areas of concentrated poverty. Many more combine both poor and middle-class residents.

2.3 Spatial Geography of Greater Accra

This reflects neighborhood-level variation within Electoral Areas. Many wards are comprised of a combination of multiple types of neighborhoods. Importantly, even as the middle class has grown, slum neighborhoods have also continued to expand in close proximity to wealthier enclaves. Overall, the number of residents living in Greater Accra's slums remains larger than in middle- and upper-class neighborhoods.[51] Slums in Greater Accra – and in many African cities – are neither temporary or transitional spaces occupied by recent migrants nor holdovers from an earlier era of urban life. The emergence of slums is an outcome of contemporary urbanization. Many are now permanent fixtures of the urban landscape. In Greater Accra, large slum areas such as Ashaiman, Nima, and Jamestown are formally recognized by the state, giving residents relatively secure land rights, and have stable settlement patterns, with some families living in these areas for multiple generations. Ashaiman has been carved off from Tema to become its own administrative district, with its own municipal government. A few of the city's large slums, especially Old Fadama (Agbogbloshie), have less secure property rights, with residents living under threat of eviction.[52]

Localized variation between slums and wealthier neighborhoods can be seen quantitatively in the census data by adapting the definition of neighborhood introduced earlier. Using the centroids of each census enumeration area as the (arbitrary) fixed points around which to take spatially weighted averages of surrounding census characteristics, I approximate the overall characteristics of all possible 500-meter radius "neighborhoods" throughout the city.[53] The proportion of adult residents that meet the definition of middle-class status ranges from 0% to 97% across these neighborhoods, with a median of 20%. In the wealthiest quartile of the city's neighborhoods, more than a quarter of the adult population fits the definition of middle or upper class. In the bottom tenth percentile, less than 10% of adults meet the definition of middle class.

With the exception of a few overwhelmingly wealthy areas, there is also variation in wealth at the individual level within neighborhoods. Poor urban residents continue to live in relatively large numbers within otherwise wealthier middle- and upper-class neighborhoods, either as

---

[51] World Bank (2015).
[52] Paller (2018) richly documents variation in the land-tenure security of these and other major slums in Greater Accra and traces the historical origins of different slum settlements.
[53] In subsequent chapters I focus only on neighborhoods calculated relative to the locations of the respondents in the survey sample.

squatters or in other types of more informal, temporary housing arrangements.[54] It is not uncommon to see dense settlements of informal housing – wood shacks with tin or tarpaulin roofs – built in vacant lots directly abutting office complexes, hotels, and single-family homes. This has long been typical of West African cities, with poor and wealthy residents often living in close spatial proximity.[55] The main exceptions to this pattern are new, gated, upper-class housing developments popular among the elite. These self-contained, walled-off communities are homogeneously wealthy, but only represent a small share of the housing stock.[56]

Diversity in the individual-level wealth of residents within neighborhoods means that there are still poor voters in wealthier areas who are potential clients of politicians. While there are exceptions, such as the Agbogbloshie slum, I show in Chapter 6 that poor residents in wealthier neighborhoods are on average more transient and less rooted in their communities than similarly poor people living in more permanent slum neighborhoods. This has implications for politicians' costs of engaging in clientelistic exchanges with voters in different types of neighborhoods.

Yet while there is variation in wealth at the neighborhood level *within* districts and constituencies, the city is actually fairly economically homogenous *across* its highest levels of aggregation: municipalities and parliamentary constituencies. This is in part an historical legacy of limited urban planning. With large sections of the city emerging over time in a haphazard fashion and limited enforcement of zoning, small squatter communities have long been able to coexist alongside middle- and upper-class residences, limiting the degree of broad economic segregation. Table 2.1 lists the proportion of adults meeting the definition of middle-class status in each parliamentary constituency of the city. There are several overwhelmingly poor constituencies, especially those

---

[54] Gough and Yankson (2011) describe one type of common informal housing arrangement that brings poor residents into wealthier neighborhoods: the use of caretakers. Wealthy residents often invite poor people to live in unfinished buildings – sometimes for years at a time – to keep watch.

[55] Studying West African cities in an earlier historical period, Gugler and Flanagan (1978) describe a similar pattern of internal heterogeneity in levels of wealth within many neighborhoods. While noting that segregated upper class neighborhoods persist in many cities in the locations of the estates of colonial officials, they argue that, in general, newer "[n]eighborhoods in which houses have been privately built [after colonialism] are frequently characterized by a certain socioeconomic diversity. Apart from the widespread pattern of landlords and their tenants living side by side, the very rapid growth of many cities has pushed more affluent groups into previously marginal residential areas" (79).

[56] Grant (2009).

TABLE 2.1: *Middle class size and ethnic composition by parliamentary constituency*

Constituency (District)	Middle Class %	Ga or Dangme %	Akan %	Northern %	Ewe %
Ablekuma Central (AMA)	20%	22%	38%	16%	17%
Ablekuma North (AMA)	21%	20%	56%	8%	11%
Ablekuma South (AMA)	23%	50%	30%	5%	11%
Ablekuma West (AMA)	24%	24%	51%	4%	17%
Adenta (Adenta)	24%	13%	39%	11%	30%
Anyaa/Sowutuom (Ga Central)	23%	12%	60%	7%	16%
Ashaiman (Ashaiman)	18%	19%	26%	15%	35%
Ayawaso Central (AMA)	21%	14%	39%	15%	24%
Ayawaso East (AMA)	15%	10%	17%	44%	17%
Ayawaso North (AMA)	16%	8%	21%	40%	21%
Ayawaso West (AMA)	50%	15%	42%	11%	24%
Bortianor Ngleshie Amanfro (Ga South)	16%	20%	46%	6%	23%
La Dade Kotopon (La Dade Kotopon)	29%	45%	28%	8%	15%
Dome-Kwabenya (Ga East)	23%	10%	54%	7%	23%
Korle Klottey (AMA)	23%	42%	30%	8%	12%
Kpone-Katamanso (Kpone-Katamanso)	22%	26%	31%	7%	30%
Krowor (Ledzokuku-Krowor)	27%	35%	39%	5%	17%
Ledzokuku (Ledzokuku-Krowor)	22%	49%	28%	5%	15%
Madina (Madina)	26%	12%	36%	17%	27%

(continued)

TABLE 2.1: *(continued)*

Constituency (District)	Middle Class %	Ga or Dangme %	Akan %	Northern %	Ewe %
Odododiodioo (AMA)	9%	37%	23%	27%	8%
Okaikwei Central (AMA)	22%	15%	**42%**	13%	23%
Okaikwei North (AMA)	21%	14%	**40%**	11%	29%
Okaikwei South (AMA)	26%	26%	**49%**	6%	13%
Tema East (Tema)	19%	29%	**44%**	7%	16%
Tema West (Tema)	31%	14%	**46%**	7%	28%
Trobu (Ga West)	19%	10%	**58%**	7%	19%
Weija-Gbawe (Ga South)	19%	18%	**56%**	5%	17%

All data is from the 2010 census after geolocating census enumeration areas to a map of constituency boundaries for the 28 predominately urban constituencies in the Greater Accra metropolitan area. Geolocatable census data is not available for Tema, preventing a disaggregation of Tema West and Tema East into the third constituency in Tema – Tema Central. There are thus 27 constituencies listed here instead of 28. The definition of middle-class status is discussed above: an indicator for having at least some secondary education, English literacy, and formal-sector employment. The plurality ethnic group in each constituency is highlighted in **bold**.

2.3 Spatial Geography of Greater Accra

that coincide with the largest slums, such as Ayawaso East, home to the Nima slum, Ashaiman, and Odododiodioo, which contains Accra's colonial-era central business district alongside large slums at Jamestown and Agbogbloshie. There is only one majority middle class constituency, Ayawaso West. Instead, middle-class residents make up roughly one-quarter of the population in most constituencies, similar to their overall percentage. Notably, this lack of aggregate district and constituency-level economic segregation runs counter to residential patterns in some other developing world cities, especially in Latin America, where wealthy and poor neighborhoods often fall into distinct local administrative and electoral units. Chapter 9 considers the implications of these differences in district-level economic segregation.

In addition to variation across space in wealth, there is variation in the ethnic composition of local communities. Table 2.1 shows that in 21 of Greater Accra's 28 urban parliamentary constituencies there is no majority ethnic group. Ethnic composition is even more varied at local levels. Figure 2.5 again displays each Electoral Area in the metropolitan

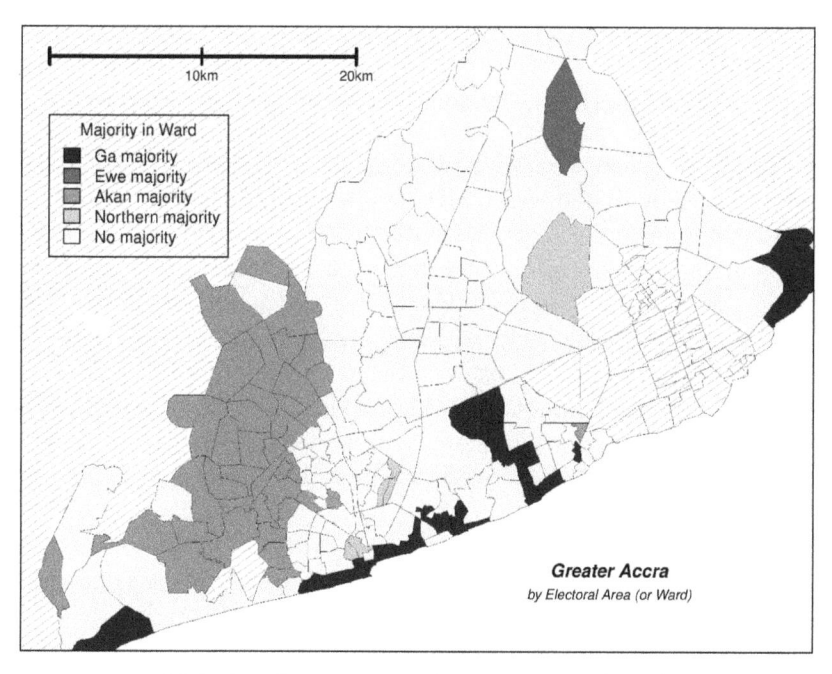

FIGURE 2.5: *Majority ethnic groups in Greater Accra:* urban Electoral Areas, or wards, shaded by whether or not there is a majority ethnic group on the 2010 census. Geocoded census data is missing for Tema and Ashaiman.

area, now shading these wards by the majority ethnic group measured on the 2010 census. While most wards also have no majority ethnic group, there are some that are more homogenous. These include a string of majority Ga areas along the Atlantic Coast in the locations of the original Ga settlements, majority Akan wards along the northwestern rim of the city, and northern-dominated areas in the location of the largest Zongo neighborhoods. There is even more localized variation in the ethnic composition when disaggregating further, down to the neighborhood level. Quantitatively, the spatially weighted averages of census characteristics around each enumeration area range from neighborhoods that are perfectly homogenous (ethnic fractionalization of 0) to neighborhoods with ethnic fractionalization of 0.87, where there is an 87% chance that two randomly selected residents come from different ethnic groups. The median neighborhood has fractionalization of 0.68. The result of this variation is that politicians in Greater Accra compete for support across local neighborhoods with very different ethnic compositions.

Importantly, ethnicity and socioeconomic class cross-cut in Greater Accra at both the neighborhood and the individual levels and can be studied independently. The city's slums and middle- and upper-class neighborhoods are internally varied in their levels of ethnic diversity, such that it is possible to consider the separate political effects of neighborhood wealth and neighborhood ethnic diversity (see Chapter 7). Calculating neighborhoods based on the centroid of each enumeration area, the neighborhood-level correlation between ethnic fractionalization and the proportion of adults in the middle class is only 0.16. As a result, the four broad categories of neighborhoods defined by the interaction of neighborhood diversity and the size of the middle class, mirroring Table 1.1, all exist in large numbers. Categorizing neighborhoods by whether they are above or below the mean value of both diversity and proportion middle class yields four nearly equally sized sets of neighborhoods. Relatively wealthy and diverse neighborhoods, with above average diversity and above average middle-class populations, are essentially just as common (26%) as poorer, more homogenous neighborhoods (25%) or poorer, diverse neighborhoods (30%). Relatively wealthy and homogenous neighborhoods, with above-average middle-class populations but below-average diversity, are slightly less common than the other three types (19%).

Moreover, at the individual level, differences in levels of wealth across ethnic groups are not so stark that it is difficult to disentangle evidence of ethnic competition from class competition, as might be the case in

TABLE 2.2: *Class status by ethnicity in urban Greater Accra*

	% of Group in Middle Class or Above	Group's Total Population Share
Ga-Dangme	20%	23%
Akan	24%	40%
Northern	16%	11%
Ewe	23%	20%
Other	25%	6%

From the 2010 census. Middle-class status is defined as above. The residual ethnic category combines various smaller ethnic groups and resident expatriates.

a more ethnically unequal society, such as South Africa. Table 2.2 lists the percentage of the city's residents on the 2010 census by each major ethnic category who meet the definition of middle class status described above. There are marginally more Akans in the middle class than Gas and especially than Northerners, but all ethnic groups have a mix of both higher and lower socioeconomic status residents.

Finally, there is also variation in the presence of state service provision throughout the city. While many neighborhoods suffer from the service deficits outlined earlier, there are some areas where service provision is much better – with paved roads, functioning sewers, running water, and nearby public schools and hospitals. This is primarily the case in earlier-settled neighborhoods of Accra, especially in residential neighborhoods within the city of Accra (the AMA) that surround the central business district. Higher levels of service provision in these neighborhoods are a historical legacy of successful efforts at urban planning in the early postcolonial period. But similarly successful attempts at urban planning in Greater Accra became rare over time. Shortcomings in public service provision are far more dramatic in newer-settled areas that have emerged in the past several decades beyond the boundaries of Accra itself.

2.4 COMPARISON TO URBAN GROWTH ELSEWHERE IN AFRICA

The growth of the middle class and rising ethnic diversity in Greater Accra mirror transformations in urban areas across sub-Saharan Africa. In this section, I outline major patterns of urban change in Africa and discuss three scope conditions for the book's main argument that arise from comparing urban Ghana to other cases. To the extent that urban

Ghana deviates from continent-wide trends in urbanization, it primarily does so in ways that make it a *harder case* for the argument in Chapter 1, with relatively more favorable conditions for a transition toward programmatic competition than other cases.

There were one billion new urban residents across the developing world between 1990 and 2015, *excluding* the well-documented urban growth in China.[57] Urban growth has been particularly extensive in sub-Saharan Africa. Table 2.3 shows urban growth in a selection of African countries and provides a comparison to growth rates in other world regions. Table 2.4 shows rates of growth in the largest cities within each of the countries in Table 2.3. East and West Africa were the second- and third-fastest urbanizing regions in the world between 2010 and 2015, behind only East Asia. Near majorities of the population in West and Central Africa now live in cities, even in the absence of significant industrialization, joining Southern Africa as heavily urbanized subregions of the continent.

Urbanization in Africa has coincided with the reintroduction of multiparty elections. As of 2015, the 29 sub-Saharan countries listed in Table 2.3 were democracies or competitive authoritarian regimes with regular elections.[58] The urban population has grown in all but one country in Table 2.3 since 1990, and at least one-third of the electorate now lives in cities in two-thirds of Africa's democracies and hybrid regimes.[59] Urbanization amidst democratization has not been unique to Africa. Outside of China, more than 80% of the urban growth between 1990 and 2014 in the developing world has come in democracies or hybrid regimes that hold contested elections.

Alongside democratization, urban growth in Africa has developed hand-in-hand with the longest period of sustained economic growth since independence in many countries.[60] The majority of sub-Saharan African countries have had average annual GDP growth rates above 3% over the past three decades. While the gains from growth have been unequal,

---

[57] See United Nations (2014). There were another 470 million new urban residents in China alone over the same period.

[58] These are countries in which the study of elections is important for explaining political outcomes, even if they are not all fully democratic (Levitsky and Way 2010). I define the set of countries in Table 2.3 based on Freedom House (2014) scores of "Free" or "Partly Free" or Polity IV (2014) scores greater than 0.

[59] The urban population instead declined in Liberia during this period due to the country's civil war.

[60] Radelet (2010).

2.4 *Comparison to Urban Growth Elsewhere in Africa* 67

TABLE 2.3: *Urban population in sub-Saharan Africa's democratic or hybrid regimes*

Country:	% Urban (1965)	% Urban (1990)	% Urban (2015)	Recent Annual % Change (2010–2015)
Benin	12.5	34.5	44.0	1.0
Botswana	3.8	41.9	57.4	0.4
Burkina Faso	5.2	13.8	29.9	3.0
Burundi	2.3	6.3	12.1	2.5
Cote d'Ivoire	24.5	39.3	54.2	1.4
DRC	23.4	30.6	42.5	1.2
Djibouti	56.1	76.0	77.3	0.1
Gabon	23.8	69.1	87.2	0.3
Ghana	**26.1**	**36.4**	**54.0**	**1.3**
Guinea	13.0	28.0	37.2	1.3
Guinea-Bissau	14.3	28.1	49.3	1.7
Kenya	8.6	16.7	25.6	1.7
Lesotho	6.4	14.0	27.3	2.0
Liberia	22.1	55.4	49.7	0.8
Madagascar	12.4	23.6	35.1	1.9
Malawi	4.9	11.6	16.3	0.9
Mali	12.6	23.3	39.9	2.1
Mozambique	5.8	25.0	32.2	0.8
Namibia	20.0	27.7	46.7	2.3
Niger	6.8	15.4	18.7	1.3
Nigeria	16.6	29.7	47.8	1.9
Senegal	26.4	38.9	43.7	0.7
Sierra Leone	20.4	33.3	39.9	0.9
South Africa	47.2	52.0	64.8	0.8
Tanzania	6.0	18.9	31.6	2.3
Togo	15.0	28.6	40.0	1.3
Uganda	5.5	11.1	16.1	2.1
Zambia	23.4	39.4	40.9	1.1
Zimbabwe	14.6	29.0	32.4	−0.5
Sub-Sah. Africa (all countries)	20.6	31.3	40.4	1.4
Subregion:				
West Africa	16.6	30.2	45.1	1.6
Central Africa	19.7	32.2	44.0	1.2
Southern Africa	42.9	48.8	61.6	0.8
East Africa	8.9	17.9	25.6	1.7
Comparison Regions:				
South America	55.8	74.1	83.3	0.3
Central America	50.2	65.1	73.8	0.4

(continued)

TABLE 2.3: *(continued)*

	% Urban (1965)	% Urban (1990)	% Urban (2015)	Recent Annual % Change (2010–2015)
Caribbean	42.5	57.9	70.4	0.8
Mid-East (W. Asia)	40.4	61.1	69.9	0.5
East Asia	25.0	33.9	60.0	2.0
Southeast Asia	19.9	31.6	47.6	1.4
Central Asia	40.8	44.6	40.5	0.0
South Asia	18.4	26.5	34.8	1.2

Population figures and subregion classifications from United Nations (2014). Region totals include all countries, including autocracies. Individual countries listed are the subset within regions with either Freedom House (FH) ratings of at least "partly free" or Polity IV scores over 0. These are the countries where the electoral behavior of urban residents is politically relevant. The table excludes small island nations (e.g., Seychelles).

this has lifted millions of people into the urban middle class.[61] Similar to the estimates for the size of Ghana's urban middle class given earlier, I employ DHS surveys to compare the size of the urban middle class across countries in Figure 2.6, using the same definitions of middle class.[62]

Figure 2.6 shows that Ghana now has one of the largest urban middle classes on the continent. This forms the first scope condition for the book's argument. The puzzle in Chapter 1 is less puzzling in countries where the urban middle class remains much smaller than in Ghana. I also expect less variation across urban neighborhoods in patterns of political behavior where there is less variation across neighborhoods in levels of wealth. But each of these differences makes Ghana a useful case to study – Ghana can provide insights about what is coming in other countries as their urban middle classes continue to grow.

While the size of its urban middle class puts it at the forefront of trends on the continent, the high levels of ethnic diversity in Greater Accra are more typical of other large African cities. In Table 2.4 I identify the 25 largest cities in the 29 sub-Saharan African countries in Table 2.3 that are democracies or hybrid regimes. Returning to the DHS data, I subset to survey respondents from each city and examine the ethnic composition

---

[61] Lofchie (2015) and Resnick (2015b).
[62] Using the most recent full DHS survey conducted in each country, I calculate the proportion of respondents in urban areas who fit either definition of the middle class plotted in Figure 1.2 in Chapter 1. The most recent DHS surveys range from 2010 to 2014 across countries. I rely on the DHS's own classification of "urban" locations.

TABLE 2.4: Twenty-five largest cities in African countries with competitive elections

City, Country:	Metro Area Pop. (1985)	Metro Area Pop. (2015)	% Change (1985–2015)	Ethnic Diversity (DHS)	Locally Competitive?
Lagos, Nigeria	3,500,000	13,123,000	275%	High	Yes
Kinshasa, DRC	2,812,000	11,587,000	312%	High	–
Johannesburg, S. Africa	3,446,000	9,399,000	173%	–	Yes
Dar es Salaam, Tanzania	1,137,000	5,116,000	350%	–	Yes
Abidjan, Cote d'Ivoire	1,716,000	4,860,000	183%	High	Yes
Greater Accra, Ghana	**1,431,000**[a]	**4,010,000**[a]	**180%**	**High**	**Yes**
Nairobi, Kenya	1,090,000	3,915,000	259%	High	Yes
Cape Town, S. Africa	1,925,000	3,660,000	90%	–	Yes
Kano, Nigeria	1,861,000	3,587,000	93%	Low	Yes
Dakar, Senegal	1,162,000	3,520,000	203%	High	Yes
Ibadan, Nigeria	1,436,000	3,160,000	120%	Low	Yes
Durban, S. Africa	1,446,000	2,901,000	101%	–	No
Ouagadougou, Burk. Faso	424,000	2,741,000	546%	Low	No
Antananarivo, Madag.	742,000	2,610,000	252%	–	Yes
Kumasi, Ghana	532,000	2,599,000	389%	Medium	No
Bamako, Mali	608,000	2,515,000	314%	High	–
Abuja, Nigeria	204,000	2,440,000	1,096%	High	Yes
Lusaka, Zambia	636,000	2,179,000	242%	High	Yes
Pretoria, S. Africa	763,000	2,059,000	170%	–	Yes
Lubumbashi, DRC	588,000	2,015,000	243%	Low	–

(continued)

TABLE 2.4: (continued)

	Metro Area Pop. (1985)	Metro Area Pop. (2015)	% Change (1985–2015)	Ethnic Diversity (DHS)	Locally Competitive?
Mbuji-Mayi, DRC	509,000	2,007,000	294%	Low	–
Conakry, Guinea	766,000	1,936,000	153%	High	Yes
Kampala, Uganda	595,000	1,936,000	225%	Medium	Yes
Harare, Zimbabwe	778,000	1,501,000	93%	–	Yes
Benin City, Nigeria	480,000	1,496,000	212%	Medium	Yes

Population figures from United Nations (2014) for "urban agglomerations" around each city. *a*: Population for Greater Accra is adjusted using 2010 census data to include Tema and other surrounding urban districts, as discussed in the text. The UN figures underreport Accra's population by excluding these districts. Local political competitiveness is calculated using the most recent election for which results are available. Local results were not available for the DRC and Mali. Ethnic diversity is calculated based on the size of the largest ethnic group in the DHS sample. If over 75% of respondents are from a single group, diversity is "Low"; if a majority but less than 75% are from a single group, diversity is "Medium"; if less than 50% are from a single group, diversity is "High."

2.4 Comparison to Urban Growth Elsewhere in Africa

Urban Middle Class: Education/Employment

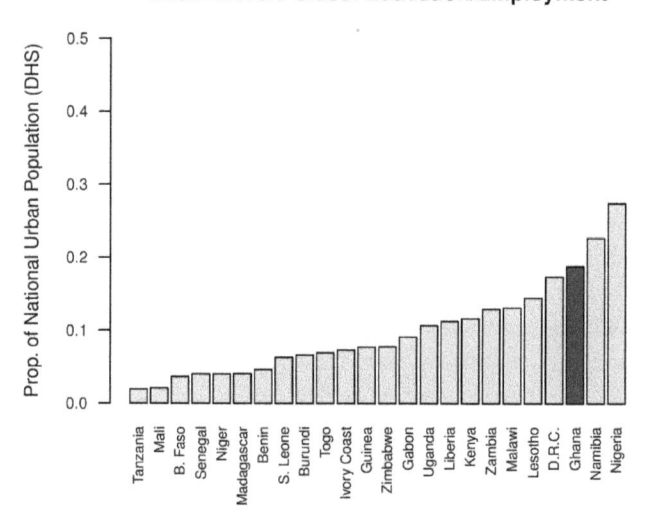

Urban Middle Class: with Housing Quality

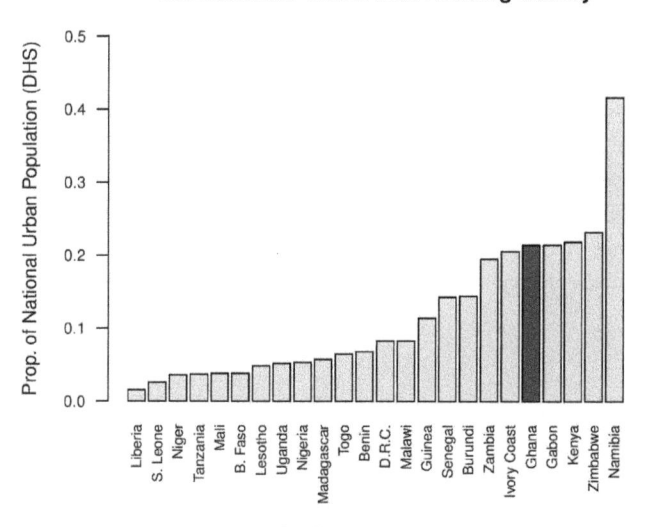

FIGURE 2.6: *Comparison in size of urban middle class from DHS surveys:* The first panel defines middle class status as any urban DHS respondents with completed secondary education, literacy, and nonmanual/formal sector employment (see above for definition). The second panel defines middle class status as any urban DHS respondents with electricity, drinkable or running water, and a flush toilet as well as at least two of the three education and employment characteristics. Calculated from the most recent full DHS survey in each country (as of 2016).

of each sample.⁶³ The first column of Table 2.4 shows that the majority of large African cities are similarly as diverse as Accra, with no majority ethnic group in 10 of the 18 cities for which DHS data is available. Only in five of these cities does a single ethnic group make up more than 75% of population.

These differences in levels of ethnic diversity create a second scope condition for the argument. Where cities are more homogenous, the puzzle in Chapter 1 is once again less puzzling – there should be less of an expectation of differences in ethnic competition when cities are not diverse. But Greater Accra again provides a harder test: the expectations in the existing literature described in Chapter 1 that the nature of ethnic competition will change in cities relative to rural areas should be more pronounced in cities that are more diverse.

Finally, urban growth in other countries is also occurring in contexts in which governments are potentially even less able than in Greater Accra to address the demands for basic public services created by a growing population. I compare the capacity of urban governments to address the challenges of urbanization using the "Bureaucratic Quality" index from Political Risk Services Group (2014). While this measure is imperfect and collapses across the more nuanced theoretical distinctions between low-quality governance, state implementation capacity, and scarcity that I draw in Chapter 1, it is one of the only available cross-national measures of related concepts with which to make cross-case comparisons.⁶⁴ While Ghana's bureaucratic quality is low relative to advanced democracies on this measure, Ghana is tied with Malawi for the highest level of bureaucratic quality among the 29 African counties in Table 2.3 above.⁶⁵

---

[63] This is calculated from DHS survey data after using geocoded sampling locations to subset the most recent DHS survey in each country to the sampling clusters that fall within each metropolitan area. The DHS provides representative samples at the province level, not the metropolitan-area level, but these are often coterminous for larger cities. The sample sizes in each metropolitan area are very large, with 2,000 to 3,000 respondents in many of these large cities. This allows for a rough approximation of each metropolitan area's characteristics even if the survey sample is not fully representative. This is the only readily available cross-national source from which to estimate the ethnic composition of multiple cities; Afrobarometer surveys have as few as 100 respondents in many of these cities.

[64] The Bureaucratic Quality Index is among the most common measures of state capacity in existing literature. See Hendrix (2010) and Kasara and Suryanarayan (2015).

[65] Ghana scores 2.5 on this 0 to 4 index, with 4 being the highest-quality states (e.g., Germany, Sweden).

This has implications for a third scope condition. With one of the relatively highest-quality bureaucracies on the continent, politicians in urban Ghana should have an easier time keeping pace with the service-delivery challenges created by urban growth than their counterparts in most other African countries. Moreover, Ghanaian politicians likely face relatively weaker constraints on what they can credibly offer to voters as compared to most other African politicians. Both are again consistent with Ghana providing a hard case for the book's argument.

2.5 GHANA'S POLITICAL SYSTEM

The remainder of the chapter introduces Ghana's political system and places it in comparative perspective. I highlight two key features that are important for later chapters: first, the presidential election is the most important in Ghana in determining access to local state spending; and second, all votes in the presidential election count equally everywhere throughout the country, such that there are not incentives for strategic voting depending on the particular local areas in which voters live. I then introduce Ghana's party system, documenting how the country's major ethnic cleavages graph onto the main partisan cleavage to produce patterns of ethnic voting.

2.5.1 Ghana's Electoral and Administrative Systems

Ghana has had one of the most successful transitions to democracy in Africa after the end of the Cold War. Multiparty democracy was formally reintroduced in 1992 and the country has now held competitive presidential elections every four years, beginning in 1996, with peaceful transitions in power between parties after the 2000, 2008, and 2016 elections. Presidential elections use a majoritarian run-off system in which all votes count equally in a single national constituency. Members of Parliament (MPs) are elected concurrently by plurality rule in 275 single-member constituencies.

Ghana's president is the dominant political actor throughout the political system. Parliament is weak, similar to most other new democracies in Africa. MPs do not introduce independent legislation or engage in significant executive oversight.[66] While MPs control a small discretionary development fund to spend within their constituencies, control over the large majority of state resources depends on the presidential election

---

[66] Barkan (2008), Lindberg and Zhou (2009), and Lindberg (2010).

in the country's "winner-take-all" political system. Presidential elections determine control over every local government in the country. The president appoints a local leader from his political party to be the District Chief Executive (DCE), akin to a mayor, of each of the country's 216 districts.[67] In practice, the DCE has considerable control over determining how state spending on the provision of club and private goods is allocated within each district. A legislative body equivalent to a city council, called the District Assembly, serves below the DCE and is, at least in theory, supposed to approve district spending decisions. Thirty percent of these assembly members are appointed by the president and the remainder are elected to four-year terms from each Electoral Area, the single-member wards displayed in Figures 2.4 and 2.5. I examine the district assemblies in more detail in Chapter 8.

These features of the political system make neighborhoods the appropriate unit of analysis in the subsequent chapters. As I will document further in Chapters 6 and 8, the political party that wins the presidential election gains direct control over every local government through the appointment of the DCE (mayor) in each district, who then has the power to control highly localized distributive decisions. Moreover, much of the opportunity for favoritism in the allocation of state resources becomes a choice by ruling party leaders over which neighborhoods to target *within* districts, not across them. Disbursements from the national government to each district are mostly formula-based allocations subject to limited political interference.[68] But district-level leaders have significant local-level discretion in how and where they spend these resources. This has important consequences for voting behavior: expectations about the *very local* provision of state resources can shape voter behavior in national-level presidential elections, as voters' access to resources from even local tiers of government is most dependent on the outcome of the presidential election, not local or parliamentary elections.

2.5.2 Ghana's Party System

Two political parties dominate Ghanaian politics: the National Democratic Congress (NDC), in power 1992–2000 and 2009–2016, and the New Patriotic Party (NPP), in power 2001–2008 and 2017–present. The NDC was the ruling party and the NPP was in opposition during

---

[67] District Chief Executives are called Municipal or Metropolitan Chief Executives (MCE) in larger districts, but these terms are used interchangeably in common parlance.
[68] See Banful (2011) and Williams (2017).

collection of all data analyzed in the subsequent chapters.[69] Recent presidential elections have had razor-thin margins between these parties, with the NDC candidate winning in 2012 by less than three percentage points and in 2008 by less than one percentage point.

The NDC and NPP are both highly institutionalized and embedded in society, giving Ghana one of the most institutionalized party systems in Africa. Riedl (2014) describes the emergence of a strong two-party system in Ghana as an outcome of the country's transition away from autocracy in 1992. The NDC emerged from the PNDC (Provisional National Defense Council) military government of Jerry Rawlings, who created the party as he prepared to contest the 1992 election. As an autocrat managing a transition to democracy, Rawlings created high barriers to entry for other parties in Ghana, both through explicit legal rules and through competitive incentives; the NPP, which quickly emerged as the main opposition party in 1992, was forced to build a nationwide organization to be able to successfully compete against a strong ruling party that could draw on resources and pre-existing nationwide mobilization networks developed during a decade of authoritarianism. As Ghana's two-party system has solidified, competitive pressures between the parties have produced further institutionalization; any steps either party takes to further strengthen and embed its grassroots organization are usually quickly mirrored by the other.[70]

The NDC and NPP have elected committees of local activists at every polling station, parliamentary constituency, and region (province) who form a permanent roster of local party campaign agents throughout the country.[71] Both presidential and parliamentary candidates heavily rely on these pre-existing local organizations for their campaign activities. Each party also remains active even when in opposition; both have access to private sector financing to continue party activities and some patronage distribution to supporters. But the resources that a party controls increase dramatically if it wins the presidential election and takes control over each district government.

The DCEs who govern each district are usually drawn from the leadership ranks of these constituency-level party organizations, as are most of

---

[69] The NPP returned to power in January 2017 after winning the December 2016 election.
[70] For example, see the history of the adoption of primary elections in Öhman (2004) and Ichino and Nathan (2012).
[71] See Fobih (2010). Competitive internal elections are held to select these constituency-, regional-, and national-level party leaders, and local party members also vote in primary elections to select both parliamentary and presidential candidates.

the appointed members of each district assembly.[72] In addition, despite their weak influence over national policy making, MPs are key actors within local party organizations. Rather than their formal duties as legislators, it is their informal role as the main local decision maker for their party within each parliamentary constituency that gives MPs much of their importance in the Ghanaian political system. MPs often wield de facto control over the constituency party branch, becoming the public face of and chief mouthpiece for their party's presidential campaign in their constituency and exercising lobbying influence over local government appointments and the allocation of national government resources within their district if their party wins the presidential election.

Importantly, the structure of these party organizations reinforces the focus on neighborhoods in the subsequent chapters. Leaders of constituency-level party organizations, including the relevant MP, have significant autonomy in allocating party resources and effort within their parliamentary constituencies, including for their party's presidential campaign. Because campaign strategy decisions are made in a disaggregated fashion by local ruling-party leaders at the constituency level, the most appropriate scale at which to study differences in the targeting of campaigning appeals and effort is *within* individual parliamentary constituencies. Moreover, because all votes count equally everywhere in Ghana's presidential elections – the most important election for determining control over state resources – pursuing a marginal additional vote has the same value to constituency-level party leaders in every neighborhood within their constituency. There are no neighborhoods that a party can safely ignore in a competitive presidential election.

Similar to many parties in sub-Saharan Africa, the NDC and NPP draw on support from distinct coalitions of ethnic groups. Neither is an explicitly "ethnic party," as defined by Horowitz (1985), Chandra (2011), and Elischer (2013), however. The parties do not advocate for ethnocentric interests, court support only from specific groups, or rely on ethnically exclusionary messaging. Instead, both parties go out of their way to publicly appear diverse, including members of many of the country's major ethnic groups in national party leadership committees and presidential cabinet appointments, and, at least publicly, disavowing openly ethnocentric rhetoric.[73]

---

[72] Elected district assembly members also often serve simultaneously as local party executives, even though assembly elections are technically nonpartisan. See Chapter 8.

[73] Posner (2005) demonstrates that looking for whether there is explicit ethnic campaign rhetoric or whether party leadership committees are ethnically diverse is not an effective

Some recent scholarship builds from observations of multi-ethnic party leadership and the lack of explicit ethnic campaign rhetoric to argue that ethnicity is now a subsidiary consideration in Ghanaian elections and is insufficient to account for Ghanaian partisanship.[74] I demonstrate empirically in Chapter 7 that this is true to some extent. Ethnicity is not a universal predictor of vote choice in Ghana, and elections are by no means an "ethnic census," as defined by Horowitz (1985).

But ethnicity remains a central determinant of partisanship for many voters in Ghana. Recent literature risks going too far in downplaying its role. For example, Hoffman and Long (2013) argue that the importance of ethnicity has been exaggerated because only two viable candidates, from two specific ethnic groups, compete in each presidential election, and thus by default many Ghanaian voters have no co-ethnic candidate in the race and technically cannot engage in ethnic voting. This significantly understates the role of ethnicity in Ghana's party system, however, and would do so in any ethnically diverse country where the electoral system creates incentives for a small effective number of parties. In countries with majoritarian electoral systems, there is often no single ethnic group large enough to win a national majority on its own.[75] This includes Ghana, where the largest ethno-linguistic group – the Akan – comprise 47% of the national population, and are themselves somewhat politically divided among subgroups. Parties in these settings can instead draw on coalitions of ethnic groups for support. The presidential candidate is only from one group at a time, but members of other groups in the coalition can still engage in significant ethnic bloc voting for the candidate from their affiliated party.[76] Kenya provides a classic example of this logic. The minority Kalenjin ethnic group has voted en masse – at levels well over 90% – for Luo and then Kikuyu presidential candidates in recent elections after presidential candidates from these groups formed

---

means by which to measure the electoral importance of ethnicity. Drawing on observations of a very similar phenomenon in the Zambian case, Posner (2005) shows that *specifically because* ethnicity is already so important for vote choice, many parties attempt to present a public nonethnic or cross-ethnic facade. Parties that are already secure in their support from core ethnic groups do not have to use explicit ethnic rhetoric – they can attempt to publicly signal cross-ethnic credentials in the hopes of adding additional support on the margins from other groups.

[74] For example, see Fridy (2007), Elischer (2013), Hoffman and Long (2013), and Osei (2016).

[75] See Ferree (2010) for further discussion of the implications of group size for the types of ethnic coalitions that can form.

[76] Arriola (2012) documents the creation of similar multi-ethnic coalitions across Africa.

coalition alliances with Kalenjin leaders. Kalenjin voters were still indisputably voting along ethnic lines in these elections, even though they did not vote for a direct co-ethnic.[77]

Similarly, Ghana's parties still rely on ethnic coalitions for support even though they are not classic "ethnic parties." The ethnic affiliations of the NDC and NPP have long historical roots. The NPP draws its strongest support from Kumasi, the country's second largest city, and the rural cocoa farming belt in the center of the country, particularly in the Ashanti and Eastern Regions. These areas are home to the Akan, Ghana's largest ethno-linguistic group, which forms the majority across much of southern and central Ghana. The NPP's main base is the Ashanti (Ashanti Region), Akyem (Eastern Region), and Akuapem (Eastern Region) subgroups within the Akan, as well as many of the smaller Akan subgroups. The partisan alignment between predecessor parties of the NPP and the Akan dates back to Akan opposition to Kwame Nkurmah in the independence era.[78]

The NDC draws strong support from the Ewe from Ghana's Volta Region, the ethnic group of its founder, Jerry Rawlings, which comprises 14% of the national population. The NDC's overwhelming support among the Ewe has persisted even though the party has not nominated an Ewe as its presidential or vice-presidential candidate since 1996, indicative of the coalitional nature of the party's ethnic attachments.[79] The NDC also draws support from many of the predominantly Muslim groups from Ghana's three northern regions. This is especially because the NDC president from 2012 to 2016, John Dramani Mahama, was from the Northern Region. The connection between northern ethnic groups and the NDC does not hold for every northern group, but dates to extensive patronage from the NDC to northern Ghana under Jerry Rawlings in the 1980s and 1990s, as well as strong ties between the Rawlings regime and northern migrants in southern Ghana.[80] The NDC historically has also drawn most votes of the Ga and Dangme (including Krobo), which together comprise roughly 7% of the national population.

---

[77] This suggests a bloc-voting definition of "ethnic voting," rather than a narrower definition focusing only on the direct match of ethnicity between a voter and a candidate. I explain how I define ethnic voting in more detail in the analysis of voting behavior in Chapter 7.

[78] Rathbone (2000).

[79] In the NDC in the 2000, 2004, and 2008 elections in Ghana, the NDC's presidential candidate came from an ethnic group outside the party's core ethnic coalition.

[80] For example, see Kobo (2010).

A series of smaller ethnic groups, such as those comprising the Guan category on Ghana's census and some non-Muslim northern ethnic groups, such as the Konkomba, are not closely linked to either party.

These links between ethnic groups and the parties are not absolute and are often complicated by variation at the subgroup level. For example, the Fanti subgroup of the Akan, concentrated in Ghana's Central Region, have at times been less aligned with the NPP than other Akan subgroups. This is largely because John Evans Atta Mills – the NDC presidential candidate in the 2000, 2004, and 2008 elections and sitting president from 2009 to 2012 – was a Fanti from Central Region and had brought a core group of Fanti elites, sometimes referred to in the popular press as the "Fanti Confederacy," into senior NDC leadership positions. After Mills' death and the subsequent diminished influence of Fanti elites within the NDC government, however, the Fanti began more closely mirroring the pro-NPP voting behavior of other Akan subgroups.[81] Elsewhere, partisan alignments vary at a subgroup level due to politicized chieftaincy conflicts and land disputes, especially among groups in the rural north.[82] Despite these intra-ethnic divisions, northern migrants who live in southern Ghana are largely viewed as affiliated with the NDC and organize politically around a shared northern identity. Northern migrants in the south often live in the segregated Zongo neighborhoods described earlier, which are seen as major NDC strongholds.

It is important not to mistake this complexity for ethnicity not mattering in electoral behavior, however. Aggregating up from these subgroup differences, there are still broad correlations between ethnicity and vote choice. Existing research shows a clear overall pattern of support among each of these groups for their ethnically affiliated party, while also

---

[81] The clear majority of Fanti voters captured in the survey data analyzed in the subsequent chapters voted for the NPP in the 2012 election, held after Mills' death. In the 2016 presidential election, the NPP won 20 of 23 parliamentary constituencies in the Fanti-dominated Central Region, consistent with significant ethnic voting. This is a sharp departure from the 2008 elections, when Mills was last the NDC candidate and the NDC won more than half of these same constituencies. The return of the Fanti to voting more like the other Akan subgroups represents the largest single difference in Ghana's nationwide electoral map that helped the NPP win the 2016 election.

[82] The most prominent example of this is the Dagomba, the largest ethnic group in northern Ghana. The majority (approximately 80%) are from the Andani "gate" (or clan), which is strongly aligned with the NDC. But a smaller rival gate/clan within the Dagomba, the Abudu, has become closely tied to the NPP because the NPP (and its predecessor parties) has historically supported the Abudu in their pursuit of the violently contested Dagomba paramount chieftaincy (MacGaffey 2006).

indicating that some voters from these groups cross between the parties.[83] In the survey data from Greater Accra examined in the subsequent chapters, I find that 80% of Akans supported the NPP in the 2012 presidential election, including 71% of Fantis, while 84% of Ewes, 67% of Northerners, and 73% of Gas supported the NDC. Ultimately, a more important issue than establishing whether ethnicity matters overall in Ghanaian elections is to explain why it matters to some voters but not others even as they choose among the same candidates in the same election. I explore these questions in Chapters 5 and 7.

The close links between parties and ethnic groups in Ghana mean that Greater Accra – which now has large populations from each of these major ethnic groups – has become very politically competitive. The Greater Accra Region contained one-fifth of the registered voters nationwide in the 2012 election and has at least one-sixth of the national population. In 2012, the NDC won 50.6% of the presidential vote in the metropolitan area's 28 urban constituencies, compared to 48.8% for the NPP, similar to the 50.3% and 47.8% won by each party, respectively, in 2008.[84] Figure 2.7 shades the Electoral Areas within the metropolitan area by 2008 presidential election results. Each party has stronghold neighborhoods throughout the metropolitan area, primarily in areas where their affiliated ethnic groups are numerically dominant. Other areas are very competitive, however, and the parties are closely matched in most of the city's parliamentary constituencies; MPs won their seats with less than 55% of the vote in more than half of the metropolitan area's parliamentary constituencies in 2012.

Finally, in addition to drawing on ethnic bases, the NDC and NPP are similar to many other African political parties in that they do not have clearly differentiated policy platforms.[85] Both parties have publicly claimed different ideological mantles for themselves: NDC leaders often describe their party in socialist terms, in line with the revolutionary rhetoric of their founder, Jerry Rawlings; the NPP claims that they are center-right and pro-business and the party maintains a significant advantage in support among the country's wealthiest business elite. Consistent with these self-proclaimed ideological orientations, Elischer

---

[83] See Weghorst and Lindberg (2013) and Ichino and Nathan (2013a). Even Hoffman and Long (2013) show that ethnicity is a significant predictor of vote choice for many voters from these affiliated ethnic groups, including those without a direct co-ethnic candidate.
[84] Provisional results from 2016 show the NPP winning Greater Accra Region with 52% of the presidential vote vs. 47% for the NDC.
[85] See Riedl (2014) and, more generally, van de Walle (2007).

2.5 *Ghana's Political System*

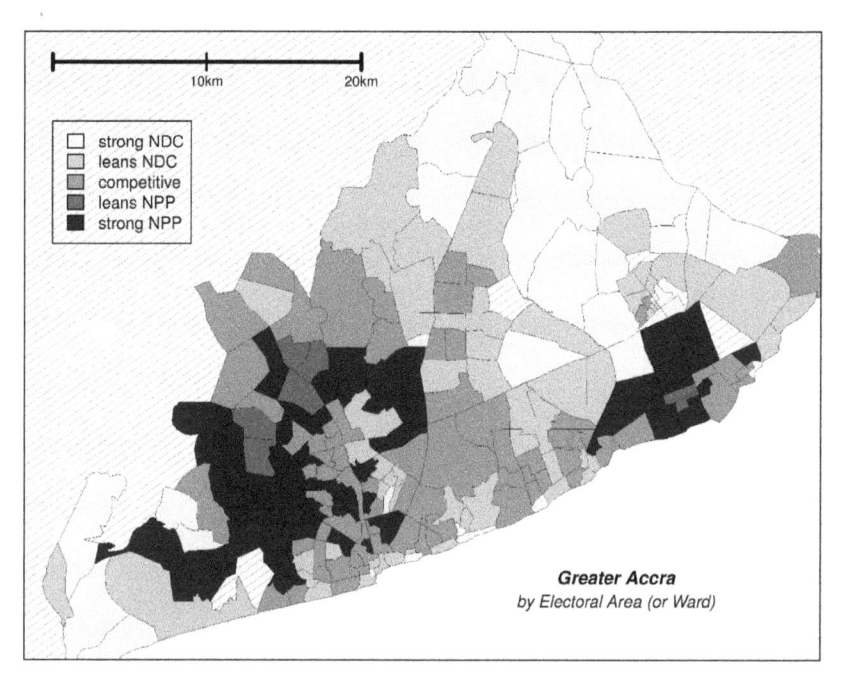

FIGURE 2.7: *Levels of competitiveness within Greater Accra:* Electoral Areas in Greater Accra shaded by 2008 presidential vote share. "Strong" areas are where a party received more than 65% of the vote, "lean" where a party received between 55% and 65%, and "competitive" where neither received more than 55%. The 2008 results are used because of missing data at the Electoral Area level for 2012. Where 2012 data is available, vote shares at the Electoral Area level are highly correlated with 2008 vote shares.

(2013) suggests that the NDC and NPP platforms did begin as somewhat ideologically differentiated in Ghana's first elections after the return to multiparty democracy in the 1990s – an observation I partially confirm with data from party manifestos in Chapter 4. But the records of recent NDC and NPP governments belie any coherent ideological classification and suggest that to whatever extent these parties may have begun as ideologically distinct, that is long a thing of the past – and was never particularly meaningful in terms of the actual policy outcomes each party delivered. Despite its socialist rhetoric, the NDC oversaw neoliberal structural adjustment in the 1980s and 1990s, with widespread privatization of the economy and reductions in the size of the existing welfare state. After taking power in the 2000 election, the "conservative" NPP then (re)created much of Ghana's contemporary (very limited) welfare state, including a national health insurance system, and centered its 2012 campaign manifesto on a pledge to make secondary schooling free, a redistributive policy that benefits the poor. Despite their earlier differences, the parties' policy proposals are now so similar in content that senior NPP leaders have complained that the NDC has literally plagiarized the NPP's manifesto.[86] Both parties also have a significant history of adopting each other's proposals as their own once in office. I demonstrate in Chapter 4 that there is now such a large degree of overlap in the content of the parties' campaign promises that Ghanaian voters have no real basis to expect that these parties will govern in line with distinct policy orientations.

2.6 EXTENSIONS TO OTHER POLITICAL SYSTEMS

In many respects, Ghana's political system is typical of other African democracies. For example, similar "winner-take-all" systems are common in much of sub-Saharan Africa. Strong presidents dominate local-level governments, and local-level leaders, even when they are not directly appointed by the national government, remain dependent on national government transfers for their budgets.[87] In addition, very few African democracies – other than perhaps South Africa and Namibia – have a sustained history of ideologically differentiated parties offering voters differentiated policy platforms.[88] There are several ways in which the Ghanaian political system deviates from most other cases, however. These differences again primarily make Ghana a harder case for the main argument.

Ghana's party system may be the dimension along which it differs most from other African countries that hold regular elections. The unusually high degree of institutionalization of Ghana's party system should in theory reduce the costs politicians face in making policy-based appeals relative to more inchoate party systems where parties rarely last beyond a single election. Weaker parties will be even less able to make credible policy-based appeals than institutionalized parties with strong party labels that are easier to hold accountable at the ballot box. Low levels of party institutionalization may thus exacerbate the credibility problems and class-based differences in participation I describe in Chapters 3

---

[86] For example, see "NPP Could Declare 2016 Election Results" (2016).
[87] For example, see van de Walle (2003), Olowu and Wunsch (2004), Prempeh (2008), and Lambright (2014). There are notable exceptions, however, such as the Nigerian federal system.
[88] Elischer (2013) and Riedl (2014).

and 4, further discouraging transitions to policy-based competition in cities despite the growth of the urban middle class.

Ghana's high level of party institutionalization also raises other external validity concerns. In settings with less-institutionalized parties, grassroots party organizations may be less extensive in poor urban neighborhoods, reducing the capacity of parties to engage voters in clientelistic relationships at an individual level.[89] Under the argument presented in Chapter 5, this could reduce incentives for ethnic voting in poor, ethnically diverse neighborhoods within cities if voters are less closely bound to parties in individual-level patronage relationships.

But there are reasons to doubt whether this is a serious issue. First, Chapter 5 suggests that the costs to building dense party organizations are lower in poor urban slums compared to other areas, especially rural areas where traditional leaders provide an alternative structure for voter mobilization. Even if party organizations on the whole are weaker in another country than in Ghana, there may still be a relative difference in party capacity for clientelism between urban and rural areas that produces similar differences in voting behavior as predicted in Chapter 5; the one area of a country in which otherwise weakly institutionalized parties have strong grassroots organizations may still be urban slums. Moreover, party substitutes that can maintain clientelistic relationships with individual voters often emerge in urban slums and play similar roles to Ghana's party organizations, even where parties are formally weak. For example, LeBas (2013) describes how politicians employ criminal gangs, rather than networks of party agents, to enforce clientelistic transactions in Kenyan slums, a country with a much less institutionalized party system than Ghana. More broadly, there may still be strong clientelistic brokers in noninstitutionalized party systems who play a similar role on the ground as Ghana's party agents, but instead of being permanent members of a stable organization they may be freelancers, switching allegiances from election to election. Indeed, many theories of clientelism assume that typical clientelistic brokers have independent sources of authority and can switch from one party to another.[90] These types of brokers can sustain individual-level clientelistic relationships even where formal

---

[89] By contrast, party institutionalization does not appear to be a serious constraint on ethnic voting or expectations of ethnic favoritism in Africa. Rates of ethnic voting and voters' expectations of ethnic favoritism remain very high in countries such as Kenya and Zambia, even though they have much more unstable parties.

[90] For example, see Camp (2017) and Gottlieb and Larreguy (2015).

party organizations are weak. If independent brokers are playing similar roles as Ghana's party agents, the predictions for vote choice in Chapter 5 would remain largely the same even in a less institutionalized party system.

Ghana's high level of political competition is an additional dimension along which it deviates from some other African countries that hold regular elections. At a local level, the high level of competitiveness in Greater Accra is by no means unusual among major African cities. There is an oft-repeated claim that many African cities are opposition strongholds,[91] but this has been exaggerated. Almost all of the largest cities in African democracies are politically competitive. Using the same list of the 25 largest cities in Africa's democracies and hybrid regimes as in Table 2.4, I code whether a single party won more than 65% of the vote in the most recent national election (presidential or parliamentary) for which results are publicly available.[92] The final column of Table 2.4 shows that in all but 3 of these 25 large cities, no party reached this threshold.[93] But at the national level, Ghana is noticeably more competitive than countries dominated by a single hegemonic party, such as Uganda, Tanzania, or Botswana. Greater political competition should make a programmatic transition in the face of a wealthier population *more likely* in Ghana than in other countries. Weitz-Shapiro (2014) and Kitschelt (2007) both suggest that competition makes parties more sensitive to the potential downsides of clientelism, while parties that are less threatened by electoral defeat can more easily persist with current forms of electoral appeal even if demographic conditions have changed. In this respect, Ghana once again provides a harder test for my argument.

A final scope condition pertains to the salience of ethnicity in the political system. In the subsequent chapters, I assume as a starting point that ethnic electoral competition is widespread – as is the case in many African countries – and then consider whether the middle class and ethnic diversity in urban areas reduce the political salience of ethnicity in cities. But there are some African countries where ethnicity has never been widely

---

[91] For example, see Resnick (2011).
[92] A list of election results used for each city is available on request.
[93] Moreover, in two of three cases where a single party dominates, it is the ruling party, not the opposition party. The exception is Kumasi, Ghana, where the NPP won 70% of the vote in the last presidential election (though it has now become the ruling party again). If the threshold is lowered to 60% of the vote, only two additional cities would be coded as strongholds of a particular party: Anatananarivo, Madagascar, and Lusaka, Zambia. The ruling party won in Lusaka; the opposition party in Anatananarivo.

politicized, such as Mali or Senegal.[94] The arguments throughout the book about ethnicity will be less relevant in these countries.

2.7 SUMMARY

This chapter introduced the book's main empirical case. The first half of the chapter documented the growth of the middle class and the changing ethnic composition in Greater Accra. I introduced the measurement strategy for examining neighborhood-level variation and demonstrated that there is significant localized variation within Greater Accra in terms of wealth and ethnic composition. The second half introduced key features of Ghana's political system, including the national-level control of local governments and the ethnic nature of the party system. Both halves placed the Ghanaian case in comparative perspective, arguing that to the extent Ghana deviates from common patterns in Africa, it primarily does so in ways that make the puzzle in Chapter 1 more puzzling than it would be in other settings.

---

[94] For Mali, see Dunning and Harrison (2010). For Senegal, see Koter (2013). Posner (2004) documents these distinctions across African countries in his index of "Politicized Ethnic Cleavages." Ghana is near the middle of the distribution in the extent of its politicized ethnic cleavages.

PART II

THE MIDDLE CLASS AND PROGRAMMATIC POLITICS

3

Class and Preferences

"Give out loans to traders like myself."
– Survey respondent, Gbawe, Greater Accra, November 2013

"Put up universities in each region."
– Survey respondent, Lapaz, Accra, November 2013

Wealthier and better-educated people are often expected to place different demands on politicians than the poor, rendering middle-class voters relatively less susceptible to nonprogrammatic, patronage-based appeals, especially direct individual-level clientelism. For this reason, the demand-side theories of party-voter linkages described in Chapter 1 expect that politicians will place more emphasis on programmatic appeals when there are more middle-class or wealthy voters. Has the emergence of a large middle class led politicians in Greater Accra to adapt their electoral appeals?

Before this question can be answered, it is necessary first to see whether the initial condition in demand-side theories holds: do members of the middle class make different demands on politicians than the poor? This chapter shows that – in key ways – they often do. I examine the demands that poor and middle-class residents place on governments using data from an original, representative survey of Greater Accra that allows me to distinguish between two broad categories of preferences: demands for *particularistic* goods or for *universalistic* policies.[1]

---

[1] I do not attempt to characterize the preferences of the wealthy elite, who may make distinct demands from the middle class, given the significant data limitations of observing

The difference between these is whether a preference can be satisfied in a patronage exchange with a politician. Particularistic preferences – exemplified by the survey respondent's demand for a personal loan in the first quote above – leave voters susceptible to nonprogrammatic appeals, including clientelism, that address their preferences in a politically targeted fashion. By contrast, universalistic demands – exemplified by the second quote above, demanding a major expansion of Ghana's public university system – require policy solutions that necessarily affect large numbers of people, with benefits that cannot be easily targeted as patronage. As voters' demands become more universalistic, it should be increasingly difficult for politicians to win elections based only on clientelism and other nonprogrammatic strategies.

Middle-class residents in Greater Accra are significantly more likely than the poor to demand universalistic policies from their elected representatives. They are also much less likely than the poor to demand private goods – the subcategory of particularistic benefits that can be traded for support in individual-level clientelistic relationships with politicians. As a result, individual-level clientelism may be nonviable among most middle-class residents, a majority of whom do not report demands on politicians for private goods. Moreover, demands for universalistic policies are significantly higher among survey respondents in Greater Accra than among respondents in a companion survey of five rural constituencies of southern Ghana. This suggests that urban politicians are likely to face particularly significant pressure to deliver universalistic policies compared to rural politicians, as the new middle class is overwhelmingly concentrated in urban areas.

The demands urban residents make are not uniform throughout Greater Accra, however. I also find variation in preferences across the city's neighborhoods due to differences in existing state presence. Respondents from all socioeconomic backgrounds are less likely to demand universalistic policies, and more likely to demand particularistic goods, particularly club (local public) goods, when living in areas where government provision of basic services is lacking. Although urban middle-class residents are on average much more likely than the urban poor to demand universalistic policies, most middle-class residents who live in underserved neighborhoods still have strong preferences for

---

elite preferences and behavior. Wealthy elites make up a very small share of the urban population, however. In robustness tests (see Section 3.5) I drop any survey respondents who might be wealthy elites and show that the findings are unaffected.

particularistic club goods that address shortcomings in neighborhood infrastructure. As a result, many middle-class residents are still vulnerable to nonprogrammatic appeals that politically target club goods to address infrastructural deficits.

This is the first of two chapters in Part II. I begin in this chapter by showing that the urban middle class does make different demands on politicians than the urban poor in some ways, consistent with the expectations of a large existing literature. In Chapter 4, however, I show that these demands are *not* producing changes in electoral competition, as urban politicians do not face sufficient supply-side pressures to change their appeals in response.

3.1 PARTICULARISTIC VERSUS UNIVERSALISTIC PREFERENCES

I conceptualize people as having two broad categories of preferences that could be addressed by politicians: demands for particularistic goods, or for universalistic policies. The key distinction is whether a demand could potentially could be satisfied by a politician providing a targeted patronage benefit in the form of a private or club good. Particularistic preferences encompass demands for private goods, potentially targetable as clientelistic transfers to individuals (e.g., cash payments, jobs, loans), and demands for local public, or club, goods, which can be geographically targeted as patronage to small communities (e.g., a paved road, a community borehole).[2] Demands for universalistic policies involve actions that will necessarily affect many other people, with benefits that cannot be isolated based on partisanship, ethnicity, or specific location. These include demands about policies concerning tax rates, the welfare state, inflation, foreign investment and trade policies, natural resource management, major national infrastructure, corruption, national education policy, price controls, and subsidies to industries or agriculture, among other examples.[3] Importantly, the distinction between these two categories does not assume anything about the motivations of the person making

---

[2] Club goods have benefits that are locally nonexcludable, but which generally do not extend to residents who live outside the catchment areas in which they are sited. As a result, they can be delivered as patronage to spatially clustered groups – for example, all those living in a particular village or small neighborhood. See Ichino and Nathan (2013a), Gottlieb and Larreguy (2015), and Ejdemyr et al. (2017).

[3] Some universalistic policies disproportionately benefit specific interest groups. For example, changes to civil service laws will benefit civil servants. Income tax cuts might

the demand. Particularistic and universalistic preferences could both be rooted in pocketbook concerns.[4] What is distinct is whether a demand could be satisfied in a direct exchange between a politician and voter (or small cluster of voters), or instead requires a broader policy solution.

This distinction affects which electoral strategies are viable for politicians. Universalistic policies almost always involve programmatic distribution, while particularistic goods can be distributed either programmatically or nonprogrammatically, depending on whether they are distributed as part of a formal program with well-defined eligibility rules or distributed informally by politicians in a manner that favors specific, narrow groups of people as part of a patronage transaction.[5] Consider the examples from the two epigraphs to this chapter. Loans to individual traders in informal markets could be disbursed by the government as part of some programmatic welfare state program. But loans could also be given out as individual patronage benefits in a clientelistic exchange – as they regularly are in urban Ghana. On the other hand, building new public universities in every region of Ghana would benefit tens of thousands of potential students across the country by expanding access to public tertiary education. Absent a major shift in Ghana's public university admissions and tuition policies, students are unlikely to be systematically excluded from studying at the new universities based on partisanship, ethnicity, or current residential location.[6]

As a result, when many voters demand particularistic benefits, patronage-based, nonprogrammatic appeals remain viable. Politicians can choose to build support by selectively distributing (and withholding) particularistic benefits to different groups based on political criteria. By contrast, where a large number of voters have universalistic preferences,

---

disproportionately benefit the wealthy. But these benefits accrue to large groups of people with little possibility for any form of individualized patronage transaction. There is a qualitatively meaningful distinction between policies that affect broad categories of people and goods that can be targeted or withheld from narrow groups based on political criteria.

[4] A civil servant could ask the government to raise the salaries of civil servants because it directly affects her finances, just as a cash handout would. But raising civil service wages can only be satisfied by a change to public sector policies that will affect many other people, of many ethnicities and partisan persuasions, while a cash handout could be targeted individually to one civil servant.

[5] See Chapter 1 for the definition of programmatic distribution used throughout the book.

[6] The respondent's motivations are not relevant to this definition. Even if she thinks she might benefit personally – perhaps she failed to earn admission to the existing public universities – large numbers of other citizens from around the country would also benefit.

patronage-based appeals no longer offer an exclusive means to win elections; universalistic preferences necessitate that politicians compete for support – at least in part – based on their policy proposals and their performance in addressing universalistic issues.

3.2 EFFECTS OF CLASS ON PREFERENCES

Demand-side explanations for programmatic competition are rooted in the expectation that the middle class and the wealthy will have different preferences than the poor.[7] Wealthier people, including those in the middle class, should be more likely than the poor to demand universalistic policies over particularistic goods. The existing literature suggests several reasons why this might be the case. First, the poor are often assumed to gain greater marginal utility from the particularistic benefits that politicians can provide. A broad class of formal models of distributive politics building from Lindbeck and Weibull (1987) and Dixit and Londregan (1996) make this assumption. Consistent with these models, a large body of research establishes that political exchanges of individualized particularistic benefits are disproportionately focused on the poor.[8] Second, the poor are often more risk averse and have shorter time horizons than the wealthy. Poorer people may thus prefer upfront, targeted particularistic benefits that address immediate needs over promises of future policy changes that are uncertain to be implemented and may have only indirect benefits.[9] Third, and relatedly, the higher levels of education associated with higher socioeconomic status may allow people to develop more sophisticated and wide-ranging policy preferences, especially as greater participation in the formal-sector economy frees them from focusing on immediate needs.[10] Fourth, even in the absence of the other three factors, differences in preferences could emerge based on variation in where members of different socioeconomic classes live. Within cities, the

---

[7] For summaries of these arguments, see Kitschelt and Wilkinson (2007) and Hicken (2011).
[8] For example, Brusco et al. (2004), Calvo and Murillo (2004), Bratton (2008), and Gonzalez-Ocantos et al. (2012). Weitz-Shapiro (2014) suggests that disproportionate targeting of the poor through clientelism could emerge even without underlying differences in preferences because wealthier voters may judge clientelism as normatively unacceptable and punish politicians seen engaging in it as corrupt. I do not collect data on respondents' normative attitudes about different modes of distribution, however, so cannot test this claim.
[9] Kitschelt (2000).
[10] Inglehart (1997).

poor often live in neighborhoods with fewer economic opportunities and more scarcity in basic services, with more acute needs for some types of particularistic goods.

This fourth argument suggests that there should not be a perfect correspondence of class and preferences. As Chapter 2 explained, there can be stark variation within cities in the quality of basic services, such that many middle-class voters live in neighborhoods with shortcomings in provision of club goods such as paved roads, sewers, water, and local security. Wealthy elites can afford to provide many of these privately, substituting for the state at great personal cost. But doing so remains prohibitively expensive for many in the middle class, who still rely on state provision. As a result, both poor and middle-class voters may place strong demands on the state for particularistic club goods when living in areas where basic services are lacking – even as the middle class demands few private goods that could be targeted through individual-level clientelism.[11] Nonetheless, I still expect that after controlling for differences in local access to public services, higher socioeconomic status will be positively correlated with greater demand for universalistic policies relative to all types of particularistic goods.

3.3 THE SURVEY DATA

I examine the relationship between class and preferences using an original survey of residents of Greater Accra that is analyzed in each subsequent chapter in the book. The survey interviewed a representative, random sample of 1,008 adults from metropolitan Greater Accra in November–December 2013. The sample includes 21 respondents living in each of 48 small sampling clusters, each roughly corresponding to a separate neighborhood, in 10 parliamentary constituencies within the metropolitan area.[12] The sample was selected after stratifying all parliamentary constituencies in the metropolitan area by wealth, ethnic

[11] Some local communities may organize collectively to provide basic services to themselves in the absence of the state (Bodea and LeBas 2016). But self-provision often provides very imperfect, temporary solutions to needs for basic services. I assume that voters in such communities will generally still place demands on the state to provide services directly.

[12] Thirteen interviews are dropped from all analyses due to enumerator errors, leaving $N = 995$. The parliamentary constituencies are Ayawaso East, Ayawaso North, Ablekuma North, Ablekuma Central, and Okaikwei Central, within the city of Accra (AMA), and Weija-Gbawe, Bortianor-Ngleshie Amanfro, La Dade Kotopon, Ledzokuku, and Krowor, in the surrounding metropolitan area.

diversity, and 2012 NDC vote share, and then selecting random geocoded start points within constituencies after stratifying census enumeration areas on wealth and ethnic diversity.[13] From each of the 48 start points, respondents were selected via a standard random walk procedure.[14]

As discussed in Chapter 2, I measure the class status of survey respondents using an index based on whether a respondent has at least some secondary education, is fluent in English, and is employed in the formal sector. Rather than indicating a middle position in an income distribution, this definition captures the extent to which someone has reached a middle tier in the broader structure of the economy, with the skills and employment to escape basic poverty and compete in the modern formal sector economy.[15] The main variable for class used in all analysis is a continuous index: either the first dimension of a factor analysis of questions on education, literacy, and employment, or a count variable of how many of these characteristics each respondent has. All results are robust to either measure; I report results with the factor index, which is scaled in standard deviations from a mean of 0. Continuous measures are preferable to a binary classification of middle class and poor, which risks introducing bias from measurement error by misassigning respondents to the wrong categories; my measure assumes only that respondents with more of these characteristics are more likely to be in the middle class.[16] Separately, in all analyses I also control for an index of basic household assets.[17]

---

[13] See the Appendix for more detail on the sampling procedures.
[14] Forty percent of interviews were conducted on weekends and holidays so that employed middle-class respondents were more likely to be available. Interviews alternated by gender and were conducted in one of four languages (English, Akan/Twi, Ga, or Ewe) by local enumerators using smartphones.
[15] As discussed in Chapter 2, measures of education and employment status are too crude to distinguish the elite from the middle class. But wealthy elites are not well-represented in the data; they represent a small fraction of the population to begin with, and are those least likely to consent to face-to-face household survey interviews. As a result, higher socioeconomic status in my data should primarily overlap with membership in the middle class.
[16] For example, a respondent may be literate and well educated, but working in the informal sector. A continuous measure would count such a respondent as more likely to be in the middle class than a respondent with none of these three characteristics, rather than counting both respondents as lower class. I also conduct robustness tests using a dichotomous measure of class status similar to Thurlow et al. (2015) that incorporates measures of housing quality alongside the information on education and employment. I find substantively identical results for all analyses reported here.
[17] The assets index is based on a factor analysis of indicators for: owning a car, television, and computer; having running water, a flush toilet, electricity, and a security gate.

While my main theoretical and empirical focus is on intra-urban comparisons, I also compare responses from the main survey of Greater Accra to a companion survey conducted in five villages or towns each in five rural parliamentary constituencies, randomly selected from all rural constituencies in five regions of southern Ghana.[18] This does not provide a representative sample of all of rural Ghana, but the rural respondents were asked the same questions about preferences as the urban respondents, allowing for a rough comparison in prevalence of different types of preferences between urban and rural areas.

3.4 MEASURING DEMANDS

Respondents' preferences for government actions were measured as simply as possible: each respondent was asked in an open-ended question to list up to three issues that he or she most wants the government to address.[19] A similar question is also on the Afrobarometer and is frequently used to examine policy preferences in Africa.[20] Enumerators recorded verbatim sentence-long answers instead of coding their responses into predefined topical categories, as in previous surveys, allowing for more flexible interpretation of the responses along a series of different dimensions.

Each of the three responses per respondent was subsequently blind-coded as indicating a particularistic or a universalistic demand. Using the definition described earlier, the coding rules count all demands that could be satisfied through a targeted patronage transfer that benefits an individual voter or small geographically clustered group as particularistic. Particularistic preferences are further broken down into two subcategories: preferences for private or for club (local public) goods. Demands that could only be addressed by a major public policy are instead coded as universalistic. Because respondents gave up to three responses each, the coding is not mutually exclusive within respondents. I operationalize

---

[18] The sampling frame and selection procedures for the rural survey are described in the Appendix. There were 510 respondents in 25 sampling locations.
[19] The question was: "In your opinion, what are the most important issues or problems that you think the government should address?" This question was asked before all other questions on the survey about politics, to avoid priming partisan responses. A level of government was never specified to allow unprompted responses and to avoid response or desirability effects. If asked for clarification, the enumerators indicated that responses could address issues at the national, local, or personal level.
[20] For example, see Lieberman and McClendon (2013), Mattes (2015), and Gottlieb et al. (2018).

universalistic preferences both as an indicator for whether a respondent named any universalistic (particularistic) preference among her three responses and as the percentage of her total responses that were universalistic (particularistic). This produces what is at best only a crude measure of preferences. But evidence of aggregate differences across groups in their self-reported demands should still be indicative of qualitatively important variation in overall preferences.

The most common preferences in the urban survey are presented in Table 3.1. Fifty-five percent of respondents named at least one universalistic policy among the three issues they wanted the government to address. More than one-third of respondents (35%) listed at least two universalistic policies. The most common universalistic demands concerned changes to utility and fuel prices (for which a single price is fixed nationally), taxes, inflation and other national-level economic issues, national education policies, and support for anticorruption efforts. Particularistic preferences were split between demands for club goods (64% demanded at least one) and private goods (53% demanded at least one). The most common club goods demanded were improvements to neighborhood sanitation, water supply, and roads. The most common private goods demanded were personal employment, as well as scholarships and assistance for family education expenses, loans to start informal businesses, and help finding housing.

Demands for universalistic policies were significantly more common in Greater Accra than among the rural respondents interviewed in the companion survey conducted in rural areas. Compared to 55% of the urban respondents, only 38% of rural respondents named at least one universalistic policy among their three demands. Universalistic policies represented at least half of the demands for only 23% of rural respondents, less than the 35% in Greater Accra. By contrast, 75% of rural respondents demanded at least one club good, seeking benefits such as clean water, paved roads, and public schools at a higher rate than in the urban area, where average levels of existing service provision are higher. The overall levels of demand for private goods were similar among the urban and rural respondents.

Several clarifications are necessary regarding how these responses are coded. First, the coding scheme is agnostic about respondents' motivations – whether respondents are motivated by pocketbook concerns does not speak to whether their demands can be addressed by a targeted patronage transfer. Second, the question does not solicit preferences over the preferred mode of distribution. A respondent demanding

TABLE 3.1: *Typical voter demands by category and topic*

Category:			
Universalistic (Public)			
Rates and taxes (34%)	"reduce water and electricity bills"	"reduce taxes"	"reduce import duty"
Economy (20%)	"better polices … to check prices"	"create more industries in ghana"	"…deal with…foreigners in our markets"
Education (9%)	"free secondary and tertiary education"	"train more…teachers"	"put up universities in each region"
Petroleum prices (7%)	"reduce prices of fuel"	"reduction of fuel prices"	"reduce rates of fuel"
Corruption (5%)	"deal with corruption in civil service"	"fight corruption"	"posts to those who deserve, not politically"
Wages/pensions (4%)	"…better pension policies"	"increment in gov't workers' salary"	"increase teachers' salary"
Health (3%)	"NHIS should cover all diseases …"	"the health insurance is not working"	"health care system is bad in the country"
Particularistic (Club/Local Public)			
Category:			
Sanitation (31%)	"construct community gutters"	"proper waste dump"	"build toilet facilities"
Water supply (27%)	"lay more pipelines here"	"we need water here"	"pipe problem here"
Infrastructure (27%)	"construct roads here"	"provision … of streetlight"	"tar the community road"
Education (8%)	"build a JHS for us"	"…public school in my locality"	"build…school in the area"

Particularistic (Private)

Category:			
Unemployment (56%)	"we need job"	"provide youth employment"	"provide more job opportunities"
Education (19%)	"supply free education materials"	"give scholarships"	"skills training … for the youth"
Loans (7%)	"give out loans to traders like myself"	"give loans to businessmen"	"support to open our own businesses"
Housing (3%)	"reducing of rent fee"	"housing facilities must be built"	"reduce rent"
Social welfare (3%)	"assist the aged financially"	"support … in terms of food"	"solve financial problems"

Within each type (public, club, private) responses were coded into a list of more than 20 topics, using the same topics as the Afrobarometer and Lieberman and McClendon (2013). The most common topics are listed here, with the percentage within each broader type in parentheses. "JHS" is a Junior High School (middle school). "NHIS" is the National Health Insurance Scheme. Lightly edited for spelling and length.

that the government "assist the aged financially" could want a Social Security-style welfare program, could be requesting direct assistance from a politician, or could be satisfied by either as long as she gets the help. In the first case, she cannot be won over through patronage, but in the latter two cases she could be, so this is still coded as a particularistic preference.[21]

3.5 DIFFERENCES BY CLASS AND LOCATION

Belonging to the middle class is a strong predictor of having universalistic preferences in Greater Accra. Table 3.2 reports coefficients from a series of multilevel regressions in which the outcome variable is either an indicator for naming any universalistic policy among each respondent's answers, or the percentage of universalistic policies listed by each respondent. Intercepts are partially pooled by the 48 sampling clusters in the urban survey to account for the clustering in the sample design.[22] The education/employment index is the continuous measure of middle-class status described earlier. It is scaled in standard deviations from mean 0, with higher values indicating that a respondent is more likely to be in the middle class. At an individual level, I control for an index of basic household assets, age, gender, membership in each major ethnic group in Ghana, and an indicator for being Muslim. I also include controls for a series of other factors that could affect the preferences that respondents report: a measure of the percentage of each respondent's life lived in Greater Accra, an indicator for whether the respondent prefers state spending be targeted to a home rural region instead of her current

---

[21] This becomes more ambiguous with demands for "free secondary education." Viewed in context, these demands are direct references to the NPP's main 2012 campaign policy slogan, which promised to eliminate tuition for all public secondary schools (see Chapter 4). Any direct references to "free SHS" are thus coded as universalistic because they appear to be explicit demands for the NPP's proposed universalistic policy. Other demands for assistance with educational expenses (e.g., "give scholarships") are still coded as particularistic because they could be satisfied with patronage to individuals. Importantly, all results detailed here (and in Chapter 4) are robust to dropping respondents who are coded as having universalistic preferences based only on statements about education.
[22] Gelman and Hill (2007). These results are robust to using clustered standard errors by sampling cluster. The model is a logistic regression when the outcome is binary and OLS otherwise. I also replace the percentage measure with a count of universalistic preferences per respondent (from 0 to 3) and replicate Table 3.2 using an ordered logistic regression, finding similar results.

3.5 Differences by Class and Location

TABLE 3.2: *Universalistic preferences, by socioeconomic status and local need*

Outcome	1 Binary	2 Percentage	3 Binary	4 Percentage
Education/Employment Index	0.176*	0.041***	0.177*	0.041***
	(0.084)	(0.012)	(0.083)	(0.012)
Assets Index	−0.114	−0.013	−0.117	−0.015
	(0.085)	(0.012)	(0.087)	(0.013)
Pop. Change 10 Years (500m)			−0.012	−0.003
			(0.026)	(0.004)
Neighborhood Wealth (500m)			0.275	0.043
			(0.177)	(0.027)
Running Water (by cluster)			0.708*	0.119*
			(0.341)	(0.052)
Paved Road (by cluster)			0.462†	0.071†
			(0.255)	(0.039)
Pop. Density (by cluster)			0.017**	0.002*
			(0.006)	(0.001)
Individual-level Controls	Y	Y	Y	Y
N	987	987	987	987

*** $p < 0.001$, ** $p < 0.01$, * $p < 0.05$, † $p < 0.1$. Columns 1 and 3 are logistic regression coefficients, columns 2 and 4 are OLS. Intercepts are partially pooled by sampling cluster, following Gelman and Hill (2007). The outcome is either a binary indicator for listing at least one universalistic policy (column 1 and 3) or the percentage of total preferences that were universalistic (columns 2 and 4). For readability, population density is scaled as 1000s / sq. km. Data from the urban survey only.

neighborhood, and an indicator for moving to the current neighborhood to satisfy preferences for club goods.[23]

I estimate from Table 3.2 that a respondent in the middle class – with at least some secondary education, English literacy, and formal sector employment – is 10.7 percentage points (95% CI: 0.7, 20.6) more likely to list at least one universalistic policy among her preferences than a respondent without these characteristics.[24] While preferences are by no means overwhelmingly polarized by socioeconomic class, this is a

---

[23] Two additional indicators in all models in the text control for interview quality and measurement error: whether enumerators made logistical errors during the interview (12% of interviews), and whether enumerators noted respondents were cooperative with the survey interview (90%).

[24] All first differences in the text are conducted as in Hanmer and Kalkan (2013), holding all covariates at their observed values in the data.

substantively large difference consistent with many members of the middle class making qualitatively different demands on politicians than the poor.

In a separate model, I also find that respondents in the middle class are significantly less likely than the poor to demand private goods – the subcategory of particularistic benefits that can most easily be exchanged with voters through clientelism. I estimate that middle-class respondents are 15.2 percentage points (95% CI: 4.4, 25.3) less likely to mention at least one private good among their demands than poor respondents.[25] Overall, the majority of respondents meeting the full definition of middle-class status – with formal sector employment, literacy, and some secondary education – do not list any private goods among their responses. This suggests that middle-class residents should be, on average, less susceptible to direct clientelistic exchanges with politicians that deliver private goods in return for support.

Differences in access to basic service provision in each respondent's neighborhood also predict preferences, consistent with the idea that preferences respond to local needs. As a result, most middle-class respondents who do not have access to adequate services in their neighborhood still place demands on the government to deliver services in the form of club goods that can be targeted through nonprogrammatic appeals. Indeed, a majority (68%) of respondents meeting the full definition of middle-class status demand at least one club good among their listed preferences. I show how demands vary across neighborhoods in columns 3 and 4 of Table 3.2 by adding a series of neighborhood-level predictors. These include the percentage change in population in the immediate geographic area around each respondent between 2000 and 2010, to measure strain on local infrastructure;[26] an index from a factor analysis of census variables measuring neighborhood wealth in the immediate area around each respondent;[27] the percentage of respondents in each sampling cluster who report that running water is regularly available; an indicator for whether the largest road in each sampling cluster is paved; and a measure

---

[25] Middle-class and poor respondents are equally likely to demand at least one club good among their responses, however.
[26] This is calculated by overlaying geocoded 2010 census enumeration area data on the 2000 census to measure changes over the 10-year period in total population in the 500-meter radius around each respondent. The use of a 500-meter radius to define neighborhood characteristics is described in Chapter 2 and the Appendix.
[27] The construction of this neighborhood wealth index is described in more detail in Chapter 6 and in the Appendix.

3.5 Differences by Class and Location

of the population density in the census enumeration areas covered by each survey sampling cluster.[28]

Respondents are more likely to demand universalistic goods when living in areas of the city with better existing service provision – regardless of socioeconomic class. Simulating from column 3, I estimate that all respondents are 15.2 percentage points (95% CI: 1.2, 28.4) more likely to express at least one universalistic preference when in a sampling cluster in which every respondent reported that there is running water than when living in a sampling cluster in which no respondents reported running-water access. Similarly, all respondents are 9.7 percentage points (95% CI: -0.9, 19.5, $p = 0.07$) more likely to list a universalistic demand when living in a sampling cluster in which enumerators recorded that the main road was paved. But controlling for these and other measures of current service provision, columns 3 and 4 show that higher socioeconomic status respondents are still more likely to have universalistic policy demands than poor respondents.

These results are robust to several concerns. First, there could be concern that my measure of middle-class status includes whether a respondent is employed in the formal sector, while demands for employment are a common particularistic preference in Table 3.1, putting employment on both sides of the regression. To address this, I re-estimate Table 3.2 after redefining middle-class status based only on education and literacy, or instead after dropping all respondents who reported demands for employment, and find similar results. Second, there could be concern that some respondents whom I identify as middle class are actually upper-class wealthy elites. While I cannot directly distinguish middle-class and elite respondents based on education, literacy, and employment sector, I attempt to identify the respondents most likely to be economic elites indirectly based on the enumerators' reports of each respondent's housing quality: 35 respondents were marked as living in "luxury" housing.[29] Re-estimating Table 3.2 after dropping all of these respondents returns

---

[28] Population density can also proxy for neighborhood need for club goods. The densest parts of the city are in the original downtown, where existing endowments of infrastructure are overwhelmingly concentrated. Less dense neighborhoods on the periphery of the city usually have significantly less existing infrastructure provision.

[29] This is at best a very rough measure of which respondents are in the upper class. Only 26 of these 35 also score in the top 75th percentile on the education/employment index, for example. Ultimately, as described in more detail in Chapter 2, I lack the ability to sufficiently distinguish upper-class respondents to estimate their preferences separately from the middle class. But the small number in luxury housing suggest that the proportion of total respondents in the survey in the upper class is likely very small.

identical results for the relationship between the education/employment index and preferences.

3.6 SUMMARY

Middle-class residents in Greater Accra place noticeably different demands on their elected leaders than most poor residents. They are more likely than the urban poor to have universalistic preferences – seeking broad policy changes that cannot be address through nonprogrammatic, patronage-based appeals. They are also significantly less likely than the urban poor to demand private benefits, making middle-class voters much less susceptible to individual-level clientelism. Despite these differences, however, most urban middle-class voters do still demand particularistic club goods, especially when there are low levels of service provision in their neighborhoods.

With the middle class now making up such a large share of Greater Accra's population, do politicians offer new types of electoral appeals to address the universalistic demands of many middle-class residents? Chapter 4 will argue that politicians in Greater Accra largely do not. Facing supply-side constraints on their ability to address universalistic preferences, politicians in Greater Accra instead double down with patronage-based appeals. In turn, residents with universalistic preferences are more likely to opt out of the electorate, both because they are less likely to be mobilized to participate and because they are more disillusioned than others about not being offered credible options on the ballot to address their preferences. Despite the differences in demands documented in this chapter, Chapter 4 will cast doubt on the ability of the emerging middle class to transform modes of electoral competition in urban areas in new democracies.

4

Credibility, Patronage, and Participation

"We don't believe in anything they are telling us."
– Accountant, Odorkor, Accra, October 2013

"My focus is on those who are susceptible to the deceits of politics."
– NPP parliamentary candidate, Greater Accra, July 2012

Chapter 3 shows that the middle class has different preferences than the poor, with significantly more demand for universalistic policies that cannot be addressed through patronage. With approximately one-quarter of adults in Greater Accra now in the middle class, the number of residents with universalistic preferences should be large enough to swing competitive parliamentary and local elections in the city, and to help determine which party wins the presidential election in the Greater Accra Region – one of the main swing areas in national elections. Winning their votes could mean diversifying electoral appeals to engage in more programmatic, policy-based competition alongside nonprogrammatic appeals. Such a transformation would be consistent with a broad literature that has linked economic development and the growth of the middle class to transitions away from patronage-based politics.[1] It would also be consistent with the expectations of many policymakers and journalists about the political effects of Africa's urban middle class described in Chapter 1.

But the universalistic policy demands of many middle-class voters in Greater Accra are not creating a shift toward programmatic competition.

---

[1] For example, see Stokes et al. (2013).

Instead, parliamentary candidates and local party leaders differentially ignore urban middle-class voters during their campaigns – even as their numbers grow – and concentrate on the poor. Voters who demand universalistic policies are disproportionately abstaining from electoral politics, not forcing changes to modes of electoral competition. The reasons why are rooted in the supply-side costs of offering new electoral appeals. In a context of low state capacity, politicians are unable to credibly commit to delivering on campaign promises to voters who want major changes to universalistic public policies. This creates short-term incentives for politicians to avoid wasting campaign effort on middle-class voters, whom politicians perceive to be most difficult to convince. As a result, voters who want universalistic policies become more likely to opt out of participation than voters with exclusively particularistic demands, both because they are less likely on average to be mobilized to turn out and because they are less likely to trust that their preferences will be addressed by any party on the ballot. Electoral participation remains dominated by voters most susceptible to patronage-based appeals, which only helps perpetuate incentives for politicians to under-supply policy-based competition relative to demand for it in the population.

I explore this argument in the context of the 2012 presidential and parliamentary elections in Greater Accra. I combine the survey data from Chapter 3 with multiple other sources, including interviews with parliamentary candidates and local party leaders and a content analysis of each party's manifestos from the 1996 elections through 2012. Although most of this evidence is cross-sectional, I draw direct links between politicians' inability to make credible commitments with voters with universalistic preferences and politicians' decisions to under-mobilize middle-class voters in their campaigns, as well as between politicians' campaign behavior and lower participation by policy-demanding voters. Moreover, analysis of changes in manifestos over time suggests that electoral competition in Ghana is not becoming any more programmatic as the urban middle class grows, at odds with the expectation that the new middle class will trigger a shift into greater policy-based competition.

This chapter highlights central features of the trap described in Chapter 1. Despite the emergence of a large urban middle class, supply-side constraints on politicians mean that the nature of electoral competition is not changing. As politicians in Greater Accra avoid engaging with middle-class voters whom they perceive to be too difficult to convince, competition remains overwhelmingly patronage-based. This contradicts many of the more dramatic claims about the effects of Africa's new middle class, and demonstrates the limits of demand-side theories that attribute changes in the nature of electoral politics to socioeconomic and demographic shifts. The chapter also contributes to our understanding of the determinants of class-based turnout differences in new democracies. I offer a new explanation for why better-educated, wealthier voters may participate less than the poor in many new democracies, arguing that such a difference may primarily reflect underlying voter preferences, with turnout differences rooted in the inability of politicians to credibly commit to addressing the demands of voters who value programmatic politics.

4.1 THE CREDIBILITY PROBLEM

The universalistic policy demands of the urban middle class do not trigger a transition toward programmatic competition for several reasons. First, politicians in new democracies can face a significant credibility problem with voters, lacking the ability to commit to universalistic policies that many in the urban middle class demand. Second, differences in turnout and participation across voters with different types of preferences – a partial outcome of this credibility problem – further align politicians' incentives against changing their appeals. This section discusses the conditions under which a self-reinforcing cycle emerges in which electoral appeals remain overwhelmingly nonprogrammatic even as urban residents increasingly demand universalistic policy.

4.1.1 Supply-side Constraints to Addressing Universalistic Preferences

In a new democracy where most voters are initially poor, the politicians and parties that are initially most successful will be those who best target patronage to key constituencies and ethnic bases to satisfy voters' particularistic preferences, not those with strong policy commitments. When there is a subsequent rise in universalistic preferences in the population tied to the growth of the middle class, politicians and parties that have already specialized in patronage-based appeals can respond in two ways: (1) they can diversify their approach and begin making real policy promises; or (2) they can "stay the course" with patronage-based appeals, making only cursory efforts to address universalistic preferences. Each entails costs: the first, the transaction costs of making policy appeals credible; the second, the opportunity costs of foregoing votes from those demanding universalistic policies. In cities in new democracies, especially in Africa, the second choice will often be less costly than the first, even as the middle class comes to represent a large share of the urban population. I demonstrate this by considering the costs of each option in turn.

Choosing the first option means diversifying appeals to address some of the universalistic policy issues demanded by many in the middle class even as politicians also continue with nonprogrammatic appeals aimed primarily at the poor. Chapter 2 shows that there are no large African cities in which the middle class is the full majority; it is unlikely that any politician would fully abandon efforts to secure support from the urban poor.[2] But even if middle-class voters with universalistic preferences do not yet form a majority, their votes are still valuable in elections in which small swings in vote-share determine outcomes. This is especially the case if the candidates or parties have competed to a draw among the poor, or in settings with considerable ethnic voting – many expect middle-class voters to be less susceptible to ethnic appeals and instead to become a key swing constituency.

Ex ante, if the costs of mobilizing support among voters with universalistic preferences were similar to the costs of engaging with voters with particularistic preferences, politicians should begin catering to the new policy demands of many in the middle class, as long as doing so does not inhibit politicians' ability to also win votes from poorer voters with more particularistic demands. Programmatic and nonprogrammatic electoral strategies are sometimes theorized as mutually exclusive, but a large body of literature from a wide range of developing countries demonstrates that these appeals regularly coexist.[3] "Mixed" or "dual" appeals are thus possible, such that it should not be prohibitively difficult for politicians to address at least some key universalistic preferences without abandoning many existing patronage-based strategies. Rather than the risk of losing poor voters' support, a more binding constraint on whether politicians choose to diversify their appeals will be the costs of addressing universalistic preferences.

---

[2] Exceptions in which urban politicians might consider catering exclusively to middle-class preferences would be in fractured multiparty or multicandidate elections with low thresholds to win seats – as in local District Assembly (city council) elections in Greater Accra – or in settings where the wealthy and poor are starkly segregated into different electoral jurisdictions – as in municipal elections in some Latin American and South African cities. I examine the former situation empirically in Chapter 8, and discuss the implications of the latter in Chapter 9.

[3] For example, Levitsky (2003), Scheiner (2006), Kitschelt and Wilkinson (2007), Kitschelt (2007), Thachil (2014), Resnick (2014), and, especially, Luna (2014).

4.1 The Credibility Problem

A key determinant of these costs is a credibility problem that politicians who have specialized in patronage distribution face when transitioning to policy-based appeals.[4] To successfully win votes based on programmatic policy, politicians must both distinguish their policy promises from those of rival candidates, such that voters have some policy basis by which to make a choice, and, most importantly, convince voters that they are committed to following through on these policy promises in office. Making these commitments credible is very difficult in new democracies where patronage-based appeals have long been prevalent and there is little prior history of ideologically rooted or policy-based competition.[5]

The credibility problem has several dimensions that raise the transaction costs to investing in programmatic, policy-based appeals. Most important is low state capacity, which constrains politicians' ability to deliver on many policy proposals. Even if they are firmly committed to them, it is often unlikely that the state apparatus beneath policy-oriented politicians can successfully implement their proposals. Governments in Africa regularly fail to implement major policy reforms because of budget crises and weak bureaucracies. Local officials and politicians tasked with implementation fail to deliver promised goods, siphon off program funds, or target supposedly universalistic benefits as patronage.[6] The list of widely touted policy changes that never materialize amidst corruption allegations is very long.

Secondary factors that limit the credibility of some universalistic promises arise from collective action problems within the government. Individual politicians who are dedicated to a universalistic policy agenda often cannot act on their own – they need the cooperation of other legislators, local government officials, and/or bureaucrats who may block or pervert the implementation of new policies.[7] These problems are particularly likely when the main demand for universalistic policies comes from a middle class that is overwhelmingly concentrated in cities, as is the case in most of Africa. Even if some urban politicians want to address the preferences of these voters, delivering national-level policy reforms means convincing rural politicians who face electorates with very few middle-class voters to go along with policies that they may not similarly

---

[4] Keefer and Vlaicu (2008).
[5] See Keefer and Vlaicu (2008) and Keefer (2007) for related examinations of commitment problems bedeviling programmatic competition in new democracies.
[6] Among many examples, see van de Walle (2001), Reinikka and Svensson (2004), and Franck and Rainer (2012).
[7] For example, see Persson et al. (2012).

see as a priority. Unlike low state capacity, which creates a more general constraint, these coordination problems do not affect all universalistic policies, as not all universalistic policies demanded by the urban middle class directly conflict with the interests of rural politicians or necessitate a trade-off between urban and rural interests. But for those that do, coordination constraints also limit the ability of urban politicians to commit to policy reforms.[8]

The inability of urban politicians to act alone is greatest in settings with little political and fiscal decentralization. Where local governments have fiscal and political autonomy, local politicians can become policy entrepreneurs, introducing new policies at a local level that address middle-class preferences, even if politicians elsewhere focus on patronage.[9] But where power remains highly centralized and local governments lack autonomy to pursue their own policy agendas, urban politicians often do not have the latitude to experiment with new policies.

Given these hurdles, it is reasonable for voters to expect that most programmatic promises to deliver new universalistic policies are noncredible. Voters will be skeptical in general because they believe the state is not capable of implementing policies as proposed, having grown disillusioned by a long history of previous policy failures amidst budget crises, corruption, and favoritism. In some cases, voters may also realize that individual politicians do not actually have the political power needed to carry out their promises, or may not trust that politicians have the commitment necessary to follow through. Voters who demand universalistic policies may be those least likely to see promises about these policies as credible: better-educated middle-class voters who are more likely to demand universalistic policies are also those most aware of past policy failures and most likely have the greatest understanding of the limits of the state.[10]

---

[8] In cases where demands of different constituencies are not mutually exclusive, politicians in the same party may have strong incentives to coordinate on addressing universalistic demands that will result in more urban votes for their party. In this way, coordination problems cannot explain the entire credibility problem. While low state-implementation capacity is a more general constraint, coordination problems only limit urban politicians' ability to commit in specific cases where there are clear conflicts with the interests of copartisan legislators representing other segments of the electorate.

[9] This is a common element of "dual linkage" politics in many Latin American democracies, where powerful mayors have been shown to specialize their appeals depending on the wealth of their municipalities. See Chapter 9.

[10] Similarly, Mattes (2015) finds that the urban middle class in South Africa is much less trusting than the poor in respect of the government's ability to deliver promised policies.

Voters with these expectations will discount most attempts to woo them with programmatic policy proposals as "cheap talk." Reversing their beliefs requires costly long-term investments from politicians in building reputations of policy credibility, through some combination of sustained successful policy implementation, major anticorruption initiatives, improved bureaucratic capacity via state reform, or the forging of strong rural–urban political coalitions. Each can take more time than a politician seeking to win the next election in a competitive political system usually has available.

By contrast, choosing the second option above – sticking with existing nonprogrammatic, patronage-based appeals – allows politicians to avoid costly investments in building policy credibility. The main constraint on the second option is the opportunity cost of ignoring voters with universalistic preferences. This cost is high if a politician's opponents start making credible policy-based appeals, thereby cornering these votes. But in settings with little prior history of programmatic politics in which all parties are initially patronage-based – as is the case in most African democracies – all other parties and politicians likely face the same credibility problems in building support based on policy. When every party is also constrained, politicians can get away in the short term with ignoring voters with universalistic preferences.

Moreover, because significant scarcity in access to public services in many African cities means that many middle-class voters still demand particularistic club goods for their neighborhoods (see Chapter 3), urban politicians can still secure at least some middle-class votes by selectively targeting club goods to neighborhoods with poor service provision. Continued demands for patronage goods among a section of the middle class reduces the need to diversify appeals.

But a particularly important reason politicians can afford to "stay the course" with nonprogrammatic appeals even as the middle class grows may be a lack of participation from people who demand universalistic policies. In advanced democracies, the wealthy and the middle class are more likely to participate in politics than the poor.[11] The preferences of the wealthy are then better represented in policy.[12] Kasara and Suryanarayan (2015) demonstrate that this pattern reverses in many developing countries, however, with wealthier citizens reporting lower

---

[11] Rosenstone and Hansen (1993) and Verba et al. (1995); but also see Ansolabehere and Hersh (2012).
[12] Gilens (2012).

turnout than the poor. The reasons for this reversal in turnout inequality are subject to debate.[13] One possibility is that class-based differences in turnout emerge from people with universalistic preferences not believing any politician will address their demands. The same credibility problem that makes universalistic appeals difficult for politicians can also depress the participation of people with universalistic preferences, which can then feed back into further reducing the risks to politicians of choosing the second option in the choice mentioned earlier.

I expect differences in participation for two reasons. Neither is directly about socioeconomic status itself, but about the preferences that voters of different socioeconomic classes are likely to hold. First, people with universalistic preferences – who are disproportionately represented in the middle class – may become disillusioned by the significant constraints on politicians' ability to deliver universalistic policy. Believing that no options on the ballot credibly promise to deliver what they want, they may simply stay home.[14] Second, people with universalistic preferences may also become less likely to vote if politicians invest less effort in mobilizing their turnout – in expectation that winning their support is too difficult – compared to voters politicians perceive to be more likely to have particularistic preferences and thus to be easier to convince. An important determinant of turnout is whether individual voters, or everyone in a voter's surrounding neighborhood, are mobilized to turn out by politicians.[15] Turnout buying and other individual-level campaign strategies can sometimes inflate the turnout of poor voters with particularistic preferences through provision of private goods that many in the middle class do not value. Absent other simultaneous forms of mobilization targeted at the middle class, turnout disparities can result.[16]

---

[13] Kasara and Suryanarayan (2015), Croke et al. (2016), and Amat and Beramendi (2016).

[14] Research from Latin America similarly shows that voters who are disillusioned with systemic corruption and believe they cannot create real change through voting are less likely to turn out (McCann and Dominguez 1998, Davis et al. 2004, Chong et al. 2015).

[15] See Rosenstone and Hansen (1993), Gerber and Green (2000), Fedderson (2004), Nichter (2008), and Cho and Rudolph (2008).

[16] Nichter (2008). The existence of patronage distribution does not imply that the poor will necessarily turn out at higher rates than the middle class and the rich. Using inducements to encourage voting among the poor does not preclude also mobilizing the middle class and the rich through policy appeals and other means. In Argentina, for example, the poor have typically *not* turned out at greater rates than the middle class and the rich (Fornos et al. 2004, Jaitman 2013) even though parties engage in turnout buying of poor supporters (Nichter 2008). This is because parties are also simultaneously mobilizing the nonpoor through other means (Levitsky 2003, Calvo

4.1 The Credibility Problem

The abstention of universalistic policy-demanding voters can extend to other arenas of participation. Where party organizations are built around the distribution of patronage, people who do not value patronage benefits may avoid them.[17] The reward structure to participation in such an organization is unlikely to be aligned with the goals of people seeking to advance specific policy agendas. And where the primary mode of interaction constituents have with local representatives such as MPs and city councilors is through the demand and exchange of narrow particularistic benefits, especially private goods,[18] voters with primarily universalistic preferences may be more likely to avoid these interactions as well.

A feedback loop can result, with voters' decisions to exit the electorate looping back into politicians' incentives to avoid addressing universalistic preferences in the first place. If voters who want universalistic policies abstain from participating, even on the margins, the electorate remains more heavily weighted to those preferring particularistic benefits. A lag can emerge between demographic changes that increase the extent of universalistic preferences in the population and the extent to which politicians feel electoral pressure to address these preferences. The middle-class voters who remain in the electorate will disproportionately be those who still demand particularistic goods, especially club goods, that can be targeted selectively through nonprogrammatic appeals. Party organizations, which select which politicians get to contest for office in the first place, will also remain dominated by those seeking patronage, not policy. The voters that urban politicians interact with on a regular basis are also far more likely to be patronage- than policy-demanding.[19] When each of these is the case, politicians can win office while continuing to forego costly investments in making their universalistic appeals credible, even as the middle class grows. But this may only encourage more of those who want universalistic policies to stay away in the future, creating a

---

and Murillo 2004). "Turnout buying" of the form Nichter (2008) examines will only produce class-based turnout differences if politicians also choose to differentially ignore middle-class voters in their campaigns.

[17] Party members in patronage-based political systems are thought to primarily join in pursuit of rents rather than ideology or policy (Bob-Milliar 2012).

[18] For example, see Lindberg (2010).

[19] It is possible that voters with universalistic preferences remain active in other ways. Research on India, for example suggests, that while less likely to turn out or participate in party organizations than the poor, the middle class remain active in civil society groups (Chatterjee 2004, Harriss 2006). But even if this allows for indirect lobbying regarding government decision-making, these voters will not affect politicians' behavior through explicit channels of electoral accountability.

spiral that further broadens the disconnect between aggregate preferences in the population and the electoral pressures politicians actually face.

Politicians might still make surface-level claims about universalistic issues during campaigns. When politicians are aware of the credibility problem and know that few voters trust that they will follow through, it becomes essentially costless to include rhetoric about universalistic policy in platforms and manifestos in the hope that it sways some voters on the margins. But this is mostly cheap talk. Beyond posturing, politicians in such an environment face incentives against focusing serious effort on addressing the universalistic preferences of many middle-class voters.

This feedback loop will eventually break down. A shock, such as an economic crisis, could spark greater turnout, or the middle class may eventually grow so large that politicians have no choice but to address universalistic preferences to form viable electoral coalitions. But in the medium term, even if economic growth increases aggregate preferences for universalistic policy, patronage politics can be very "sticky," with the form of political competition lagging well behind the demands of the underlying population.

4.1.2 Alternative Arguments

There are several possible objections to this argument. First, perhaps politicians ignore the universalistic preferences of many in the middle class simply because the median voter is poor and has particularistic preferences. Spatial models of elections that assume that voter preferences are arrayed along a unidimensional issue space expect politicians to converge on the median voter. It is problematic to extrapolate from spatial models to electoral contexts such as those I consider here, however. In general, these theories do not apply as easily where there is little to no ideological competition or redistributive taxation – the main dimensions in most applications of spatial models.[20] The particularistic and universalistic preferences in Chapter 3 instead appear to be arrayed along entirely separate dimensions. More importantly, the expectation of convergence to the median in spatial models arises from an assumption that politicians can only commit to a single point on the issue dimension. Spatial models consider which point is the dominant strategy. But I argue that

---

[20] For example, consider the models building from Downs (1957) or Meltzer and Richard (1981). Kasara and Suryanarayan (2015) describe the inapplicability of the Meltzer and Richard (1981) framework to most developing countries.

it is possible for politicians to diversify and at least partly combine programmatic and nonprogrammatic appeals, catering to universalistic and particularistic preferences simultaneously by offering different types of benefits to different voters. Where diversified appeals are possible, it no longer follows that converging to a single type of appeal is necessarily the best strategy.

Instead, it is better to conceptualize the electorate in this context as comprised of different blocs of voters with different interests. Politicians must pull together some combination of these blocs to form a winning coalition by appealing to the interests of each group. These blocs can be defined by class, but also by geographic location or ethnicity. A middle class that forms a significant minority of such an electorate can still become a pivotal bloc in competitive elections, depending on how much support each candidate or party anticipates from the other blocs. This is especially true if we assume that voters with universalistic preferences are less likely to vote along ethnic lines and thus are more "swingable."[21] When viewed in this way, politicians *should* go after middle-class voters with universalistic preferences – in combination with pursuing other blocs of voters – even if they are not the majority, as long as the costs to doing so are not too high. Politicians will not do so, however, when credibly supplying programmatic appeals that address universalistic demands is much more difficult relative to winning with support only from voters with particularistic preferences.

A median voter theory also provides distinct predictions for electoral districts within cities in which politicians can win with middle-class votes alone and the median voter likely does make universalistic demands. If politicians are simply converging on the median, they should employ more programmatic appeals in these areas. My argument predicts that politicians will still focus instead on overwhelmingly particularistic appeals in these areas because the credibility problem continues to bind. The evidence below – and in my examination in Chapter 8 of municipal elections in which there are many local wards in which a politician could win a multi-candidate race with exclusively middle-class support – is much more consistent with the latter prediction.

---

[21] Such an assumption is broadly consistent with instrumental theories of ethnic voting (e.g., Posner 2005, Ferree 2006) and with modernization theories that make more expressive assumptions about ethnic voting. In an instrumental framework, voters with universalistic preferences should place less weight on the patronage benefits that accrue from ethnic favoritism. In modernization theories, wealthier voters should place less emphasis on ethnic identity in their behavior.

Second, it may seem implausible that high levels of electoral competition do not push some candidate or party to cater to universalistic preferences. Weitz-Shapiro (2014) considers whether mayors in Argentina respond to the demands of nonpoor voters in their districts. She shows that politicians often persist with individual-level clientelism despite large nonpoor populations when elections are not competitive, but that competition forces politicians to be sensitive to the preferences of the middle class and wealthy to avoid losing re-election. But competition can only force an otherwise clientelistic politician to cater to demands for programmatic politics when these voters actually have the ability to punish such a politician by voting for a nonclientelistic alternative. Argentina already has a mix of programmatic and nonprogrammatic parties on the ballot.[22] In competitive districts, voters usually face a real choice between a politician who will engage in clientelism and one not expected to do so. But consider the case where there is no prior history of programmatic competition and *all* parties and candidates cannot credibly commit to delivering on universalistic policy in the short term. Here, even if one candidate starts including rhetoric about universalistic issues in his platform, most voters will view this as cheap talk and noncredible. Competition will not force politicians with short time horizons to be responsive to universalistic preferences.[23]

This raises a third possible concern – that new candidates within existing parties or an entirely new party will emerge to offer the universalistic policies many in the middle class demand. Barriers to entry for new candidates or parties offering programmatic appeals can be very high, however. Candidates seeking nominations within existing parties must get selected by party organizations dominated by poor voters who demand particularistic benefits. These organizations will select for politicians based on their ability to deliver patronage, not policy.[24] Disaffected voters could instead organize a new party committed to universalistic issues. But staying home and abstaining from participation is a much lower-cost response in the face of large collective action problems,

---

[22] See Calvo and Murillo (2004) on the Argentinian party system.
[23] In this sense, competition may instead be a key element that incentivizes politicians to ignore demands for programmatic politics, in the opposite of Weitz-Shapiro's (2014) findings. Where the credibility problem is more binding than in Argentina, it can be easier for politicians facing a serious risk of electoral defeat to double down on nonprogrammatic appeals in the short-term to win the next election than to make costly investments in building policy credibility.
[24] Ichino and Nathan (2012) and Ichino and Nathan (2013b) show that primary elections in Ghana select for nominees best able to deliver patronage to party members.

particularly if voters with universalistic preferences are dispersed across neighborhoods, cross-cut the main ethnic cleavages in society, and are not already embedded in organizations that provide a framework for collective organization.[25] In addition, an outside entrepreneur with a policy-based appeal could emerge. But this is unlikely in the near future in more institutionalized party systems, such as in Ghana, where Riedl (2014) shows that the procedural and financial barriers to fielding a successful outside campaign can be significant.[26] Moreover, any new party or other political newcomers will still face the same (or worse) constraints as existing politicians to making credible policy appeals.[27] Voters may find it even more difficult to trust the policy credibility of an outsider running for office for the first time under the banner of a brand new party with no history in government.[28] If a credible outside option addressing the universalistic preferences of middle-class voters does manage to emerge, however, the differences in participation predicted here should decline and the feedback loop described above should stall.

4.2 DATA SOURCES

I examine this argument using several data sources. First, I use the same representative survey of residents of Greater Accra analyzed in Chapter 3 to measure political participation and reports of politicians' campaign

---

[25] Magaloni (2006) describes the significant "coordination dilemmas" activists seeking to create programmatic opposition parties face when confronting a deeply entrenched patronage-based political system. These include the fact that they may not agree on which policies to pursue. The universalistic preferences in Chapter 3 span a wide range of locations on the ideological spectrum, such that there would likely be real disagreement about what the platform of a new party should be. This bedeviled the Mexican opposition for much of the twentieth century. Despite clear popular demand for programmatic politics from a sizable minority of the population opposed to Mexico's patronage-based, single-party regime, programmatic opposition politicians were unable for decades to coordinate to present a viable alternative because of their internal ideological disagreements (Greene 2007).

[26] The closest examples of insurgent policy-based campaigns in Africa are the populists documented by Resnick (2014), such as Michael Sata in Zambia, who emerged in a significantly less institutionalized party system. Fusing policy appeals with standard forms of clientelism, Sata targeted his message to the urban poor, not the middle class, and would not have ended the turnout disparities predicted here.

[27] Keefer and Vlaicu (2008) describe how the credibility problem can create an equilibrium in this way in which policy-based parties never emerge.

[28] Arriola (2012) shows that insurgent opposition parties in Africa are most successful when they are able to use private-sector financial resources to bring in blocs of supporters through the pre-election distribution of patronage benefits, not when they have the most compelling policy platforms.

behavior. The survey also includes an embedded experiment on attitudes about the credibility of politicians' promises. The survey is supplemented by interviews conducted before and after the 2012 election with local-level political party executives and parliamentary candidates in Greater Accra, as well as focus groups with city residents. These focus groups were conducted in a cross-section of neighborhoods in the Greater Accra metropolitan area, selected nonrandomly to produce variation in ethnic diversity and wealth. Participants were randomly selected within each neighborhood using a random walk procedure.[29] More detail about these data sources is in the Appendix. Finally, I conduct a content analysis of the manifestos of both major parties – the NDC and NPP – from the 1996 through 2012 elections to examine the extent to which they attempt to make programmatic appeals. While most of this data is cross-sectional, the manifestos allow me to examine changes over time.

4.3 EVIDENCE

The evidence unfolds in multiple steps. First, I show that electoral competition is not programmatic and is not becoming more programmatic as the middle class grows. Second, I show that many residents of Greater Accra doubt the credibility of the policy promises politicians in urban Ghana make, and that voters with universalistic preferences are the most skeptical. Third, I document that politicians in Greater Accra are aware of this commitment problem and believe that middle-class voters – whom they perceive as those most likely to have universalistic preferences – are difficult to convince. As a result, politicians under-invest in mobilizing middle-class voters in their campaigns while focusing on poor voters they believe can be more easily swayed with particularistic, especially private, benefits. Fourth, and finally, I show that voters with universalistic preferences are more likely to abstain from electoral participation.

While I present these outcomes in this order for expositional clarity, the argument above suggests that each outcome is related to the others in a loop. Politicians' decisions to differentially ignore middle-class voters whom they expect to have universalistic preferences are likely both a cause and at least a partial outcome of differences in turnout

---

[29] Each focus group was mixed gender, with between 4 and 7 participants. There was a range of socioeconomic status among these participants, but none were wealthy elites.

and participation. And as more of the voters who demand universalistic policies exit the political arena, politicians face less pressure to deliver programmatic appeals – connecting the final outcome in this section back to the first.

4.3.1 A Lack of Programmatic Competition

There is little evidence that any transition toward programmatic competition is underway. On the surface, this may not immediately appear to be the case. The NDC and NPP both release manifestos outlining policy commitments. The promises in these manifestos are included in campaign speeches and media appearances made by each party's presidential candidate and in televised presidential debates. At the local level, parliamentary candidates and members of each party's grassroots organization emphasize these same messages as part of their on-the-ground voter mobilization efforts,[30] with parliamentary candidates in particular serving as the main local mouthpieces for their party's national platform. Some scholars have taken these types of policy statements as evidence of programmatic competition, whether in Ghana or in similar political systems elsewhere.[31] But the existence of this rhetoric is not evidence of programmatic competition. Almost all political parties everywhere make at least some policy promises during campaigns. Policy rhetoric can be cheap talk – noncredible promises on which most voters do not expect politicians to deliver. For policy rhetoric to affect voting behavior, voters must both be able to distinguish between parties' competing policy promises – with some actual basis to choose whom to support based on policy – and must also trust that these promises are credible enough to provide real indicators of how a party will govern.[32]

Neither appears to be the case in Ghana. Neither has become more true over time. The result is that both parties now promise to implement largely identical platforms and there are strong reasons for voters to doubt the credibility of either's promises. I examine whether promises are differentiated through a content analysis of each party's manifestos for every election from 1996 to 2012.[33] For each party, I count the promises they make about domestic policy issues and code each on

---

[30] Brierley and Kramon (2015).
[31] Elischer (2013) and Resnick (2014).
[32] See Kitschelt et al. (2010) and the definition of programmatic competition in Chapter 1.
[33] The 1992 manifestos are not available. I stop in 2012, the main election for which I measure the other outcomes in the chapter.

several dimensions. These manifestos are long lists of commitments – with as many as 396 domestic policy promises made by the NPP in 1996 and an average of 230 per manifesto.[34] While not all items in each manifesto will receive equal emphasis on the campaign trail, these documents provide the universe of promises that each party made before each presidential and parliamentary election.[35] Summary statistics for each party's 2012 manifesto are in Table 4.1.

The manifestos indicate that Ghanaian voters should have little ability to differentiate between the parties based on their policies for several reasons. First, the majority of promises in every election beginning in 2000 have been about "valence" issues – universally good things about which there is no disagreement. Bleck and van de Walle (2012) demonstrate that many African parties focus primarily on valence issues, noting that "[r]ather than proposing a specific policy position, parties will say they are for something good (like development, education, democratic practices) or against something bad (like corruption or colonial interference)" (1414). This contrasts to "position taking," characteristic of programmatic political systems, in which parties "advocate for ... specific polic[ies] that could be debated" and about which there could be real disagreement (Bleck and van de Walle 2012, 1415). The NDC and NPP both provide excellent examples of valence-based campaigns. Table 4.1 indicates that nearly two-thirds of each party's promises in 2012 were promises to deliver on valence issues around which there is likely no disagreement rather than representing positions on contestable topics. Examples in the NDC's 2012 manifesto include promises to provide "quality education, ensuring children who are not in school gain access," to deliver "an average GDP growth rate of at least 8%," and to "investigate corruption."[36] No party would disagree with these goals. The prevalence of valence issues in the manifestos has increased over

---

[34] In total, I code information for 2,299 promises. For the 2012 manifestos, each party provided an "executive summary" of its core pledges – 56 for the NDC and 77 for the NPP. I focus on these core promises for 2012. For the other years, the manifestos have no summary section and are long lists of hundreds of promises with no clear rank ordering, so I code information for all promises.
[35] MP candidates typically do not have separate platforms of their own beyond supplementing their party's national message with localized promises about specific particularistic goods they will deliver to their constituents.
[36] The NPP's 2012 manifesto similarly emphasized the party's commitments to "raise the quality of education at all levels," create a "better economy," "fight against corruption," and provide "good leadership." See New Patriotic Party (2012) and National Democratic Congress (2012).

TABLE 4.1: *Overlapping manifestos: NDC and NPP 2012 campaign pledges*

Party	Valence Issues	Ideological Content	Overlaps Other Party	Clear Disagreement	Targets Specific Class Group
NDC Total: 56	Valence: 66% (37) Position: 34% (19)	Left: 13% (7) Right: 7% (4) Nonideological: 80% (45)	Identical: 43% (24) Similar: 27% (15) Unique: 30% (17)	Yes: 2% (1)	No specific class: 50% (28) Poor: 32% (18) Middle class: 13% (7) Business: 16% (9)
NPP Total: 77	Valence: 62% (48) Position: 38% (29)	Left: 17% (13) Right: 13% (10) Nonideological: 70% (54)	Identical: 51% (39) Similar: 27% (21) Unique: 22% (17)	Yes: 9% (7)	No specific class: 44% (34) Poor: 36% (28) Middle class: 11% (9) Business: 19% (15)

Coding rules are in the Appendix. The percentages in the final column do not sum to 100% because the categories are not mutually exclusive; some promises would benefit multiple specific class groups.

time, with the parties now staking out far fewer positions on contested issues than in 1996, when only 36% and 48% of the NDC and NPP's promises, respectively, were about valence issues.

In addition, the promises each party makes mostly lack any ideological content. To the extent that the parties do stake out ideological stances, they occupy overlapping spaces on a standard left-right spectrum, with no obvious separation. I code each domestic policy promise for whether it represents a generally left-wing or right-wing approach regarding support for redistribution and state intervention into the market.[37] Table 4.1 shows that the promises of both parties were all over the ideological map in 2012, with no evidence of an ideological cleavage despite the NPP sometimes being described as more business-oriented and conservative and the NDC as socialist (see Chapter 2). The large majority of promises (80% for NDC; 70% for NPP) were coded as having no ideological content. Of the remainder, both parties emphasized similar mixes of left- and right-leaning policy stances. Moreover, the top two panels of Figure 4.1 show that the parties have never been particularly ideologically distinct and may be becoming less so over time. In every election since 1996, the majority of each party's promises have lacked ideological content. The supposedly conservative NPP has made a similar proportion of left-leaning pro-regulation, pro-intervention promises as the nominally socialist NDC in every election until 2012 – when the NPP made noticeably more left-wing promises than the NDC.[38] The NPP's manifesto now includes numerous proposals to expand the welfare state and intervene in the free market to protect industries from foreign competition.

This lack of ideological differentiation is not surprising because there is a remarkable degree of overlap in the promises each party makes.

---

[37] I define left vs. right on an interventionist/redistributive vs. pro free market dimension. Left-wing proposals included pledges about redistribution to the poor; expansion of the welfare state; state intervention into or regulation of the economy; support for state-owned enterprises; and protectionist trade policy. Right-wing proposals included statements about support for the private sector, deregulation of the economy, tax cuts, support for free markets, privatization of state-owned enterprises and service delivery, and free trade. Nonideological statements were any promises about providing basic public infrastructure (schools, roads, hospitals, etc.), supporting good governance and human rights, or producing positive economic outcomes without describing how (economic growth, better cocoa farming yields, more jobs, etc.).

[38] Elischer (2013) argues that the parties were more ideologically distinct in the early 1990s, but there is only limited evidence of this in the manifestos. The NDC appears to have gone to great lengths in its early manifestos – especially in 2000 – to signal its commitment to the private sector and free markets and highlight its role in privatizing the economy during the 1990s.

4.3 Evidence

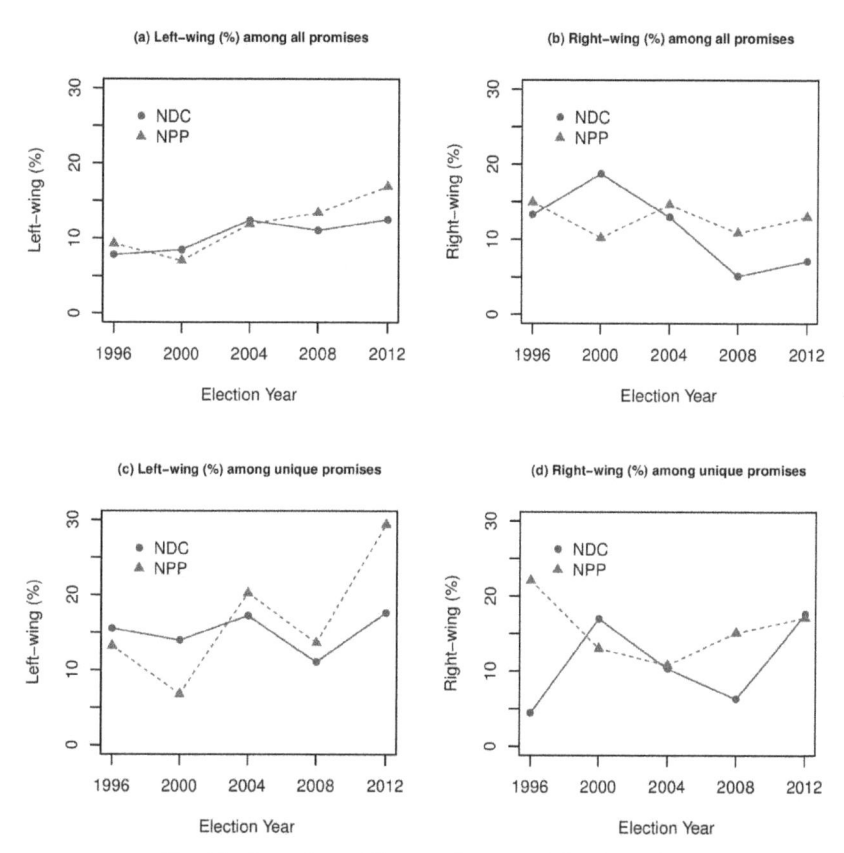

FIGURE 4.1: *The ideological muddle:* Panels (a) and (b) show the proportion of promises that reflect a left-leaning or right-leaning proposal. Panels (c) and (d) show the proportion of *unique* promises – not appearing in the other party's manifesto for that year – with each ideological orientation.

Nearly 80% of the promises in the NPP's 2012 manifesto also appear in the NDC's 2012 manifesto, while 70% of the NDC's promises appear in the NPP's manifesto. In Table 4.1, I break this overlap down into two subcategories: (i) promises that are identical in the other manifesto; and (ii) promises that are similar in intent, but involve slightly different proposals.[39] Table 4.1 shows that the majority of this overlap involves

---

[39] Examples of similar, but not identical, promises include an NDC pledge to "establish a GHc10 million Jobs and Enterprise Development Fund to encourage and support young people ... and create sustainable jobs" matched by an NPP promise to "introduce and improve upon existing skills training programmes [sic] ... and other existing youth employment programs." These policies share the same goal and would result in similar

Overlapping promises between parties

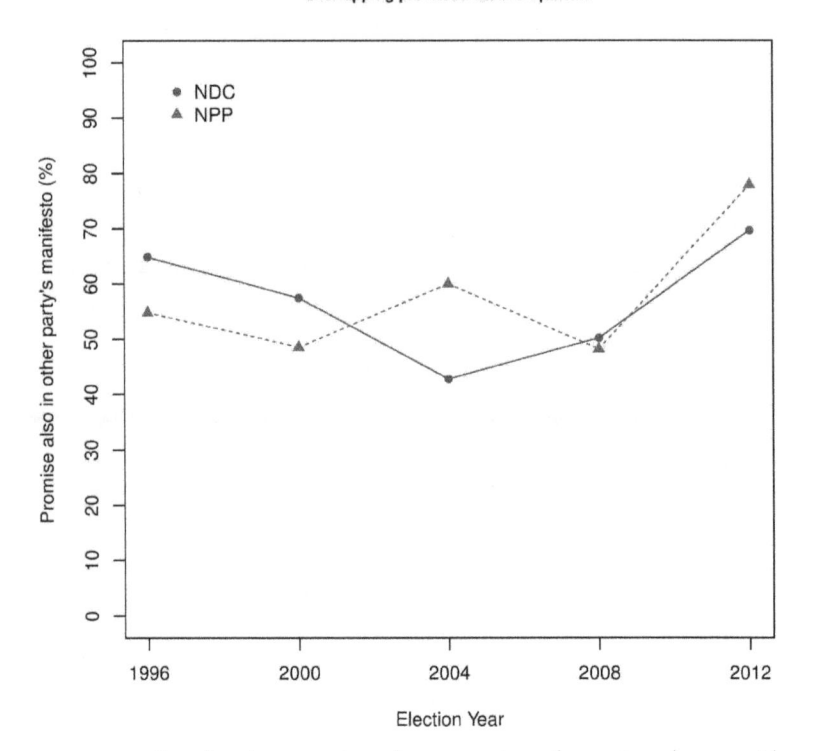

FIGURE 4.2: *Overlapping promises:* the proportion of promises that are either identical or similar to promises in the opposing party's manifesto in the same election year.

promises that are completely identical.[40] Figure 4.2 plots changes in the degree of overlap over time and shows that the parties had their most similar platforms to date in the 2012 election. Rather than becoming increasingly differentiated over time, as would be expected if they were placing greater emphasis on policy issues as the middle class grew, the parties were offering almost the same set of policies.

Moreover, most unique promises made by only one party are about issues over which there is no obvious disagreement. Many appear to be

---

job and training programs, even if they would take somewhat different forms. See New Patriotic Party (2012) and National Democratic Congress (2012).

[40] For example, the NDC promised to "increase power generation ... to 5,000 megawatts by 2016" while the NPP promised to "complete the generation expansion program ... to 5,000 [megawatts]"; an NPP promise to "support the passage of the Freedom of Information Act" was matched by an NDC promise to "prioritise the passage of the Freedom of Information Act."

ideas that the other party just did not happen to emphasize.[41] Panels (c) and (d) of Figure 4.1 examine the ideological content of the unique promises in each manifesto. Each party stakes out positions both to the left and the right when making promises that are not copied by the other. To the extent that there has been change over time, the supposedly conservative NPP now stakes out more unique left-wing positions than the NDC.

There were only a handful of issues in the 2012 campaign in which each party took clearly opposed positions, and only one among the NDC's core 2012 promises. This disagreement was about how to expand secondary education. The NPP proposed making all public secondary schools free. The NDC criticized this proposal for being unrealistic and instead proposed building 200 new secondary schools in underserved areas. But even on this issue, the parties ended up at the same position shortly after the election. After winning, the NDC adopted the NPP's proposal as its own, with President Mahama announcing in 2013 that he would attempt to implement the same free secondary school policy he had criticized.

In addition to not being clearly differentiated, most of these policy promises are not particularly credible. Ghana's parties both have long histories of coming up short on their commitments.[42] Consistent with the credibility problem described above, this gives voters – especially those with universalistic preferences seeking major policy changes – significant reasons to doubt whether each party will follow through on its rhetoric. Much of this limited credibility is due to low state capacity: low professionalization and weak performance incentives of the bureaucrats tasked with implementing policies, the government's persistent budgetary constraints, and the limited checks against corruption and misallocation of state spending. It is simply not possible for the government to deliver on many of the more grandiose proposals the parties make during campaigns. And even when the government is committed to seeing a policy through, contractors are often not paid on time, delaying work for years,

---

[41] For example, the NDC made a unique promise in 2012 to "construct two National Science Parks to spread the benefits of technology across Ghana." The NPP made a unique pledge to restart a stalled NDC program to create a functioning national system of street addresses.

[42] Party leaders admit this in moments of candor. During the 2016 campaign, a senior NDC leader was quoted justifying his party's inability to meet past promises by arguing that manifestos are not "binding" and it is not "a crime" to break them. He continued: "[T]he first manifesto in the world was the Ten Commandments. That is God's manifesto he gave to Moses. Have we complied with that?" See Essuman (2016).

budgeted funds get siphoned off due to corruption by local bureaucrats and politicians, or major projects are left unfinished due to coordination problems between bureaucrats and local politicians tasked with implementing them.[43] In other cases, the government is forced by financial realities to do the opposite of what was promised – such as when the NDC had to significantly raise electricity, water, and fuel prices in 2013 in contradiction to a campaign promise because state utilities lacked funds to continue operating.

Recent examples illustrate this lack of credibility. Some promises in each manifesto represent sweeping claims on which no government could plausibly deliver.[44] Others may appear more manageable on their face, but nothing ever happens after the election or programs that are implemented come up short of what was claimed. As one indicator of this inability to follow through, dozens of promises recur in each party's manifesto from election to election, even after that party has been in power for four years and could have tried to implement them. The prominent debate about secondary school access in the 2012 campaigns provides a fitting example. Despite quickly switching to claim it would carry out the NPP's free public secondary school policy in 2013, the NDC government had still not implemented the policy by the 2016 campaign. The program had been held up by the same budgetary constraints that the NDC had itself pointed to on the campaign trail in 2012 to discredit the NPP's proposal. Both parties entered the 2016 campaign with identical promises to end secondary school fees.[45] Moreover, between 2012 and 2016, the NDC downgraded their 2012 election promise of 200 new secondary schools to a claim that they had built 123 (or 73, depending on the pronouncement), even as media investigations revealed that as few as ten had opened. During the 2016 campaign, the NDC again reiterated its promise for the full slate of new schools and the NPP now also campaigned on the same promise – boasting that they, instead, would see to the construction of the secondary schools.[46]

Another example relates to Ghana's power crisis. Rolling blackouts – called "dum sɔ" in Twi – have occurred for years. A central pledge

---

[43] Luna (2016), Brierley (2016), and Williams (2017).
[44] As a fitting example, in the 2008 election the NPP promised that "the entire environment including air, water, foliage as well as the varied impact of living organisms will be managed to avoid pollution and contamination of all forms." See New Patriotic Party (2008).
[45] As of this writing, the NPP has begun implementing this policy after winning the 2016 election.
[46] See, for example, Allotey (2016); "Mahama's 200 Day Schools in Limbo" (2016).

in the NDC's 2008 and 2012 platforms was to increase the national power supply to end blackouts. After the election, President Mahama (of the NDC) made a series of public pronouncements promising to end "dum sɔ" by a specific date, only to break each promise and make a new one a few months later, to much derision in the press.[47] Periodic blackouts have continued under the NPP since the 2016 election – which also campaigned on a promise to end them.

For other promises, voters have strong reasons to believe that benefits that parties claim will be programmatically distributed will actually be given out as patronage. The NPP campaigned in 2012 in large part on its record of creating several major nationwide antipoverty programs when it was in power prior to 2008. The most significant was a national health insurance system, the National Health Insurance Scheme (NHIS).[48] By the end of the NPP's term in 2009, the NHIS was hitting logistical roadblocks, with health providers sometimes turning away policyholders because of delayed reimbursements.[49] In addition, because enrollees must pay upfront registration fees to join the scheme, paying for the enrollment of poor voters has become a patronage good used by both parties.[50] Other examples of supposedly programmatic programs implemented in reality as clientelism are the National Youth Employment Programme (NYEP), introduced by the NPP to provide subsidized employment and job training for unemployed youth, and a series of related microfinance and training programs implemented by the NDC after the 2008 election. Despite being described in manifestos as programmatic, these programs

---

[47] See Ansah (2016). A fitting example comes from my own experience in Accra in March 2016. On the same day that a senior government minister declared on the floor of Parliament that Mahama had finally solved the power crisis, much of Accra suffered a 12-hour blackout. I only read news coverage about the claimed end to the power crisis late that night, when the power finally came back on. See Gadugah (2016).

[48] As an example of the lack of differentiation between the parties, a proposal for a public insurance program like the NHIS originally appeared in the NDC's 1996 and 2000 manifestos; the NPP's 1996 and 2000 manifestos do not mention it. But in 2003 the NPP passed the legislation creating the NHIS – based on a pilot program started by the previous NDC government – and the NHIS became a core element of the NPP's 2004, 2008, and 2012 campaigns.

[49] For example, see Zakaria (2009); "NHIS must promptly pay claims – healthcare providers" (2013); "Rejection of NHIS Cards at Hospitals" (2013). As of 2015, the government restricts NHIS coverage to a single hospital or clinic per policyholder because it cannot afford to provide broader universal coverage. Many Ghanaians believe that despite NHIS membership they will receive substandard service, or be denied altogether, without the ability to pay in cash (Dalinjong and Laar 2012). Also see Mensah (2014).

[50] Interview with NDC executive, Ayawaso West constituency, Greater Accra, July 23, 2012; interview with district assembly member, Okaikwei Central constituency, February 25, 2014.

have long been seen as patronage slush funds for the ruling party.[51] The NYEP – rebranded by the NDC as GYEEDA – succumbed to a corruption scandal in 2013 that revealed that dramatically fewer people had benefited from the program than both parties had claimed when in office, and that much of the program's funding was siphoned off as corruption.[52]

4.3.2 Survey Experiment: Perceptions of Credibility

The previous section suggests that Ghana's major parties are not offering differentiated or credible policy proposals that would allow voters with universalistic preferences to choose candidates based on policy. I now examine the credibility problem from the perspective of potential voters. Residents of Greater Accra, especially those with universalistic policy demands, are skeptical of each party's policy messaging.

Participants in focus groups conducted throughout Greater Accra after the 2012 election generally did not trust either party's promises. One participant in a middle-class neighborhood said of the NPP's main promise to make secondary school free, "They will 'chop' [*steal*] the thing, and the benefits will not be extended to the poor. So its not going to be free at all."[53] A woman in another middle class area similarly argued, "You can say you will bring free education, but when you win, you will not do it."[54] An accountant in the Odorkor neighborhood argued, "When they promise ... we don't believe in anything they are telling us."[55] A hairdresser in Adenta explained that "this [MP candidate] will say this today and then tomorrow he does another thing. The other one too ... he says this and then he will not even do anything ... So there is no need for me to vote."[56] Instead of trusting candidates' promises, middle-class

---

[51] This is described in the interviews and focus group in Chapter 6. Also see "Teach the Foot Soldiers How to Fish" (2010). Other programs such as LESDEP (the Local Enterprise and Skills Development Programme) and MASLOC (the Micro-finance and Small Loans Centre) have also faced persistent allegations that they primarily serve as opportunities to funnel patronage to ruling party supporters despite official claims that they are programmatic.

[52] GYEEDA is the Ghana Youth Employment and Entrepreneurial Development Agency. For example, see "The GYEEDA Report" (2013); Gyasi (2013).

[53] Focus group, Dzorwulu, Ayawaso West constituency, Greater Accra, June 21, 2013.

[54] Focus group, Adenta, Adenta constituency, Greater Accra, August 7, 2013.

[55] Focus group, Odorkor "Official Town," Ablekuma North constituency, Greater Accra, October 1, 2013.

[56] Focus group, Adenta, Adenta constituency, Greater Accra, August 7, 2013. Much of the discussion in these focus groups centers on interactions with candidates for parliament

4.3 Evidence

participants emphasized their self-reliance. A statement from a nurse in Dzorwulu is typical: "We struggle for ourselves. They [politicians] think about themselves, we also think about ourselves."[57] A middle-class participant in Odorkor tied his disillusionment to the fact that he does not want particularistic goods: "I'm not looking at the MP to do something for me. I can help myself. But that's what they've [MPs] been doing to get the illiterate people."[58] Some focus group participants pointed to this lack of trust in the parties as their reason for staying home on election day.

Local party leaders and parliamentary candidates in Greater Accra interviewed during the field research also recognized this lack of trust. An NDC parliamentary candidate describing his reception while campaigning said, "I think there is a collapse of trust in politicians generally ... The complaint we usually get is that we've voted for this party for 16 years, nothing has come out of it. What are the guarantees that you will be different from the rest?"[59] An NPP constituency executive noted this distrust and tied it to turnout: "People were peeved, because they didn't get what they expected from us [when NPP was in power] ... Some of them didn't vote at all. A lot of people didn't vote because they were not happy."[60] Others readily acknowledged that voters did not see policy messages in their platforms as credible. Local executives from both parties complained about how they performed poorly despite having the "better message."[61] As one NPP activist said after describing his party's promise about free secondary education: "I don't want to be misleading ... The fact is Ghanaians don't vote on issues. That's what every politician, that's what the NDC knows." Along with many other local activists, he believed that vote choice is explained by particularistic preferences, not policy.[62]

A vignette experiment embedded in the main survey allows me to test more systematically which voter characteristics explain beliefs about the

---

because they are the main local figure from their party campaigning on behalf of both the presidential candidate and themselves in each local area of the city.

[57] Focus group, Dzorwulu, Ayawaso West constituency, Greater Accra, June 21, 2013.
[58] Focus group, Odorkor "Official Town," Ablekuma North constituency, Greater Accra, October 1, 2013.
[59] Interview with NDC parliamentary candidate, Greater Accra, June 20, 2012.
[60] Interview with NPP constituency executive, Greater Accra, July 29, 2013.
[61] Interview with NDC constituency executive, Greater Accra, March 25, 2014; interview with NPP constituency executive, Greater Accra, March 4, 2014; interview with NPP constituency executives, Greater Accra, August 6, 2013.
[62] Interview with NPP party agents, Greater Accra, August 1, 2013.

credibility of common campaign promises. Each respondent was read two sets of paired vignettes about hypothetical parliamentary candidates competing in an election.[63] The candidates in the vignettes randomly varied along three dimensions: their ethnicity, cued via names;[64] their professional background;[65] and policies they promised to deliver after the election. Each campaign promise was randomly selected from among two examples of universalistic policies or two examples each of pledges to deliver club or private goods to the respondent's community, with one promise made by each hypothetical candidate in the vignette.[66] After being asked to vote in a mock election between the two candidates in each pair, respondents were asked a follow-up question about one randomly selected candidate per pair: "Do you think a politician like [NAME] will actually deliver on a promise like [PROMISE]?" This question provides a measure of each respondent's beliefs about the credibility of politicians' promises to deliver the policy in the vignette.

Overall, few respondents saw these promises as credible. Only 28.4% of respondents answered "yes" to the question about credibility, with 27.2% believing the politician would follow through on the promised universalistic policy. This general level of distrust across all respondents indicates the low credibility environment in which politicians operate. But low credibility is not an insurmountable constraint for nonprogrammatic appeals. Voters can easily observe whether or not they receive narrow particularistic benefits. These benefits can either be targeted

---

[63] The design is similar to a conjoint experiment (Hainmueller et al. 2013). The experiment did not explicitly cue partisanship. A party cue may have overwhelmed the other treatments, with reflexively favorable answers about preferred parties creating ceiling effects.

[64] Names unambiguously cue membership in one of the four major ethnic categories: as Akan, Ga, Ewe, or Muslim northerner. Two names were used per ethnicity to average over idiosyncratic features cued by specific names. Full texts of the vignettes are in the Appendix, with balance statistics.

[65] These were doctor, lawyer, businessman, and university lecturer.

[66] The example policies were chosen from answers to a pilot of the survey question on preferences analyzed in Table 3.1. For universalistic goods, the treatments were "lobby for keeping the price of fuel and utilities low so that everyone in Ghana can continue to afford fuel and electricity" or "lobby for construction of new water production facilities in Ghana, so the water flows more regularly around the country." For club goods, "construct and tar more of the roads in the constituency" or "build new classroom blocks and resource centers at schools in the constituency." For private goods, "find jobs for some of the youth in the constituency" or "provide scholarships to some families in the constituency to pay school fees."

upfront, before elections, or through repeated personalized exchanges in which the credibility of specific promises can be more easily assessed, even among voters who are distrustful of politicians in general. But skepticism about credibility creates a significant hurdle for politicians seeking to reach voters with universalistic preferences through policy-based appeals.[67] Implementation of universalistic policy takes place over a longer time frame and is less observable. Policy platforms will only build support if voters trust that they will be implemented over time.

But I find that the voters with the greatest preferences for universalistic policies – those most likely to care about the details of a party's platform – are the voters least likely to believe in a politician's promise to deliver on these policies. In Table 4.2, I analyze responses using multilevel models similar to those in Chapter 3, while also including indicators for each treatment condition as controls. I estimate results separately for each type of promise (universalistic, club, and private).[68] I find that the respondents who actually demand universalistic policies are those least likely to believe that politicians' promises are credible. Simulating from column 1 of Table 4.2, respondents who demand at least one universalistic policy are 6.4 percentage points (95% CI: −0.9, 13.4, $p = 0.07$) less likely to believe the promise to deliver a universalistic policy than respondents who only want particularistic goods.

Columns 1–4 in Table 4.2 also show that there is a co-ethnicity treatment effect in the experiment, with respondents significantly less likely to trust campaign promises from non-co-ethnic politicians compared to co-ethnics (as signaled by the politicians' names). This suggests that ethnicity is also an important factor urban voters use to evaluate the credibility of promises. Many respondents may not have believed that universalistic policies promised by candidates from other ethnic groups would actually be universalistic as implemented, but instead would become patronage that favored the other group. Entrenched voter expectations of favoritism create an additional hurdle for the credibility of policy-based appeals. I further explore the impact of beliefs about favoritism on voting behavior in Chapters 5 and 7.

---

[67] See Kitschelt (2000) for a similar discussion.
[68] At the neighborhood level, I control for wealth, ethnic fractionalization, population density, and competitiveness in the surrounding ward (or Electoral Area) in the 2008 election.

TABLE 4.2: *Survey experiment: credibility of MPs' campaign promises*

Promised Good	1 Public	2 Public	3 Club	4 Club	5 Private	6 Private
Universalistic Preferences (binary)	−0.354† (0.198)		−0.437* (0.192)		−0.390* (0.197)	
Universalistic Preferences (percentage)		−0.418 (0.309)		−0.759* (0.305)		−0.493 (0.304)
Co-ethnic Candidate	0.496* (0.200)	0.477* (0.200)	0.451* (0.195)	0.441* (0.195)	0.274 (0.200)	0.259 (0.199)
Example 2: Low Utility Prices	0.063 (0.196)	0.066 (0.195)				
Example 2: New Classrooms			0.078 (0.190)	0.056 (0.190)		
Example 2: Scholarships					−0.009 (0.192)	−0.011 (0.192)
Education/Employment Index	0.038 (0.119)	0.039 (0.119)	0.093 (0.111)	0.106 (0.112)	0.064 (0.113)	0.067 (0.114)
Assets Index	0.047 (0.120)	0.047 (0.120)	0.092 (0.114)	0.091 (0.113)	0.123 (0.117)	0.120 (0.117)
Individual-level Controls	Y	Y	Y	Y	Y	Y
Neighborhood-level Controls	Y	Y	Y	Y	Y	Y
Name and Background Controls	Y	Y	Y	Y	Y	Y
N	611	611	611	611	613	613

*** $p < 0.001$, ** $p < 0.01$, * $p < 0.05$, † $p < 0.1$. The outcome is whether a respondent believes the MP in the vignette will actually deliver the cued good after the election. Columns 1–2 are for the public goods treatments (promise: water production or lower utility prices), columns 3–4 are for the club goods treatments (promise: construct roads or build classrooms), columns 5–6 are for the private goods treatments (promise: jobs for youth or scholarships to families). All models are logistic regressions with intercepts partially pooled by sampling cluster, following Gelman and Hill (2007), and include the same individual-level controls as in Table 3.2 and the neighborhood-level controls described in the text. I also include indicators for each possible candidate name (among 8 options) and each candidate background (among 4 options). Two-thirds of respondents received a prompt about each type of good.

4.3.3 Differential Mobilization and Engagement by Class

Politicians in Greater Accra are well aware of the correlation between class and preferences demonstrated in Chapter 3. In interviews, parliamentary candidates in the 2012 elections and local party leaders from Greater Accra clearly indicated that they knew that the middle class is growing, now represents a meaningful portion of the electorate in their constituencies, and has different preferences than the poor. But these politicians were also aware of the credibility problem indicated in Table 4.2: they knew that voters with universalistic preferences are especially hard to convince. As a result, middle-class voters are often ignored during each party's voter mobilization efforts in expectation that these are the voters among whom the credibility problem is most binding.

Importantly, interview respondents largely did not justify ignoring the middle class because of its limited size. Instead, they describe using class as a heuristic for which voters are convincible, avoiding middle-class voters in pre-election mobilization efforts because they do not believe they can credibly engage with voters who demand policy – even when they know there are many such voters in their constituencies.[69] For example, an NPP parliamentary candidate indicated that he realized the middle class had different preferences, but suggested that he lacked the ability to convince them to support him. When asked about his approach with middle-class voters, he said "People are more aware of what they really want than before. Before you could use money to change their minds, but ... your money can't buy most of them now like it used to." As a result, "you don't convince [middle-class voters] much at all. They know what is going on." But, he argued, "the poor people ... somebody brings them a big bag of sugar, tomorrow rice – what they eat is what they are thinking about," and went on to describe efforts to engage with poor voters by distributing private goods.[70] A local NPP party executive made a related argument, emphasizing the credibility problems inherent in engaging middle-class voters before elections: "I would say they are politically awakened, so they can discern now more than before. Formerly, people could fool them. But now you cannot fool them ... They know exactly

---

[69] Moreover, while it could be the case that it is more logistically difficult for politicians to find and engage with middle-class voters, given their busier work schedules and different types of housing, interview respondents specifically emphasized that middle-class voters are not disproportionately ignored simply because they are harder to reach, but because politicians believe they are harder to convince.

[70] Interview with NPP parliamentary candidate, Greater Accra, June 6, 2012.

what is happening when you come to them, whether you are deceiving them or not ... You must be very careful if you are dealing with them."[71] Another NPP executive similarly emphasized that his party focused instead on poor voters more dependent on politicians for access to particularistic benefits – especially private goods – the party could actually provide: "Yes, we have [wealthier and middle-class voters] ... But we don't normally follow them so much ... Most of the people want to see their MP assisting their wards, for example, getting school admissions, getting employment and other things" – typical particularistic benefits delivered in clientelistic exchanges in urban Ghana.[72]

These responses were best crystallized by the NPP's 2012 parliamentary candidate in the Ayawaso West constituency of Accra – the wealthiest area in Ghana and the one constituency in the metropolitan area in which middle- and upper-class residents make up the clear majority of the population (see Chapter 2). Despite being the candidate with the single greatest incentive to focus on the preferences of the urban middle class, he described focusing his campaign effort on poor voters, citing his inability to change the minds of higher-class voters as his reason for doing so.[73] The candidate argued,

When people have a certain level of education, they are able to clearly understand the issues. I don't mind whether they support me or they support the NDC, but they have some logical arguments to make their choices. So I really don't worry about that. My focus is on those who are susceptible to the deceits of politics ... I am focusing my effort in the informal communities.[74]

NDC politicians described similar difficulties campaigning among middle-class voters. When discussing differences between middle-class and poor neighborhoods, an NDC activist reported, "Somewhere like the Zongo and other places where poverty is high, everybody is trying to reach out for [benefits]. They do understand you when you talk. But the residential [neighborhood], when we go there they don't listen to

[71] Interview with NPP constituency executive, Greater Accra, June 26, 2012.
[72] Interview with NPP constituency executives, Greater Accra, August 6, 2013.
[73] This runs directly at odds with an alternative argument rooted in median voter theory, as described earlier. Rather than switching to cater to the middle class where it is the median, the parliamentary candidate emphasized a credibility problem to justify continuing to focus on the poor.
[74] "Informal" communities refers to those in informal housing. Interview with NPP parliamentary candidate, Greater Accra, July 16, 2012.

you ... Before you go in they tell you we have made up our mind, we know what we're doing."[75] These voters may be particularly unreceptive because politicians usually campaign at the local level with a message that does not address preferences for universalistic policies. While the presidential candidates of each party popularize their national-level policy promises in their speeches and media appearances, parliamentary candidates and party agents claimed that they often intentionally downplay their parties' main universalistic promises when mobilizing turnout before the election, instead focusing on promises of small-scale particularistic goods for individual voters in specific neighborhoods because they believe voters will find these more credible.[76]

The themes from these interviews can be seen more systematically in the survey data. The survey of Greater Accra examined campaign mobilization before the 2012 election in Greater Accra by asking respondents about campaign activities in their neighborhood.[77] Table 4.3 shows significantly less effort from the parties to mobilize turnout among middle-class voters. This is consistent with class serving as a heuristic for politicians about the likely preferences – and thus difficulty of convincing – different sets of voters.

In columns 1–2 of Table 4.3, the outcome is an indicator for whether a respondent reports that she saw party agents going door-to-door in her neighborhood before the election. In columns 3–4 of Table 4.3, the outcome is an indicator for reporting that she either saw or "heard about" a party distributing private gifts before the election. The models are multilevel logistic regressions with the same individual-level predictors as in Table 3.2 and Table 4.2. I also include several additional predictors that may affect the campaign strategies to which voters are exposed: competitiveness in each respondent's Electoral Area (ward),[78] population density, ethnic fractionalization around each respondent, and a neighborhood

---

[75] A "Zongo" is a Muslim slum. Interview with NDC ward-level executive, Greater Accra, March 1, 2014.
[76] Interview with NDC constituency executive, Greater Accra, February 27, 2014.
[77] The questions are: "Think back to before the elections last year. Did any political parties come door-to-door in this neighborhood to meet with voters in their homes?" and "Think back to before the elections last year. Do you remember if any of the political parties gave out any gifts, such as t-shirts, food, or money to some people in this neighborhood?" Overall, 69% of respondents reported seeing or hearing about gifts being distributed and 67% reported door-to-door campaigning.
[78] This is the absolute value of the difference in two-party vote share between the NDC and NPP in 2008.

TABLE 4.3: *Campaign mobilization, by neighborhood wealth and socioeconomic status*

Outcome	1 Door-to-Door	2 Door-to-Door	3 Private Gifts	4 Private Gifts
Education/Employment Index	-0.004 (0.090)	-0.008 (0.091)	-0.163† (0.092)	-0.186* (0.093)
Assets Index	-0.219* (0.090)	-0.216* (0.090)	0.029 (0.092)	0.053 (0.093)
Universalistic Preferences (binary)		-0.199 (0.157)		0.190 (0.162)
Neighborhood Wealth (500m)	-0.486** (0.161)	-0.513** (0.164)	-0.096 (0.173)	-0.150 (0.170)
2008 Competitiveness (by Electoral Area)	-2.558* (1.098)	-2.980** (1.119)	-1.427 (1.262)	-1.500 (1.241)
Ethnic Fractionalization (500m)	-0.337 (1.267)	-0.601 (1.283)	-1.935 (1.503)	-1.561 (1.471)
Pop. Density (by cluster)	0.001 (0.007)	0.001 (0.007)	0.020* (0.008)	0.018* (0.008)
Individual-level Controls	Y	Y	Y	Y
Constituency FEs	Y	Y	Y	Y
N	930	923	930	923

*** $p < 0.001$, ** $p < 0.01$, * $p < 0.05$, † $p < 0.1$. The outcome is knowledge of door-to-door campaigning in columns 1 and 2 and gift distribution in columns 3 and 4. Logistic regression coefficients with intercepts partially pooled by sampling cluster, following Gelman and Hill (2007). For readability, population density is scaled as 1000s / sq. km. Note that competitiveness is higher when the competitiveness variable is smaller (absolute difference in vote shares between NPP and NDC in each Electoral Area), such that there is more mobilization in places that were more competitive in the last election.

wealth index.[79] I include parliamentary constituency fixed effects to control for baseline differences in campaign strategies across constituencies, as party organizations, local campaign budgets, and the actors making campaign strategy decisions are all organized by constituency (see Chapter 2).

In Table 4.3, I find that respondents are less likely to report door-to-door mobilization efforts in wealthier neighborhoods, consistent with politicians placing less effort on mobilizing middle-class voters. From column 1, respondents are 10.1 percentage points (95% CI: 3.4, 17.1) less likely to report door-to-door mobilization after increasing local neighborhood wealth by one standard deviation. The predicted level of reports of door-to-door mobilization in the poorest neighborhoods in the sample is 77%, compared to only 34% in the wealthiest neighborhoods. While some campaign activity thus still happens even in the wealthiest neighborhoods, a difference of this size reflects qualitatively meaningful differences in voters' experiences with campaign mobilization.[80] Middle-class respondents were also significantly less likely to be exposed to individual gift giving before the last election, which is another means the parties use to mobilize turnout. From column 3, respondents who are in the middle class are 8.8 percentage points (95% CI: −1.1, 19.2, $p = 0.07$) less likely to report gift distribution than poor respondents. While politicians cannot easily observe individual-level preferences when deciding whom to approach, they can observe socioeconomic class – they are less likely to go door-to-door canvassing voters in middle- or upper-class neighborhoods in the first place, and are differentially less likely to offer gifts when they do interact with middle-class voters, consistent with the evidence in Chapter 3 that most middle-class voters do not demand these private benefits.

The outcomes in Table 4.3 represent the main activities used to encourage voter turnout before elections in Ghana, suggesting that parties under-invest in mobilizing middle-class turnout. In the interviews, *all* parliamentary candidates and campaign agents mentioned door-to-door canvassing in particular as one of their core voter mobilization tactics.[81]

---

[79] These latter variables are defined in the Appendix. The decision to calculate neighborhood characteristics around respondents based on census characteristics falling within a 500-meter radius is described in more detail in Chapter 2.

[80] Because these models all control for population density, this difference is not simply due to there being more voters living in poorer neighborhoods for parties to interact with.

[81] Interview respondents also described other activities, such as campaign visits to church services and trade associations and constituency-wide rallies. But few of these other

Canvassing is also not a tactic that is inherently only valuable among the poor. Turnout buying and the distribution of patronage sometimes occur as politicians canvass, but Brierley and Kramon (2015) emphasize that this is not always the case. Canvassing also serves as one of the main means by which Ghana's parties try to get the word out about campaign promises. But Table 4.3 suggests that the parties are much less likely to try to get the word out in neighborhoods where they believe many voters will not view these promises as credible.

In addition, the parties do not appear to differ significantly in the extent to which they emphasize universalistic policy messages targeted at the urban middle class on the campaign trail. In the analysis of manifestos given earlier, I also code whether each policy promise would primarily affect members of a specific class group – the poor, the middle class, or the business elite – or instead would affect all classes equally.[82] The final column of Table 4.1 shows that each party made a similar number of proposals aimed at the middle class in 2012, with 13% and 11% from the NDC and NPP, respectively. Moreover, neither party has substantially increased its focus on middle-class issues as the urban middle class has grown. For example, the NPP included a similar proportion of promises (9%) that would mainly affect the middle class back in its 1996 manifesto, at a time when Ghana's urban middle class was much smaller.

4.3.4 Effects on Turnout and Participation

I argue above that if voters with universalistic preferences are less likely to find politicians' campaign promises credible and also less likely to be actively mobilized to turn out to vote, they will participate in electoral politics at lower rates. This may further reduce politicians' incentives to

---

activities explicitly target the middle class. Moreover, in interactions at church services or other community forums, the credibility problems politicians report facing when engaging with voters who demand universalistic policies still hold. Importantly, none of the politicians interviewed ever mentioned broadcast or online media when asked to describe campaign activities, indicating that this is unlikely to represent a significant alternative channel through which the parties are separately mobilizing turnout and support from middle-class voters in urban areas. Political TV advertising remains in its infancy in Ghana.

[82] Promises in the manifestos that I code as primarily affecting the middle class are those that will mainly benefit people with secondary education and formal-sector employment, consistent with the definition of middle-class status in Chapter 2. Examples include expanding access to tertiary education, increasing the salaries of civil servants, and creating mortgage finance institutions to enable home buying.

invest in making credible policy appeals. Consistent with this argument, the survey data shows lower rates of participation by voters with universalistic preferences. This is likely due to a combination of the factors shown in the previous two sections: the credibility problem demonstrated in the survey experiment, and the parties' decisions to downplay the mobilization of middle-class voters – and by extension those most likely to have universalistic preferences.

In columns 1–4 of Table 4.4, I estimate similar multilevel logistic regressions to those in Table 4.3 in which the outcome is now self-reported turnout in the 2012 presidential and parliamentary elections.[83] The main explanatory variable is either the binary or percentage measure of universalistic preferences used in Chapter 3. I include the same controls as Table 4.3.

There is not total abstention by voters with universalistic preferences. But in columns 2 and 4 of Table 4.4, I find that respondents who list at least one universalistic preference in their response to the question about the issues they want the government to address are 7.1 percentage points (95% CI: 2.6, 11.6) less likely to vote than respondents with only particularistic preferences.[84] Respondents who list exclusively universalistic preferences are 7.8 percentage points (95% CI: 0.7, 15.7) less likely to vote than respondents with only particularistic preferences. Crucially, it is not the case that middle-class respondents in general are less likely to vote – instead, only those middle-class respondents with universalistic preferences are less likely to vote. This is consistent with the argument that middle-class respondents who still want many particularistic goods – especially club goods for their neighborhood – will still believe that these preferences can be addressed by politicians who target patronage to different areas of the city; voters with universalistic

---

[83] Turnout is measured by asking if respondents voted in the December 2012 elections: 84% reported turning out, compared to an official rate of 76% in the same parliamentary constituencies in the survey sample. Desirability bias likely leads to some over-reporting, such that the aggregate level of self-reported turnout overstates the true extent of participation. But wealthier and better-educated respondents are thought to be those most likely to over-report voting (Karp and Brockington 2005, Ansolabehere and Hersh 2012, Kasara and Suryanarayan 2015). This *biases against* my results if those preferring universalistic policies overreport turnout relative to poorer, less-educated voters who want particularistic goods.

[84] This cannot be explained by differences across socioeconomic classes in the costs of voting. Election day is a holiday, such that workers in the formal sector will have no greater difficulty finding time to vote, and voter registration takes place over several weeks, with ample opportunity to register.

TABLE 4.4: *Turnout and participation, by universalistic preferences*

Outcome	1 Turnout	2 Turnout	3 Turnout	4 Turnout	5 Withdrawal	6 Withdrawal
Universalistic Preferences (binary)	−0.532** (0.200)	−0.600** (0.199)			0.381* (0.156)	
Universalistic Preferences (percentage)			−0.484† (0.286)	−0.589* (0.281)		0.381† (0.230)
Education/Employment Index	−0.071 (0.111)	−0.063 (0.111)	−0.077 (0.112)	−0.066 (0.111)	0.199* (0.088)	0.199* (0.089)
Assets Index	0.153 (0.118)	0.126 (0.115)	0.154 (0.118)	0.130 (0.115)	−0.127 (0.092)	−0.129 (0.092)
Neighborhood Wealth (500m)	−0.036 (0.194)	0.020 (0.190)	−0.039 (0.194)	0.007 (0.188)	0.154 (0.158)	0.152 (0.156)
2008 Competitiveness (by Electoral Area)	−2.565† (1.349)	−1.867† (1.031)	−2.442† (1.344)	−1.763† (1.015)	0.223 (1.120)	0.115 (1.104)
Ethnic Fractionalization (500m)	0.871 (1.615)	0.383 (1.300)	0.983 (1.615)	0.505 (1.280)	−0.342 (1.326)	−0.477 (1.303)
Pop. Density (by cluster)	0.010 (0.009)	0.012† (0.007)	0.009 (0.009)	0.010 (0.007)	−0.003 (0.007)	−0.003 (0.007)
Individual-level Controls	Y	Y	Y	Y	Y	Y
Constituency FEs	Y	N	Y	N	Y	Y
N	986	986	986	986	919	919

*** $p < 0.001$, ** $p < 0.01$, * $p < 0.05$, † $p < 0.1$. The outcome in columns 1–4 is self-reported turnout in the 2012 presidential and parliamentary elections. The outcome in columns 5–6 is an indicator for doing only 1 or 0 of the 5 forms of participation discussed in the text. All models are logistic regressions with intercepts partially pooled by sampling cluster, following Gelman and Hill (2007). Constituency fixed effects are included, except in columns 2 and 4. Note that competitiveness is higher when the competitiveness variable is smaller (absolute difference in vote shares between NPP and NDC), such that there is more participation in places that were more competitive in the last election.

preferences are those whose demands are not credibly addressed by any options on the ballot. This result, however, is inconsistent with any alternative arguments pointing to other more general features of the middle class as explanations for differences in participation.

Voters with universalistic preferences are also especially unlikely to turn out to vote when they live in a neighborhood that is not subject to campaign mobilization by the parties. In an additional model similar to that in Table 4.4, column 4, I interact universalistic preferences with the percentage of respondents in each survey sampling cluster reporting door-to-door mobilization by either party before the 2012 election. In the sampling clusters with the minimum reported canvassing, respondents who want universalistic policies are dramatically less likely to turn out to vote than those preferring exclusively particularistic goods (28.4 percentage points less likely, 95% CI: 1.5, 56.9). By contrast, in areas with the maximum reported canvassing, respondents with universalistic preferences are not significantly less likely to turn out than other voters (95% CI: −8.7, 13.9). While this evidence is only suggestive, it indicates that politicians' decisions to differentially undermobilize certain areas of the city may feed back into incentives to continue ignoring these areas in the future.

I also identify respondents who abstain from other forms of political participation in general. I make an indicator for whether a respondent has done none, or only one, of the following five key forms of participation: voted in the 2012 election, is an active member of a party, knows a local party agent, knows or has met with her district assembly member (city councilor), and/or participates in a nonparty association (such as a church, trade, civil society, or neighborhood association) that discusses political issues at least "some of the time." More than a third (36%) of respondents are what I label "minimum participators," i.e. people who have done none or only one of these activities.[85] I use a binary indicator for being a minimal participator in politics as the outcome variable in columns 5–6 of Table 4.4. Respondents who want at least one universalistic policy are 8.5 percentage points (95% CI: 2.4, 14.2) more likely to refrain collectively from these forms of participation than those who only want particularistic goods. In addition, middle-class respondents are more likely to abstain from these activities in general. Simulating from column 5, respondents with

---

[85] 74% of these "minimum participators" vote but have done none of the other participation activities.

English literacy, at least some secondary education, and formal sector employment are 10.5 percentage points (95% CI: 0.8, 20.2) more likely to broadly abstain from participation than respondents without those characteristics.

I address several alternative arguments for this result. First, breaking down the outcome variable in columns 5–6 of Table 4.4 into its individual components helps allay concerns that residents with universalistic preferences may be offsetting lower electoral participation through other, more informal, forms of participation.[86] Rather than participate through other channels, the middle class in Greater Accra is in general more likely to disengage from the other forms of associational life that could provide alternative paths to political participation. Middle-class respondents are 11.4 percentage points (95% CI: 2.9, 19.8) less likely than the poor to be members of a civic association that discusses or engages in political issues. Middle-class respondents are also 7.1 percentage points (95% CI: -0.5, 14.2, $p = 0.07$) less likely to be political party members than poor respondents. This means that the membership of local party organizations is almost entirely poor, even in the wealthiest parts of the city. This is especially important because local party members are the most immediate people to whom politicians in Ghana are accountable, serving as the voters in primary elections to select presidential and parliamentary candidates, as well as local and national party leaders.[87]

Second, Kasara and Suryanarayan (2015) provide an alternative explanation for class-based participation differences in developing countries such as Ghana that is important to address. Kasara and Suryanarayan (2015) argue that when the rich are not threatened by redistributive taxation in new democracies with low capacity to tax individual incomes, they abstain from politics because they no longer need to participate to prevent redistribution of their wealth to the poor. Consistent with this argument, Ghana has relatively low tax capacity cross-nationally, such that the threat of taxes that expropriate the wealth of the middle class is far lower than in most advanced democracies where redistribution is a central feature of political competition. But this does not

---

[86] Wealthy elites likely retain considerable influence on policy through nonelectoral channels. They serve as the ruling political class, fund campaigns, and are business leaders who can lobby the government. But I do not examine their behavior, as explained in the previous chapters.
[87] Ichino and Nathan (2012).

mean middle-class residents in Greater Accra are not upset about their tax burden. Complaints about taxes and government-imposed fees for services are the primary universalistic demand in the data on preferences in Chapter 3 (Table 3.1). If the lower risk of redistributive taxation is what depresses the turnout of wealthier voters in new democracies, as Kasara and Suryanarayan (2015) argue, survey respondents who still complain about their tax burden should be more likely to turn out to vote than those who do not view taxes and government fees as a particularly salient issue. But I find the opposite pattern. I replicate the model in column 2 of Table 4.4, replacing the indicator of universalistic preferences with an indicator of naming a universalistic preference about tax rates and government fees only. Respondents who complain about their tax burden are 7.7 percentage points (95% CI: 2.4, 13.5) less likely to turn out to vote than those who do not appear sensitive to tax issues, contrary to the implications of Kasara and Suryanarayan (2015). Ultimately, tax capacity and the presence of nonprogrammatic competition are likely highly correlated across countries. States with low tax capacity are also those with generally lower state capacity in which the credibility problem described earlier may constrain the emergence of programmatic politics. Some of the cross-national variation observed in Kasara and Suryanarayan (2015) could be due instead to incentives created by clientelistic traps like the one examined here.

Third, and finally, there could be concern that voters with universalistic preferences become more likely to disengage from electoral politics not because of a credibility problem, as argued earlier, but because the two parties offer largely identical policies. Convergence may simply make voters with universalistic preferences more indifferent between the parties than voters who want particularistic benefits. This is likely true to some extent. But it is an insufficient explanation for the results on its own. The parties' lack of policy differentiation is itself a plausible outcome of the credibility problem. In a context in which most universalistic promises are noncredible, parties have little to gain from developing more concrete and differentiated proposals. Rather than invest in clear policy brands that commit to policy-oriented voters over time, the parties likely feel free to converge on cheap talk valence appeals – in which they promise voters similar slates of commitments to do a wide-ranging set of universally "good things" – *because* it is costless to do so in a context in which party leaders know there is little expectation that their promises will be binding.

4.4 SUMMARY

In this chapter, I show that while the growing urban middle class wants universalistic public policies from the government, Ghana's parties are not addressing these preferences with credible programmatic appeals. Politicians in Greater Accra do not believe they can convince these voters to support them. Less likely to be mobilized to turn out, and more likely to believe that neither party will address their preferences, urban voters with universalistic policy preferences are differentially abstaining from participation. While their exit from the electorate is by no means absolute, abstention undermines the electoral weight of voters with universalistic demands. This allows urban politicians to continue winning elections based almost entirely on patronage-based appeals despite increases in wealth and education that the existing literature suggests should lead to greater programmatic competition.

While levels of wealth and programmatic competition are correlated cross-nationally, these patterns emphasize that the connection between demographic and political change can be very indirect.[88] Chapter 3 shows differences in voter demands by socioeconomic class that are broadly consistent with demand-side theories about the end of clientelism, but these accounts are too eager about the political changes that will result. They do not adequately consider politicians' incentives to respond to new voter preferences.

The persistence of nonprogrammatic forms of competition has implications for how we understand voting behavior in urban areas. I show that Ghana's parties have staked out largely overlapping positions on policy issues, giving voters with universalistic preferences no clear option to rally behind. But this also affects voters with particularistic preferences: with both parties promising to do largely identical things if elected, voters can only differentiate between the parties based on who they expect to do a better job of following through on them. Local- and national-level candidates in Ghana often center campaign speeches around pledges to perform "better" than their opponents. But "better" can be very subjective. In a political system in which many voters do not trust politicians' promises and expect state resources to be distributed as patronage, vote choice ends up having much more to do with voters' expectations about *who* is most likely to benefit from each politician's "performance" than the specific content of *what* politicians promise to do. And as already

---

[88] Also see Kitschelt and Kselman (2013).

4.4 Summary

hinted at by the results for ethnicity in the survey experiment in this chapter (Table 4.2), expectations about who is most likely to benefit from each party's performance are still rooted in ethnicity. If voters expect ethnic favoritism in the allocation of particularistic benefits that they value, the other main political change expected in urban areas highlighted in Chapter 1 – the erosion of ethnic politics – will also not occur. The next part of the book pursues this argument, examining the interaction of distributive politics and voting behavior in Greater Accra with a focus on how patronage distribution shapes the political importance of ethnicity.

PART III

NEIGHBORHOODS AND ETHNIC COMPETITION

5

Ethnic Competition across Neighborhoods

The persistence of nonprogrammatic appeals leads directly to the persistence of ethnic competition in much of urban Ghana. Part II suggests that in the absence of real policy competition between the major parties, elections in Greater Accra are more about *who* than *what* – determined by who benefits from the particularistic goods that all politicians promise to distribute, rather than what policies politicians claim they will pursue. In such a context, ethnicity can become a key feature of electoral competition if it shapes who expects to be favored in the distribution of particularistic goods by each party.

Part III turns to the role of ethnicity and considers the second element of the puzzle in Chapter 1: the persistence of ethnic competition in much of the city despite the growth of the middle class and high levels of ethnic diversity. Ethnicity is often expected to have reduced importance in urban areas in Africa in comparison to rural areas. This expectation is typically rooted – whether explicitly or implicitly – in an expressive, or affective, theory of ethnic politics, which holds that voters support co-ethnics as an expression of social identity. An expressive theory expects differences in the political salience of ethnicity because of individual-level variation in voters' socioeconomic characteristics that affect their attachments to ethnic identities.[1] Echoing an earlier generation of modernization theories,[2] urban voters have been said to give less emphasis to ethnicity than rural voters because wealthier and better-educated voters place less value on ethnic ties, because interethnic assimilation in diverse cities has led

---

[1] Horowitz (1985). Also see the summary of this theory in Ferree (2006).
[2] Lerner (1958) and Lipset (1960).

to increased identification with class-based or national identity groups rather than ethnic groups, or because urban voters are freed from attachments to traditional rural ethnic elites and social institutions – especially chieftaincy – that incentivize investments in group membership.[3]

Part III will show that there appears to be less ethnic voting overall in Greater Accra than in rural Ghana, seemingly consistent with existing narratives.[4] But rather than uniformly less, there is a wide range of variation in ethnic voting within the city. This intra-urban variation has been ignored by existing studies comparing urban and rural areas.[5] There are neighborhoods in Greater Accra where ethnicity and vote choice are essentially uncorrelated, such that knowing a voters' ethnicity provides little information about how she is likely to vote. But there are also many other neighborhoods where virtually all voters support ethnically aligned parties and ethnicity is the central dimension of electoral competition. This second set of neighborhoods is just as "modern" as the first, not an anachronistic holdout from an earlier era.

It is impossible to explain overall differences in ethnic competition between rural and urban areas without also being able to account for this intra-urban variation. Part III demonstrates that the major explanations offered for overall rural–urban differences in ethnic politics – especially those rooted in the socioeconomic characteristics and identities of voters – fall apart when confronted with intra-urban variation. Differences in the extent to which ethnicity predicts vote choice in Greater Accra also persist even after controlling for the core variables in expressive theories of ethnic politics.

Instrumental theories of ethnic politics offer a more promising means of explaining intra-urban variation. Instrumental theories argue that ethnic voting is a means to an end, not an expression of identity.[6] Voters disproportionately support co-ethnic candidates or ethnically affiliated

---

[3] For example, Conroy-Krutz (2009), Severino and Ray (2011), Green (2014), Resnick (2014), and Robinson (2014). As already described in Chapter 1, such expectations run counter to an earlier strand of research on urban Africa, which argued that ties to ethnic groups were heightened in urban areas (e.g., Epstein 1958, Cohen 1969, Bates 1974, Wolpe 1974, Schildkrout 1976).

[4] As described in Chapters 1 and 2, I define ethnic voting throughout the book using a "bloc-voting"-based definition: as support for a party associated with a voter's ethnic group, not as a one-to-one match between the ethnicity of each candidate and voter. In this framework, a high level of ethnic voting means that ethnicity is highly correlated with vote choice.

[5] In a closely related argument to the one developed here, Ichino and Nathan (2013a) also show that there is variation in ethnic voting in rural Ghana, such that it is equally problematic to characterize rural areas as having uniformly high rates of ethnic voting.

[6] Chandra (2004), Posner (2005), Ferree (2006), and Ichino and Nathan (2013a).

parties because they expect better performance from them – in this case, performance in providing access to the scarce particularistic goods that most urban voters demand. In line with this view, I show that variation in the political importance of ethnicity in cities arises from patterns of favoritism in distributive politics, which determine voters' expectations regarding the prospective benefits of electing ethnically aligned politicians.

I begin Part III by expanding existing instrumental theories to better link politicians' incentives across different urban neighborhoods to voters' expectations of ethnic favoritism and, consequently, their incentives to vote along ethnic lines. While nonprogrammatic competition prevails in all neighborhoods of the city for the reasons explored in Part II, the specific forms that nonprogrammatic appeals take differ across poor and middle class neighborhoods and between ethnically diverse neighborhoods and ethnically homogenous neighborhoods. In turn, variation in politicians' behavior defines the incentives that otherwise similar voters face to support ethnically aligned parties when living in different places, even after holding voters' socioeconomic status and ethnic social identification constant. After the present chapter develops the theory, Chapter 6 provides empirical support for the claims about neighborhood-level variation in distributive politics. Chapter 7 provides empirical evidence for effects on voters' expectations and behavior. Chapter 7 also rules out a series of alternative explanations and extends the argument to an exceptional case of one ethnic group in Greater Accra among whom politicians have different incentives for distributive politics – the Ga.

Overall, Part III demonstrates that ethnicity remains a key element of urban politics despite the growth of the urban middle class and high levels of ethnic diversity because politicians still have supply-side incentives to engage in ethnic favoritism in many urban neighborhoods. This builds on the argument from Part II that political behavior can be as much a response to what politicians supply as to what voters demand: I show that as long as ethnicity remains a salient factor in how politicians decide who will benefit from valuable state resources, many voters will have instrumental incentives to continue supporting ethnically aligned parties, even if these voters have become wealthier and well educated, have close social connections to other ethnic groups, or place less emphasis on their ethnic identities in daily life.

This explains the next main step in the trap in Figure 1.1. Part II argues that politicians across the city persist with nonprogrammatic appeals despite the growth of the urban middle class. In turn, Part III will show that ethnic favoritism continues in the distribution of state resources.

152   *Ethnic Competition across Neighborhoods*

This ethnic favoritism directly encourages ethnic voting among large segments of the urban population. In this way, the arguments of Part II and Part III are linked: persistent nonprogrammatic appeals create incentives for persistent ethnic competition.

The chapter begins by considering a puzzle: neighborhood-level variation in ethnic voting in Greater Accra that cannot be accounted for by existing theories of voting behavior. In Sections 5.2 and 5.3, I develop a theoretical argument about how variation in patterns of distributive politics across different types of urban neighborhoods shapes voter behavior and the nature of ethnic competition. The final section considers extensions to the theory that account for the targeting of unaligned or swing voters, the effects of alternative electoral or political institutions, and differences between rural and urban areas.

5.1 A PUZZLE: NEIGHBORHOOD-LEVEL VARIATION IN GREATER ACCRA

Whether you think there is ethnic voting in Greater Accra depends greatly on where you look for it. Figure 5.1 provides snapshots of four sampling clusters in Greater Accra from the survey analyzed in Chapters 3 and 4. Each pair of panels in Figure 5.1 shades census Enumeration Areas (tracts) in the area surrounding each sampling cluster along two indices: ethnic fractionalization and neighborhood wealth.[7] The neighborhoods in the first column are both relatively ethnically diverse, while the neighborhoods in the second column are much more homogenous.[8] Both neighborhoods in the top row are middle class, while the neighborhoods in the bottom row are slums. The points in Figure 5.1 represent the locations of all survey respondents in each cluster who both turned out to vote in 2012 and have an ethnically aligned party – and thus could have voted along ethnic lines. The extent of ethnic voting – whether these voters reported supporting their ethnically aligned party in the 2012 presidential election – is listed at the top of each panel.[9]

In one of these neighborhoods – La-Wireless – respondents were nearly as likely to vote across ethnic lines for the other party as to

---

[7] Both indices are defined in Chapter 6 and the Appendix.
[8] For purposes of the example, I am using "neighborhood" loosely to refer to each cluster of respondents. In Chapter 2, I develop a formal definition of "neighborhood" used to quantify specific characteristics of each area for the analysis. This approach is also described in detail in the Appendix.
[9] Chapter 7 describes how vote choice is measured.

5.1 A Puzzle: Neighborhood-level Variation in Greater Accra 153

vote for the party affiliated with their group. Only 55% supported their aligned party. In what was essentially a two-party election, knowing a voter's ethnicity in this neighborhood would have provided almost no information about how she was likely to have voted. But in the other three neighborhoods, ethnic voting was extensive, with overwhelming majorities reporting support for aligned parties. Simply knowing a voter's ethnicity in Tweneboa, Mamobi, or Nungua-Kinsgway would have allowed you to predict her vote choice with considerable confidence.

Existing theories of voting behavior do not do a good job of explaining why La-Wireless is so different from the other three neighborhoods in Figure 5.1. I consider four sets of theories. First, many plausible explanations can be dismissed easily by the fact that voters in each location in Figure 5.1 faced the exact same choice, voting at the same time and choosing among the same presidential candidates in an election in which their votes all counted equally. The four areas also all share a labor market – they are within commuting distance of each other – and had experienced the same broader economic trends leading into the 2012 election. To whatever extent electoral rules, macroeconomic performance, the personalities or ethnicity of presidential candidates, or the policy proposals of each party affect vote choice in Ghana, they are held constant in Figure 5.1 and thus cannot explain the different voting patterns.

Second, another class of explanations would focus on individual-level differences between residents in each area. For example, perhaps respondents in La-Wireless are simply wealthier or better educated, or identify less with their ethnic groups, than respondents in the other three sampling clusters. In Chapter 7, however, I consider these individual-level explanations directly and find that voters' wealth, education, employment status, and social ties to or identification with their ethnic groups do not predict variation in ethnic voting in Greater Accra at all. Neighborhood-level differences such as those in Figure 5.1 persist when controlling for these variables. That many of these individual-level characteristics of voters are unlikely to account for Figure 5.1 can already be guessed from the figure itself. Consider voter wealth. Modernization theories would claim that there is little ethnic voting in La-Wireless because it is a middle class area and most voters there are likely relatively wealthy and well educated. But Tweneboa – the top-right panel of Figure 5.1 – is a similarly middle class neighborhood, yet 93% of voters in Tweneboa supported their ethnically affiliated party.

"La–Wireless"
La Dade Kotopon constituency
55% ethnic voting

Ethnic Fractionalization — **Wealth**

"Mamobi"
Ayawaso North constituency
89% ethnic voting

Ethnic Fractionalization — **Wealth**

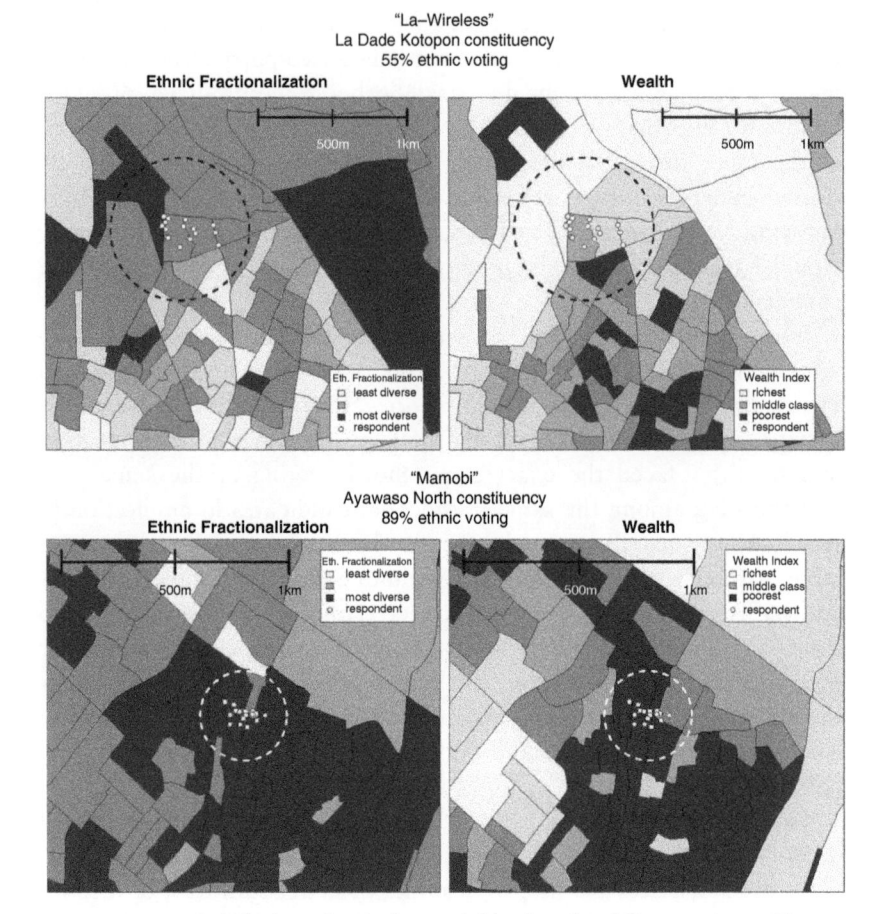

FIGURE 5.1: *Ethnic voting in four neighborhoods of Greater Accra:* The polygons represent census Enumeration Areas (tracts), shaded by ethnic fractionalization (left column in each pair) or the wealth index (right column in each pair). The points are survey respondents.

A third category of explanations argues that features of neighborhood context produce different behaviors from otherwise individually similar voters. Studies of political behavior in the United States have argued, for example, that voters' local ethnic contexts shape their behavior through psychological mechanisms of either "racial threat" or social contact.[10] But both of these theories are at odds with the patterns in Figure 5.1. If

[10] For example, Key (1949), Allport (1954), Bobo and Hutchings (1996), Oliver and Wong (2003), and Enos (2017).

5.1 A Puzzle: Neighborhood-level Variation in Greater Accra 155

"Tweneboa"
Ablekuma North constituency
93% ethnic voting

Ethnic Fractionalization — **Wealth**

"Nungua–Kingsway"
Krowor constituency
88% ethnic voting

Ethnic Fractionalization — **Wealth**

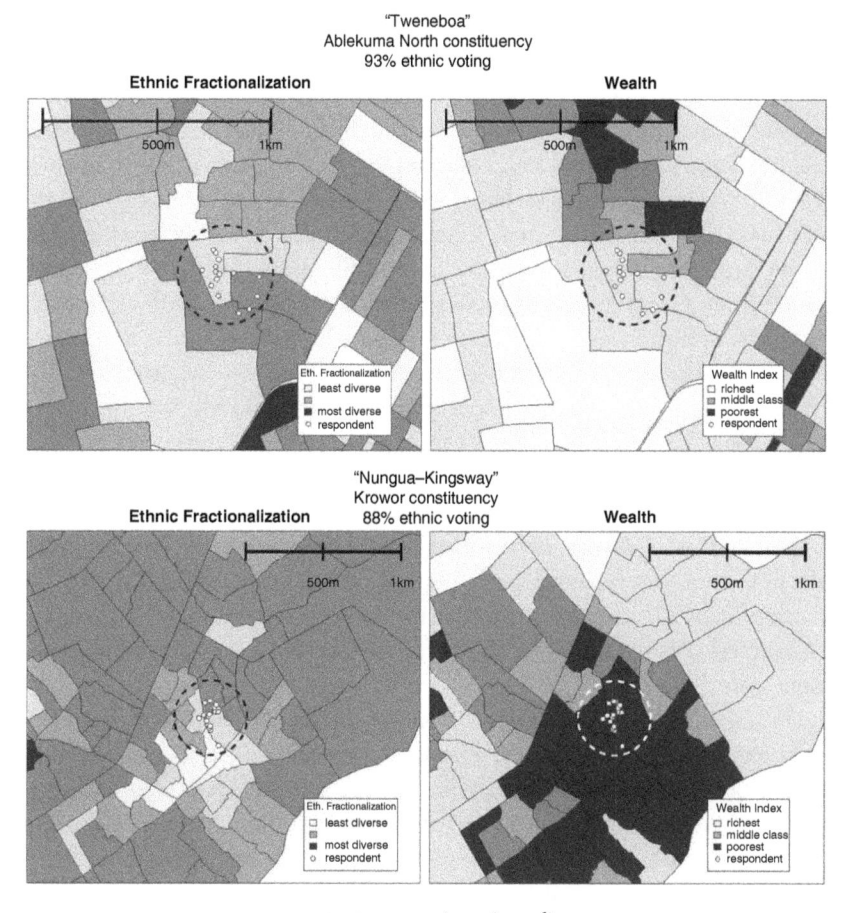

FIGURE 5.1: *(continued)*

psychological perceptions of group threat were at play, there should be more ethnic voting in more diverse neighborhoods, where there is more direct contact and competition between groups. But Figure 5.1 shows less ethnic voting in La-Wireless than in Tweneboa, even though La-Wireless is significantly more diverse. Social contact theories make an opposite prediction: less ethnic voting in more diverse areas where greater interethnic social interactions reduce the salience of ethnicity. But there is still substantial ethnic voting in the very diverse Mamobi, a dense slum neighborhood in which neighbors from different ethnic groups live in closer proximity and likely have greater daily social contact than in the wealthier La-Wireless.

A final set of explanations for Figure 5.1 can be drawn from instrumental theories of ethnic voting that tie support for co-ethnic politicians to voters' expectations of benefiting from ethnic favoritism, often through patronage distribution or clientelism.[11] Building on an instrumental framework, Ichino and Nathan (2013a) argue that voters in rural Ghana support politicians based on expectations of favoritism in the delivery of club goods such as schools and roads. Voters in homogenous areas expect politicians from the party affiliated with the locally dominant ethnic group to benefit their area with club goods, while politicians from the opposing party are likely to ignore it, favoring areas dominated by their own groups instead. An implication of this argument is that voters should have weaker expectations of ethnic favoritism in diverse areas where politicians cannot easily favor specific ethnic groups with club goods, resulting in less ethnic voting.[12]

Alternatively, there could be less ethnic voting in La-Wireless under an instrumental theory because middle- and upper-class voters simply do not value the types of particularistic goods that politicians provide as favoritism. If wealthier voters care more about universalistic policy, instrumental considerations about favoritism will have less influence on their vote choices.

But neither of these arguments is sufficient on its own. Targeting club goods to benefit specific ethnic groups should be just as impossible in the very diverse Mamobi as in La-Wireless, but ethnic voting in Mamobi remains high. Moreover, in contrast to an explanation for La-Wireless rooted in the demands of middle-class voters, ethnic voting is widespread in Tweneboa, an equally wealthy neighborhood. And, importantly, while Chapter 3 shows that many middle-class residents of Greater Accra demand universalistic policies, Chapter 4 shows that the residents who are least likely to be susceptible to particularistic appeals rooted in ethnic favoritism are those most likely to have abstained from voting – thereby dropping out of the denominator in Figure 5.1. Chapter 4 shows that the middle class voters in areas such as La-Wireless and Tweneboa are disproportionately those who still value particularistic goods – especially club goods – that politicians can target selectively. This subset of

---

[11] Bates (1983), Chandra (2004), Posner (2005), Ferree (2006).
[12] Ichino and Nathan (2013a) do not examine this prediction in rural Ghana because there are so few diverse communities in rural areas, as demonstrated by Figure 1.3. Ejdemyr et al. (2017) provide evidence from Malawi, however, that politicians are less likely to favor diverse communities with club goods, consistent with the argument in Ichino and Nathan (2013a).

the middle class is still susceptible to instrumental incentives to vote along ethnic lines.

5.2 WHERE IS THERE ETHNIC FAVORITISM IN CITIES?

Instrumental theories come closest to accounting for the patterns in Figure 5.1. But we need a more complete theory than in Ichino and Nathan (2013a) for how ethnic favoritism differs across neighborhoods in urban areas to fully explain the differences between La-Wireless and the other three sampling clusters. This means explaining neighborhood-level variation in how politicians distribute both club goods and private goods – the two types of particularistic resources that Chapters 3 and 4 show that the large majority of voters in Greater Accra demand.

This section begins by considering why politicians in countries such as Ghana often favor core ethnic groups when allocating particularistic goods. I then discuss why the extent of favoritism in urban areas is likely to differ by neighborhood wealth in the distribution of private goods and differ by neighborhood ethnic diversity in the distribution of club goods. I combine these elements into specific predictions for how the distribution of particularistic goods unfolds across the different types of urban neighborhoods exemplified by Figure 5.1.

5.2.1 Why Favoritism at All?

I build on a standard assumption in the study of African politics that parties largely seek to favor co-ethnic voters and stronghold, co-ethnic areas with the particularistic benefits that they control.[13] In a context in which partisanship and ethnicity are closely intertwined, an assumption of ethnic favoritism implies a core-voter as opposed to a swing-voter model of distributive politics.[14] The extent to which assuming favoritism to core, ethnically aligned voters and core, ethnically aligned areas is reasonable depends on how we conceptualize the relationship between ethnicity and partisanship.

If the link between ethnic groups and parties is largely expressive or identity based, an assumption of core favoritism can seem unreasonable for strategic, vote-maximizing politicians.[15] Identity-based voting can be

---

[13] Bates (1983), Posner (2005), Kimenyi (2006), and Franck and Rainer (2012).
[14] Golden and Min (2013).
[15] That is, unless we assume politicians themselves allocate particularistic goods on a primarily expressive and nonstrategic basis, as would be the case if ethnic favoritism

modeled similarly to ideology or partisanship in standard probabilistic voting models, such as Lindbeck and Weibull (1987) and Dixit and Londregan (1996), with voters' utility functions a combination of the exogenous, innate benefits of electing a co-ethnic party and the separate monetary benefits from distributive transfers from each party. Voting for an ethnically aligned party in this framework potentially trades off against the patronage benefits that each party allocates.[16] In this approach, parties should be able to take core, co-ethnic voters for granted. Because core voters innately value electing a party affiliated with their identity group, they have built-in incentives to support that party regardless of whether it gives them patronage. Meanwhile, unaligned swing voters have no innate preference for a particular party and choose parties based only on the transfers they receive. They are thus more susceptible to patronage-based appeals. Parties can treat core voters as captured, concentrating scarce resources among unaligned voters and swing areas where there will be greater returns.[17]

But modeling core voters as primarily being driven by innate biases in favor of co-ethnics is inappropriate if ethnic voting and ties between ethnic groups and parties are largely instrumental. In an instrumental theory of ethnic voting, ethnicity and distributive politics do not trade off against each other. Instead, ethnicity matters because of what it signals about the particularistic goods that voters will receive if a party is elected.[18] Diaz-Cayeros et al. (2016) develop an alternative model of distributive politics that makes the core status of voters in patronage-based democracies endogenous to the patronage that they receive.[19] Their approach can be extended to justify an assumption of ethnic favoritism. In this framework, core co-ethnic voters only support a party *because*

---

emerges primarily from social obligations to co-ethnics (Ekeh 1975, Chabal and Daloz 1999).

[16] Some studies model the influence of ethnicity on voting behavior in this fashion even without explicitly aligning themselves with expressive theories of ethnic politics. For example, see the theories in both Wantchekon (2003) and Casey (2015). More broadly, Carlson (2015) classifies these and related studies as "additive models" of voting behavior in which factors such as ethnicity and performance (including performance in delivery of particularistic goods) are assumed to have independent effects on voters. By contrast, Carlson (2015) describes instrumental theories of ethnic voting as "interactive models," in which the effects on voting behavior of ethnicity and performance in the delivery of particularistic goods are jointly determined.

[17] Dixit and Londregan (1996). Kasara (2007) applies this logic to African cases.

[18] Posner (2005) and Ferree (2006).

[19] Gottlieb and Larreguy (2015) provide another framework for endogenizing the core status of voters as an outcome of past favoritism.

5.2 Where Is There Ethnic Favoritism in Cities?

they expect to benefit from it. These expectations are sustained through repeated delivery of particularistic benefits. The core status of voters can erode over time – with core voters becoming swing voters – if parties stop providing favored access to these benefits. Because core status can erode, parties must continue targeting core voters with at least some resources to maintain their support and cannot take them for granted.

A second reason core supporters are likely to be favored – especially in the allocation of private goods to individuals – rests on a more technological mechanism. Targeting patronage resources to core voters can become a better strategy than pursuing unaligned, swing voters if core voters are those whom a party "knows better," and hence with whom a party can carry out more efficient patronage exchanges. Even under an expressive, identity-based theory of ethnic voting, Dixit and Londregan (1996) imply that core voters will be favored if parties are significantly more knowledgeable about core voters and better able to enforce clientelistic relationships with them.

The underlying assumptions for both of these explanations for favoritism more closely fit the empirical reality of many African democracies than an assumption that expressive, identity-based support from ethnically aligned voters can be taken for granted. Overall, the evidence for expressive, identity-based voting in Africa is weak.[20] Instead, a large body of research suggests that ethnic voting is endogenous to voters' information and beliefs about politicians' performance, including in the distribution of particularistic goods.[21] I will show in Chapter 6 that politicians and party agents in Greater Accra describe particularistic goods distribution to core supporters in terms directly akin to Diaz-Cayeros et al.'s (2016) theory – as something they must do to keep existing supporters from defecting. In addition, Chapter 6 will also suggest that Ghana's parties are more embedded in social networks with core ethnic groups, increasing their ability to engage in efficient individual-level patronage exchanges with core voters compared to unaligned voters or those from ethnic groups that typically support an opposing party.

Despite these theoretical reasons to expect ethnic favoritism, empirical evidence of favoritism in Africa is mixed.[22] This is problematic if

---

[20] Posner (2005), Ferree (2006), Ichino and Nathan (2013a), Conroy-Krutz (2013), and Carlson (2015) all provide evidence that is inconsistent with such a theory.
[21] Most recently, see Conroy-Krutz (2013) and Carlson (2015).
[22] Kasara (2007), Kramon and Posner (2013), Burgess et al. (2015), and Ejdemyr et al. (2017).

we have to assume that strategies of core- and swing-voter targeting are mutually exclusive. The argument in this chapter does not depend on such a hard claim, however. Instead, building from literature demonstrating that parties can use mixed strategies – favoring core voters with some resources, even as they pursue swing voters with others[23] – I make a more relaxed claim about ethnic favoritism. In reality, parties engage in some complex mix of core and swing targeting, drawing on different types of particularistic resources and engaging different types of voters at different points in the electoral cycle. My predictions rest on two less restrictive assumptions: first, that parties never play *pure* swing-voter strategies, such that at least some benefits go disproportionately to core supporters and stronghold areas to keep their attachments to the party from eroding; and second, that whatever the overall mix between core and swing targeting, core supporters and stronghold areas of the *opposing* party are likely to be differentially excluded.[24]

5.2.2 Neighborhood Wealth and Favoritism in Private Goods Delivery

The extent to which core ethnic groups are favored in the nonprogrammatic distribution of the two types of particularistic goods – private and club goods – should vary with the characteristics of urban neighborhoods. I focus first on the distribution of private goods to individual voters. Ethnic favoritism in the allocation of private goods can be common in poor urban neighborhoods, while rare in upper- and middle-class areas of a city, even among poor voters who still live there.

I focus on the two main ways private goods are distributed nonprogrammatically in most new democracies: what Nichter and Peress (2017) term *relational clientelism*, or more *episodic* forms of unmonitored transfer. The key difference is whether private goods are distributed as part of a sustained patronage relationship, with expectations that benefits will be reciprocated with support, or as a single-shot transaction. The goal of relational clientelism is to bind voters to a party through the repeated distribution of individualized benefits that can be terminated if parties believe voters have stopped supporting them. For this to work, a party needs to be able to identify specific needs of individual voters, guess their likely partisanship with reasonable confidence, and monitor

---

[23] For example, see Albertus (2013) and Diaz-Cayeros et al. (2016).
[24] This second assumption is a prediction of both core and swing models of distributive politics (Cox and McCubbins 1986, Dixit and Londregan 1996).

them for indicators that they may have defected. This does not necessarily require directly violating the secrecy of the ballot.[25] Instead, a broad body of evidence suggests that through sustained interpersonal relationships with voters, parties' local agents can generally identify who their likely supporters are (with some error) and still carry out clientelistic relationships.[26] Doing so successfully requires a dense grassroots party organization (or equivalent) that penetrates the social fabric of local communities to engage with large numbers of individual voters over time.

By contrast, unmonitored, episodic private goods distribution is more akin to gift-giving than clientelism and does not require a dense party organization. Parties can distribute gifts even among groups that they are not able to monitor or engage with in a sustained fashion.[27] These goods are delivered as one-off payments, usually immediately before elections. The goal is not to bind voters to a party or directly buy support, but to motivate turnout, gain an audience, or signal credibility and capacity to perform in the future.[28] Importantly, because parties do not attempt to monitor recipients, parties are likely to distribute relatively less-valuable private goods in these single-shot transactions – such as small amounts of cash, food, or clothing – compared to what is distributed via relational clientelism. The most valuable private benefits a party controls that have long-term benefits to recipients – such as patronage jobs in the municipal government, school scholarships, or loans for small businesses – are more likely to be distributed to voters with whom parties expect to engage repeatedly over time. Relational clientelism should then be relatively more important for vote choice than the distribution of single-shot, pre-election gifts because more valuable benefits are at stake.

---

[25] In general, theoretical claims that clientelistic transactions depend on parties' direct ability to monitor vote choices have been overstated. Numerous studies document the empirical persistence of clientelism sustained by imperfect monitoring despite formal ballot secrecy (e.g., Auerbach 2016, Koter 2016, Nichter and Peress 2017). Examples include the historical United States, where forms of relational clientelism persisted in urban areas long after ballot reforms rendered the direct observation of individual votes impossible (e.g., Banfield and Wilson 1963, Erie 1988).

[26] For example, Auyero (2000), Brusco et al. (2004), Auerbach (2016), and Schneider (2017). Signals of partisanship that locally embedded party agents can use to intuit who is a loyal supporter include seeing how voters speak in favor of a party in the course of their daily lives, who displays party paraphernalia at their homes, who attends party rallies and meetings, and various other signals that can be observed from sustained social interaction. Moreover, Ferree and Long (2016) suggest that voters in areas where parties have dense organizations sometimes believe party agents can violate ballot secrecy – and behave accordingly – even when this is false.

[27] Kramon (2016).

[28] Nichter (2008), Munoz (2014), and Kramon (2016), respectively.

Expectations of ethnic favoritism are especially likely to emerge from relational clientelism. Where partisanship and ethnicity overlap, parties can be better at engaging in sustained relationships with ethnically aligned voters than those from other ethnic groups, making monitoring costs lowest among these core voters. The local agents that parties employ are often disproportionately drawn from core ethnic groups, even in areas where core groups comprise the minority of the local population, and will be more embedded in social networks with voters from those groups. Voters from the core ethnic groups of opposing parties, by contrast, often remain less legible to a party's agents.[29] On the other hand, the costs to parties of engaging with core versus unaligned voters are much more similar in episodic, pre-election gift-giving. Without a need to engage with individual recipients over time, there is no particular reason why it is easier to give private goods as single-shot gifts to one ethnic group over another.

Understanding where ethnic favoritism in the distribution of private goods is most likely within a city thus requires understanding where relational clientelism is most likely. Some studies assume that clientelism will be very difficult for parties to conduct in urban areas in general, arguing that the population density and anonymity of cities make sustaining relationships with individual voters too costly.[30] More specific to African cases, Koter (2016) suggests that clientelism is less viable in urban areas because the traditional elites, such as chiefs, that parties often use as clientelistic intermediaries in rural areas are much weaker – or even nonexistent – in cities. But neither of these factors are nearly as significant constraints on clientelism as is claimed. Instead, there is clear evidence that clientelism regularly thrives in developing world cities, particularly in slum neighborhoods.[31]

Relational clientelism is viable in poor slums neighborhoods because these communities have social structures that lower parties' costs to

---

[29] Along these lines, Schneider (2017) examines the ability of grassroots politicians in India to identify and provide information about voters in their communities. While local agents struggle to observe and monitor the partisanship of voters who support opposing parties, they appear quite good at identifying the vote choices of core supporters, with whom they have closer social ties. These findings suggest that clientelism will be more viable with core than swing voters, complementing the claim by Dixit and Londregan (1996) that core targeting becomes more likely when there are efficiency advantages in a party's ability to engage with core voters.

[30] Magaloni (2006) and Stokes et al. (2013).

[31] Among many examples, see Auyero (2000), Levitsky (2003), Auerbach (2015), and Paller (2018).

building interpersonal ties with voters. In fact, urban slums may be the areas within a country where individual-level clientelism between parties and voters *is most likely*. Rather than discouraging clientelism, the density of slums helps encourage it. Slums have large concentrations of vulnerable poor voters who highly value and demand private benefits from parties and depend on politicians for access to scarce state resources. Party agents embedded in slums have regular opportunities for interactions with voters that facilitate identifying individual needs and monitoring behavior. Contrary to Stokes et al. (2013), residents in poor urban neighborhoods are often not anonymous to each other. Instead, residents in slums in African cities live in very close daily proximity, sharing compound houses alongside multiple other families, as well as cooking facilities, toilets, bathing areas, water pumps, and various other public spaces. Each allows for regular interactions with party agents who live alongside them. In addition, the informal community leaders who sometimes emerge in slums in place of traditional chiefs – landlords, trade association leaders, and even pastors – can be coopted into party organizations and empowered in a symbiotic relationship with parties, enhancing their stature in their neighborhoods by gaining access to more benefits to distribute in return for helping parties organize support and keep track of voters.[32] Slums are also areas where organized crime thrives. These neighborhoods can be controlled by gangs that can be employed by parties to help enforce and monitor patronage relationships.[33]

By contrast, relational clientelism is much costlier for parties to sustain in middle- and upper-class neighborhoods. Because few middle- or upper-class voters demand private goods from politicians (Chapter 3), fewer voters overall in middle- and upper-class neighborhoods will be susceptible to relational clientelism. Chapter 2 explains that middle- and upper-class neighborhoods in African cities are usually not homogeneously wealthy, however, such that some poor voters who demand private goods still live there. But with only a fraction of the electorate demanding private goods, it is much less cost effective than in slums for parties to sustain a dense network of agents embedded in the community who can engage with individual voters. Residents in these areas are also often much more socially atomized from their neighbors than residents in slums, with few ties to powerful community leaders, and live in

[32] Paller (2014).
[33] LeBas (2013).

separate lots in single-family houses surrounded by high walls and gates. Poor residents in middle- and upper-class neighborhoods in particular are scattered as squatters in informal housing on unfinished lots, rather than concentrated in communal compound houses. These poor residents can also be more transient, often with even weaker property rights than similarly poor residents in slums, living in temporary structures and moving from plot to plot as workers or caretakers hired on a temporary basis. This constrains opportunities for parties to interact with individual voters, even those voters still susceptible to clientelism. As a result, there should be significantly more ethnic favoritism in private goods delivery in poor neighborhoods than in middle- and upper-class neighborhoods.

5.2.3 Neighborhood Diversity and Favoritism in Club Goods Delivery

There are also differences across urban neighborhoods in the effectiveness of favoring core ethnic groups with club goods. Unlike private goods, club goods can be used to build support in both poor and middle-class neighborhoods, as most middle-class and poor voters both demand club goods from the government (Chapters 3 and 4). Instead of neighborhood wealth, the electoral effectiveness of targeting club goods as favoritism depends on the ethnic composition of neighborhoods – especially whether an area is ethnically homogenous or diverse.[34]

Club goods have benefits that are geographically, but not individually, excludable. All residents within the catchment area of a club good such as an elementary school, water well, or local sewer system can benefit from it. But everyone beyond generally will not. A strategy of ethnic favoritism in the distribution of club goods is only viable in homogenous neighborhoods. In areas dominated by a party's aligned ethnic groups, a party can reach many co-ethnics with a club good with few benefits wasted on voters from ethnic groups who will likely support the opposing party. But a party cannot specifically target its co-ethnics by building a club good in an ethnically diverse neighborhood. Voters from many different groups will benefit, including those aligned with the opposing party. Moreover, in homogenous neighborhoods dominated by an opposing party's aligned ethnic groups, club benefits are largely wasted on nonsupporters absent a substantial, sustained investment of resources over time that can offset

---

[34] Ichino and Nathan (2013a) and Ejdemyr et al. (2017).

these others voters' pre-existing expectations that they are more likely to benefit from the election of their own ethnically aligned party.

The result is that homogenous areas dominated by the ruling party's core groups will be favored in the distribution of club goods if parties have chosen a strategy of ethnic favoritism. Diverse neighborhoods or homogenous areas dominated by politically unaligned groups could still receive club goods if parties pursue a mixed strategy that also involves targeting perceived swing voters or swing neighborhoods. But homogenous areas dominated by the core groups of opposition parties will be largely excluded.

5.2.4 Ethnic Favoritism across Neighborhoods

These separate discussions of private and club goods can be combined into joint predictions about where parties are most likely to favor their core ethnic groups. This can be demonstrated most directly by considering a simplified example of a city with two ethnic groups – A and B – and neighborhoods that vary in their diversity and wealth, as in Figure 5.1 and Table 1.1. By defining the ethnic composition of each neighborhood in terms of the populations of groups A and B, this city can be thought of as containing the six more specific types of neighborhoods in Table 5.1. In Chapter 2, I document that each type of neighborhood in Table 5.1 exists in Greater Accra. Some neighborhoods are mostly homogeneous and made up of each ethnic group, while others are diverse. Within these sets of neighborhoods (diverse, A-dominated, B-dominated), some are poor slums, while others are middle or upper class. I assume that most residents are poor themselves in poor neighborhoods, while upper- and middle-class neighborhoods have a mix of both wealthier and poorer residents, consistent with Chapter 2.

Each group has an ethnically affiliated political party – party A or party B – competing in a single election. All votes count equally, such that the value of an additional vote is the same regardless of which neighborhood it comes from. As they compete in this election, the parties do not offer differentiated policy proposals, but attract support through patronage and service delivery, by distributing – or promising to distribute if elected – some mix of private and club goods. The neighborhoods in Table 5.1 can be interpreted as collectively comprising one urban administrative district or other local government unit in which allocative decisions are being made by a single decision maker who is an official

TABLE 5.1: *Ethnic favoritism from the perspective of a Group A voter.*[35]

	Favoritism from Perspective of a Group A Voter		
	i. Ethnically Diverse Neighborhood	ii. Homogenous, Group A-dominated Neighborhood	iii. Homogeneous, Group B-dominated Neighborhood
1. Middle- or Upper-class Neighborhood	Club: *No favoritism* Private: *No favoritism*	Club: *Favored by Party A* Private: *No favoritism*	Club: *Favored by Party B* Private: *No favoritism*
2. Poor or Slum Neighborhood	Club: *No favoritism* Private: *Favored by Party A*	Club: *Favored by Party A* Private: *Favored by Party A*	Club: *Favored by Party B* Private: *Favored by Party A*

from the party that wins the election.[36] Some of this decision maker's budget is fungible and can be transferred across neighborhoods, but I assume that there is still a minimum amount that must be spent in each neighborhood, such that there are no neighborhoods that get no spending at all after the election.[37]

---

[35] Note that this table predicts where one party is more likely to provide each benefit than the other, not the overall volume of goods distributed in each place.

[36] This parallels how distributive decisions are made in urban Ghana and many other African countries, in which municipal-level politicians have considerable discretion in allocating funds sent down from the national government (Chapter 2). The overall amount available to distribute in each district may depend on how much is also being allocated to other districts by the national government or higher-level party leaders. There may be higher-level favoritism in overall budgetary allocations across broad regions of the country, for example. The argument here assumes only that there is still some minimum, nonnegligible amount spent in each district.

[37] While formal models typically assume that politicians' budgets are fully liquid, this is rarely true in practice. Municipal governments in Ghana typically set aside a minimum amount of funds for each local Electoral Area (or ward) of the district, such that at least some resources are spent in all areas of a city, even if a much greater share of the overall budget is invested in some than in others. At the end of the chapter, I consider how Table 5.1 would differ if politicians could fully sort all of their budget among neighborhoods.

5.2 Where Is There Ethnic Favoritism in Cities?

Table 5.1 considers where a voter from group A is likely to be favored in access to each type of particularistic good. The ethnic composition of neighborhoods should influence where each party engages in ethnic favoritism in club goods distribution, while the wealth of neighborhoods affects where there is likely to be ethnic favoritism in the clientelistic distribution of private goods. In A-dominated neighborhoods (column *ii* of Table 5.1), party A will invest more than party B in club goods, while party B will invest significantly more than party A in club goods to B-dominated neighborhoods (column *iii*). In diverse neighborhoods (column *i*), however, the parties cannot target club goods as favoritism to specific ethnic groups. Even if the parties invest in club goods in these neighborhoods for other reasons, there is no reason to expect that one party is systematically more likely to favor diverse neighborhoods after the election. In wealthier neighborhoods (row 1), there will be little relational clientelism targeted at core ethnic groups. In poorer neighborhoods (row 2), by contrast, relational clientelism is more feasible, especially among each party's core ethnic groups, and ethnic favoritism in access to private goods will be common.

The effectiveness of private goods versus club goods distribution varies with a party's ability to engage with individual voters in long-term patronage relationships. In neighborhoods where parties do not have the organizational capacity for relational clientelism, club goods distribution is relatively more cost effective than private goods distribution.[38] Parties can reach many voters at once with a club good and monitor their behavior through aggregate election results, rather than wasting private benefits in single-shot transactions in which they cannot ensure that voters will comply with support. But in the poor slum neighborhoods where long-term, individual-level patronage relationships are easier to sustain, private goods distribution can become more viable. Parties can efficiently target specific voters with benefits and lock in their support without wasting benefits on others who live nearby but are unlikely to support the party.

This trade-off is especially clear in poor neighborhoods where many voters who would benefit from a club good are from the ethnic group affiliated with the other party. I expect parties to substitute away from club goods distribution in poor, diverse neighborhoods (row 2, column *i*) and poor neighborhoods dominated by an opposing party's co-ethnics

---

[38] Chandra (2004), Gottlieb and Larreguy (2015), Rueda (2015), and Ejdemyr et al. (2017).

(row 2, column *iii*) to instead target private benefits to voters from core groups. Party *A*'s local organization may be relatively weaker in neighborhoods where it has fewer co-ethnics, especially in row 2, column *iii*, and the party may commit fewer resources to these neighborhoods overall. But because all votes count equally everywhere in the election and some minimum amount must be spent in each cell of Table 5.1, party *A* still benefits from targeting some private goods to co-ethnics who live in these neighborhoods to maintain their support. The party's budget that must be spent in these areas can be more valuably channeled as private goods to the party's co-ethnics who still live there rather than wasted by providing clubs that benefit co-ethnics of the other party.

By contrast, in poor neighborhoods where a party's co-ethnics predominate (row 2, column *ii*), distributing government resources after the election as club goods may be relatively more efficient for party *A* than private goods distribution. Club goods in poor, *A*-dominated neighborhoods will primarily benefit *A* voters and allow party *A* to avoid organizational costs of individual-level clientelism. One implication of this trade-off is that individual group *A* voters in poor, *A*-dominated neighborhoods (row 2, column *ii*) may be less likely to receive private benefits through relational clientelism from party *A* after the election than if they lived in a more diverse neighborhood (row 2, column *i* or column *iii*) where more private goods may be distributed by party *A* relative to the size of the pool of potential group *A* recipients.

5.3 PATTERNS OF ETHNIC VOTING

When the extent of ethnic favoritism differs across neighborhoods of a city, otherwise identical voters – with the same individual-level characteristics – will have different incentives to support each party based on where they live. In this section, I connect neighborhood-level variation in distributive politics to neighborhood-level variation in voting behavior.

5.3.1 Expectations of Favoritism

Neighborhood-level variation in ethnic favoritism creates neighborhood-level variation in vote choice if voters support the party they expect to benefit from most in the distribution of particularistic goods after the election. Research on vote choice in Africa suggests that a central consideration for voters is performance – both evaluations of past performance and, especially, expectations about how politicians will perform in the future. This may be a party's macrolevel performance managing the economy,[39] but often means performance at a much more micro level in the distribution of particularistic goods.[40]

Voters' prospective expectations of benefiting from politicians' performance in delivery of particularistic goods are rooted in past experiences with goods distribution. There is not necessarily a perfect correspondence between voter expectations and each party's exact record, however. Voters cannot observe all distribution that occurs, especially in places where they do not live, and it is not always easy to accurately attribute credit.[41] Voters' beliefs that ethnic favoritism is occurring in the allocation of a particular state resource can also sometimes be false.[42] In the absence of perfect information, well-known associations between parties and different ethnic groups provide voters with valuable heuristics about the people and places most likely to benefit from each party.[43]

As a result, even if parties do not always distribute particularistic goods exactly in line with Table 5.1, voters will still believe they are more likely to benefit from the election of an ethnically aligned party in some neighborhoods but not others as long as they expect that parties generally engage in ethnic favoritism. These expectations produce incentives for ethnic voting even when voters do not personally receive many resources, in an absolute sense, from their ethnically aligned party. What matters most is the *relative difference in voters' expectations* of benefiting from the competing parties.[44] But there will be little instrumental incentive for ethnic voting if voters live in an area where they expect no difference in the resources they will receive from each party after the election, or expect that they are actually more likely to benefit from the election of a non-co-ethnic party.[45]

5.3.2 Predictions for Voter Behavior

Specific predictions about where ethnic voting is most likely can be derived from the simplified example above. Neighborhood-level

---

[39] Posner and Simon (2002) and Bratton et al. (2011).
[40] Ichino and Nathan (2013a), Weghorst and Lindberg (2013), and Harding (2015). Importantly, only this latter type of performance can explain neighborhood-level variation in voting; macroeconomic performance is constant between neighborhoods. Aspects of economic performance that have highly localized impacts usually pertain to the delivery of club or private goods and fall within the theory here.
[41] Harding (2015).
[42] Posner (2005) and Carlson (2016).
[43] Ferree (2006).
[44] Padro i Miquel (2007).
[45] Ichino and Nathan (2013a).

variation in ethnic voting occurs in this framework as long as voters hold two beliefs: (i) that the parties will engage in some ethnic favoritism in the distribution of private and club goods after the election; and (ii) that few private goods will be distributed as clientelism by any party in middle- or upper-class neighborhoods. Neither belief requires that voters make complex inferences about politicians' behavior.

Returning to Table 5.1, consider voters from groups A and B voting in an election between parties A and B in a city with the same six types of neighborhoods. As described earlier, all votes count equally and the winning party takes power in all six neighborhoods after the election, such that group A voters cannot take a party A victory for granted just because they live in an A-dominated neighborhood. Voters choose between parties based on their combined expectation of which party is most likely to benefit them with private and club goods.

If a group A voter expects some degree of ethnic favoritism in club goods delivery, she will expect different benefits depending on the ethnic composition of her neighborhood. A group A voter's expectation of benefiting from club goods in diverse neighborhoods (column *i*) will not depend on the ethnic profile of each party because the neighborhood receives similar benefits regardless of which party wins. But party A will be expected to deliver the most club goods in A neighborhoods (column *ii*). When living in a B-dominated neighborhood (column *iii*), party B will instead be expected to be more likely to deliver club goods, which will benefit a group A voter living there.

An A voter's private goods expectations will depend instead on the wealth of her neighborhood. In middle- or upper-class neighborhoods (row 1), she expects few private goods from either party through relational clientelism after the election, even if she is poor. Benefiting from private goods distributed as clientelism by party A is much more likely, in contrast, when a similar A voter lives in a poor neighborhood (row 2). This is even the case in poor neighborhoods where the A voter is in the local minority (row 2, column *iii*). As one of the few group A residents, an A voter in a poor B neighborhood may be one of the first in line in the area to gain from party A's victory, receiving benefits that party A gains control over distributing in the area after the election.

Predictions for vote choice in Table 5.2 come from combining each voter's likely expectations of favoritism in each cell of Table 5.1. Rather than ethnic voting being uncommon across the entire city, support for party A by A voters will be low in two types of neighborhoods. First,

5.3 Patterns of Ethnic Voting

TABLE 5.2: *Vote choice for a Group A voter.*

	Vote Choice for a Group A Voter		
	i. Ethnically Diverse Neighborhood	ii. Homogenous, Group A-dominated Neighborhood	iii. Homogeneous, Group B-dominated Neighborhood
1. Middle- or Upper-class Neighborhood	**Less ethnic voting**	Ethnic voting for A	**Cross-ethnic voting for B**
2. Poor or Slum Neighborhood	Ethnic voting for A	Ethnic voting for A	Ethnic voting for A (if private goods > club goods)

in wealthier, diverse neighborhoods (row 1, column *i* of Table 5.2), there is no difference in the club or private goods an *A* voter expects from either party, making her indifferent between parties in expectations of particularistic goods. In this type of neighborhood, which corresponds to the example of La-Wireless in figure 5.1 at the beginning of the chapter, I expect ethnic voting to mostly fade away, with voters supporting ethnically aligned and unaligned parties in roughly equal proportions.[46] Second, in middle- or upper-class *B*-dominated neighborhoods (row 1, column *iii* of Table 5.2), an *A* voter receives few private benefits from either party, but club goods from party *B*, encouraging cross-ethnic voting for party *B*.[47] In this second type of neighborhood, I expect enough voters from group *A* to cross ethnic lines and support party *B* such that there are either no longer differences in rates of support for each party, or group *A* voters now vote relatively more for party *B*.

---

[46] In a two-party election, an ethnic group splitting votes between the two parties 50–50 is equivalent to "nonethnic voting," as there is then no correlation between ethnicity and vote choice.

[47] Ichino and Nathan (2013a). The overall extent of ethnic voting in row 1, column *iii* should still be high as a percentage of the total voters. By definition, group *A* voters make up only a minority of the population. Local majority *B* voters will still be supporting party *B*. From their perspective, the neighborhood is instead equivalent to row 1, column *ii* in Table 5.2.

Both of these predictions rest on an assumption that few voters continue to vote for their co-ethnic party based on a purely expressive, or affective, logic when they no longer have instrumental incentives to do so. Empirically, it is unrealistic that *all* voters would choose parties based only on instrumental incentives. But the relative extent to which instrumental incentives dominate expressive considerations is testable, at least in the aggregate: if there was still significant voting based on expressive ethnic attachments even in the absence of instrumental incentives, or if a large number of voters perceived some sort of psychological cost to breaking ranks and supporting a non-co-ethnic party, any reductions in ethnic voting in these two cells of Table 5.2 should be muted, or even nonexistent. But an empirical finding of substantively large reductions in ethnic voting in these two types of neighborhoods would suggest that, at least for most voters, instrumental incentives dominate expressive attachments to identity groups.

In the other four neighborhoods in Table 5.2, however, I expect that a group A voter still has incentives to support her co-ethnic party at a much higher rate than the other party. Where there are many other A voters (column ii), the voter will expect significantly more particularistic goods from party A than B regardless of neighborhood wealth. This corresponds to Tweneboa and Nungua-Kingsway in Figure 5.1, where voters in the local ethnic majority voted overwhelmingly for their aligned party. In poor, diverse neighborhoods (row 2, column i), even though the group A voter expects no difference in the club goods she will receive after the election, the voter expects more private benefits from party A than B, pushing her to support party A. This corresponds to Mamobi in Figure 5.1, where there was also significant ethnic voting.

Finally, in poor, B neighborhoods (row 2, column iii), an A voter will expect more club goods from party B, but expect more private goods if party A is elected. Whether a group A voter in this final type of neighborhood votes for party A or party B depends on whether she places greater value on private goods or club goods. Many poor voters will value private goods that address immediate personal needs more highly than club goods for their broader neighborhood. A targeted private benefit can have a significantly larger and more direct effect on a voter's personal well-being. Where this is the case, there will be significant ethnic voting by group A voters in poor, B-dominated neighborhoods as well. Empirically, I do not have data to measure a direct trade-off between the value each voter places on private versus club goods. But the survey question on demands analyzed in Chapter 3 suggests that many poor voters do value private goods as much or more than club goods: the majority of poor survey respondents in Greater Accra listed either as many, or more, demands for private goods among their three responses to the question on preferences as demands for club goods.

5.4 EXTENSIONS

This argument makes several simplifying assumptions for expositional clarity. In this section, I explore what happens to the main predictions if these assumptions are relaxed to allow politicians to employ more complicated distributive strategies, to change underlying features of political institutions, or to consider rural rather than urban contexts.

5.4.1 More complex distributive strategies

Table 5.2's predictions do not require parties to play pure core-voter strategies or engage in absolute ethnic favoritism. Parties could engage in forms of swing targeting alongside core favoritism. Doing so does not change the predictions for vote choice unless each party completely stops favoring their own core ethnic group(s) relative to the core group(s) of the opposing party.

A swing targeting strategy in the example in Tables 5.1 and 5.2 would take the form of each party investing a greater share of its overall resources in politically competitive neighborhoods – the diverse areas in column i.[48] Such an approach would predominately involve club goods distribution rather than relational clientelism, given the differential costs to each party of engaging the other ethnic group in sustained relationships. In a competitive election in which both parties adopt this strategy, however, the aggregate effects on vote choice will cancel out. There will be no reason for voters living in diverse neighborhoods to expect systematically more from one party or the other. Moreover, even if one party – e.g., the incumbent – can spend much more on club goods in diverse neighborhoods before the election, voters' prospective expectations regarding which party will benefit the neighborhood the most after the election are unlikely to differ across parties, as the opposition party could begin spending more if it were to win.[49]

---

[48] I have assumed away unaligned ethnic groups; both ethnic groups – A and B – are affiliated with one of the parties.
[49] If vote choice is purely retrospective and one party has a large funding advantage in the present, there could be a universal shift toward this more dominant party among all

Swing targeting would also occur if there were some third group – C – aligned with neither party. Tables 5.1 and 5.2 can be extended to a third group by adding a fourth column for C-dominated neighborhoods. Pursuing swing C voters would now mean investing club goods in C-dominated neighborhoods and attempting, to the extent possible, to build individual clientelistic relationships with C voters. If both parties converged on pursuing group C, however, their efforts in C-dominated neighborhoods would largely cancel out from the perspective of group A and B voters, such that the new fourth column would look much like the current column i. And as long as both parties also continued to favor their own core group relative to the core group of the opposing party, relative expectations of favoritism would remain unchanged among group A and B voters in the other neighborhoods.

In addition to pursuing competitive neighborhoods or swing ethnic groups, the parties might choose to employ episodic private goods distribution alongside relational clientelism, distributing some private benefits before elections in an unmonitored fashion, as described in Kramon (2016). This is also unlikely to alter the predictions in Tables 5.1 and 5.2. A group A voter's expected benefits from any private goods distributed as episodic gifts before the election are likely much less important for her vote choice.[50] I argue that the small private benefits often distributed as gifts immediately before elections are usually much less valuable than the longer-term private benefits voters can receive through sustained clientelistic relationships after the election. In neighborhoods where both modes of private goods distribution occur, expectations about relational clientelism should outweigh any voter expectations created by episodic gift-giving. And even if episodic, pre-election goods distribution occurs in neighborhoods where there is no relational clientelism, as in row 1 of Table 5.1, this is unlikely to systematically swamp voters' expectations about club goods delivery. Not only will these private benefits be of relatively low value, but when they are provided through unmonitored, non-repeated exchanges, there is little risk to voters from taking the benefits and voting however they would have anyway. Moreover, if

---

voters in diverse neighborhoods. But this would not necessarily create observable differences in ethnic voting, especially in row 1, column i. For every A voter that becomes more likely to vote for party A, a B voter would also become more likely to cross ethnic lines towards party A in response to receiving club benefits.

[50] Weghorst and Lindberg (2013) and Guardado and Wantchekon (2017) similarly argue that unmonitored pre-election gift-giving in Africa often may have little direct effect on voting behavior.

the distribution of single-shot pre-election gifts is not targeted by ethnicity, there will be little reason for a voter to expect to receive systematically more from one party or the other in the future, creating no particular instrumental incentive for ethnic voting even if gifts improve the overall reputation of the particular candidate distributing them.

5.4.2 Differences in the Institutional Environment

I also consider two ways in which the institutional environment could differ. First, I assume that all votes count equally in the election, such that parties do not gain extra benefits from additional votes in competitive compared to noncompetitive neighborhoods. The predictions for all but one of the six cells in Table 5.2 would remain the same if the election instead occurred under a voting rule in which winning competitive areas (column i above) was more important. The only difference would be that parties would no longer have strong incentives to invest effort in maintaining grassroots organizations capable of relational clientelism in poor neighborhoods dominated by the other party's ethnic group. This means that an A voter in row 2, column iii may no longer expect favoritism from party A in private goods distribution. The prediction in this cell in Table 5.2 would flip to cross-ethnic voting by A voters for party B, similar to row 1, column iii.

In addition, I assume that parties have to spend at least some of the resources they gain control over after the election in each cell of Table 5.1. Eliminating this assumption again primarily affects the delivery of private goods by party A to group A voters in poor, group B neighborhoods (row 2, column iii). If a party can fully move resources away from neighborhoods dominated by the co-ethnics of the opposing party, it is possible it will not find it cost effective to maintain patronage networks at all in these areas, and will concentrate relational clientelism in the other types of poor neighborhoods in row 2. This would have the same effects on vote choice in this cell of Table 5.2 as changing the electoral system. Predictions in all other cells of Table 5.2 would remain the same, however.

5.4.3 Comparison to Rural Areas

The predictions about urban neighborhoods in Table 5.2 differ somewhat from the related argument developed for rural areas in Ichino and Nathan (2013a), which is more similar to row 1 of Table 5.2, with predictions of cross-ethnic voting when voters live in areas dominated by an ethnic group affiliated with a different political party and less ethnic voting by all voters in diverse areas where neither party can favor specific ethnic groups with club goods. While I expect these same patterns in middle- and upper-class neighborhoods in cities, I make a different prediction for urban slums. In poor urban neighborhoods, voters' expectations of favoritism in access to private goods distribution via relational clientelism will still produce significant ethnic voting regardless of the ethnic composition of the neighborhood.

These divergent predictions are rooted in the likelihood of relational clientelism. Rural voters – especially those living in small villages where everyone knows everyone else – may in fact be easiest for parties to identify, monitor, and engage with over time. Despite this, I expect that fewer rural voters receive valuable private goods directly from each party through relational clientelism in comparison to voters in urban slums. This seeming paradox is explained by the availability of alternative forms of voter mobilization in many rural communities, which allow parties to engage with rural voters in a different manner.

In many rural areas, parties can draw on powerful traditional elites, such as chiefs, to serve as intermediaries instead of party agents. These traditional leaders largely either do not exist or are not influential in cities.[51] Rather than investing substantial party resources in maintaining a large network of party agents to engage in direct relationships with individual voters, parties can work through local notables who already have built-in sources of socioeconomic authority that give them significant leverage over voters. Chiefs and other traditional elites can help parties build support in the absence of direct ties with voters in two ways. They can serve as clientelistic brokers on behalf of parties, identifying recipients for private benefits, monitoring behavior, and using their power to enforce patronage transactions.[52] In a less clientelistic fashion, chiefs can serve as key opinion leaders whose endorsements have significant influence over community members.[53] Through either mechanism, the ability to work through, or pay off and secure endorsements from, chiefs and other rural elites allows parties to substitute away from identifying and monitoring private goods recipients at an individual level and forego the – potentially quite significant – costs of employing a network of their own agents to engage in relational clientelism.

---

[51] Chapter 7 explores a key exception: indigenous urban ethnic groups among whom traditional elites remain powerful in the city.
[52] Ntsebeza (2005), Koter (2016), and de Kadt and Larreguy (2018).
[53] Baldwin (2015).

Indeed, existing literature suggests that many parties in African democracies have not developed the grassroots organizations in rural areas needed to engage in sustained relationships with a large numbers of individual clients (van de Walle 2007, Kramon 2016).[54] Even where parties still have nominal organizations in rural villages, few valuable individual-level clientelistic benefits may flow through these organizations when existing rural elites provide a powerful and effective substitute form of voter engagement. In addition to the availability of substitutes, the marginal value to a party of empowering a grassroots party worker in a rural village to serve as a clientelistic intermediary is simply lower than in an urban slum – there are many fewer potential clients for each party agent to reach.

The ability to work through rural elites also makes club goods distribution relatively more attractive than private goods distribution in the first place. Rather than identifying and targeting private benefits to individual voters, parties can secure support of a small, ethnically homogenous village all at once by targeting a club good to the whole village, with the intermediary coordinating support for the party in return – either via direct pressure (e.g., Koter 2016) or through an influential endorsement (e.g., Baldwin 2015). Community-level exchanges in which an entire village coordinates support behind a candidate or party in return for benefits are common across rural Africa.[55] In the rural villages where social structures are most conducive to these forms of coordinated, community-level exchanges, there is less need for parties to invest in individual-level clientelism. As a result, fewer private goods may be distributed as clientelism than in urban neighborhoods where similar exchanges are less possible, given the absence of similar social institutions that could coordinate votes.

If there is less relational clientelism, row 2 in Tables 5.1 and 5.2 becomes more similar to row 1. This is especially clear for column *iii* – cases in which a group A voter lives as a local ethnic minority in a B-dominated area. I argue above that an A voter may still expect to benefit from relational clientelism from party A in poor urban neighborhoods (row 2, column *iii*), producing ethnic voting for party A if the poor voter values private benefits over club goods. This will not be the case

---

[54] Similarly, Ferree and Long (2016) suggest that parties in Ghana are less able to monitor individual voters in rural than urban areas.
[55] Lindberg (2010), Gottlieb and Larreguy (2015), and Conroy-Krutz (2017) all document the logic underlying these forms of rural vote coordination.

if no relational clientelism occurs or, instead, if many of the private benefits that are delivered are funneled through chiefs or other community leaders. Local minority *A* voters may be disproportionately cut out of benefiting from private goods in the latter scenario, as community leaders in a *B*-dominated village will almost certainly be from group *B*, and have closer ties to *B* voters. Moreover, even if chiefs and other local leaders are not used as intermediaries, *B*-dominated villages in rural areas are also the places where it is least likely that party *A* will have developed its own strong local network of party agents capable of monitoring individual voters. Expecting few private benefits from party *A* for these reasons, group *A* voters in *B*-dominated villages have incentives to vote across ethnic lines in anticipation of benefiting from club goods distributed by party *B*. This is the core prediction in Ichino and Nathan (2013a).

5.5 SUMMARY

This chapter suggests that intra-urban variation in ethnic competition emerges from intra-urban variation in distributive politics. Otherwise similar voters – of the same socioeconomic class, with the same social attachments to their ethnic groups, and who make the same demands on politicians – behave differently in different neighborhoods of a city because they have different expectations of favoritism.

In addition to accounting for intra-urban variation in voting behavior, this argument makes distinct claims from those of earlier attempts to explain the causes of overall rural–urban differences in ethnic politics. At its heart, this chapter presents a supply-side argument for ethnic competition. If there is less ethnic voting overall in cities than in rural areas, it will be because politicians face higher costs to supplying particularistic goods as ethnic favoritism in cities, *not* because voters' demands or individual socioeconomic characteristics differ. I expect less ethnic voting in diverse, middle-class neighborhoods of cities both because it is too difficult for politicians to target club goods as favoritism and because it is too costly for politicians to engage in relational clientelism with individual core supporters who live there, even those who still strongly demand private benefits. This differs sharply from demand-side claims that there will be less ethnic voting in cities because voters are wealthier, better educated, are more ethnically assimilated, have weaker ties to their ethnic groups, or are freed from the control of traditional elites.

I explore this argument empirically in the next two chapters using cross-sectional data, focusing primarily on variation across neighborhoods of Greater Accra. But the supply-side nature of the argument developed in this chapter also has implications for thinking about the future trajectory of ethnic competition as urbanization continues. Greater urbanization in Greater Accra and other African cities may mean an even larger urban middle class and even more overall ethnic diversity. But as long as ethnic segregation persists at a neighborhood level and slum neighborhoods continue to grow apace alongside the middle class, ethnic competition will remain a key feature of urban politics – not disappear – unless there are large shifts in politicians' incentives to supply ethnic favoritism.

6

Distributive Politics in Urban Areas

> *"It's like a blackmail situation ... [They] brought a protestation that they would switch to the NPP based on failed promises ... The deal was that I had to get them jobs. So that's what I'm doing."*
> – NDC party agent, La Dade Kotopon constituency, Greater Accra, February 2014

> *"When such things are given, they rather give it to those parts, the slum areas surrounding here."*
> – Focus group participant, Dzorwulu, Ayawaso West constituency, Greater Accra, June 2013

Chapter 5 predicts that parties favor core voters in some neighborhoods within a city, but not others. This chapter examines whether this is the case, showing that voters in Greater Accra are likely to expect ethnic favoritism in the allocation of many state resources and that the strength of these expectations should depend on the neighborhoods in which they live.

This chapter presents descriptive evidence in support of six elements of the argument in Chapter 5. First, while the parties do not employ pure core-voter strategies and ethnic favoritism is not absolute, core voters are disproportionately favored by each party in the distribution of many types of benefits, especially outside of campaign periods. Second, this favoritism occurs for two reasons: because parties believe they must continue benefiting core voters to keep their electoral base intact, and because parties have efficiency advantages in sustaining clientelistic relationships with ethnically aligned voters. Third, the targeted distribution of valuable private goods through clientelism is concentrated in poor neighborhoods of the city, while almost nonexistent in middle- and upper-class areas. Fourth, at the same time, however, club goods are targeted to poor and middle-class neighborhoods alike, such that vote choices in middle-class neighborhoods can still be affected by expectations about which party is more likely to deliver club goods even if there is little distribution of private goods. Fifth, I document the housing patterns and social structures that help make clientelism too costly for parties in wealthier neighborhoods, even among the poor voters who live there and still strongly demand private goods.

Finally, the last section of the chapter examines the extension to the theory in Chapter 5 to rural–urban differences. I show that individual-level clientelistic relationships directly linking parties and voters appear to be more common in urban slums than in most rural villages, in contrast to common arguments that clientelism is less viable in cities.[1]

The particularistic, patronage-based appeals described here are not the only ways in which Ghana's parties seek support in urban areas – they are combined with the policy rhetoric described in Chapter 4, as well as with messaging about macroeconomic performance and the personal characteristics of different candidates. But given the credibility problems that Ghana's parties face in building support based on policy appeals, this chapter documents many of the main methods through which politicians persuade and mobilize voters in urban areas in the absence of more substantive programmatic competition.

6.1 MIXED TARGETING OF PARTICULARISTIC GOODS

The NDC and NPP do not engage in exclusive ethnic favoritism in Greater Accra. Local party executives, polling-station agents, and parliamentary candidates, as well as ordinary residents participating in focus groups, describe in detail how each party distributes particularistic goods in multiple ways, with multiple beneficiaries. Two forms of distribution in particular were highlighted in the interviews and focus groups: unmonitored pre-election gift-giving, which is targeted widely, and postelection clientelism, which disproportionately benefits core, ethnically aligned supporters. In this section, I show that each party engages in unmonitored distribution of particularistic benefits in the campaign period before elections – reaching both core and unaligned voters with

---

[1] Magaloni (2006), Stokes et al. (2013) and Koter (2016).

relatively low-value benefits. But the ruling party and elected MPs also systematically favor core voters and those with whom their party agents have sustained relationships in the distribution of more valuable benefits that they gain control over once in office.[2]

6.1.1 Pre-election Distribution

Both parties distribute particularistic goods widely in campaign periods before elections, benefiting ethnically aligned and unaligned voters alike in the delivery of private and club goods. The private goods described by interview respondents and focus group participants as distributed most commonly before the 2012 elections were small amounts of cash and food, clothing, and basic household supplies (soap, cooking oil, etc.).[3] Both major parties were said to distribute these gifts. A resident of Kpone explained, "Last year [*before the election*], they had a campaign team that goes house-to-house to do their campaign ... They give money. They buy drinks ... It's not only the NDC, [but also the NPP]."[4]

This pre-election distribution is not vote buying. Focus group participants did not believe that accepting these benefits means entering an enforceable contract, emphasizing that their vote choices remain secret and that they can take gifts and still vote however they want.[5] A resident of Kpone said, "Normally they do go around and give people things to convince them ... [But] at the end of the day, when I come to the booth, it's between me and God. They may not know whether I voted for them."[6] A focus group participant in the Ashaiman slum described it similarly: "The MP will come and say 'take these Ghana cedis' ... and since that person has taken that money, they will say 'oh I will vote for you.'" But this is not sincere: "It's [still] up to you to decide who you want to vote for."[7] Participants in the Kaneshie neighborhood of Accra expressed similar sentiments: one said, "I will just collect it, but it will

---

[2] Faller (2013) and Brierley and Kramon (2015) both suggest that there are similar temporal differences across the electoral cycle in whether core or swing voters are favored by Ghana's parties.
[3] This corresponds to the survey data on gift-giving examined in Chapter 4, which shows that 69% of the representative sample of residents of Greater Accra had knowledge of gifts being distributed in their neighborhoods before the election.
[4] Focus group, Kpone, Kpone-Katamanso constituency, Greater Accra, June 19, 2013.
[5] Ferree and Long (2016) suggest by contrast that some Ghanaian voters, including in urban areas, do believe that ballot secrecy can be violated by parties and thus do sometimes view gift exchanges as enforceable vote buying.
[6] Focus group, Kpone, Kpone-Katamanso constituency, Greater Accra, June 19, 2013.
[7] Focus group, Zongo Laka, Ashaiman constituency, Greater Accra, July 3, 2013.

never have any influence on you"; another argued, "Even though I don't want the person to win, I will collect it if they bring it." Lindberg (2010) similarly suggests that many urban voters treat campaign periods as a "harvesting season" for nonbinding handouts they can collect from party agents and parliamentary candidates.

The party agents who personally distribute these gifts are well aware that they do not create binding commitments. One NPP party agent complained, "We say 'take it, vote for me' ... Some people do it ... But some ... [they] still won't vote for you. 'I'll take it, but I'll not vote for you. Because when I get to the polling booth, I'm the only person there. It's only me and God.' This is our complaint. 'Hey, I voted for you', but it's a lie!"[8] Other party agents similarly complained that they had no way of monitoring vote choice.[9]

Instead, distributing pre-election benefits is aimed more at creating reputations of performance and generosity.[10] Some local party leaders justified gift-giving as a means to develop a reputation as serving the interests of the community and as a way to signal respect for voters. An NDC constituency executive in the Okaikwei Central constituency argued that campaign season gifts are primarily meant to improve the party's local reputation:

[We] don't give money like "I am sharing money, take this and vote for me." No ... For example there is a church here and I want to speak to the church people so that they vote for me. After speaking to them ... I will acquire some paint and get the place painted. And they will announce it at church. 'He has painted the church. Praise God. The NDC has painted our church.'

When campaigning door-to-door, private gifts show respect: "You can't invite somebody ... sit them down, talk to them ... then when you finish you say, okay, let's see you tomorrow. At least some motivation – something to drink or something to eat" must be given.[11]

Another motivation for distributing pre-election gifts may be fear of the electoral consequences of *not* doing so. In a competitive election in which the opposing party is also distributing gifts and poor voters have

---

[8] Interview with NPP party agent, Madina constituency, Greater Accra, June 29, 2012.
[9] E.g., interview with NPP party agent, Okaikwei Central constituency, Greater Accra, March 19, 2014.
[10] Kramon (2016) and Munoz (2014).
[11] Interview with NDC party executive, Okaikwei Central constituency, Greater Accra, February 27, 2014.

been habituated to expect gifts, disappointing voters by not passing out benefits can damage a party's reputation. An NDC parliamentary candidate in Accra described his gift distribution on the campaign trail mostly as a means to satisfy persistent demands from voters: "What I do [when going door-to-door] is I have a wad of notes [*flashes a thick wad of cash from his pocket*]. When I get pestered too much while campaigning, here's something small ... just get off my back so we can move on."[12] An NPP party agent in Madina spelled out the competitive risks of refusing to provide gifts: "if [our parliamentary candidate] says he doesn't have, they'll go and say 'Oh, that man is a bad man!' ... So that makes the politicians think they must bribe the people with money. If they don't give out, they won't vote for you."[13]

These gifts are sometimes distributed to voters well outside each party's core ethnic coalition. An NPP parliamentary candidate said he most often gave out small gifts during the 2012 campaign in neighborhoods where he knew his co-ethnics – Akans – were *least* numerous, even though he realized he had no guarantee the recipients would support the NPP. "I target most where our people are not many because I know if I win just a little there to add to where my people are ... I will have won."[14] Participants in a middle-class area of Kaneshie also made clear that this gift distribution reaches voters with whom a party otherwise has little long-term relationship. As one participant explained, "During the elections, they came to give chairs, furniture, and some bags of rice ... So they just brought these things to flatter us during the election." But the participant continued, "It's only during the election ... After the election, nothing. You won't even see them [the party agents], let alone their shadow."[15] Data from four regions of Ghana in Brierley and Kramon (2015) similarly suggests that the two major parties, especially the incumbent NDC, targeted pre-election canvassing and gift-giving widely during the 2012 campaign, rather than only focusing effort in stronghold constituencies and ethnic bases. In media coverage of Ghanaian campaigns, national party leaders frequently urge local party activists to focus their

---

[12] Interview with NDC parliamentary candidate, Ablekuma North constituency, Greater Accra, July 23, 2012.
[13] Interview with NPP party agent, Madina constituency, Greater Accra, June 29, 2012.
[14] Interview with NPP parliamentary candidate, Madina constituency, Greater Accra, June 6, 2012.
[15] Focus group, Kaneshie, Okaikwei South constituency, Greater Accra, June 26, 2013. These recipients are not core supporters who otherwise regularly interact with the local party organization.

main campaign efforts – and implicitly, their distribution of pre-election gifts, a key component of house-to-house campaigning – on "floating voters," rather than the party's core supporters.[16]

Similar dynamics are also paralleled in small-scale club goods distribution by both parties during campaign periods. In similar language to that used in the discussion of pre-election private gifts, focus group participants described parties and MP candidates fanning out across the city during campaigns to re-pave streets, put up streetlights, and clear litter-filled gutters, benefiting voters with whom they otherwise have little direct connection. A participant in Odorkor said, "They will do some small work within the period that the election is coming on and they will come and clear the gutters and everything ... Then after that, you vote, and they are gone."[17] Participants in the Mataheko neighborhood of central Accra described how an NDC MP candidate brought a backhoe to their neighborhood shortly before election day to level out unpaved streets.[18] Opposition NPP MP candidates described providing club goods – such as new boreholes in neighborhoods without running water access – as a core part of their campaign activity.[19]

6.1.2 Post-election Favoritism

The distribution of pre-election benefits does not mean each party's core ethnic groups have no reason to expect to benefit from ethnic favoritism, however. Pre-election gift-giving coexists alongside favoritism, especially after the campaign period is over. These strategies appear to be intertemporal complements across the electoral cycle – parties are free to focus on voters outside their core in their final campaign appeals because they have already shored up the support of their ethnic bases prior to the campaign beginning.

Both the focus group participants and local politicians described significant private goods distribution also occurring after elections, with

---

[16] For example, see "Target Floating Voters – Amissah-Arthur Charges Campaign Team" (2016).
[17] Focus group, Odorkor "Official Town," Ablekuma North constituency, Greater Accra, October 1, 2013.
[18] They complained that the candidate's work crew accidentally burst a water main, destroying the road he had meant to fix. The damage had not been repaired by the time of our focus group, 10 months after the election. The participants said they had not voted for him. Focus groups, Mataheko, Ablekuma Central constituency, October 1, 2013.
[19] E.g., interview with NPP parliamentary candidate, Madina constituency, Greater Accra, June 6, 2012.

core supporters of the ruling party the main beneficiaries. Unlike with campaign gifts, these exchanges were typically described as involving repeated interactions benefiting voters who are "in" a party or that a party already "knows" and is "close to." In a context in which outright statements in favor of co-ethnic favoritism are taboo, language about voters who are "close to" or "know" a party can be a euphemistic way to indicate that voters with the strongest ties to a party are most likely to benefit. Moreover, the private goods described as distributed in this second group of patronage exchanges were typically more valuable than the small gifts of cash or food described as pre-election gifts, and often funded through government resources and programs.

As an example of the opportunities that can open up to core supporters once their party wins, an NDC party leader in Accra described how he helped find civil service jobs for core supporters in his neighborhood after the NDC took power: "People in my community, they need job ... So when they come to me I say, 'I've learned [the Prison Service] is doing recruitment. If you are interested ... I'll go and lobby for you.' This is what we did."[20] NPP party agents in Ledzokuku constituency similarly described how core party supporters would expect jobs from the district government if the NPP had won in 2012: "When you are in the party and ... the party gets into power, definitely there are positions. Automatic positions for you. You see Ghana politics is a winner-take-all system. Like LEKMA Assembly, there are so many positions and they are going to be automatic for you in the party when your presidential candidate wins."[21] Core party supporters who own small businesses would also be first in line to receive contracts from the district governments if their party takes power. As the NPP party agent in Madina described it, "This man [*gesturing to an NPP supporter*], he's a ... [cement] block maker. So if you want somebody to buy blocks from, where are you going to go and buy the blocks from? That contract will go to him." He continued: "We have carpenters [who support the party]. If there's any contract, our carpenters go ahead" of non-NPP carpenters.[22] Similarly, numerous media reports after the NDC took power in 2009 described core NDC "foot soldiers" being quickly moved in to various positions providing

---

[20] Interview with NDC constituency executive, Ayawaso West constituency, Greater Accra, July 23, 2012.
[21] LEKMA is the Ledzokuku-Krowor Municipal Assembly, the district government in the area. Interview with NPP party agents, Ledzokuku constituency, Greater Accra, August 1, 2013.
[22] Interview with NPP party agent, Madina constituency, Greater Accra, June 29, 2012.

small services to the district governments – from gangs of NDC youth gaining control of charging fees for the use of public toilets in urban slums to favoring certain women hired to prepare food at public schools as part of the government's School Feeding Programme.[23]

MPs also distribute private patronage benefits to core supporters once they take office, even if they are not in the national ruling party.[24] An NPP executive in Weija constituency described how the NPP MP invested in the small businesses of supporters: "The women who are poor. You see? They expect that when you come to power, you will help them ... Our MP was giving money to the women to trade. 100 Ghana cedis each. About 200 women."[25] NPP constituency executives from Okaikwei North in Accra described how the MP in their constituency provided long-term financial support for poor market traders and paid health insurance registration fees for supporters after winning the election: "If you go to the markets, she did a lot for the market women ... When we come to health insurance ... many people were not able to afford registering for the NHIS. About 4000 people, she registered for them. She pays the fee."[26] This patronage distribution is sometimes formalized; NPP executives in a nearby constituency described running a microfinance loan scheme for loyal party supporters directly from their branch office in collaboration with the NPP MP.[27]

The focus group participants had clear expectations that these benefits would go to core supporters. A nurse in the Dzorwulu neighborhood of Accra argued that most benefits the parties distribute "are given to the party members, to those they already know. It's not everybody it comes to."[28] A participant in the Mataheko neighborhood said, "Things like this ... the distribution of the money, it will go to the people who are close to the party."[29] A participant in the Kpone focus group agreed:

---

[23] For example, Mensah (2009).
[24] Lindberg (2010). Each MP controls a discretionary development fund to distribute as they choose within their constituency.
[25] Interview with NPP constituency executive, Weija constituency, Greater Accra, July 29, 2013.
[26] NHIS is the "National Health Insurance Scheme," introduced in Chapter 4. Interview with NPP constituency executives, Okaikwei North constituency, Greater Accra, August 6, 2013.
[27] Interview with NPP constituency executive, Okaikwei Central constituency, March 4, 2014; interview with district assembly member and former NPP constituency executive, Okaikwei Central constituency, March 12, 2014.
[28] Focus group, Dzorwulu, Ayawaso West constituency, Greater Accra, June 21, 2013.
[29] Focus group, Mataheko, Ablekuma Central constituency, October 1, 2013.

"Here it is a political environment ... So if for example, if you're from party A ... if you come to power, I know that you'll help me out. But if you come to power and ... [I'm] not part of your party, it will be difficult."[30] Another explained, "Some people have been put into trading by the [NDC] MP. He's trying to let them get something to do on their own. They're in the training process. So some of them, he volunteers to give them machines, hair driers for the hair dressers, so it will help them ... With regards to those who sew, he gave them machines." The participant continued: "But he hasn't done it for everybody. It's some few people," indicating that NDC supporters were favored in this assistance.[31]

These expectations extend to benefits from government antipoverty programs, such as youth employment and loan and microfinance programs. There are persistent accusations in the press, as described in Chapter 4, that benefits from these programs favor core voters of the ruling party. Focus group participants had similar expectations. When asked about one of these government microfinance programs, a resident of Odorkor responded, "MASLOC? I've heard of it. It came under the NPP time ... I had a friend who was part of the NPP team and he got the MASLOC loans. But people like us ... who are not part of the party, didn't get it ... If it wasn't for him, I wouldn't even know that there was MASLOC." Another participant in the same focus group concurred: "If you are not a member ... when the loan comes and you want to get some, they wouldn't give it to you."[32] A resident of Tema had similar expectations about government job programs: "If you go for a job and you don't have a party card, they never give you a job. It's about who you know."[33]

6.2 THE ROOTS OF FAVORITISM

Why do local party organizations funnel these benefits after the election to voters who already support the party? Chapter 5 identifies two main reasons why core voters are likely to be favored: because parties must continue providing ethnically aligned voters with benefits to keep their

---

[30] Focus group, Kpone, Kpone-Katamanso constituency, Greater Accra, June 19, 2013.
[31] Focus group, Kpone, Kpone-Katamanso constituency, Greater Accra, June 19, 2013.
[32] MASLOC is the government's "Micro-finance and Small Loans Centre." Focus group, Odorkor "Official Town," Ablekuma North constituency, Greater Accra, October 1, 2013.
[33] Discussion with pilot survey respondents, Tema Community 8, Tema Central constituency, Greater Accra, August 23, 2013.

6.2 The Roots of Favoritism

support from eroding,[34] and because parties have informational and efficiency advantages in engaging in patronage exchanges with voters from core ethnic groups.[35] Both are borne out in the interview evidence.

Local politicians in Greater Accra described their reasoning for providing patronage to existing party supporters in terms that closely match Diaz-Cayeros et al.'s (2016) argument (see Chapter 5) that favoring core supporters is necessary to ensure that they continue to be core supporters. An NDC party agent explained this logic bluntly: "It's like a blackmail situation." Supporters threaten to leave their party if they do not receive enough patronage. The party agent described a recent incident in which he provided patronage jobs to core NDC voters in his neighborhood:

I had to get some jobs for them yesterday, for the youth in the constituency ... This lady ... marshaled 20 people to me, to bring a protestation that they would switch to the NPP based on failed promises from [the NDC MP]. And I had to plead with them, but the deal was that I had to get them jobs. So that's what I'm doing.[36]

Discussions of similar "blackmail situations" are common in the press. Core supporters clearly believe they are entitled to benefits from their party if it wins the election, and protest and threaten to defect if they do not receive them.[37] Shortly before the 2016 presidential campaign was to begin in earnest, for example, some core NDC supporters in the Nima slum – the main northern ethnic stronghold of the NDC in Accra – said they would refuse to help the party during the upcoming campaign unless they were first given more patronage. When NDC leaders came to the neighborhood to distribute cash to quell these complaints, party supporters were unsatisfied. As one supporter explained, they wanted more valuable, longer-term benefits in return for their continued support, not the cash given out to regular voters as gifts: "We prefer jobs to money because money wouldn't last like the jobs which would provide us daily bread for a good living ... Why would I support a party that can't give me a job?"[38]

---

[34] Diaz-Cayeros et al. (2016).
[35] Dixit and Londregan (1996).
[36] Interview with NDC party agent, La Dade Kotopon constituency, Greater Accra, February 27, 2014.
[37] This is similar to Nichter and Peress's (2017) description of clientelism as "request fulfilling."
[38] "NDC foot-soldiers reject GHC10,000" (2016). As another example, see "NDC foot soldiers join NPP" (2016).

These threats are credible enough to work specifically because the relationship between ethnicity and partisanship in Ghana is responsive to voters' instrumental calculations, not innate and fixed. While Nima is an NDC stronghold made up predominately of voters from northern ethnic groups closely affiliated with the party, not all northerners in Nima support the NDC. The party cannot take the uniform support of the neighborhood for granted, even as it runs a co-ethnic northerner (President Mahama) as its candidate. Only continued patronage can ensure these voters will remain core supporters into the future.

In addition, a second reason proposed in Chapter 5 for favoritism in relational clientelism is that parties have efficiency advantages in targeting benefits to ethnically aligned voters. Local party organizations in Greater Accra are deeply embedded in the social fabric of some urban neighborhoods, capable of identifying individual party supporters, targeting personalized support, and repeatedly interacting with them over time. Ghana's parties have active committees of agents at each polling station in most urban neighborhoods reporting to ward-level (Electoral Area-level) coordinators, who in turn report to constituency-level executives and MPs. Under these polling station committees there can sometimes be informal networks of party members ("foot soldiers" or "party boys") who assist local party leaders with various activities. As noted by Paller (2014), informal community leaders in slums often simultaneously serve as leaders within these party organizations. Ward-level city councilors (district assembly members; see Chapter 8), who serve as formal neighborhood leaders, are also often simultaneously party executives at the constituency or polling-station levels.

Party leaders regularly claimed that they are confident that they can identify and target individual core supporters within neighborhoods where party networks are extensive.[39] Much of this ability grows out of the interpersonal social networks that each party's local agents bring into the party organization. For example, an NDC leader in Accra described how he relies on grassroots party agents to help him identify NDC supporters in his constituency: "Every polling station is a branch. We encourage the [party agents] to identify the people there [at the polling station]. So in every house when I enter the house, I already know that in this house we have 10 NPP, 5 NDC."[40]

---

[39] Importantly, this is a claim about identifying their own core supporters, not a claim that they can identify *all* voters. This mirrors evidence in Schneider (2017) on partisan differences in the voter identification abilities of grassroots party workers in India.

[40] Interview with NDC party executive, Okaikwei Central constituency, Greater Accra, February 27, 2014.

6.2 *The Roots of Favoritism*

In other cases, the parties try to supplement the localized knowledge of grassroots agents with rudimentary forms of data collection. An NPP MP candidate and a constituency executive each separately described going through official voter rolls in an attempt to identify likely supporters based on the ethnicity of their surnames.[41] The NPP MP candidate also described using additional data collection to help ensure that his core co-ethnic supporters registered to vote before the 2012 election: "Before the voter registration we went to houses, wrote their names, which party they belong to, did you vote last time, or are you a new voter ... We did all the statistics. So before we move into voting registration we knew how many new voters were coming in and where they are from."[42] In the most extreme example of this type of data collection, which occurred after the field research for this book concluded, the NDC created an official register and database of all of its members shortly before the 2016 election, issuing formal party ID cards to core supporters in each community. This database was subsequently discarded by the NDC after the 2016 elections, however, amid concerns that it was rife with inaccuracies.[43] This suggests that these formal data-collection efforts are at best only imperfect complements for the more detailed personal knowledge of party agents.

Together, these forms of information on supporters are used to target benefits. An NDC party agent in La Dade Kotopon constituency described using a database of local supporters to allocate jobs after the party won the 2012 election: "I've made a database of all our people, I'm updating it, what skills do you have ... So per this database, we can know who wants work, what skill sets you have, and then we can match you to a job. We can look at the vacancies and push for you. So that's what we are doing for our people."[44]

Importantly, local party organizations in Greater Accra appear to have the most information about supporters from their core ethnic groups. While representative data on the composition of party organizations is

---

[41] The candidate showed me his printed copy of the voters' register, which had check marks by each Akan name. Interview with NPP parliamentary candidate, Greater Accra, June 6, 2012; interview with NPP constituency executive, Okaikwei Central constituency, Greater Accra, March 4, 2014.

[42] Interview with NPP parliamentary candidate, Greater Accra, June 6, 2012.

[43] Djabanor and Kwakofi (2017).

[44] Interview with NDC party agent, La Dade Kotopon constituency, Greater Accra, February 27, 2014.

not available, the interviews made clear that polling station-level party executives and grassroots party agents are mostly drawn from each party's core ethnic groups. To the extent that personal social networks remain rooted in ethnicity, this overrepresentation of core ethnic groups within party branches means that local party organizations will have more information on co-ethnics than on other voters, facilitating targeting of core ethnic groups with private goods when they give out benefits to the voters that "they know" best.[45]

The large majority of NPP party agents and leaders interviewed were Akans; nearly all from the NDC were Gas, Ewes, or Northerners. When asked explicitly about the ethnic composition of their agents, NPP leaders, even in historically Ga-dominated areas of Accra, indicated that most grassroots agents were Akans.[46] One party leader took out her constituency's "album" – a list of all polling-station executives in the constituency – and went through the names one by one. Almost all were Akan, even though her Electoral Area contains large Northern and Ga populations.[47] An NDC constituency executive similarly claimed that most of his polling station executives and party agents were non-Akan, even though he worked in a heavily Akan constituency. He believed the NDC's aligned ethnic groups dominated the local party organization because they had secured an early foothold in the party and were unwilling to relinquish positions to outsiders. Potential Akan members then stayed away from the NDC organization because they did not feel welcome. "The Akan people ... feel that this party [the NDC], and for that matter these people, 'they are not us, they are not like us, they don't like us. So let's stay at our side' ... Very few in my branch executives are Akans," he said. He continued:

---

[45] While the parties engage in some of the forms of data collection described earlier, the interviews did not suggest that this data collection was sophisticated enough to fully substitute for the localized knowledge of party agents in informing targeting decisions in the distribution of resources.

[46] Interview with NPP ward coordinator and former constituency executives, Krowor constituency, Greater Accra, February 15, 2014. The former constituency chairman, himself a Ga traditional elder, complained that he had lost his constituency leadership position in the NPP because Ga party members were significantly outnumbered by Akans: "The other tribes took the opportunity and have more people there [as polling station executives]. So if you go and contest [for a constituency executive position] they will say, I won't vote for you, you are not my brother."

[47] Interview with NPP regional executive and district assembly member, Okaikwei Central constituency, Greater Accra, March 12, 2014.

My people at the grassroots ... they have a thinking that if they give these people [Akans] a chance, they may take over their branch positions from them. And therefore they have a certain barrier that they have created around themselves. So all the time [in internal party elections] it's "Oh don't vote for these people – these people are not the NDC people."[48]

6.3 NEIGHBORHOOD CHARACTERISTICS AND PARTICULARISTIC GOODS DISTRIBUTION

The aggregate effect of these two modes of distribution – unmonitored pre-elected gift-giving and postelection clientelism – is that there is ethnic favoritism in the distribution of particularistic goods in some, but not all, areas of the city. Chapter 5 argues that favoritism in the distribution of private goods through relational clientelism should be concentrated in poorer areas, where building individual-level patronage relationships with core voters is cost effective, but be largely absent in middle- and upper-class areas. By contrast, pre-election gift-giving is possible anywhere that there are poor voters who could be influenced by it, including in otherwise wealthy neighborhoods. In addition, Chapter 5 argues that club goods distribution should be used to attract support in both poor and middle-class neighborhoods. Instead, ethnically homogenous neighborhoods dominated by the ruling party's aligned ethnic groups should be favored with club goods. I find support for each of these claims except the last one, for which the analysis is limited by data constraints.

6.3.1 Analysis by Neighborhood

The survey data shows systematic differences in the distribution of private goods across levels of neighborhood wealth. In addition to the questions about door-to-door campaigning and pre-election gift distribution in Chapter 4, the survey included questions about the distribution of private benefits in nonelection periods, which better measure the presence of clientelism. Respondents were asked open-ended questions about whether they knew of any benefits local politicians, including the MP, had delivered to residents of their neighborhood.[49] Up to four

---

[48] Interview with NDC constituency executive, Ablekuma North constituency, Greater Accra, March 25, 2014.
[49] This involved two separate questions: "Think about your MP. Do you know of any activities or projects your MP has done for people here? This could be to help the whole

verbatim responses were recorded for each respondent and subsequently blind-coded as representing club goods or private goods. Table 6.1 lists common responses to the open-ended questions about activities of local politicians in the neighborhood. Overall, 36% of the respondents could report at least one activity engaged in by local politicians in their area; 30% of respondents could name at least one club good provided, while 10% named at least one private good. The most common private goods mentioned were support for education (typically tuition assistance), help finding jobs, and provision of loans and other direct financial support for small businesses. The private goods that most respondents reported in these open-ended questions are consistent with the more valuable clientelistic benefits described earlier – jobs, scholarships, loans for businesses – not with the much smaller-scale gifts commonly passed out during campaigns, such as small amounts of food or cash.[50] This suggests that the open-ended questions in Table 6.1 measure goods distribution that is separate from handouts provided during campaigns.

Respondents were also asked whether they knew about anyone in their neighborhood benefiting from government antipoverty programs, including key job and loan programs through which the government allocates valuable private benefits with long-term effects to individual voters.[51] Overall, 30% of respondents knew or had "heard about" a beneficiary of one of these antipoverty programs in their local area.

Reports of private goods distribution were much more common in Greater Accra's poorer neighborhoods. Figure 6.1 plots summary statistics for the open-ended questions on private and club goods delivery, the

---

community or to help individual people here. Can you give examples?"; immediately followed by: "Think about other politicians in this area. Do you know of any activities or projects other politicians have done for people here in the community? This could be to help the whole community or to help individual people here. Can you give examples?"

[50] Overall, the survey respondents appear to view small pre-election handouts in a categorically different manner from the private goods in Table 6.1. The majority of respondents (69%) reported knowing about distribution of pre-election gifts when asked about it directly, but almost none mentioned small gifts of food, cash, or clothing in response to the open-ended questions about politicians' activities.

[51] "Do you know anyone in this neighborhood here who has received a job or loan facility through a government program, such as NYEP, GYEEDA, MASLOC, or LESDEP?" The NYEP is the "National Youth Employment Program," created under the NPP government and renamed GYEEDA ("Ghana Youth Employment and Entrepreneurial Development Agency") by the NDC government. MASLOC, discussed earlier, is a microfinance loan program. LESDEP is the "Local Enterprises and Skills Development Program," which also provides microfinance and job training.

TABLE 6.1: *Typical goods delivered by local politicians*

Private Goods
Category:

Education (21%)	"help in paying school fees"	"send some people to school"	"school uniforms"
Unemployment (19%)	"jobs for the youth"	"help to acquire jobs"	"send youth to train in trade of their choice"
Money (17%)	"helped some youth financially"	"financial support"	"given money to some people"
Health (11%)	"paid people's health insurance"	"solve some [people's] medical problems free"	"bringing doctors to check our health"
Support business (7%)	"help the market women"	"help hairdressers … acquire machines"	"sharing of tailoring machines to the youth"

Club Goods
Category:

Infrastructure (48%)	"construction of roads"	"provided some streetlights"	"tarring of road"
Sanitation (23%)	"cleaning of gutters"	"built some drainages"	"sweeping the community"
Education (8%)	"school building"	"computers to some schools"	"cement to build Arabic school"
Water Supply (6%)	"water storage tanks"	"laying of pipes"	"borehole for the community"
Health (6%)	"construction of hospital"	"building of polyclinic"	"supply of hospital equipment"

Within each category (private, club) responses were coded into a list of more than 20 topics. The most common topics are listed here, with each topic's percentage within the broader category listed in parentheses. Responses are lightly edited for spelling and length.

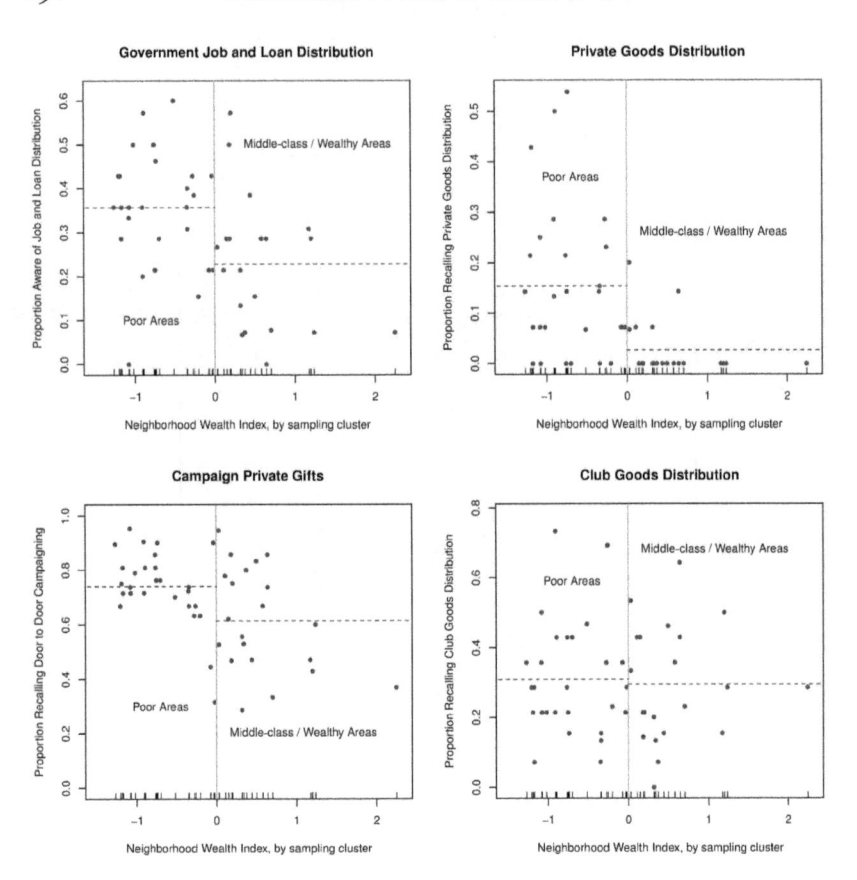

FIGURE 6.1: *Reported goods delivery by survey sampling cluster*: Each panel plots the percentage of respondents in each of the 48 sampling clusters, or neighborhoods, in the urban survey who reported knowledge of the outcome listed at the top of each panel. The x-axis is for the average value of the neighborhood wealth index for each sampling cluster. The mean neighborhood in Greater Accra is a 0 on this index. The hashed lines plot the averages across locations to the left and right of the city-wide mean.

question on whether respondents know about beneficiaries of government job and loan programs, and the question on whether respondents knew about the distribution of pre-election gifts during the campaign period. Responses are aggregated by each of the 48 sampling clusters in the survey.[52] The x-axis is the average value of a neighborhood

---

[52] There are 20 or 21 respondents per sampling cluster. See Chapter 3 and the Appendix for more detail on the sampling procedure.

6.3 Neighborhood Characteristics and Goods Distribution

wealth index calculated for each cluster of respondents.[53] The neighborhood wealth index is calculated from the first dimension of a factor analysis calculated over spatially weighted averages of census characteristics in 500-meter radii ("neighborhoods"; see Chapter 2) around each respondent. The index includes data on household assets, education, and employment.[54] The index is scaled in standard deviations from a city-wide mean of 0.

The top two panels of Figure 6.1 are consistent with relational clientelism being concentrated in poorer neighborhoods. On average, 36% of respondents in the poorer (below average) survey locations – and as many as 60% in one location – knew recipients of the government antipoverty programs, as shown in the top-left panel of Figure 6.1. Only 23%, on average, knew about recipients in the middle- and upper-class neighborhoods (above average), with fewer than 10% aware of recipients in the wealthiest neighborhoods, as measured by the neighborhood wealth index. For the open-ended question on private goods delivery (top-right panel), an average of 15% of respondents in poor neighborhoods could name specific instances of private goods distribution by politicians, compared to just 3% in the middle- and upper-class neighborhoods. Zero respondents reported any private goods distribution at all in more than three-quarters of the middle-class and wealthy locations – even poor respondents who live in these neighborhoods and still demand private goods.

The bottom-left panel of Figure 6.1 shows that while there are relatively more reports of gift-giving by the parties in poor neighborhoods during the campaign, some gift-giving occurs in both poor and wealthier neighborhoods. A majority of respondents are still aware of this gift distribution in most neighborhoods with wealth above the city-wide average. This is consistent with parties being able to engage in unmonitored gift giving in a less-targeted fashion even in places where they have greater difficulty sustaining relationships with individual voters. The final

---

[53] I aggregate individual respondent-level scores on this index to the sampling cluster level in Figure 6.1 for visualization purposes only.
[54] The index includes: % with running water (which can be privately provided by wealthier residents via tanker or borehole in absence of state provision), % with a flush toilet, % with electricity (available to all who can afford a connection), % in a single-family home (excluding informal structures), % with a computer; % adults with more than a middle school education, and % adults employed in the formal or public sectors. Variables that exclusively measure service provision are excluded from the index so that it primarily captures differences in the private wealth of residents. This index is described in more detail in the Appendix.

panel shows that local politicians were reported to deliver club goods at fairly equal rates in poorer and middle- and upper-class neighborhoods. This is consistent with the claim in Chapter 5 that the distribution of club goods should be a key feature of distributive politics in both slums and middle-class areas of a city.

These differences persist after controlling for individual-level characteristics of the respondents and for other characteristics of their neighborhoods. Table 6.2 reports the results of a series of multilevel logistic regression models in which the outcome variables are binary indicators for the questions in Figure 6.1. The models include a series of individual-level controls and parliamentary constituency fixed effects, to account for baseline differences in distributive strategies across constituencies, as the main party leaders controlling the microlevel targeting of particularistic goods are at the constituency and district level (see Chapter 2).[55] I also control for population density and 2008 presidential vote share in the Electoral Area (ward) of each sampling cluster, to account for possible partisan patterns in goods distribution. The key explanatory variable in columns 1–3 is the neighborhood wealth index. The main explanatory variable in column 4 is the percentage of residents in the respondent's neighborhood from ethnic groups traditionally aligned with the NDC, the ruling party at the time of the survey.[56]

Similar to Figure 6.1, I find that neighborhood wealth predicts whether respondents report private goods distribution, but not club goods distribution. Simulating from column 1, as a respondent moves from a neighborhood one standard deviation below the city-wide mean in wealth to a neighborhood one standard deviation above, the respondent is 12 percentage points (95% CI: $-1.7, 25.3, p = 0.08$) less likely to be aware of people in her neighborhood benefiting from the government job or loan programs. Simulating from column 2, as a respondent moves from a neighborhood one standard deviation below the city-wide mean in wealth to a neighborhood one standard deviation above the mean, the

---

[55] As noted in Chapter 2, constituencies nest within districts. The individual-level controls are age, gender, an indicator for being a Muslim, indicators for each major ethnic category, the education/employment and assets indices described in Chapters 2 and 3, and two indicators for the quality of the survey interview: whether respondents were reported as being cooperative and whether the enumerator made errors in filling out the survey form.

[56] This is the combined Northern, Ewe, and Ga population percentages. The 2008 presidential vote share control variable is dropped when the ethnicity share variable is included because these are strongly correlated.

6.3 Neighborhood Characteristics and Goods Distribution

TABLE 6.2: *Respondent reports of goods distribution (urban sample)*

Outcome	1 Jobs and Loans	2 Private Goods	3 Club Goods	4 Club Goods
Neighborhood Wealth Index (500m)	−0.324† (0.188)	−1.362† (0.696)	0.101 (0.179)	0.181 (0.189)
NDC-aligned groups % (500m)				2.786 (1.848)
NDC 2008 Pres. Vote Share (by ELA)	−2.419 (1.744)	−4.375 (4.344)	1.901 (1.625)	
Population Density (by sampling cluster)	0.017* (0.007)	0.026 (0.017)	0.014† (0.007)	0.016* (0.007)
Years in Neighborhood	0.016* (0.008)	0.003 (0.012)	0.015† (0.008)	0.013† (0.008)
Age	0.001 (0.008)	0.011 (0.013)	−0.010 (0.008)	−0.009 (0.008)
Muslim	0.735* (0.366)	0.544 (0.534)	−0.150 (0.373)	−0.116 (0.371)
Male	0.111 (0.185)	0.318 (0.308)	−0.034 (0.183)	−0.034 (0.182)
Ewe	0.207 (0.244)	0.115 (0.438)	−0.134 (0.245)	−0.106 (0.244)
Northerner	−0.685† (0.389)	−0.394 (0.566)	−0.175 (0.390)	−0.169 (0.385)
Ga-Dangme	−0.168 (0.246)	0.717† (0.414)	0.407† (0.231)	0.401† (0.228)
Education/Employment Index	−0.050 (0.108)	0.074 (0.177)	0.158 (0.105)	0.153 (0.105)
Assets Index	0.048 (0.111)	−0.260 (0.197)	−0.145 (0.109)	−0.139 (0.108)
Constituency FEs	Y	Y	Y	Y
N	669	669	669	669

***p < 0.001, **p < 0.01, *p < 0.05, †*p* < 0.1. Multilevel logistic regressions with intercepts partially pooled by sampling cluster, as in Gelman and Hill (2007). All models include parliamentary constituency fixed effects. The outcome in column 1 is whether a respondent is aware of people in the neighborhood benefiting from government job and loan programs. The outcome in column 2 is whether a respondent listed any private good among the goods she is aware of local politicians delivering in her neighborhood. The outcome in columns 3 and 4 is whether a respondent listed any club good among the goods she is aware of local politicians delivering in her neighborhood. These questions were only asked to a randomly chosen two-thirds of respondents in each location. Akan is the omitted ethnicity category. Results for the corresponding model for the question on pre-election gift-giving are in Chapter 4.

respondent is 18 percentage points (95% CI: −0.4, 34.8, $p = 0.051$) less likely to name at least one private good in response to the open-ended question about activities by local politicians. Importantly, these differences persist even when restricting the models in columns 1 and 2 to poor respondents only; the poor respondents who live in middle- and upper-class neighborhoods are still significantly less likely to be aware of private goods delivery by politicians than similarly poor respondents in poor neighborhoods. In addition, because I include constituency fixed effects, each model examines variation in the distribution of private goods across neighborhood wealth *within* each jurisdiction. Columns 1 and 2 suggest that the clientelistic allocation of private goods is concentrated in the relatively poorest neighborhoods within each constituency.

In Column 3, however, I find that neighborhood wealth does not predict whether respondents report club goods delivery, consistent with politicians distributing club goods in both poor and middle- and upper-class neighborhoods. The estimated change in the probability that a respondent reports club goods distribution between a neighborhood one standard deviation below the city-wide mean in neighborhood wealth and a neighborhood one standard deviation above is only 3.6 percentage points, with a 95% confidence interval of −9.8 to 17.2 ($p = 0.57$).

Finally, column 4 explores the other main prediction about neighborhood characteristics and distributive politics in Chapter 5: that ethnically homogenous neighborhoods at all levels of wealth that are dominated by groups aligned with the ruling party will be favored in the allocation of club goods. Column 4 shows that respondents are 24.2 percentage points more likely to be aware of club goods distribution by politicians in a neighborhood in which 75% of the population is from the NDC's aligned ethnic groups than in a neighborhood in which only 25% of the population is from aligned groups, but this result is not statistically significant (95% CI: −9.3, 51.2, $p = 0.13$). The open-ended questions on goods delivery on the survey at best provide only a very noisy test for possible favoritism in club goods distribution because respondents' self-reports do not distinguish which level of government delivered a particular good. Chapter 2 explains that local governments and MPs, who can be from different political parties, simultaneously distribute separate sets of funding for club goods. If opposition MPs and the ruling party leaders who control local governments target different sets of voters, aggregate patterns of favoritism in survey responses can become muddled. Despite this data limitation, I show in Chapter 7 that survey respondents have strong expectations that the ruling party will engage in ethnic favoritism in distribution of club goods, especially in ethnically homogenous neighborhoods dominated by its aligned groups.[57]

6.3.2 Costs of Clientelism across Neighborhoods

Poor residents of middle- and upper-class neighborhoods in Greater Accra demand private goods from politicians at similar rates as poor residents in poor neighborhoods. If politicians' distributive strategies were a simple function of voter demands, the result that private goods distribution is rarely reported in wealthier neighborhoods – even by poor respondents – should not hold. But politicians in Greater Accra face significantly higher costs to sustaining successful clientelistic relationships with the poor voters who live in middle- and upper-class areas compared to poor voters in slums.

When asked who benefits from the jobs and loans distributed through government antipoverty programs, a poor focus group participant in Dzorwulu, a wealthy neighborhood in Accra, said: "This area consists of high-class people of the society. So when such things are given, they rather give it to those parts, the slum areas surrounding here, because they are in need. It seems like sometimes the government thinks, 'These people ... they don't need such things, so why not channel it to the slum zones?'" But the participant noted that despite living in a wealthier area, he himself was just as poor as those in the slums (he lived in a temporary wooden structure) and he also wanted these benefits. "Government thinks that because you are here, in this residential area, you have money," he said.[58]

The reason he is excluded may have more to do with the costs of maintaining individual-level patronage relationships with poor voters in wealthier neighborhoods than misperceptions about his poverty. Poor voters in wealthier neighborhoods can be more transient and often live in less communal forms of housing than poor voters in slums, providing less opportunity for daily interaction with others in the community. Both make it difficult for local party agents to "know" poor voters in the ways described earlier, increasing the costs of sustaining relational clientelism. Many poor residents who live in wealthier neighborhoods in Greater Accra are there as household staff, laborers on construction

---

[57] Chapter 8 uses data on flows of particular club goods most likely to be controlled by district (municipal) governments to show that benefits are targeted to co-ethnic and ruling-party neighborhoods.

[58] Focus group, Dzorwulu, Ayawaso West constituency, Greater Accra, June 21, 2013.

projects, or street-side shopkeepers. Others live as "caretakers," invited to squat on property under construction to keep watch.[59] The remaining poor residents are squatters, often in temporary structures in empty or uncompleted lots.

On average, residents of Greater Accra's slums have lived in their neighborhoods for much longer than similarly poor residents living in otherwise middle- or upper-class neighborhoods.[60] I subset the survey data to the lowest socioeconomic status respondents in the survey sample as measured by the education and employment index used in Chapters 2 and 4.[61] Poor respondents in neighborhoods with below-average scores on the neighborhood wealth index had lived in their community for a median of 15 years. By contrast, similarly poor residents in neighborhoods with above-average wealth had lived in their community for a median of only 6 years, just 1.5 electoral cycles in Ghana.[62] The poorest residents in neighborhoods with above-average wealth were also 3.5 times more likely to report living as "caretakers" (15.3% vs. 4.4%) and 1.7 times more likely to report living as squatters than similarly poor residents in slums (8.8% vs. 5.1%). In the interviews, party agents argued that the transience of poor voters in middle- and upper-class neighborhoods renders sustained relationships more difficult; a local NPP activist in a middle-class area noted that there is little guarantee that a poor caretaker or roadside shopkeeper who receives financial support from him will even be in the area to vote for the party by the next election.[63]

In addition, poor residents living outside of slums are much harder for parties to monitor than poor residents in slums. The poor in slums often live in compound houses, sharing cooking areas and toilet facilities with many other families, facilitating regular interaction with local party agents, while poor voters in wealthier neighborhoods are more likely to live separately in single-family accommodations, leaving them

---

[59] Gough and Yankson (2011).
[60] Despite these average differences between poor residents in slums and in wealthier neighborhoods, Paller (2018) shows that the security of property rights varies across different slums within Greater Accra, with illegal settlements such as Agbogbloshie where residents live under regular threat of eviction alongside more permanent slums where residents have relatively secure property rights, such as Nima, Jamestown, and Ashaiman.
[61] These are respondents who have no secondary education, no English literacy, and no formal-sector employment.
[62] These differences also hold when calculated as a percentage of each respondent's life.
[63] Interview with NPP party agent, Okaikwei Central constituency, Greater Accra, March 19, 2014.

less easily observable and less socially connected to neighborhood life. More than three-quarters (77%) of the poorest respondents in neighborhoods with below-average wealth on the survey lived in compound houses, compared to only 35% of the poorest respondents in neighborhoods with above-average wealth. The poorest respondents in wealthier neighborhoods were nearly twice as likely to live in uncompleted, temporary structures, such as wooden kiosks, than the poorest respondents in slums (25.5% vs. 13.3%), and more than three times as likely to live in single-family homes (29.2% vs. 9.6%).

6.4 COMPARISON TO RURAL AREAS

These overall patterns of distributive politics differ in rural areas in a manner consistent with the extension of the argument in Chapter 5 to rural areas. Comparing urban and rural areas reveals several key differences. First, there appears to be less direct individual-level clientelism between parties and voters in most rural villages than in poor urban neighborhoods, although this is less true in large rural towns, which are more similar to urban slums. Second, parties interact with rural voters through intermediaries more often than they do in urban areas. Third, parties place relatively more emphasis on club goods than private goods distribution in rural areas, as the greater levels of ethnic homogeneity in most rural communities allow parties to more efficiently target entire communities with club benefits while avoiding the organizational costs of individual-level clientelism.

Rural areas in Ghana have several distinct features that alter politicians' incentives for distributive politics. Rural communities are far more ethnically homogeneous on average than cities, as shown in Chapter 1. Although there can be settlers and migrants from other ethnic groups, the typical rural village is dominated by a single indigenous ethnic group. Ethnic homogeneity means that targeting club goods to entire villages and monitoring those villages' subsequent aggregate election results becomes a more efficient means to target benefits to blocs of voters and monitor their compliance than developing direct relationships with large numbers of voters at an individual level.

In addition, chiefs and other traditional leaders from the locally dominant group typically own the agricultural land in each rural district and have other social and economic authority in the community that makes them far more influential in local affairs than in urban areas, where chiefs are absent among most ethnic groups.[64] The presence of these traditional elites provides parties with intermediaries they can use to coordinate support within villages without having to directly engage with voters on an individual level. Population density is also much lower than in cities, with fewer voters per community for party agents to mobilize. This is especially the case in rural villages, but less true in larger rural towns, where population densities and housing arrangements are more similar to urban slums.

The implications of these characteristics for distributive politics were well summarized in an interview with an NDC constituency executive who had a unique perspective on how his party engages with voters differently in the city versus the countryside. He led the NDC's local organization in Krowor, an urban constituency in Greater Accra, from 2005 through the 2008 election and then switched to being a constituency party executive in his ancestral home area, the rural Akropong constituency in the Eastern Region. When asked about differences in how the party engages with voters in these constituencies, he explained:

> In Akropong [*the rural area*] the money [distributed to voters] will not be so much like in Krowor [*the urban area*]. In Krowor, the money is more. Because in Akropong you have 11 or 12 villages comprising the constituency ... You need to travel from one town to another town, some villages are up on mountains ... If they need something you can go help them by, let's say, building a public toilet ... In Accra here people will be coming to you differently ... People will be coming to you because almost everybody knows you. In Akropong, they wouldn't know you. The village leaders will know this man is good, so let's go support him, and then they [the voters] all follow. But in Accra it's not like that. In Accra you have to work so hard house to house ... In Akropong Township it's done like that, but just in the main town ... But in some villages where it's not a big place, you tell the NDC coordinator who is in that village to organize people who love your party to come for a meeting and then you can go and talk to them together. You don't go to each house. You go to somebody's house in the villages if the person is an opinion leader, just for really important people. But in Greater Accra you need to move to all the individual work places, shops [to interact with voters].[65]

The party leader highlighted several rural–urban contrasts. First, he said it is more difficult for the party to engage with individual voters in far-flung villages in the rural constituency than in the urban constituency, or

---

[64] Chapter 7 explores an exception: ethnic groups in urban areas that have powerful chiefs in the city.
[65] Interview with former NDC constituency executive, Krowor constituency, Greater Accra, March 19, 2014.

6.4 Comparison to Rural Areas

in the larger rural town. Instead, he described the party engaging with voters in rural villages all at once, either by providing a club good that brings benefits to an entire village (building a public toilet) or by working through existing village leaders. Second, while the party leader still noted a strategy of favoring core supporters, gathering those "who love your party" for rallies or meetings in each village at which attendees are often given gifts and small amounts of money, his description does not suggest that the local party organization is directly engaging with these supporters through sustained clientelistic relationships. But he suggested that direct relationships with party agents can be common in the urban area.

These differences can be seen more systematically in data from the companion survey in rural areas analyzed in Chapter 3. I focus first on the reports of club goods delivery. Rural respondents were significantly more likely to report the delivery of club goods than urban respondents, consistent with the argument of the NDC leader about the greater importance of club goods distribution in villages. Overall, 42% of respondents reported a club good for the open-ended questions about politicians' activities compared to 30% of urban respondents. Rural respondents were particularly likely to report that politicians had delivered club goods to their communities when they lived in smaller, less-developed villages in comparison to larger rural towns. This can be seen after splitting the rural responses by the same neighborhood wealth index used above. In rural areas, this index captures differences in the overall levels of development between communities. Large towns typically have better infrastructure and better-educated populations and thus score higher on the index than small villages. In rural sampling locations with below-median values on the neighborhood wealth index, 54% of rural respondents reported knowing about club goods distribution by local politicians. Only 32% of respondents reported club goods distribution from rural sampling locations with above-median values on the index, similar to the urban average.[66]

Responses about private goods delivery also differ between urban and rural areas. While urban and rural respondents were similarly likely overall to report that private goods had been delivered (10% urban vs. 9% rural), the response rate in urban areas includes wealthier neighborhoods where little private goods distribution is reported (see Figure 6.1). The

---

[66] There are similar differences in the summary statistics when splitting sampling locations by total population.

distribution of private goods was reported in the poorest urban neighborhoods at significantly higher rates than in almost all of the rural survey locations. For example, in five of the poorest urban survey locations more than 30% of respondents reported that these types of private goods had been delivered to residents, higher than the percentage reporting private goods in all 25 rural survey locations. In six rural survey locations, no respondents reported any private goods delivery at all, similar to the many wealthier survey locations in the urban sample where no private goods delivery was reported (see Figure 6.1).[67]

There may be less direct private goods distribution from parties to voters in rural areas for two reasons, both outlined in Chapter 5. First, parties have less reason to invest in building relationships with individual voters if they can rely on powerful local elites to serve as intermediaries. Consistent with this difference, the urban and rural respondents reported significantly different rates of interaction with traditional leaders. Only 15% of urban respondents in Greater Accra reported meeting with a chief or other traditional leader in the last year, with many of these responses coming from the indigenous Ga ethnic group. By contrast, 42% of rural respondents reported interactions with a traditional leader in their local community in the last year. Second, although Ghana's parties do have similar committees of party activists at rural polling stations, it is less efficient for the parties to empower grassroots agents to serve as clientelistic intermediaries, with control over the distribution of valuable private goods, in less densely populated rural villages compared to large rural towns or urban slums, where a single party agent can reach many more voters. This is especially true given the presence of readily available substitutes in many villages that already have other built-in forms of influence over voters.

Table 6.3 provides quantitative evidence consistent with these two reasons for an urban–rural difference in private goods distribution. In models similar to Table 6.2, I regress binary indicator variables for whether the rural survey respondents know about the different types of goods delivery on a series of individual characteristics of respondents, as

---

[67] Episodic pre-election gift-giving remains common in rural areas, however. In the rural areas, 86% of respondents knew about or "heard about" the distribution of small gifts during the campaign, more than the 69% who knew of these handouts before the election in urban areas. Unconditional gifts can be given even in areas where a party does not have a dense local organization because this does not require longer-term relationships with voters.

TABLE 6.3: *Respondent reports of private goods distribution (rural sample)*

	1	2
Outcome	Private	Jobs/Loans
Neighborhood Wealth Index (2km)	−0.167	1.069*
	(0.525)	(0.450)
Met Chief	0.794†	0.276
	(0.455)	(0.302)
Party Member	0.694	0.588†
	(0.468)	(0.352)
Age	−0.024	−0.008
	(0.017)	(0.010)
Male	0.399	0.179
	(0.446)	(0.291)
Muslim	0.862	0.087
	(0.993)	(0.672)
Ewe	−1.919†	0.756
	(1.109)	(0.613)
Northerner	−1.144	−0.397
	(0.841)	(0.599)
Education/Employ. Index	0.029	0.087
	(0.212)	(0.141)
Assets Index	0.343†	−0.048
	(0.198)	(0.147)
Constituency FEs	Y	Y
N	321	321

*** $p < 0.001$, ** $p < 0.01$, * $p < 0.05$, † $p < 0.1$. Multilevel logistic regressions with intercepts partially pooled by sampling cluster, as in Gelman and Hill (2007). The outcome in column 1 is whether a respondent listed any private good among the goods she is aware of local politicians delivering in her neighborhood. The outcome in column 2 is whether a respondent is aware of people in the community benefiting from government job and loan programs. These questions were only asked to a randomly chosen two-thirds of respondents in each location. Akan is the omitted ethnicity category. Ga-Dangme is also omitted because all Ga-Dangme respondents were in one constituency (Lower Manya Krobo).

well as the neighborhood wealth index.[68] In each column of Table 6.3, I also include indicators for whether each respondent is a member of a political party and has met with a traditional chief in the last year.

---

[68] Because rural communities can be much more spatially dispersed than urban neighborhoods, I now calculate the neighborhood wealth index as a weighted average of census characteristics in a 2km radius around respondents, rather than the narrower 500m radius used for the urban sample.

Voters with direct ties to traditional chiefs were more likely to be among the small minority (9%) of rural respondents who reported private goods delivery in the open-ended questions about politicians' activities. In column 1 of Table 6.3, I estimate that respondents in each rural constituency are 6.4 percentage points (95% CI: −0.5, 14.3, $p = 0.08$) more likely to report private goods delivery if they have met with a traditional chief in the past year. The probability of reporting private goods delivery on the open-ended questions is nearly zero among rural respondents who did not interact with their local chief in the last year. This is consistent with many of the private goods that do reach rural voters being delivered through chiefs who serve as intermediaries for parties. In addition, in a similar model in which the outcome is an indicator for whether the respondent knew about the distribution of small gifts during the campaign period, rural respondents who had interacted with chiefs were significantly more likely to be aware of these activities. But contact with traditional chiefs does not predict whether respondents knew about politicians distributing either type of private goods in similar models among all non-Ga respondents in the urban survey.

In column 2 of Table 6.3 I analyze the question about whether respondents knew recipients of the official government job and loan programs – such as NYEP and MASLOC – described earlier. Rural respondents were significantly more likely to know recipients of these programs in more developed sampling locations – the rural towns – than in less developed villages. Respondents are 29.0 percentage points (95% CI: 5.7, 49.3) more likely to know recipients of the government job and loan programs in the most developed town (Kpando, Kpando constituency) compared to the least developed village in the rural survey (Apatem, Offinso North constituency). This is the exact opposite of the pattern for urban areas, seen in Figure 6.1 and Table 6.2, where respondents were most likely to know about these valuable private benefits being distributed by the government in the poorest neighborhoods. But as described in the quote above from the NDC party leader, the parties may only distribute these types of benefits in major towns in rural areas where they have invested in organizations capable of maintaining relationships with individual recipients.

The results in Table 6.3 have implications for differences in voting behavior between rural and urban areas. If these patterns of private goods distribution inform voters' expectations, poor voters in rural villages and poor voters from local ethnic minority groups who do not have close ties to local chiefs should not expect many private benefits from the government regardless of which party wins the election. Chapter 5 suggests that these voters' expectations about club goods will become most important in their voting decisions. Cross-ethnic voting can emerge along the lines of Ichino and Nathan (2013a) when voters live in rural villages where they expect more club goods after the election from a party aligned with other ethnic groups, but expect few private benefits from their own ethnically aligned party. While Chapter 5 argues that similar behavior is likely in wealthier urban neighborhoods, another area where I show that few private goods are distributed as direct clientelism, this differs from urban slums, where voters can expect favoritism in access to private goods through clientelistic relationships with party agents. I explore vote choice in urban areas in Chapter 7.

6.5 SUMMARY

This chapter provides descriptive evidence of several key features of distributive politics in Greater Accra. First, I document that Ghana's major parties engage in two different types of private goods distribution in the city – episodic gift-giving and relational clientelism – that have different goals, target different types of voters, and are used at different points in the electoral cycle. Second, I present evidence that the latter form of private goods distribution – relational clientelism – is concentrated in poor urban slums, while largely absent in Greater Accra's middle- and upper-class neighborhoods. The chapter also describes how the ways in which parties engage with voters in the city differ from their approaches in rural areas, suggesting that there may be more individual-level clientelism in Greater Accra's slums than in the typical rural village in Ghana.

This evidence helps explain the next link in the trap outlined in Figure 1.1. Chapter 4 shows that nonprogrammatic appeals persist despite the growth of the urban middle class. The present chapter shows the common forms those nonprogrammatic appeals take at the local level. Chapter 7 demonstrates the connection between these nonprogrammatic modes of distribution and the continued importance of ethnic competition in urban politics.

7

Neighborhood Context, Expectations of Favoritism, and Voting

> "We have tried since the elections to ask ourselves why the results did not favor us ... Verbally, my candidate was superior ... The development that NDC did far outweighs what NPP did ... But all in all, it could not sway them ... Some of the Akans feel that they were worse off under the NDC – that they were the <u>worst</u> off."
>
> – NDC constituency executive, Ablekuma North constituency, Greater Accra, March 2014

In 2014, an NDC constituency executive explained why he thinks his party lost the 2012 elections in Ablekuma North, an Akan-majority constituency in Accra. This had been his first election serving in party leadership and he was (perhaps naively) optimistic during the campaign that the NDC could significantly expand its support in the constituency. The party had nominated a young, charismatic parliamentary candidate, who the party leader was certain had a more compelling message than the incumbent NPP MP. He also believed that the performance of the national NDC government would sway voters to his party's side, describing several club goods the NDC had delivered to the constituency during the campaign period, such as paved roads and new gutters to prevent flooding. But none of this seemed to work. The NDC lost Ablekuma North in 2012 with 38.5% of the presidential vote, essentially identical to the 38.1% they secured in 2008, when the party was in opposition and had invested fewer resources there.[1]

---

[1] The NDC's parliamentary candidate won 38.3% in 2012 compared to 38.1% in 2008.

The party leader's explanation for why nothing changed (quoted above) came down to ethnicity: most Akans in his area still would not support the NDC. He did not accuse them of blindly supporting the NPP – the party with which their ethnic group is traditionally aligned. Instead, he thought Akans in Ablekuma North stuck with the NPP because they felt that they were worse off under the NDC government than they would have been under the NPP, and, in fact, had been the "worst off" under the NDC government of any ethnic group. "They have still not forgiven us," he said, for favoring other groups. His party's campaign efforts had not been enough to overcome Akan voters' expectations of favoritism.[2] Despite everything the NDC had done for the constituency, Akan voters in Ablekuma North still expected they would get even more from the NPP if it were elected instead. Not everywhere in Greater Accra was like Ablekuma North, however. Even as this NDC party leader lamented his inability to convince Akan voters to move away from the NPP, there were other parts of Greater Accra in 2012 where many Akan voters did *not* support the NPP presidential candidate and instead crossed ethnic lines to back the NDC.

Chapter 5 argues that voters' *relative expectations* of which party is most likely to benefit them in the distribution of particularistic goods are a key factor in voting decisions and suggests that these expectations vary depending on where voters live within a city. In turn, this can produce significant neighborhood-level variation in ethnic voting, depending on the wealth and ethnic composition of voters' local contexts.[3] In areas dominated by a single ethnic group – such as the many Akan-majority neighborhoods within Ablekuma North – voters will expect to receive more club goods after the election from the party affiliated with that dominant group. Moreover, in slum neighborhoods, where Chapter 6 shows that relational clientelism favoring core supports is common, voters will expect more private benefits if their affiliated party is in power. But there are other types of neighborhoods where Chapter 5 predicts that similar voters should be less likely to support an ethnically aligned party: (i) diverse, middle- and upper-class neighborhoods, where voters should

---

[2] Interview with NDC constituency executive, Ablekuma North constituency, Greater Accra, March 25, 2014.

[3] As discussed in Chapter 2, I define ethnic voting as whether a voter supports an ethnically aligned political party, not only as the match between the ethnicity of voter and candidate. Below I note, however, that the results in this chapter are also robust to using a narrower definition of ethnic voting that restricts the analysis only to voters from the same ethnic categories as each presidential candidate.

expect to receive similar amounts of club goods regardless of which party wins and have little expectation of receiving valuable private benefits after the election from any party; and (ii) neighborhoods where a voter's ethnic group is a local minority, especially when these areas are wealthier, where a voter can expect to benefit more from club goods targeted to her neighborhood by a nonaligned party and may not expect private goods from any party.

This chapter examines this argument using data from the main survey analyzed throughout the book, including an original survey experiment on voters' expectations of favoritism. The analysis focuses primarily on voting in presidential elections to study the contest with the greatest influence on distribution of state resources, and to hold candidate characteristics – such as ethnicity, policy programs, and economic performance – fixed, comparing voters facing the same exact choice across neighborhoods.

I find that voters in diverse, middle- and upper-class neighborhoods are less likely to support their ethnically aligned party than voters in homogenous or poor neighborhoods. Voters living as local minorities in middle- and upper-class neighborhoods dominated by ethnic groups affiliated with the opposite political party are also more likely to vote across ethnic lines. But ethnic voting remains prevalent throughout Greater Accra's slums, regardless of their ethnic composition, as well as among voters living in neighborhoods where they are in the ethnic majority. The survey experiment provides support for the hypothesized mechanism for these neighborhood-level differences, showing that voters' expectations of benefiting from each party after the election in the distribution of club and private goods vary in line with the predictions in Chapter 5.

The chapter also evaluates and rules out alternative explanations for intra-urban variation in vote choice. First, even though Greater Accra's middle class has grown significantly, socioeconomic status does not predict whether voters support ethnically affiliated parties, in contrast with modernization theories. Second, there is no evidence of less ethnic voting among voters for whom ethnic identity is less salient, in contrast to expressive theories of ethnic voting. Third, ethnic voting does not vary with indicators of cross-ethnic social interaction, in contrast to a contact hypothesis.[4] The neighborhood-level variation also runs in the opposite direction of an ethnic threat hypothesis.[5] Fourth, and closely

---

[4] Allport (1954).
[5] Key (1949).

related, these patterns are unlikely to be explained by differences in local media and information environments. Fifth, I show that voters' ties to rural homelands and ethnic migrants' associations do not explain voting behavior, in contrast to theories that regard the rural–urban migration experience as a central factor in urban political behavior.[6] Sixth, and most importantly, I show that this spatial variation in voting behavior is unlikely to have emerged from endogenous sorting into different neighborhoods.[7]

7.1 VOTE CHOICE IN PRESIDENTIAL ELECTIONS

The main analysis explores the 2012 presidential election in Greater Accra. After introducing the measurement approach and coding of the outcome variable, I document neighborhood-level variation in ethnic voting. I then test the two core predictions of the theory in Chapter 5 about where there should be less ethnic voting in urban areas. For purposes of comparison, the section ends by examining similar patterns in concurrent parliamentary elections.

7.1.1 Data and Measurement

Data on voting behavior comes from the survey of Greater Accra analyzed throughout the book. The central quantity of interest is whether a voter's ethnicity predicts how she voted. I code ethnic voting as support for the presidential candidate of the party aligned with each respondent's ethnic group.[8] For Akan respondents, this means support for the NPP; for Ewe, Ga, and Northern respondents, support for the NDC.[9] Respondents who do not have an aligned party are dropped when the outcome is ethnic voting.

The measurement of self-reported vote choices takes care to minimize misreporting bias. Respondents were asked to mark their vote choices on a confidential ballot, obscured from the enumerator, and to place it

---

[6] Gugler and Flanagan (1978) and Gugler (2002).
[7] Tiebout (1956) and Schelling (1971).
[8] I argue in Chapter 2 that this definition of ethnic voting is most appropriate for party systems in which parties are aligned with coalitions of ethnic groups that vote as blocs in favor of the same party. But the results are robust to using a narrower definition in which I restrict analysis only to Akans and Northerners, the two categories of voters with co-ethnics in the presidential race.
[9] 181 respondents reported that they are members of two ethnic groups because of mixed parentage. They are coded as members of the primary ethnic group they mentioned to enumerators when I defined ethnic voting and I then control for whether respondents also have membership in another ethnic group in the analysis.

in a sealed box, rather than being asked about these choices outright. This replicates a procedure from Carlson (2014, 2015) that has been shown to mitigate desirability and nonresponse bias in self-reported vote data. Nonresponse was only 4% using this procedure, significantly lower than in questions on vote choice in the Afrobarometer and other similar surveys. Responses in the survey closely match the real election results, suggesting that there was little post-hoc over-reporting of support for one party: 53% of respondents reported voting for the NDC and 45% for the NPP, compared to 52% and 47% in the same parliamentary constituencies in official 2012 results. Vote choice was also only measured for respondents who reported turning out to vote in the 2012 the election; the survey did not ask respondents to speculate about how they might have voted.[10]

The main explanatory variables – neighborhood wealth and neighborhood ethnic diversity – are measured from the enumeration area-level census data, as the spatially weighted averages of census characteristics in 500-meter radii around each respondent discussed in Chapter 2.[11] Neighborhood ethnic diversity is calculated from the spatially weighted ethnic group shares around each respondent as 1 minus the standard Herfindahl fractionalization index for the ten major ethnic categories on Ghana's census. Higher values correspond to a more diverse area. Importantly, because there are sufficient numbers of poor voters living amidst otherwise wealthy neighborhoods in Greater Accra (see Chapter 2), it is possible to estimate relationships between neighborhood wealth and voting while controlling for individual socioeconomic status. The wealth and ethnic diversity of neighborhoods also are not strongly correlated, such that the six types of neighborhoods in the theory in Chapter 5 exist in the sample. In areas with above-average ethnic fractionalization, the neighborhood wealth index (defined in Chapter 6) ranges from −1.1 to 2.4. In areas with below-average fractionalization, the range is −1.4 to 3.0.

7.1.2 Neighborhood-level Variation

Overall , 76% of respondents in Greater Accra reported supporting their ethnically aligned party in the presidential election. This is lower than the

---

[10] The findings are also robust to including enumerator fixed effects to account for potential effects of enumerators' own characteristics on the responses (Adida et al. 2016).

[11] This is also explained in more detail in the Appendix.

TABLE 7.1: *Vote choice for a Group A voter.*

	Vote Choice for a Group A Voter		
	i. Ethnically Diverse Neighborhood	ii. Homogenous, Group A-dominated Neighborhood	iii. Homogeneous, Group B-dominated Neighborhood
1. Middle- or Upper-class Neighborhood	*Less ethnic voting*	*Ethnic voting for A*	*Cross-ethnic voting for B*
2. Poor or Slum Neighborhood	*Ethnic voting for A*	*Ethnic voting for A*	*Ethnic voting for A (if private goods > club goods)*

85% of respondents who reported supporting their ethnically aligned party on the companion survey of rural areas examined in Chapter 6, suggestive of an overall rural–urban difference in rates of ethnic voting.[12] But there was significant variation across the 48 sampling clusters in the urban survey in rates of ethnic voting, similar to the contrasts between the four neighborhoods highlighted in Figure 5.1. In 13 sampling locations, more than 85% of respondents reported support for their ethnically aligned party, consistent with substantial ethnic voting. But in seven locations, the rate was below 60%, with little correlation between ethnicity and vote choice in a two-party election.

The theory in Chapter 5 makes two central predictions to explain this variation, seen in Table 5.2, which is repeated here as Table 7.1. First, voters will be less likely to support ethnically aligned parties in more diverse neighborhoods, primarily when these neighborhoods are wealthier. Second, there will be cross-ethnic voting when voters are surrounded by more people aligned with a non-co-ethnic party, again especially when these neighborhoods are wealthier. In terms of absolute levels rather than

---

[12] The rural survey does not provide a representative sample of all of rural Ghana, however. Direct comparisons of rates of ethnic voting on the urban survey to other available sources, such as the Afrobarometer, are not possible because of differences in how vote choice is measured. Without comparable use of the secret ballot procedure used here, self-reports of ethnic voting on Afrobarometer surveys are likely subject to significantly more social desirability bias (Carlson 2014).

relative differences, Chapter 5 expects little correlation between ethnicity and vote choice in either of these two cells of Table 7.1. I evaluate predictions for each type of neighborhood in turn.

7.1.3 Diverse, Middle-and Upper-Class Neighborhoods

I find support for the first prediction in a series of multilevel logistic regressions, which partially pool intercepts by sampling location to account for clustering in the sample.[13] I include the measures of neighborhood wealth and ethnic fractionalization around each respondent, as defined earlier, and the population density of each survey sampling cluster. All models also include a series of individual-level controls: the assets and education/employment indices, age, gender, whether the respondent is Muslim, indicator variables for each ethnic group, whether respondents or their immediate family are party members, whether a respondent reported her ethnicity as the type of identity she feels "closest to," indicators for whether a respondent found her current home through family or ethnic group ties, and the number of years each respondent lived in the neighborhood.[14] I discuss these latter three control variables in more detail in Section 7.3. In addition, I include parliamentary constituency fixed effects to control for baseline differences in party organizations and local governments. Because much of the opportunity for favoritism in the allocation of particularistic goods in Ghana comes *within districts* and campaign strategy decisions by each party are made at the constituency level, the most appropriate level at which to test the theory is across different neighborhoods within districts and constituencies.[15]

Results for presidential vote choice are shown in Table 7.1. Column 1 begins with the control variables only. I find no evidence consistent with modernization theories that suggest that wealthier or

---

[13] Gelman and Hill (2007). Results are robust to instead clustering standard errors by location.

[14] Two additional indicators control for interview quality: whether enumerators made logistical errors (12% of interviews) or noted respondents were uncooperative (10%).

[15] I include constituency fixed effects in lieu of district fixed effects because constituency and district boundaries correspond 1:1 in the outlying areas of Greater Accra. In the largest urban districts, constituency boundaries mostly correspond to submetropolitan assemblies, a subtier of municipal government. Because of the close correspondence, it would not be possible to fit a model with both sets of fixed effects at the same time, so I defer to the more localized set of boundaries (constituencies). Note that the results in Table 7.1 are also robust to not including the constituency fixed effects or to instead including district fixed effects.

better-educated voters will be less likely to vote along ethnic lines. The education/employment and household assets indices do not predict ethnic voting – middle-class voters are just as likely as the poor to support ethnically aligned parties. This nonresult fits with the results about turnout in Chapter 4. Although their abstention is not absolute, middle-class residents who demand universalistic policies from the government – and thus may be least likely to care about instrumental incentives to support co-ethnic parties – are also those relatively most likely to have opted out of voting. The large majority of middle-class respondents who do vote are those who still demand particularistic goods, especially club goods, consistent with the evidence about preferences in Chapter 3. Their vote choices should still be sensitive to expectations about which party is most likely to benefit them with these resources.

Moreover, the salience of ethnic identity at an individual level does not predict whether respondents vote for an ethnically affiliated party, inconsistent with social attachments to ethnic groups explaining ethnic voting. I measure social identification as in Eifert et al. (2010), adapting an Afrobarometer question that asks respondents which of multiple possible identity groups they feel they closest to.[16] Overall, 48.7% of respondents named an ethnic group, as opposed to religious (28.4%), occupation-based (11.0%), location-based (7.3%), or other identity. This rate of ethnic identification is lower than in the companion survey of rural areas examined in Chapter 6, in which 57% of rural respondents listed ethnicity as their most important identity, consistent with Robinson's (2014) cross-national finding that urban residents in Africa place less emphasis on ethnic identities than rural dwellers. But naming an ethnic identity as most important does not predict vote choice in Table 7.2, inconsistent with social identification serving as a key determinant of ethnic voting.

Controlling for these individual-level characteristics of voters, however, there are significant differences in ethnic voting by similar respondents living in different neighborhoods. Higher ethnic diversity in each voter's neighborhood predicts lower support for ethnically aligned parties in column 2 of Table 7.2 ($p = 0.08$). This is consistent with less ethnic voting in more diverse neighborhoods where voters should expect

---

[16] The question is "Ghanaians describe themselves in many ways. Some people describe themselves by their ethnic group or their religion, others describe themselves in economic terms such as middle class or as a farmer, and others by the place where they live. Besides being a Ghanaian, which specific group of people do you feel you belong to first and foremost?"

TABLE 7.2: *Support for ethnically aligned party in the 2012 presidential election*

	1	2	3	4
Ethnic Fractionalization (500m)		−2.513†	−3.522*	−3.506*
		(1.428)	(1.528)	(1.529)
Neigh. Wealth (500m)		−0.163	2.091†	2.066†
		(0.170)	(1.165)	(1.164)
Eth. Fract.* Neigh. Wealth			−3.396†	−3.362†
			(1.740)	(1.739)
Pos. NDC Econ. Performance				0.149
				(0.262)
Pop. Density (by cluster)		−0.007	−0.011	−0.011
		(0.007)	(0.007)	(0.007)
Education/Employ. Index	−0.092	−0.083	−0.073	−0.079
	(0.103)	(0.104)	(0.105)	(0.105)
Assets/Wealth Index	0.036	0.074	0.066	0.064
	(0.101)	(0.107)	(0.108)	(0.108)
Ethnic Identity "Closest"	−0.095	−0.083	−0.078	−0.082
	(0.179)	(0.181)	(0.181)	(0.181)
Moved for Family / Ethnicity	0.054	0.047	0.053	0.049
	(0.205)	(0.205)	(0.206)	(0.206)
Age	0.010	0.010	0.010	0.010
	(0.008)	(0.008)	(0.008)	(0.008)
Muslim	0.020	0.137	0.141	0.126
	(0.370)	(0.374)	(0.374)	(0.375)
Male	−0.084	−0.110	−0.119	−0.124
	(0.181)	(0.182)	(0.182)	(0.183)
Ewe	0.403	0.439†	0.465†	0.452†
	(0.267)	(0.266)	(0.268)	(0.269)
Northerner	−0.865*	−0.836*	−0.859*	−0.860*
	(0.386)	(0.388)	(0.389)	(0.389)
Ga	−0.356	−0.420†	−0.402†	−0.406†
	(0.232)	(0.235)	(0.236)	(0.236)
Years in Neighborhood	0.006	0.005	0.006	0.006
	(0.008)	(0.008)	(0.008)	(0.008)
Party Member	0.223	0.226	0.242	0.241
	(0.201)	(0.202)	(0.203)	(0.203)
Constituency FEs	Y	Y	Y	Y
N	797	797	797	797

*** $p < 0.001$, ** $p < 0.01$, * $p < 0.05$, † $p < 0.1$. Logistic regressions partially pooled by sampling location. The outcome is 2012 vote choice for each respondent's co-ethnic party; those who did not vote in 2012 or who do not have a co-ethnic party are dropped from this analysis. Akan is the omitted, baseline ethnicity category. Note that the minimum value of ethnic fractionalization in the data is 0.38, not 0.

7.1 Vote Choice in Presidential Elections

Effect of Local Diversity by Neighborhood Wealth

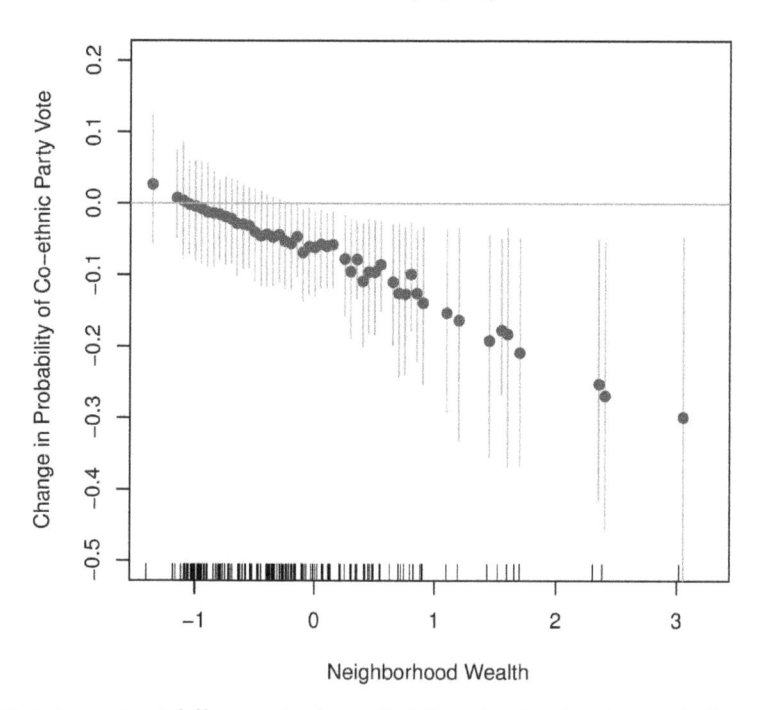

FIGURE 7.1: *First differences in the probability of voting* for the co-ethnic party after a one standard deviation increase in ethnic fractionalization in the neighborhood, across levels of neighborhood wealth, with 95% confidence intervals.

less of a difference in the club goods they receive from each party after the election. A one standard deviation (10.7 percentage point) increase in fractionalization around each respondent is associated with a 6.4 percentage point decrease in the probability of voting for an ethnically aligned party (95% CI: −12.0, −0.8).

In column 3 of Table 7.2, I interact fractionalization with neighborhood wealth. Directly in line with the first main prediction in Table 7.1, I find that ethnic voting is less common at higher levels of diversity primarily in wealthier neighborhoods ($p = 0.051$ on the interaction). Figure 7.1 plots the *change in* the probability that each respondent votes for her ethnically aligned party (y-axis) after a one standard deviation increase in ethnic fractionalization in each respondent's local neighborhood against the level of neighborhood wealth (x-axis).[17] This is similar to plotting the

---

[17] These predicted probabilities are calculated as in Hanmer and Kalkan (2013), holding covariate values, including neighborhood wealth, fixed for each respondent. As such,

regression coefficient on the relationship between neighborhood diversity and vote choice against neighborhood wealth. The rug at the bottom of Figure 7.1 gives the distribution of respondents by neighborhood wealth. Figure 7.1 shows that there is significantly less ethnic voting after a one standard deviation increase in diversity around each respondent in wealthier neighborhoods, where Chapter 6 shows that private goods distribution through relational clientelism is rare. But neighborhood ethnic diversity has no relationship with ethnic voting in the poorest neighborhoods, where individual-level clientelism remains common.

The effect of neighborhood wealth in column 3 of Table 7.2 is also as predicted. There is not a significant difference in ethnic voting from a one standard deviation increase in neighborhood wealth in the most ethnically homogeneous neighborhoods, where column *ii* of Table 7.1 predicts that respondents in both poor and wealthier neighborhoods have incentives to support ethnically affiliated parties. But there is a predicted 7.7 percentage point decrease in ethnic voting ($p = 0.051$, 95% CI: -16.3, 1.0) after similarly increasing neighborhood wealth in the most diverse neighborhoods in the sample.

These differences are large in an absolute sense. Take the example of Akan voters from the anecdote at the opening of the chapter. Simulating from column 3 of Table 7.2, I predict that an Akan respondent with covariates set at the mean among Akans in the full sample has an 82% chance (95% CI: 72%, 87%) of supporting the Akan-aligned NPP in a very poor, ethnically homogenous neighborhood, defined at the 10th percentiles of neighborhood wealth and diversity. But an identical Akan respondent has only a 50% chance (95% CI: 27%, 71%) of supporting the NPP in a neighborhood at the 90th percentiles of neighborhood wealth and diversity. This estimate is equivalent to no ethnic voting at all among Akans in the most diverse and wealthy neighborhoods; at 50% in a two-party election, a voter's ethnicity no longer provides any predictive information about her vote choice. The same simulation for an Ewe respondent – the ethnic group historically most closely associated with the NDC – yields a difference between an 88% chance (95% CI: 79%, 94%) of voting for the NDC in a neighborhood at the 10th percentiles of neighborhood wealth and diversity and only a 62% chance (95% CI: 40%, 82%) of doing so in a neighborhood at the 90th percentiles. While this suggests that Ewes remain at least marginally biased in favor of the

predicted probabilities are only identified in ranges of the x-axis where respondents exist.

7.1 Vote Choice in Presidential Elections

NDC even in the wealthiest and most diverse neighborhoods, these estimates still represent a substantively huge shift in the extent to which ethnicity predicts vote choice.

This interaction between neighborhood diversity and wealth in Figure 7.2 persists even after controlling for other variables expected to affect vote choice alongside ethnicity. In column 4, I add an indicator for whether each respondent evaluates the incumbent NDC government's economic performance positively. Positive macroeconomic performance evaluations of the NDC government are positively correlated with NDC support among all respondents, consistent with Bratton et al. (2011). But column 4 of Table 7.2 shows that controlling for performance evaluations does not alter the relationship between neighborhood characteristics and ethnic voting. Sociotropic evaluations of economic performance may cause aggregate shifts in support across the entire electorate, even as there is still neighborhood-level variation in ethnic voting based on more localized distributive incentives.[18]

7.1.4 Local Minorities in Middle- and Upper-class Neighborhoods

I also find less ethnic voting in neighborhoods where respondents live as a local minority surrounded by larger populations from ethnic groups aligned with the other party. These are neighborhoods where voters are more likely to benefit from club goods from their non-co-ethnic party. Cross-ethnic voting is especially likely in these types of neighborhoods when they are wealthier. When neighborhoods are poor, voters may still expect private goods from their ethnically affiliated party after the election. To the extent that poor voters in these neighborhoods value private goods over club goods, expectations of private benefits from a co-ethnic party in poor neighborhoods will offset incentives to vote across ethnic lines to benefit from club goods delivered by the other party. Empirically, many poor respondents in the sample appear to value access to private goods that address immediate personal economic needs at least as much as club goods that have more diffuse benefits for their neighborhoods; in the responses about preferences examined in Chapter 3, the majority of the poorest respondents demanded private goods as, or more,

---

[18] Any correlation between performance evaluations and vote choice must be interpreted with caution, however, as subjective evaluations of performance can themselves be outcomes, not causes, of vote choice (Evans and Andersen 2006, Carlson 2016).

frequently than they demanded club goods. But in middle- or upper-class neighborhoods where Chapter 6 shows that private goods distribution as clientelism after the election is rare, there is little reason to expect significant private goods from any party after the election. Voters from local ethnic minority groups then have incentives to vote for the party affiliated with the local majority in anticipation of receiving more club benefits from that party instead.

I test this second prediction by examining how support for the NDC varies with the population percentage of NDC- and NPP-aligned groups in each respondent's neighborhood. I estimate similar models to Table 7.2, but change the outcome to a binary indicator for NDC vote and replace neighborhood ethnic fractionalization with the share of the population from each major ethnic group in the 500-meter radius around each respondent.[19] I do not initially find results in line with the prediction in Table 7.1 in the full sample of respondents. But this changes once respondents from Greater Accra's indigenous Ga ethnic group are removed. The relationship between neighborhood ethnic composition and the behavior of Ga voters differs from that of other ethnic groups and is explored separately in the final section of the chapter.

Once Gas are removed, I find cross-ethnic voting in middle- and upper-class neighborhoods when voters live in an area dominated by the other party's core ethnic groups. Figure 7.2 is set up similarly to Figure 7.1. It plots the *change in* the probability that each respondent votes for the NDC after a one standard deviation increase in the population percentage of a specific ethnic group in the neighborhood (y-axis) against the wealth of the neighborhood (x-axis). The left panel of Figure 7.2 shows that increasing the NPP-aligned Akan population around each respondent predicts lower NDC support (and thus greater NPP support), but only at higher levels of neighborhood wealth.[20] In the poorest neighborhoods in the survey, increasing the Akan population percentage around each respondent has no clear impact on predicted support for the NDC. But in a middle-class neighborhood with a score on the neighborhood wealth index 1.1 standard deviations above the city-wide mean, living in a neighborhood with a 15 percentage point larger Akan population share is correlated with respondents being 11 percentage points less likely to

---

[19] Results are substantively equivalent with the outcome instead as a binary indicator for NPP vote.
[20] $p = 0.04$ on the interaction between Akan population percentage and neighborhood wealth.

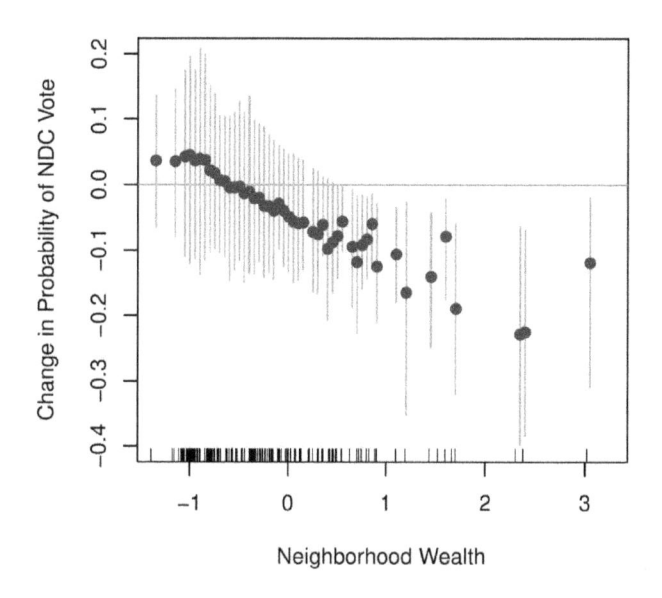

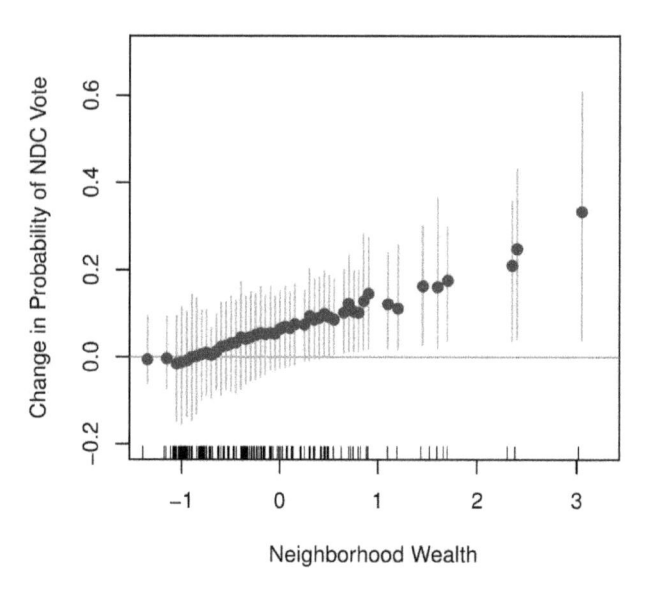

FIGURE 7.2: *Change in the probability of voting for the NDC* after a one standard deviation increase in the population share of each of the listed groups (Y-axis) across different levels of neighborhood-level wealth (X-axis), while individual-level wealth (and all other covariates) are held fixed. Includes 95% confidence intervals.

support the NDC (95% CI: 3.5, 18.0). This holds even among respondents from ethnic groups aligned with the NDC, who are more likely to vote for the NPP in middle- and upper-class Akan-dominated neighborhoods where only the NPP should be expected to deliver club goods after the election.

Similarly, the right panel of Figure 7.2 shows that a larger combined population from NDC-aligned ethnic groups in each respondent's neighborhood predicts significantly higher NDC support, but again only in middle- and upper-class neighborhoods.[21] In the poorest neighborhoods, changing the population percentage from NDC-aligned groups around each respondent has no effect on support for the NDC. But in a middle-class neighborhood with neighborhood wealth 1.1 standard deviations above the city-wide mean, a 14 percentage point larger population share from NDC-aligned groups is associated with respondents being 12 percentage points more likely to vote for the NDC (95% CI: 1.9, 23.8). This holds even among NPP-aligned Akans. Many Akan vote across ethnic lines in support of the NDC when living in middle- and upper-class neighborhoods dominated by NDC-aligned ethnic groups. But Akan voters support the NPP at high rates in poor neighborhoods regardless of ethnic composition.

Differences in the overall levels of ethnic voting predicted in Figure 7.2 are again substantively large. Returning to the example of a hypothetical Akan respondent with covariates set at the sample-wide means among Akans, I simulate the estimated level of ethnic voting from the models in Figure 7.2 for wealthy neighborhoods (90th percentile of neighborhood wealth index) in which two-thirds of the population is either Akan or instead from NDC-aligned ethnic groups. The Akan respondent has only a 9% chance (95% CI: 3%, 21%) of supporting the NDC in the Akan-dominated neighborhood. But an identical Akan respondent has a 46% chance (95% CI: 22%, 70%) of crossing ethnic lines to support the NDC in a similarly wealthy neighborhood in which two-thirds of the population is from NDC-aligned groups. This point estimate is consistent with ethnic voting nearly disappearing among local ethnic minorities

---

[21] $p = 0.06$ on the interaction between NDC-aligned ethnic group percentage and neighborhood wealth. When broken down by the population share of each ethnic group within the NDC's coalition, the result in the right panel of Figure 7.2 is particularly clear and strongly statistically significant for the Northern population share around each respondent. The incumbent NDC president at the time of the survey, John Dramani Mahama, was a Northerner, and voters may have expected Northern-dominated neighborhoods to be particularly likely to be favored if he was re-elected.

in wealthier neighborhoods. No similar-sized difference exists in very poor neighborhoods. At the 10th percentile of the neighborhood wealth index, the same Akan respondent is overwhelmingly likely to support the NPP – at rates over 70% – in a neighborhood with either ethnic composition.

7.1.5 Extension to Parliamentary Elections

I focus on the presidential election because parliamentary elections are less well-suited for examining the theory. Control over the majority of state spending, even at the local level, depends on presidential elections in Ghana (see Chapter 2). Voters may be most responsive to instrumental incentives when voting for president because much more that will directly affect their access to resources is on the line. Moreover, many parliamentary contests in Ghana are intra-ethnic, with candidates from the particular constituency's locally dominant ethnic group nominated by both parties.[22] This is often strategic, based on each party's assessment of the ethnicity most conducive to winning in a given constituency. This endogeneity of the selection of parliamentary candidates to local demographic conditions complicates any estimation of the relationship between neighborhood ethnic composition and vote choice.

Despite these limitations, I repeat the above analysis for the 2012 parliamentary elections to show that the findings are not a result of the decision to focus on the presidential contest. I switch the outcome variable in the model for Figure 7.1 to an indicator for whether a respondent voted for the parliamentary candidate from her ethnically affiliated party, and switch the outcome variable in the models in Figure 7.2 to voting for the NDC parliamentary candidate. All results are substantively identical and significant at the 90% level. This should not be surprising. Although there is often talk of "skirt and blouse" voting in the media before Ghanaian elections – the local term for "split ticket" voting – very few voters in Greater Accra split their tickets in 2012; more than 93% of respondents voted for the same party in each election.[23]

---

[22] The major parties nominated candidates from the same ethnic group in eight of the ten constituencies in the survey sample.
[23] There still could be concern that some features of the parliamentary race in each constituency have carry-over effects on presidential voting. For example, if parties both nominate parliamentary candidates from the same ethnic group, this could complicate incentives for ethnic voting. I replicate the main results controlling either for whether respondents were in a constituency where both parliamentary candidates were from the

7.2 THE MECHANISM: FAVORITISM EXPECTATIONS

The proposed mechanism for these patterns is voters' expectations about which party is more likely to benefit them with particularistic goods. I measure expectations of favoritism using a survey experiment. Each respondent was read a prompt about a hypothetical activity to be conducted by the government and asked if they expected that they or their families would benefit from it. The first randomized treatment cued whether the activity would be done by the NDC or an NPP government, had that party won the 2012 election. The second randomized treatment was the activity itself, selected from one of three examples each of either a private or a club good to be delivered to voters.[24] Collapsing across the examples, this makes four conditions (NDC vs. NPP government, delivering club vs. private goods). At the end of each prompt respondents were asked a variant of the following question: "If the NDC [NPP] government was [providing EXAMPLE], do you think that neighborhoods like this [people like you and your family] would get it or would they do it more in other places? [for other people?]"[25]

The treatment effect of interest is the difference in the proportion of respondents expecting to benefit from their ethnically aligned party versus their nonaligned party. $T = 1$ for Akans asked about the NPP and for Ewes, Northerners, and Gas asked about the NDC.[26] This is the causal effect on anticipated benefits from switching between a co-ethnic and non-co-ethnic government. The main treatment effect can also be

---

same ethnic group or for whether the parliamentary candidates for each party were from each respondent's own ethnic group. The results are unaffected.

[24] Multiple examples were used to average out idiosyncratic features of any specific example. For private goods: loans, job training, or financial assistance. For club goods: school construction, water pipes, or drains and public toilets. All are among the most common goods respondents reported politicians delivering in their neighborhoods in a pilot survey in response to the same open-response questions analyzed in Chapter 6.

[25] The full prompts are in the Appendix. To address the risk that respondents would answer more favorably about their preferred parties due to partisanship (Carlson 2016), each prompt began with a discussion of scarcity to decouple answers about the specific example from judgments about the overall virtues of a party. Each prompt began: "The national government has limited resources, so when they do something like [EXAMPLE], they can't do it everywhere. They have to do it in some places first before going to other places ..." Respondents were willing to admit they might not receive goods from a favored party: 50% of NDC voters and 52% of NPP voters said they would *not* benefit from the cued good from the party they voted for in the 2012 election.

[26] Balance statistics and regression tables for analyses of the survey experiment are in the Appendix.

7.2 The Mechanism: Favoritism Expectations

relabeled as the difference in expectations between the NDC and NPP cues for all respondents. Importantly, the quantity of interest that this survey experiment is designed to elicit is the *relative difference* in voters' expectations between the parties, not the overall amount of resources that respondents expect or actually receive in practice.[27] As a result, the analysis here focuses on marginal changes induced by the randomly assigned party cues.

Consistent with the qualitative evidence from Chapter 6, survey respondents had clear overall expectations of favoritism from their co-ethnic party in the allocation of both private and club goods. I estimate the co-ethnic party treatment effect in multilevel logistic regression models with the same predictors as in Table 7.2, but with the outcome now set to whether each respondent expects to benefit from the good in the prompt. Respondents were 13.7 percentage points (95% CI: 7.8, 19.4) more likely to expect to benefit from their ethnically aligned than their nonaligned party.

Expecting to benefit from an ethnically aligned party in the experiment is also strongly predictive of actual ethnic voting. Respondents receiving the co-ethnic party treatment in the experiment ($T = 1$) were 20.6 percentage points more likely (95% CI: 12.6, 28.0) to also vote for their co-ethnic party when answering that they expected to benefit from the example good compared to respondents who did not expect to benefit. In the reverse condition ($T = 0$), respondents were 20.7 percentage points more likely (95% CI: 11.5, 31.0) to report cross-ethnic voting for their non-co-ethnic party when expecting that this other party would benefit them than when expecting it would not.

Not only are expectations in the experiment correlated with ethnic voting, but the sizes of treatment effects vary across neighborhoods in patterns consistent with the results for vote choice. I discuss the results for the experimental prompts about club goods and private goods separately. The co-ethnic party treatment effect for club goods is significantly smaller at higher levels of neighborhood diversity. Panel (a) of Figure 7.3 shows that the expected difference in benefiting from club goods from a co-ethnic versus non-co-ethnic party declines at higher levels of ethnic diversity in each respondent's neighborhood, consistent with respondents

---

[27] The prompt describes a hypothetical situation that already presupposes that resources are being delivered. The prompts are a means to solicit information about the marginal effect of the party cue, not a method to extract accurate reports about true level of distribution.

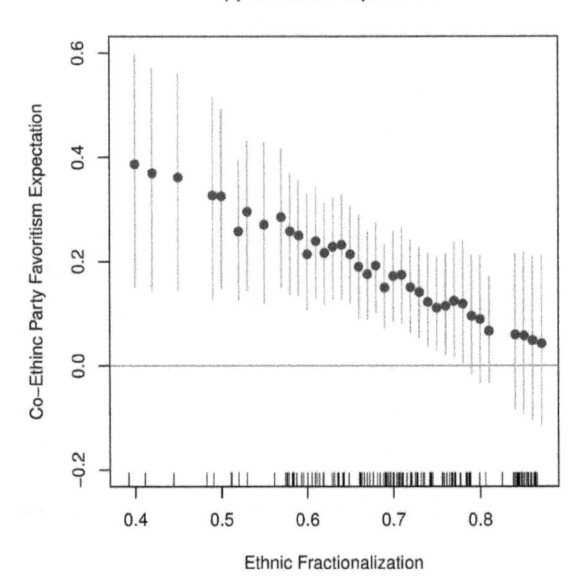

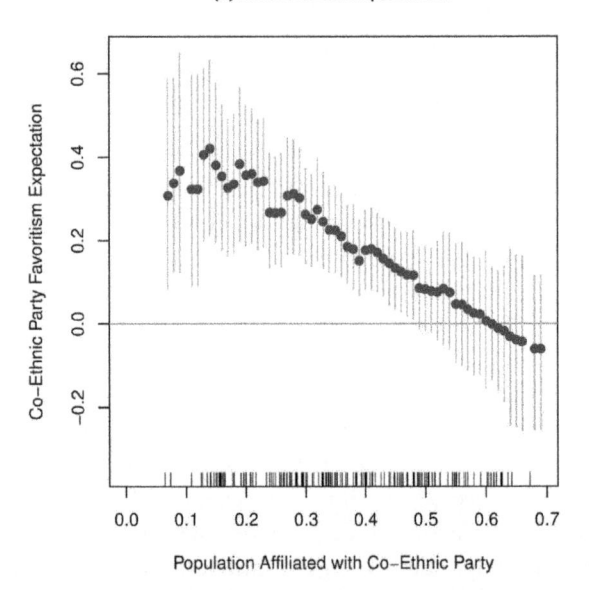

FIGURE 7.3: *First differences for the co-ethnic party treatment effect for questions about:* (a) club goods expectations, by ethnic fractionalization; and (b) private goods expectations, by percentage of population in the local neighborhood from ethnic groups affiliated with the respondent's co-ethnic party. Both panels include 95% confidence intervals.

7.2 The Mechanism: Favoritism Expectations

expecting no differences in the club goods they will get from the parties after the election in diverse neighborhoods, but significant differences in more homogeneous neighborhoods.

Respondents are also more likely to expect club goods from the party not affiliated with their ethnic group when living in area surrounded by more co-ethnics of that other party. This only holds in wealthier neighborhoods, but this is where club goods expectations are most important for vote choice under the theory in Chapter 5. Restricting to non-Gas for comparability to Figure 7.2, I reclassify the treatment effect as the difference between the NDC and NPP cues for club goods and interact an indicator for the NDC treatment with the population share of each ethnic group. I estimate these models for all neighborhoods, as well as after splitting the sample by the sample mean value of the neighborhood wealth index, to test the double interaction between neighborhood composition, wealth, and the NDC treatment.

Moving from the 10th to 90th percentile of Akan population share in neighborhoods with above-average wealth results in a predicted 26.7 point increase in expected favoritism in club goods from the Akan-affiliated NPP over the NDC ($p = 0.08$, 95% CI: -3.3, 56.8), regardless of each respondent's own ethnicity. A similar model for the population share of NDC-aligned groups around each respondent is signed in the predicted direction, but has $p = 0.12$ on this interaction. But respondents' expectations of being favored by the NDC in the delivery of club goods vary significantly with the population share from the incumbent NDC president's own ethnic group. Moving from the 10th to 90th percentile of Northern population in neighborhoods with above-average wealth results in a 31.2 percentage point shift in relative expectations of favoritism in club goods delivery in favor of the Northern-aligned NDC over the NPP ($p = 0.053$, 95% CI: -3.7, 63.4).

Results for the prompts about the private goods examples are also consistent with the theory. This is shown in three ways. First, Chapter 5 suggests that voters should have expectations of ethnic favoritism in private goods distribution in poor neighborhoods at all levels of ethnic fractionalization. Consistent with this prediction, I find that expectations of favoritism from each respondent's ethnically aligned party for the private goods cue are constant across levels of neighborhood ethnic fractionalization. Second, I find that respondents' expectations about private goods in the survey experiment are only correlated with their actual vote choices in neighborhoods where private goods distribution is actually reported to happen. This is consistent with private goods expectations primarily influencing ethnic voting in poor neighborhoods, but not in wealthier neighborhoods, where these goods are rarely distributed as clientelism.

Third, Chapter 5 argues that voters may be particularly likely to benefit from private goods distribution from their ethnically aligned party when they live in a poor neighborhood in which they are in the local ethnic minority. As one of the few co-ethnics of the government living in these neighborhoods, minority group voters may be first in line to benefit from private goods that their co-ethnic party gains control over if it wins the election. Consistent with this argument, in panel (b) of Figure 7.3, I interact the co-ethnic party treatment in the experiment with the percentage of residents in the respondent's neighborhood from ethnic groups affiliated with the respondent's ethnically aligned party. Expectations of ethnic favoritism in the distribution of private goods are largest in neighborhoods where respondents are in the local minority. This means, for example, that Akan voters particularly expect to benefit from private goods from the NPP instead of the NDC in poor neighborhoods where there are few other Akans. This can explain why there is still significant ethnic voting in poor neighborhoods even when voters are in the local ethnic minority: voters can expect access to valuable private benefits from their ethnically aligned party that outweigh the benefits of club goods expected to be distributed by the other party.

7.3 ALTERNATIVE EXPLANATIONS

There are several alternative explanations for why ethnic voting may vary across neighborhoods within a city. I already rule out two major alternatives in Table 7.2. Differences in voters' wealth and education do not explain whether they support ethnically affiliated parties in Greater Accra. Social identification with an ethnic group also does not explain vote choice. But several alternatives remain. First, the results in this chapter could be due either to cross-ethnic socialization in more diverse neighborhoods or instead to perceptions of threat from contact with other ethnic groups. Second, media environments could differ between diverse and homogenous neighborhoods in a manner that affects vote choice. Third, ethnic voting could be driven by urban voters' ties to rural homelands, a common explanation in independence-era literature on urban politics in Africa. Fourth, the selection, or sorting, process of voters into neighborhoods could confound any correlation

7.3 Alternative Explanations

between neighborhood context and vote choice. I consider and reject each possibility.

7.3.1 Socialization and Contact

A contact hypothesis could explain why there is less ethnic voting in more diverse neighborhoods.[28] Voters in more diverse neighborhoods may have more interaction with members of other ethnic groups. If these voters develop more positive views about other groups, they may become more likely to vote for parties aligned with them.[29]

But this alternative explanation should operate as much, if not more, in poor neighborhoods as in middle- or upper-class neighborhoods. The data on residential practices in Chapter 6 shows that there is more sustained interaction among neighbors in dense slums than in wealthier neighborhoods in Greater Accra, such that the negative correlation between neighborhood diversity and ethnic voting should be at least as strong in poor as in wealthier neighborhoods. But I show in Table 7.2 and Figure 7.1 that this correlation is strongest in wealthier neighborhoods and nonexistent in the poorest neighborhoods in the sample, inconsistent with contact theory.

I also measure cross-ethnic social contact in the survey data. The most direct forms of cross-ethnic contact occur when voters either have non-co-ethnic family members or share their homes with people from other groups. The survey recorded the ethnicity of the other people living in each respondent's household; 24.5% live with family or other household members from a group aligned with their non-co-ethnic party.[30] But re-estimating Figures 7.1 and 7.2 controlling for this returns substantively identical results, and living with members of other ethnic groups does not predict vote choice. The relationship between neighborhood characteristics and voting is unchanged among the respondents with the most direct, sustained contact with other ethnic groups, inconsistent with cross-ethnic socialization serving as the mechanism.

In addition, the neighborhood variables used here – such as the ethnic composition of the area 500 meters around a respondent's home –

---

[28] Allport (1954).
[29] In a related argument, Kasara (2013) shows how interethnic contact affects trust in Kenya. Ichino and Nathan (2013a) find no correlation between these same attitudes and vote choice in Ghana, however. Interethnic trust was not measured in the survey data analyzed here.
[30] This is a significantly higher rate than in the companion survey of rural areas.

would have to be proxying for voters' social networks for a socialization mechanism to explain the results. These variables are likely poor correlates of social networks, however. Most urban residents likely have regular interactions with people from other groups regardless of the specific composition of the neighborhood within 500 meters of their home. Indeed, 71% of the urban survey respondents said they had at least one close friend from another ethnic group.[31] Social networks are especially likely to differ from the ethnic composition of a respondent's neighborhood among the 36% of respondents who commute to work in a different neighborhood. If the results are only due to social ties, correlations between neighborhood characteristics and voting should be weaker for these respondents. I repeat the analysis interacting an indicator variable for commuting to work with the measures of neighborhood characteristics. I find no interactions – among those who do commute, correlations between neighborhood characteristics and voting behavior are the same as for those who do not.

Instead of cross-ethnic socialization, a related argument rooted in the American politics literature would suggest that neighborhood-level differences in ethnic voting are explained by differences in perceptions of ethnic threat. A long tradition of scholars following from Key (1949) find that white voters in the US support more racially conservative politicians when living in closer contact with black or other minority voters, acting out of a psychological threat response to the prospect of an ethnic outgroup gaining local political power.[32] But a threat hypothesis would predict *more* ethnic voting in more diverse neighborhoods, not less, in an opposite pattern from that in Table 7.2 and Figure 7.1.[33]

7.3.2 Partisan Media Environments

Closely related to a socialization mechanism is the possibility that the information about politics that voters receive, including through the media, differs across neighborhoods and alters behavior. In contrast to studies such as Casey (2015), overall differences in media availability cannot explain the results: Greater Accra forms a single media market and all survey respondents can access the same radio stations

---

[31] Controlling for having a non-co-ethnic friend has no effect on the results.
[32] For example, see Enos (2017).
[33] While this cannot explain the results for vote choice in presidential elections, I suggest in Chapter 8 that a threat response may help explain turnout by indigenous Ga voters in municipal elections as they seek to maintain control over local district governments.

and newspapers.[34] But there could still be differential exposure to media outlets by neighborhood.

Many news sources in Ghana have partisan biases. Conroy-Krutz and Moehler (2015) show in a field experiment that exposing residents of Greater Accra to hyperpartisan radio stations that favor the opposing party causes listeners to (at least temporarily) moderate their own partisanship. If a voter's media consumption is in part an outcome of the media outlets chosen by neighbors, or if information gleaned from partisan media spreads through neighborhood social networks, voters could be systematically more likely to be exposed to partisan media not aligned with their own ethnic group when living in more ethnically diverse neighborhoods or when living as local ethnic minorities.

This cannot account for the above results, however, for similar reasons why the socialization mechanism fails. The data on housing in Chapter 6 suggests that there should be more close social interaction between neighbors in poor slums than in middle- and upper-class neighborhoods; if anything, media consumption in slums should be more likely to be shaped by neighbors' listening and viewing habits than in wealthier areas, where residents live more apart from one another. But I find that the prevalence of ethnic voting does not vary with local ethnic composition in poor neighborhoods, only in middle- and upper-class neighborhoods. The signs on the interaction effect between neighborhood composition and wealth in Figures 7.1 and 7.2 are thus the opposite of what should be expected if differential access to partisan media explained differences in ethnic voting.

7.3.3 Ties to Rural Areas

Early literature on urban Africa viewed the rural–urban migration experience as a key component of urban political behavior. Summarizing scholarship from this period, Gugler (2002) notes that many urban residents in Africa have occupied a dual space between the urban and rural spheres, living in the city while maintaining financial and social ties to rural home areas where family members remain. Historically, rural–urban migrants in many African countries have also formed "ethnic youth associations" and other civic organizations that serve as the basis for political mobilization among urban migrants hailing from the same

---

[34] Conditional on wealth (already controlled for), they can all also access the same websites and TV stations.

home regions.³⁵ Respondents with stronger ties to their ethnic homelands or to ethnic associations may vote more for ethnically affiliated parties either because they care more about selecting a party that will benefit their rural home region or because they remain under the influence of rural ethnic elites. This would explain the results if survey respondents living in neighborhoods with larger populations from their own ethnic groups are also more likely to have rural ties and vote for co-ethnic parties because of them.

But most residents of Greater Accra – and the majority (55%) of the survey respondents – are no longer rural–urban migrants, having lived in cities their entire lives.³⁶ In tandem, membership in ethnic migrants' associations of the type examined in Wallerstein (1964) and discussed by Gugler (2002) is not common.³⁷ An explanation for urban ethnic voting rooted in rural–urban migration or membership in migrants' associations may be out of date with the nature of contemporary urban Ghana.

I also explicitly control for several measures of connections to rural areas. First, the results are robust to controlling for whether respondents regularly visit home regions outside Accra or send remittances to family members in another region. Second, I control for the percentage of each respondent's life lived in Greater Accra, as a measure of the recency of rural–urban migration, and find no differences in the results. Third, respondents were asked if they prefer that the government focus more resources on the community where they live now or the community "they hail from." Controlling for whether respondents prefer state resources to be targeted to rural areas outside Greater Accra does not change the findings and is not correlated with ethnic voting. Finally, membership in an ethnic association is not correlated with ethnic voting and controlling for this membership does not affect the results.

7.3.4 Endogenous Sorting

Finally, two different types of residential sorting could confound the main results. First, voters could have explicitly self-selected into neighborhoods

---

35 Wallerstein (1964), Wolpe (1974), and Gugler and Flanagan (1978).
36 Ghana Statistical Service (2008). I explain in Chapter 1 that Ghana is not unusual in this regard, but represents the overall trend in recent urbanization across the continent (Kessides 2006). The percentage of residents who are rural–urban migrants may be higher in Africa's less urbanized countries, such as in East Africa, that are currently undergoing higher rates of urbanization.
37 Less than 5% of respondents belong to such an association. Resnick (2014) finds similarly low rates of participation in these groups among poor voters in urban Zambia, where such associations were once important (Epstein 1958).

by partisanship, creating a spurious correlation between neighborhoods and voting behavior. Second, voters may have implicitly sorted if their ability to choose locations was constrained by individual characteristics that also affect voting. I test several observable implications of each type of sorting.

In the first type of sorting, Akans who support the NDC would be more likely to move to non-Akan neighborhoods. All respondents were asked open-ended questions about how they came to their current homes. None listed partisanship as an explicit motivation for choosing their location.[38] Greater Accra suffers from a housing shortage, with high rents relative to income, and real estate markets are informal, with high costs to relocation. For example, Ghanaian landlords typically require two years rent in advance and tenants have little recourse to reclaim it, significantly limiting mobility.[39] Residents face a limited menu of neighborhood options, constraining the extent to which they can explicitly sort based on noneconomic factors such as partisanship.[40] Moreover, if this type of sorting is a confounder, there should be a correlation between having moved (and thus having actively chosen a neighborhood) and vote choice. Re-estimating Table 7.2 including an indicator for whether a respondent moved shows no correlation between moving and ethnic voting.

Some respondents are better able to sort than others, however. I identify the respondents most likely to have been able to sort on nonprice factors if they had wanted to in several ways. Respondents were asked if they had considered living in other neighborhoods when searching for their current home or only considered that one neighborhood. Overall, 20.3% reported searching in multiple neighborhoods, which indicates having chosen among alternatives. There are no differences in the results when controlling for this, and explicitly choosing neighborhoods is not correlated with ethnic voting. Wealth is also a key determinant of the ability to choose neighborhoods. All analyses given here already control for measures of wealth, employment, and education. I also drop the top 25% of the sample on the assets or education/employment indices,

---

[38] 10.8% listed access to public services among their reasons for choosing a neighborhood. The main results hold when either controlling for this or dropping these respondents entirely.
[39] Arku et al. (2012).
[40] Concerns over neighborhood quality, commuting, and housing costs have been shown to trump explicit preferences for living near copartisans even in the United States, where there are fewer constraints on mobility (Mummolo and Nall 2016).

removing those likely to have had the widest range of choices and thus the greatest opportunity to explicitly sort on partisanship if they wanted to.[41] All results remain substantively similar, although some results are no longer statistically significant at conventional levels in the smaller sample.

That many residents are constrained, however, raises concern over the second type of sorting. By far the most common means of finding housing was through family members or co-ethnics; 75% came to their current locations to join family members or people from their hometown or ethnic group. This would account for the results if voters with closer ties to their ethnic group, or for whom ethnic identity is more salient, are both more likely to find housing where more family and co-ethnics live, and also more likely to vote for ethnically aligned parties. Respondents who found their homes through these ties are not more likely to live in less diverse neighborhoods, however, inconsistent with this being a confounder. All models already control for whether respondents moved for these reasons and this does not predict voting (Table 7.2). In addition, all results already control for the individual salience of ethnicity (see above) and it does not predict voting behavior.

7.4 THE GA: AN EXCEPTION THAT PROVES THE RULE?

Finally, I extend the analysis to Greater Accra's indigenous Ga ethnic group, who are dropped in the analysis for Figure 7.2.[42] Voting behavior varies across neighborhoods differently among the Ga. But these differences still appear consistent with the overall argument in Chapter 5, serving as an "exception that proves the rule": the parties face different costs to the nonprogrammatic distribution of particularistic goods among Ga voters than they do for all other ethnic groups in the city; as a result, Gas behave differently because they have different expectations of favoritism across neighborhoods. I outline key features that distinguish the Ga from other residents of Accra and present results for Ga

---

[41] Hopkins and Williamson (2012).
[42] I consider voters from the closely related Dangme-speaking ethnic groups of the broader Greater Accra region, such as the Krobo, Shai, and Ada, together with the Ga. There are too few Dangme respondents in the urban survey sample to estimate their behavior separately from other Ga voters, and Dangme share the same characteristics highlighted here for the Ga in the outlying peri-urban districts of the city where Dangmes are the indigenous group. The Ga-Dangme are also counted together as a single higher-order ethnic category in the census data that is used to calculate neighborhood ethnic composition.

7.4 The Ga: An Exception that Proves the Rule?

respondents. Chapter 8 analyzes the unique position of the Ga in the local politics of Greater Accra in more detail.

7.4.1 Differences from Other Ethnic Groups

The Ga are now a minority throughout Greater Accra, including in Accra itself (see Chapter 2). But because of their indigeneity to the city, the Ga differ from other ethnic groups in two key ways that should affect politicians' incentives for distributive politics, and, in turn, Ga voters' expectations of the benefits they can receive.

First, the Ga are easier for parties to engage with at an individual level than voters from other ethnic groups. Ga survey respondents had lived in their current neighborhood for a median of 20 years, compared to only 8 years for non-Gas. This extends to wealthier neighborhoods; Ga respondents had lived double the amount of time on average as non-Ga respondents in neighborhoods with above-average scores on the neighborhood wealth index. Ga respondents were also dramatically more likely to live in houses that they own or which are owned by a family member (61%) compared to non-Gas (36%), and far less likely than non-Gas to live in the more temporary housing arrangements, such as living as caretakers on unfinished plots, that make sustained patronage relationships difficult for parties. In addition, Ga respondents were more likely than other residents of the city to live in compound houses, typical of the city's older housing stock, in which multiple families share cooking spaces and bathrooms, rather than live in the greater social anonymity of single-family housing.[43]

These characteristics imply that Ga voters are less transient and more monitorable than other city residents. As a result, Ga voters may receive relatively more private benefits through clientelism than other voters, even in middle- and upper-class neighborhoods where there is less private goods distribution overall, for the reasons Chapter 6 argues that it is easier for parties to sustain long-term clientelistic relationships with poor voters in slums compared to similarly poor voters in wealthier neighborhoods.

Second, Ga chiefs and other traditional elites, such as family-lineage heads, are politically active and influential within Greater Accra and

---

[43] Chapter 2 shows that Gas are not particularly different from other groups in terms of individual-level wealth, however. Socioeconomic class and ethnicity largely cross-cut in Greater Accra.

the Ga are more connected to traditional ethnic social institutions than other urban residents. Ga traditional leaders can play similar political roles among the Ga community as chiefs in rural areas, as described in Chapters 5 and 6.[44] They serve as key opinion leaders whose influential endorsements shape voters' expectations about which parties are most likely to serve in their best interest. They also can become clientelistic intermediaries through which parties bind individual voters to support them. In addition, the city's original Ga neighborhoods feature prominent chiefs' palaces and traditional family houses which serve as focal meeting points for extended Ga families, akin to lineage groups or clans. These family houses serve as the sites of traditional festivals and monthly family meetings, helping to maintain ethnic network ties within the Ga community that can be leveraged by politicians to mobilize electoral support and build patronage relationships with individual voters.

Party agents describe campaigning through Ga traditional leaders as a central part of voter mobilization efforts in Greater Accra.[45] While some local party leaders were skeptical of how influential traditional leaders truly are over voters' decisions, others were adamant that campaigning through Ga elders helps coordinate support in a way that simply is not possible among other groups. One NDC party agent explained, "They do influence [voting decisions]. Let's say, for example, I am the head of this family. When I talk to my people, 'let's go this way,' they will all listen to me. So they have real influence over their people."[46]

Traditional elites are mostly not similarly influential among other ethnic groups in the city – their authority is confined to other areas of the country. For example, when asked about the role of traditional elites in a focus group in Ashaiman, the largest non-Ga slum in Greater Accra, one participant noted that traditional leaders from various ethnic groups live in the community but have no real social or political power: "The chiefs are many here. They have more than 20 northern tribal chiefs ...We barely see them. Even if a chief is passing by you, you would never know it's a chief." Instead, the strongest community leader in his

---

[44] Also see Baldwin (2015) and Koter (2016).
[45] Interview with NPP party agents, Krowor constituency, February 15, 2014; interview with NDC party agent, La Dade Kotopon constituency, February 27, 2014; interview with NPP party agent, La Dade Kotopon constituency, February 18, 2014; interview with NPP party agent, La Dade Kotopon constituency, March 5, 2014; interview with NDC party agent, La Dade Kotopon constituency, March 26, 2014.
[46] Interview with district assembly member and NDC party agent, La Dade Kotopon constituency, Greater Accra, February 14, 2014.

7.4 The Ga: An Exception that Proves the Rule? 239

neighborhood is an elected official working directly for the NDC: "[The assemblyman] is the person who has the kind of cohesion of everyone. It's the assemblyman who is the more important leader."[47] Similarly, while residents of other ethnic groups may return to ancestral home regions outside the city for traditional festivals and family-lineage group events (see Section 7.3.3), they usually do not have anywhere near the same level of explicit ethnic-based social organization within the city itself.

The NDC has the strongest connections to influential Ga chiefs and family heads. The constituency-level leadership of NDC party organizations throughout the city includes many Ga elites, and the Ga are often described as a core voting bloc for the party as a result. At times, the NPP has been able to siphon off Ga votes by securing endorsements of particular Ga leaders, including by aligning with particular factions in internal Ga chieftaincy disputes. For example, when the NPP first swept to power in the 2000 election, they won Greater Accra Region for the first time in part because they were able to peel off a significant portion of Ga voters. The NPP even won the parliamentary seat in the Odododiodioo constituency, which contains Ga Mashie, the original Ga community at the heart of central Accra, by nominating the nephew of one of the rivals in a Ga chieftaincy dispute as their parliamentary candidate and then leveraging the support of his faction into votes.[48] But the NPP has not had sustained success with these tactics – the party has lost Odododiodioo in every subsequent election, for example – and Ga chiefs and family heads remain primarily aligned with the NDC.

As a result of these links between traditional elites and the NDC, Ga voters who have close ties to traditional leaders may be particularly likely to vote for the NDC, irrespective of the demographic characteristics of their neighborhoods.[49] Moreover, Ga voters living in the core Ga enclaves of the city – the original precolonial Ga villages that Greater

---

[47] Focus group, Zongo Laka, Ashaiman constituency, Greater Accra, July 3, 2013.
[48] Interview with former MP and former NPP parliamentary candidate, Odododiodioo constituency, Greater Accra, July 28, 2011.
[49] In rural areas, chiefs are typically only active in the home regions of their groups, where that group is, essentially by default, the local ethnic majority. Rural voters may only expect access to private goods passed down through chiefs when living among the local majority in home regions in which the chief is from their own group. By contrast, Ga chiefs can be active in neighborhoods even where the Ga have now become the local ethnic minority. This gives Ga voters with connections to chiefs less of an incentive to vote across ethnic lines than rural ethnic minorities.

Accra has grown up around – may be particularly likely to expect private benefits from the NDC because these are the neighborhoods in which traditional Ga ethnic social institutions, such as the family houses described earlier, are still most active.

7.4.2 Analysis for Ga Respondents

These features carry over into different patterns of voting behavior among the Ga respondents. Similar to other ethnic groups, Ga respondents appear more likely to support their ethnically aligned party, the NDC, when living in neighborhoods with larger population shares from their own ethnic group, although this result is not statistically significant at conventional levels ($p = 0.11$).[50] But Ga respondents appear much less sensitive to the population shares of other ethnic groups around them – the results in Figure 7.2 do not hold among Gas. Instead, the strongest predictor of vote choice among Ga respondents is their ties to traditional leaders. Reporting contact with a traditional chief in the past year is associated with a 22.7 percentage point greater probability of NDC support (95% CI: 5.1, 33.8) among Ga respondents, but is not correlated with vote choice for the other respondents.

The Ga may be less sensitive to neighborhood ethnic composition because they can expect to receive private goods in a broader range of neighborhoods than other voters, reducing the difference between the two rows in Table 7.1 (also see Tables 5.1 and 5.2). In the analysis of respondents' private goods distribution in Chapter 6, Gas were much more likely than other respondents to report private goods distribution by politicians. Simulating from the model in column 2 of Table 6.2, I find that Ga respondents were 65% (6 percentage points) more likely to be able to name at least one private good distributed by a local politician than other respondents (95% CI: −0.4, 12.8, $p = 0.08$). Ga respondents were especially more likely than others to report private goods distribution when living in areas with more Gas. Moreover, respondents of all ethnic groups who had met with chiefs in the last year were 19 percentage points (95% CI: 8.2, 29.8) more likely to know recipients of private goods through government job and loan programs in their neighborhoods than respondents without ties to chiefs, consistent with chiefs serving as intermediaries through which patronage benefits are

---

[50] All results for Ga respondents alone must be interpreted with caution, because there are much smaller sample sizes when restricting to a specific subpopulation.

targeted.⁵¹ Because these chiefs are essentially all Ga, the recipients that respondents know of through contact with chiefs will primarily be Ga voters.

These differences in reported rates of private goods distribution also appear in the survey experiment. Ga respondents had largely similar expectations about club goods in the survey experiment when compared to the other respondents: expecting less favoritism in club goods distribution in more diverse neighborhoods, just as in panel (a) of Figure 7.3, and more favoritism in club goods distribution from the NDC in neighborhoods with greater NDC-aligned populations. But the relationship between neighborhood ethnic composition and Ga respondents' expectations about private goods runs in the opposite direction of the result in panel (b) of Figure 7.3 for the other respondents. Ga respondents are especially likely to expect favoritism from the NDC in the distribution of private goods in neighborhoods where a larger share of the population is Ga. Neighborhoods with large Ga populations are the areas where the traditional Ga institutions described earlier that can be used by local NDC elites to create patronage relationships with Ga voters are most active.

7.5 SUMMARY

This chapter documents neighborhood-level variation in where voters support the parties aligned with their ethnic groups. Voters continue to vote heavily along ethnic lines in slums. They also vote along ethnic lines when living in ethnically segregated neighborhoods composed primarily of members of their own ethnic group, even when those neighborhoods are wealthy. But elsewhere, similar voters choosing among the same candidates in the same election are more indifferent between the parties, or even cross ethnic lines to vote against the candidate supported by most of their co-ethnics. This intra-urban variation cannot be explained by differences in voters' own socioeconomic characteristics, including individual-level wealth and education, as these variables are not correlated with ethnic voting. The variation also cannot be explained by voters' identification with their ethnic groups, by cross-ethnic socialization, or by how voters sorted into neighborhoods. Instead, ethnic voting appears to track voters' expectations of the instrumental benefits of electing ethnically aligned politicians.

---

⁵¹ Respondents are also signed as more likely to know about recipients of private goods in general if they have had contact with chiefs, but $p = 0.11$.

As long as voters continue to expect that access to valuable resources depends on the ethnic affiliations of different parties, ethnic voting should not be expected to fade away in African cities, even if there is a large middle class and ethnic diversity is high. Ethnicity may be salient in other contexts for reasons beyond purely instrumental considerations about access to particularistic benefits, particularly where voters are shown to support co-ethnics because of expressive, affective biases. But the empirics here do not provide any evidence that expressive affinities for co-ethnics explain vote choice among most voters in Greater Accra. Indeed, if expressive voting were still common, the neighborhood-level variation documented above should not exist and there should be a strong correlation between group identification and vote choice. In cases where there is little expressive voting, changes in the extent of ethnic electoral competition will arise more from supply-side shifts in how politicians target particularistic goods than from differences in voters' underlying demand for ethnic politics.

Together with Chapters 5 and 6, this chapter completes demonstration of the link between nonprogrammatic competition and ethnic voting presented in Figure 1.1. Continued nonprogrammatic competition, despite a growing middle class, sustains the *political* relevance of ethnicity in many, but not all, urban neighborhoods, even if the *social* importance of ethnicity may be changing in a context of rising wealth and interethnic contact.

PART IV

IMPLICATIONS FOR URBAN GOVERNANCE

8

Turnout Inequality and Capture in Municipal Elections

> "[The mayor] is appointed by the government in power. The person is only willing to help those who are on their ticket, those who are on their side."
> – District assembly member, Okaikwei Central constituency, Greater Accra, March 2014

> "[The Ga] get most of the resources ... They have a feeling that the AMA is their property, their bonafide property. Therefore they exploit it to the maximum."
> – NDC constituency executive, Ablekuma North constituency, Greater Accra, March 2014

Part II argues that nonprogrammatic appeals remain the dominant strategy for urban politicians because of a credibility problem. Urban politicians cannot commit to addressing the universalistic preferences of many in the middle class. Voters with universalistic preferences then differentially abstain from political participation. Part III shows that when nonprogrammatic appeals persist, ethnic competition remains common in much, but not all, of the city. What are the combined effects of nonprogrammatic politics, differences in participation, and ethnic competition on urban governance?

The book's final empirical chapter shifts focus from presidential and parliamentary elections to local elections for municipal governments. Local elections in Ghana have lower stakes than national elections, deciding control over less valuable state resources. This shift in focus is driven in part by data constraints.[1] But local elections are still

---

[1] With only ten parliamentary constituencies and four districts included in the main survey sample, many of the analyses reported in this chapter would not have a large enough

important: they provide a microcosm of what the "trap" in Figure 1.1 looks like when each dynamic examined in the previous chapters is taken to its extremes. Themes from the previous chapters converge in Greater Accra's district-level elections and illustrate the final steps in Figure 1.1.

There is extreme variation in turnout across the city in district-level elections, rooted in a more severe version of the credibility problem in Chapter 4. Limits on the power of local city councilors mean that there are even fewer voters whose preferences they can credibly address. The result is broad abstention from local elections by the middle class, not just those with universalistic preferences. There are middle-class areas of the city with turnout of less than 5%, yet poorer areas with turnout as high as 60% in the same election. Where participation is so low, local politicians can win with the support of small minority groups, increasing the risk that city governments are captured by narrow interests. Unaccountable to most voters, local politicians steer a disproportionate share of municipal resources to their own groups and copartisans.

But this favoritism reduces the quality of governance and deepens the government's inability to meet the many service delivery challenges created by urbanization. This feeds scarcity within cities, sustaining voter demands for particularistic goods that can be targeted as patronage. Favoritism can also exacerbate the credibility problem in Chapter 4 by further reducing voters' beliefs in the capacity of their government for programmatic politics. Despite the relatively limited powers of locally elected municipal officials, the capture of local governments has real impacts on lived experiences in the city, shaping voters' perceptions of who the government really serves. While universalistic policies can only be adopted by the national government, district governments are tasked with implementing many of these policies. It is at the district level that many grand plans of national government have historically fallen apart, amid rent-seeking, corruption, and favoritism during implementation. If local political actors face no personal electoral incentive to respond to policy-demanding voters, they will underinvest effort in building the implementation capacity needed to make national politicians' universalistic promises credible.

District-level elections in Ghana are held off-cycle from the presidential and parliamentary elections, with voters selecting nominally

---

N if replicated for parliamentary elections or the presidential selection of District Chief Executives (DCEs).

nonpartisan representatives from single-member wards to serve in district assemblies, equivalent to city councils. These wards, called Electoral Areas (ELAs), typically have 10,000 to 20,000 residents. While district-assembly members are less important than presidentially appointed District Chief Executives (DCEs), equivalent to the mayors of each district, they become official leaders of their communities and provide small-scale particularistic goods and services to their constituents, especially private goods to poor voters. Assembly members collectively also have veto power over mayoral appointments, such that who wins assembly elections helps determine the type of politician the president can appoint to make the biggest distributive decisions within each district.

Examining the 2010 and 2015 district assembly elections, I find that low turnout helps candidates from the indigenous Ga ethnic group capture disproportionate power in municipal governments. While capture by indigenous urban ethnic groups has parallels in other African cities, the Ga domination of Greater Accra's local elections demonstrates the broader ability of well-mobilized interest groups to take advantage of low turnout to distort important policy outcomes in their favor.[2] I show that within Greater Accra, turnout in district elections is lowest in wards with the largest middle- and upper-class populations. Ga candidates become significantly more likely to win district assembly seats in wards with lower turnout, allowing an ethnic group with only one-quarter of the metropolitan area's population to control the district assemblies across the city and dominate the appointment of DCEs. Ga overrepresentation reduces popular approval of local government performance: survey respondents disapprove of the performance of Ga assembly members compared to local representatives of other ethnicities, especially when living in ethnically segregated wards where Ga assembly members can target resources to small geographic areas of Ga settlement. Finally, data on the distribution of new schools, roads, and streetlights suggests that Ga overrepresentation in district governments leads to favoritism in the distribution of locally controlled club goods.

8.1 GHANA'S LOCAL GOVERNMENT SYSTEM

The are 12 predominately urban districts in the Greater Accra metropolitan area. The largest, the Accra Metropolitan Assembly, or AMA,

---

[2] For example, Hajnal and Trounstine (2005) and Anzia (2014).

corresponds to the official city of Accra.[3] Each district is headed by a District Chief Executive (DCE) who is a presidential appointee and local leader of the president's party.[4] Below the DCE is a local legislative body equivalent to a city council, called the District Assembly, for which 30% of the members in each district are appointed by the national ruling party and 70% are elected from each ELA. Assembly members are elected to four-year terms, most recently in December 2010 and September 2015.[5] There were 255 ELAs in the 12 urban districts in these elections.

Elected district assembly members are fairly minor players in the grand scheme of Ghanaian politics. Although in theory the district assembly votes on budgetary allocations within each district, the ruling party's appointed DCE controls the distribution of most local government resources with limited oversight. This makes the presidential election more influential for the distribution of local government resources than the district assembly election.

But assembly members still play several important roles that make their selection worthy of attention. First, the appointed DCE is subject to a confirmation vote from the assembly members. There is little risk of elected assembly members preventing the ruling party from eventually installing one of its local leaders as the DCE, as the 30% of voting assembly members who are appointed ensure that the national ruling party controls a majority of the seats in almost all of the assemblies. But assembly members can make demands regarding the specific local ruling-party leaders appointed, for example in terms of their ethnicity, and DCE appointments are regularly rejected. Within Greater Accra this happened most recently in Adenta in 2012, where the president had to nominate three different local party leaders as DCE before getting one confirmed.

Second, elected assembly members, especially those affiliated with the ruling party, are appointed to various subcommittees of the district assembly, such as the public works or urban roads committees, that advise the DCE on specific projects. This gives a subset of assembly

---

[3] As this book went to press, the new NPP government – in power since the 2016 election – announced it was splitting the official city of Accra (the AMA) into seven separate administrative districts, each with its own DCE and District Assembly. It is too soon to document what effects this new district creation may have on the dynamics described in this chapter. But Chapter 9 explains how institutional shifts related to further decentralization could alter the trap outlined in Chapter 1.

[4] District Chief Executives are called Municipal or Metropolitan Chief Executives (MCE) in larger districts, but these terms are used interchangeably in practice.

[5] The September 2015 elections were supposed to be held in December 2014, but were delayed until 2015 by a court case.

members more direct influence over key distributive decisions in their districts. Together, these first two roles mean that assembly elections matter for the functioning of district governments even if each individual assembly member is quite weak. Although the District Assemblies have no direct input into national policy, district governments are crucial for its implementation. Many national policies are primarily implemented by the district governments, with considerable local discretion for district leaders in de facto outcomes on the ground. To the extent that locally elected assembly members affect the incentives of DCEs through veto power over their appointments or gain more direct input into assembly decisions through committee memberships, they can have a real impact on residents' lived experiences with the implementation of national government policy.

Third, assembly leaders serve as the official leaders of their neighborhoods and become key patrons to local residents. They are the main lobbyists in each community advocating for funding from higher levels of government. They also provide basic constituent services. Part of the district budget is set aside for each elected assembly member as an annual "Electoral Area Fund," a small discretionary amount for personalized assistance or projects in the ELA.[6] Assembly members typically use their Electoral Area Funds to provide private goods or small club goods, such as putting up new streetlights or digging new gutters. For larger projects, such as building a new road or school, assembly members must lobby the DCE for funds from the general district budget.

Assembly elections are officially nonpartisan, but parties play a significant role in practice. Almost all assembly members are openly affiliated with one of the two major parties, and many simultaneously hold local executive positions in the party organizations. Candidates openly campaign as members of their parties, and elected assembly members in some districts hold party caucus meetings to decide on voting strategies before district assembly sessions.[7] But nominations are open, with no partisan candidate selection procedures. Assembly races thus often become intraparty contests; the average assembly election in Greater Accra in 2010 had 3.5 candidates, with as many as nine contesting for a single seat.

---

[6] Members of the AMA report that this fund was roughly US$5,000 per year as of 2013.
[7] Interview with assembly member and NDC executive, Okaikwei Central constituency, Greater Accra, February 27, 2014; interview with assembly member, Ablekuma North constituency, Greater Accra, March 11, 2014.

Policy platforms are entirely absent from campaigns for district assembly seats. Instead, candidates focus on promises to deliver basic constituent services and private goods. In practice, assembly members become small-scale clientelistic patrons, serving as a key cog in the grassroots party machinery that engages in relational clientelism with individual voters (see Chapter 6). In interviews, assembly members report that distributing private goods to individual voters is their main activity, both once in office and during campaigns. This includes everything from money and food as pre-election gifts, to longer-term support with health expenses and health insurance fees, school tuition, and rent payments. As one assembly member explained, he pays "money, school fees, rent, whatever ... Every weekend people come for funeral donations, and you have to do it."[8] Another assembly member said,

They ask for hospital money. If there is a dowry or engagement or marriage, if you don't go and donate they say "it's a bad assemblyman." ... There are some areas we cannot walk out in that area, because they will ask you for money ... If you don't [give], it means you're not a good assembly member and then they go after you.[9]

An NDC assemblyman described the clientelistic benefits of these payments. After paying school tuition for teenage boys in his neighborhood, "they have completed and now they are loyal to me, they respect me," and help the local NDC organization with its campaigns.[10]

The election of assembly members is a choice over which neighborhoods and which types of voters within each ELA will get this assistance. As described in Chapter 2, ELAs in Greater Accra are larger than single neighborhoods. Assembly members were open in interviews about concentrating their efforts on the subset of neighborhoods within their ELA where their own supporters live. For example, an assembly member in the Okaikwei Central constituency in the AMA described providing a series of goods to the slum where he lived, including a new drainage system and construction materials for an Islamic primary school, while not expending any resources in a middle-class neighborhood that made

---

[8] Interview with assembly member and NDC executive, Okaikwei Central constituency, Greater Accra, February 27, 2014.
[9] Interview with assembly member, Ayawaso Central constituency, Greater Accra, August 27, 2013.
[10] Interview with assembly member and NDC executive, Ayawaso West constituency, Greater Accra, July 23, 2012.

up the other half of his ELA.[11] In a neighboring ELA, the pattern was reversed: the assembly member described providing most of her budget in the middle-class neighborhood where she and her supporters lived, while ignoring the slum community nearby. "Before, all the development was concentrated on [the slum area]. They got roads in [the slum area] before I was elected ... So I'm trying to bring more development to *my* area," she argued.[12] When an assembly member's supporters are clustered in one part of an ELA, other neighborhoods may be disadvantaged in the distribution of local government resources.

8.2 LOW TURNOUT AND ITS CONSEQUENCES

Turnout in Ghana's local government elections has always been lower than in national-level elections, similar to off-cycle elections in many democracies. Only 35% of registered voters turned out nationwide in the 2010 district assembly elections, compared to 73% and 79% in the 2008 and 2012 presidential elections, respectively. Much like the credibility problem described in Chapter 4, past research has attributed low turnout and apathy in district elections to voters' beliefs that district governments will not be able to deliver the resources they want.[13] But there is significant variation in turnout in local elections, both across the country and within Greater Accra itself, suggesting that the extent of this credibility problem significantly differs across areas of the city and between types of voters.

Much of this variation can be explained with a simple assumption: those who have the most to gain or lose from the selection of municipal level officials will turn out to vote and those who have less at stake will not. Two groups of voters can expect to have relatively little on the line: middle- and upper-class voters; and opposition supporters, especially when living in opposition strongholds. Three groups have more at stake in local elections: the very poor; ruling party supporters, especially when living in ruling party stronghold neighborhoods; and the Ga, Greater Accra's indigenous ethnic group.[14]

---

[11] Interview with assembly member, Okaikwei Central constituency, Greater Accra, February 25, 2014.
[12] Interview with assembly member, Okaikwei Central constituency, Greater Accra, March 12, 2014.
[13] Ayee (1996), Crook (1999), and Wunsch (2001).
[14] Importantly, these categories are not mutually exclusive. There are both middle-class and poor Ga voters and both middle-class and poor supporters of each party. See Chapters 2 and 7.

The expectation that the middle class has little reason to vote in district elections builds directly from the argument in Chapter 4, which predicts turnout differences when voters both do not believe that any candidate will address their preferences and are not mobilized to turn out by politicians. But the credibility problem driving these two dynamics is now more extreme than in national elections. District assembly members primarily have the capacity to provide small-scale private goods to constituents, which Chapter 3 shows that many in the middle class do not prioritize. The ability of assembly members to deliver club goods – still demanded by many in the middle class – is limited compared to the DCEs, who are chosen via the presidential election, and assembly members have no control over the adoption of major universalistic policies. Similar to the MPs and party leaders interviewed in Chapter 4, politicians contesting for assembly seats see middle-class voters as those generally hardest to convince and underinvest in mobilizing their support. The combined result is that middle-class voters, even those without universalistic preferences, broadly abstain in local elections, to a much greater extent than the turnout differences observed in Chapter 4.

That middle class abstention and politicians' unwillingness to mobilize middle-class voters is a result of their perceived inability to address these voters' preferences – not a mechanical result of middle-class population size – should be even clearer in local government elections than in the national elections studied in Chapter 4. Chapter 4 argues that middle-class voters with universalistic preferences now form a large enough bloc to be pivotal in the presidential and parliamentary outcome within most parliamentary constituencies, when combined with the support of other groups. But in many of the city's local ELAs, a candidate could win an assembly seat exclusively with middle-class votes, especially in multicandidate races where less than a quarter of the vote can sometimes be enough to win. Residents with some secondary education, English literacy, and formal-sector employment make up more than 25% of the adult population in over 50 ELAs across urban Greater Accra (see Figure 2.3). In these ELAs, explicitly pursuing middle-class support can be a winning strategy. But when the credibility problem binds, assembly candidates do not pursue middle-class votes and many middle-class voters opt out.

Credibility constraints also produce partisan differences in turnout in district assembly elections. If many voters expect the district government to engage in favoritism, core supporters of the national ruling party and residents of the national ruling party's stronghold ELAs should be more likely to turn out in district elections than opposition supporters or residents of opposition stronghold ELAs. Other than distributing the small discretionary Electoral Area Fund that all assembly members receive, assembly members in opposition areas of the city have little ability to commit to providing additional resources to their constituents without the cooperation of the partisan DCE. This is especially the case for more expensive club goods (e.g., new roads and schools) for which they must lobby the DCE for funding. Partisan district leaders are unlikely to allow many extra resources to be spent in opposition neighborhoods regardless of who the assembly member is. Voters in opposition strongholds, even those who strongly demand particularistic goods, may thus see their assembly members as unlikely to have the power to make consequential distributive decisions, and thus stay home because little is at stake for their ELA in the district election.

Greater Accra's Ga residents may also turn out at higher rates than residents from other ethnic groups, for two reasons. First, as discussed in Chapter 7, Ga candidates are better able to draw upon pre-existing ethnic social organizations and traditional leaders to mobilize support and encourage turnout of their co-ethnics than candidates from other ethnic groups.[15] Second, as the city's indigenous ethnic group, the Ga perceive themselves as having much more at stake in control over the local government. Ga candidates can appeal to a shared grievance or sense of threat among their co-ethnics, especially if the group's favored position in a city's local power structure is threatened by rapid demographic changes. Paller (2015) describes how political opinion in indigenous Ga settlements in Accra is shaped by the Ga community's experiences as a minority in a territory they have traditionally controlled, and suggests that elites play upon this sense of threat to mobilize voters. The Ga community places special symbolic value on controlling local governments that they believe should belong to their group. Ethnic newcomers cannot mobilize turnout around a similar symbolic claim to rightful control over the city.

Indigenous or earlier-settled ethnic groups in other settings similarly use grievances rooted in perceptions of threat from the in-migration of new groups to mobilize participation in the quest for greater local political power. Parallels to the Ga in Accra can also be seen in urban

---

[15] For example, Paller (2014) documents the use of Ga social networks to mobilize support for a Ga parliamentary candidate in the Ga Mashie neighborhood of Accra, describing how the candidate drew on his familial ties to Ga clan heads and pastors in Ga-language churches to build support.

India, where "sons of the soil" parties – such as the Maharashtrian Shiv Sena party in Mumbai – representing indigenous ethnic groups who see themselves as under threat from large-scale in-migration of other groups have taken dominant positions in electoral politics in some cities.[16] In Nairobi's Kibera slum, Nubians – descendants of the Sudanese migrants who first populated the area – draw on similar grievance-based appeals in pursuit of local power.[17] More generally, the use of "ethnic threat" as a mobilizing issue for local ethnic groups fearing the loss of local political power has been observed far beyond the African context, such as among white voters in the United States.[18]

Low turnout has consequences. Where few voters turn out, the candidates most likely to win will be those who can best mobilize small sets of supporters. Where ethnic voting is common, candidates from ethnic groups with the highest levels of social organization and the most at stake in winning local power will be especially likely to have these advantages. In Greater Accra, Ga candidates can use the turnout advantages of their ethnic group to capture disproportionate local power.

Capture by a minority interest group then leads to the inefficient distribution of local government resources, with local politicians accountable to only a small minority of the electorate taking decisions in the interest of that group rather than the city at large.[19] District governments in Greater Accra already have limited resources and cannot meet all of the myriad service delivery challenges across the urban area. But when the local government is captured and those limited resources are distributed as favoritism, scarcity in access to basic services among most urban residents only becomes worse than it needs to be, reducing the quality of governance.

Capture by indigenous urban ethnic groups such as the Ga is not unique to Greater Accra. This can also be seen in other Ghanaian cities, such as Tamale, where chiefs from the Dagomba ethnic group dominate local politics to such an extent that they were able to expel many of the city's Konkomba residents in the 1990s after violent conflicts between the two ethnic groups. The special status of indigenous groups can also be seen in Nigerian cities, such as Lagos, where a relatively small set of

---

[16] Weiner (1978).
[17] Balaton-Chrimes (2013).
[18] Key (1949) and Hopkins (2010).
[19] This logic closely follows Chhibber and Nooruddin (2004) on the relationship between service provision and the size of minimum winning coalitions.

originally settled Yoruba families use customary land rights to extract significant rents from residents and capture control over local governments even though Lagos has long since become a diverse, multi-ethnic city.[20] It can also be seen far beyond the developing world. Hajnal and Trounstine (2005) document how newly settled urban ethnic groups that are less politically organized in many US cities, such as Latinos and Asian-Americans, become systematically underrepresented in low-turnout city council elections, reducing the quality of representation they receive from urban governments relative to longer-resident ethnic groups.

But capture is also possible in low-turnout local elections even in cases where there is no similar early-settled ethnic group. In theory, any interest group that has significant advantages in grassroots mobilization of its members will dominate local elections when credibility problems or other features of the policy system create broad abstention among other categories of voters. In other contexts, this could be candidates from a locally powerful union, trade association, or local party machine. For example, Anzia (2014) richly documents the ability of well-organized teachers' unions to capture disproportionate power in low-turnout, off-cycle elections in the US and change education policies in their favor. While the reasons turnout is low in these local elections are different than for elections in urban Ghana, the resulting capture is similar.

8.3 FAVORITISM IN DISTRICT ASSEMBLIES

I examine this argument with two sets of evidence: interviews with district assembly members, and a series of quantitative data sources on turnout in assembly elections and the performance of assembly members. I begin with the qualitative evidence. The interviews suggest that there is persistent partisan favoritism in the district governments. NPP-affiliated assembly members discussed how NDC DCEs in Greater Accra steer more of the district budget to NDC strongholds and ELAs represented by NDC-affiliated assembly members, to the point that some NPP-affiliated assembly members believe there is little chance they will get any support for projects in their ELAs. NDC assembly members leveled essentially identical accusations of favoritism for the period when the NPP was last in power (2001–2008).

---

[20] Grossman (2016) describes how these traditional ruling families in Lagos "have an outsized claim to head local governments in which their homes (physical palaces) are based" (36). Also see Peil (1991) and Akinyele (2009).

One NPP assembly member described how requests for funding for projects in her ELA are consistently delayed because the DCE is

appointed by the government in power. The person is only willing to help those who are on their ticket, those who are on their side ... So when you write to request for something, they will tell you follow up, follow up, because your party is not in power ... But when you get to an NDC assembly member's area, to their community, you will see they are having a whole lot of projects.[21]

Another NPP assembly member said that because of delays in approval for development projects in his ELA, he has stopped requesting support through the normal district budget process altogether:

The power alone resides with the Mayor. Because the president appoints him, he has everybody, so if he says to do this, they'll do it. But then your project, you have to spend years chasing it before you get the money ... I don't bother going to the mayor's office ... because the mayor has his own own political agenda ... The other [NDC] assemblymen will have finished their projects, and they'll be saying [there is] no money for you.[22]

In this context, core NPP supporters may see little reason to turn out in district elections; any NPP assembly member they would elect may not be able to do much once in office.[23]

While adamantly denying the current DCE engaged in favoritism, an NDC assembly member described similar favoritism under the NPP: "It was not easy for you to have a project in this community ... Back in that time when the NPP was in power, they did what we call [in Twi] 'pick and choose, pick and choose.' So they would pick and choose ... they would say 'oh, that project that's going in our area, we like it, so it will go there.'"[24] Another NDC assembly member echoed these comments. Describing requests for funding for his ELA under the NPP, he said, "It wasn't easy at all ... If the man is NPP, they collaborate with the assembly man. But if the assembly man is NDC, it doesn't happen." With

---

[21] Interview with assembly member, Okaikwei Central constituency, Greater Accra, March 12, 2014.
[22] Interview with assembly member, Ablekuma North constituency, Greater Accra, March 11, 2014.
[23] Similarly, Lambright (2014) describes how national ruling party politicians prevent opposition party politicians who win local elections in Uganda from exercising their local authority.
[24] Interview with assembly member, Okaikwei Central constituency, Greater Accra, February 25, 2014.

the NDC in power beginning in 2009, his access to local government resources changed: "[It's] better access. You move freely to most of the offices where you can go for development. [My ELA] gets its fair share ... He's [the DCE] a government appointee and I'm also from the same government ... He listens to the NDC assembly members more than the others. It's the norm."[25] Another NDC assembly member who also serves as a local executive in the NDC admitted that he had special advantages for securing funding for projects in his ELA: when now asking for funding, "They see me, they know 'oh, this man is our party man.' They will have time for me and sit down and talk to me."[26]

Assembly members highlighted Ga neighborhoods in particular as major recipients of local government spending. One member in the AMA argued, "Some areas are benefiting more than the other areas. For example, looking at Accra itself ... [27] the district government concentrates here. The other communities that don't even have the road tarred, they don't bring money there."[28] An NDC constituency executive went further, describing the AMA under the NDC as fully captured by Ga politicians. Gas "are the AMA," he said, continuing:

They get most of the resources ... because the mayor comes from there, the office is located around that area [Ga communities of central Accra]. They have a feeling that when you go to the various appointments, chairman of the various committees [of the assembly], you realize that they come from within that enclave ... They have a feeling that the AMA is their property, their bonafide property. Therefore they exploit it to the maximum.

He described how Ga leaders had installed Gas into most of the major bureaucratic posts: "Even the NADMO [disaster relief] coordinator, they used to have a guy who was not from that area. They maneuvered and got him out because he was not a Ga. All the departmental heads come from the Ga areas."[29]

---

[25] Interview with assembly member, Ayawaso Central constituency, Greater Accra, August 27, 2013.
[26] Interview with assembly member and NDC executive, Ayawaso West constituency, Greater Accra, July 23, 2012.
[27] Within Greater Accra, "Accra" refers to the predominantly Ga neighborhoods of the center city.
[28] Interview with assembly member, Ablekuma North constituency, Greater Accra, July 19, 2012.
[29] Interview with NDC constituency executive, Ablekuma North constituency, Greater Accra, March 25, 2014.

One of the NDC's appointed assembly members, himself a Ga leader, confirmed that Ga areas get advantages from the AMA despite only comprising a minority of the city's population. He defended this favoritism, arguing that Gas deserved extra attention from the district government because of their status as indigenes facing the threat of in-migration of outsiders:

> That's how it's supposed to be. Compare it to other regions. You go to a [rural] region, the district is made up of one tribe so when you go to the assembly, the members of the assembly were elected from that same tribe. When the benefits come, they come to that tribe's area. Now when you come to Accra ... everybody is in Accra now and ... the Ga should continue to fight to be recognized ... When you go to the real Ga areas, the indigenous areas, they are the poorest, and that is not right. We need to upgrade those areas.[30]

8.4 QUANTITATIVE DATA SOURCES

Several quantitative data sources complement the interview evidence. I use 2010 and 2015 district assembly election results at the district level for the entire country and at the Electoral Area (ELA) level for Greater Accra. ELA-level results are available for all but two districts in Greater Accra for the 2010 local government elections and for all districts in 2015.[31] In addition to measuring turnout, I use the ELA-level results to identify the ethnicity of each candidate in 2010 and 2015.[32] The ethnicities of each candidate were coded from their names by a team of Ghanaian research assistants – names are often clearly identifiable with ethnic groups in Ghana. Each name was coded by three RAs and each RA ranked one to three guesses for the ethnicity of the name. Using coding rules described in the Appendix to resolve conflicts in codings between RAs, I am able to identify the major ethnic category of 91% of the candidates and sitting assembly members in 2010. These are coded as belonging to one of four major ethnic categories: Ga (including

---

[30] Interview with assembly member and NDC constituency executive, Okaikwei Central constituency, Greater Accra, February 27, 2014.
[31] District assembly election results are not centrally collated by Ghana's Election Commission at the ELA level and had to be individually collected by district. Records of the 2010 election results are no longer available in Ga South and Ledzokuku-Krowor districts, but I am still able to identify the names of the winning assembly members in these districts.
[32] It is not possible to systematically code partisanship of assembly candidates because this is not listed in any results or on the ballot.

Dangmes), Akan (all subgroups), Ewe, and Northern. The remaining 9% of names are dropped from all analysis.

The election results are combined with the 2010 census data. There is no official map of ELA boundaries available in Ghana with which to link ELAs to the census enumeration areas. ELAs are only defined as a written list of the village or neighborhood names and also by the names of polling stations.[33] I manually create a digitized map of ELA boundaries in Greater Accra by tracing the boundaries of ELA using official lists of community names alongside a random sample of polling stations physically located by research assistants. To calculate demographic characteristics at the ELA level, I then overlay this map of ELA boundaries on the digitized map of census enumeration areas.[34] I use this data to calculate two measures of the size of the middle-class population in each ELA. First, I calculate the same neighborhood wealth index examined in the previous chapters. Second, I create a continuous education/employment index similar to the main survey measure used throughout the book using the individual-level census data in each enumeration area. I count the proportion of each ELA's population falling above the mean value of this index.

The ELA-level census data is combined with data from two surveys: the main survey of Greater Accra examined in the previous chapters and a separate, smaller survey on club goods distribution in the immediate vicinity of a representative, random sample of the city's polling stations.

8.5 ANALYSIS

I establish several patterns using this data. First, turnout in assembly elections is lower nationwide in urban than rural areas and in districts with larger middle-class populations. Within Greater Accra, turnout is lowest in the wealthiest ELAs with the largest middle-class populations. Turnout also varies with NDC vote share and the size of the Ga population in each ELA. Second, I show that low turnout allows the Ga minority to disproportionately win assembly seats in Greater Accra and,

---

[33] The Electoral Commission also has no official map of polling station locations, however (see Chapter 7).
[34] For enumeration areas that cross ELA boundaries, I sum census characteristics after weighting the census data by the proportion of the surface area of each enumeration area falling within each ELA.

in turn, helps ensure that Gas are appointed as DCEs in most of the city's districts. Third, I examine the negative implications of low turnout and the overrepresentation of the Ga on evaluations of assembly members. I end with suggestive evidence that Ga overrepresentation in the assemblies has led to favoritism toward Ga areas in the distribution of some types of club goods, while NDC areas in general are favored in the distribution of other resources.

8.5.1 Predictors of Turnout

I argue that two types of voters may be especially unlikely to participate in local government elections: middle- and upper-class voters, and core supporters of the national opposition party. At the same time, I suggest that Ga voters, regardless of their socioeconomic status, and core supporters of the national ruling party should be relatively more likely to turn out than other voters. While I do not have measures of individual-level turnout in district assembly elections, I find ecological evidence consistent with each of these patterns in aggregate election results.

I first examine turnout at the district level in the 2010 district assembly elections for the entire country. Turnout was significantly lower in urban than rural districts, and especially in districts with more middle- and upper-class residents. In Ghana's very rural Upper East, Upper West, and Northern Regions, turnout in the 2010 district assembly elections was more than 50%. In Greater Accra Region, by contrast, turnout was only 19%.[35] In Kumasi, Ghana's second largest city, it was 22%. Overall, the average turnout rate in 2010 in rural districts was 44% of registered voters, while half that – 22% – in urban districts. Ghana's middle- and upper-classes are concentrated in these cities.

I estimate a series of weighted least squares regressions for turnout by district, weighting observations by the number of registered voters.[36]

---

[35] There could be concern that turnout was especially low in 2010 because the district election was repeatedly postponed due to logistical difficulties at the Electoral Commission. But turnout in 2010 in Greater Accra was actually slightly higher than in 2006, when 16% of registered voters turned out in the metropolitan area, despite no similar delay. Turnout also remained very similar in 2015, when the election had again been significantly delayed due to court cases against the Electoral Commission. It is not clear that these delays significantly alter aggregate turnout.

[36] Districts vary widely in size. District-level turnout is available at the submetropolitan assembly level (subdistrict level) within Accra, so the unit of observation here is the district nationally and subdistrict (more equivalent in size to nonurban districts) within Accra.

I find that districts that are one standard deviation wealthier on the main wealth index analyzed in the previous chapters had 8.2 percentage points lower turnout in the 2010 district assembly elections (95% CI: 5.9, 10.4).[37] I also use the individual-level census data to calculate the proportion of residents in each district who fit the definition of middle-class status in Chapter 2 – with secondary education, formal employment, and English literacy – and find that districts with 10 percentage points more middle-class residents had 7 percentage points lower turnout in 2010 (95% CI: 3.8, 10.0).

There is also wide variation in turnout rates by ward within Greater Accra, the area of the country with the lowest overall turnout in district elections. In Taifa South electoral area in the Ga East district, only 3.4% of registered voters turned out to vote in 2010. But 58% turned out in Akweitse-Gon electoral area in the peri-urban Kpone-Katamanso district. In the 2015 district assembly elections, as few as 9% of voters turned out in several electoral areas in the Ga East and Madina districts, while more than 60% turned out in several poorer wards on the outskirts of the metropolitan area.

In Table 8.1, I examine this variation systematically by regressing turnout in each ELA in Greater Accra on similar measures of wealth, as well as each ELA's population density and ethnic or partisan composition. I estimate separate models for the 2010 and 2015 district assembly elections. I again weight observations by the number of registered voters to account for size differences across ELAs. I also include district-level fixed effects, to control for baseline differences in turnout across administrative districts.[38]

A clear pattern emerges, similar to the nationwide results. In column 1 of Table 8.1, I find significantly lower turnout in ELAs with higher scores on the neighborhood wealth index. In column 2, I count the percentage of adults in each ELA with above-average scores on the individual-level education/employment index from Chapter 2. Again, I find significantly lower turnout in ELAs with larger middle- and upper-class populations. Results for the 2015 elections in columns 1 and 2 of the second panel of Table 8.1 are similar.

---

[37] For these analyses I recalculate the same index described in Chapter 6 at the district level.

[38] Because of missing turnout data in two districts in 2010 (Ga South and Ledzokuku-Krowor) and missing geocoded census data in two additional districts for both years (Tema and Ashaiman), it is only possible to estimate these regressions for 130 ELAs in 2010 and 177 ELAs in 2015.

TABLE 8.1: *Turnout in 2010 and 2015 district assembly elections in Greater Accra*

A: 2010 District Elections (by ELA)	1	2	3	4
Neighborhood Wealth Index	−0.011* (0.005)			
% Above Mean Employment/Education		−0.118** (0.040)	−0.101** (0.037)	−0.086* (0.038)
Ga %			0.141*** (0.032)	0.102** (0.037)
NDC 2008 Pres. Vote Share				0.101† (0.053)
Ethnic Fractionalization	−0.161** (0.049)	−0.161** (0.048)	0.022 (0.061)	−0.046 (0.070)
Population Density	0.001*** (0.000)	0.001*** (0.000)	0.001*** (0.000)	0.001*** (0.000)
District FEs	Y	Y	Y	Y
R^2	0.397	0.410	0.493	0.508
N	130	130	130	130
B: 2015 District Elections (by ELA)	1	2	3	4
Neighborhood Wealth Index	−0.013** (0.004)			
% Above Mean Employment/Educ.		−0.117** (0.040)	−0.060 (0.037)	−0.036 (0.038)
Ga %			0.188*** (0.029)	0.146*** (0.033)
NDC 2008 Pres. Vote Share				0.102* (0.042)
Ethnic Fractionalization	−0.094* (0.046)	−0.098* (0.046)	0.123* (0.053)	0.047 (0.061)

(continued)

TABLE 8.1: *(Continued)*

B: 2015 District Elections (by ELA)	1	2	3	4
Population Density	0.001**	0.001***	0.001***	0.001**
	(0.000)	(0.000)	(0.000)	(0.000)
District FEs	Y	Y	Y	Y
R^2	0.305	0.303	0.446	0.465
N	177	177	177	176

***$p < 0.001$, **$p < 0.01$, *$p < 0.05$, †$p < 0.1$. The outcome is turnout as percentage of registered voters per Electoral Area (ELA) in the urban districts of Greater Accra. Weighted Least Squares regressions, with weights by number of registered voters per ELA, and district-level fixed effects. Excludes ELAs with missing census (Tema and Ashaiman districts) or turnout data (Ga South and Ledozkuku-Krowor districts in 2010 only). Population density is scaled at 1,000s per sq. km.

I also find results consistent with the other patterns discussed earlier. In column 3 of Table 8.1, I show that the proportion of an ELA's population that is Ga also predicts greater turnout in the assembly elections, consistent with Ga voters having the most to gain from participating in these elections. In column 4, I find that NDC vote share in the previous presidential election also predicts higher turnout, consistent with more turnout in ruling-NDC strongholds and lower turnout in opposition-NPP strongholds in local government elections when the NDC holds national power.

8.5.2 Who Wins Low-turnout Local Elections

Low turnout appears to open the way for ethnic capture of local governments. With turnout so low, the average winning coalition for an assembly seat in Greater Accra in 2010 was only 6.5% of each ELA's registered voters. In the Dzorwulu and Abelenkpe electoral areas in Ayawaso West constituency of Accra – both wealthy areas of the city – the winning assembly members in 2010 each won only 1.7% of registered voters in multicandidate races. Elsewhere, however, winning candidates had to bring together as many as 15% or 20% of registered voters, requiring significantly broader support to win.

Where the winning threshold is small, candidates from groups that can most easily mobilize their members can win even if they represent a clear minority of the electorate. The Ga in particular are poised to take advantage of low turnout in district assembly elections. Gas were 48% of the elected assembly members across all urban districts in Greater Accra in 2010 and 43% in 2015, compared to only 27% of the population. When combined with the additional assembly members appointed to each assembly by the ruling party, this gave Gas the majority in essentially every district assembly throughout the urban area. The overrepresentation of Gas is most extreme within the city of Accra itself. Ga candidates won 52% and 54% of the seats in the AMA in 2010 and 2015, respectively, despite comprising only 23% of the city's population. By comparison, the Akan are the most underrepresented in the district assemblies, despite being the largest ethnic group in Accra: 28% of assembly members elected in 2010 were Akan, compared to 40% of the metropolitan area's population; only 20% of members in the AMA were Akan, from 38% of the city's population.[39] Ga dominance in these assembly elections is not an outcome of the NDC being in power nationally; Ga candidates also appear to have been overrepresented in the similarly low-turnout 2006 district assembly elections, when the NPP was the ruling party.[40]

I estimate the probability that a Ga candidate won each assembly election in 2010 using logistic regressions with a Ga victory as the outcome and the same predictors as column 4 of Table 8.1. I also include the percentage turnout in each ELA as an explanatory variable. Controlling for the Ga population percentage in each ELA, which understandably predicts whether a Ga candidate wins, Gas were most likely to win assembly seats where turnout was lower. I estimate that a Ga candidate is 10 percentage points more likely to have won an assembly seat after a 10 percentage point decrease in turnout (95% CI: 0.00, 14.6). Where turnout was higher, by contrast, the winner of the assembly seat was more likely to reflect the actual ethnic composition of the ELA.

At the same time that Ga candidates are disproportionately winning low-turnout assembly elections, Ga party leaders are disproportionately

---

[39] Gas were also more likely to run for assembly seats in the first place. From the ELAs where I can code the ethnicity of all 2010 candidate names, 45% of candidates were Ga, compared to 31% Akan. At least one Ga candidate contested for more than 75% of the seats in 2010.
[40] I estimate that Ga candidates won 47% of the seats in the AMA and 42% in the larger metropolitan area in 2006 based on my own coding of these names; the 2006 winners' names were not included in those coded by the research assistants as described earlier.

nominated by the president to be the DCE of each district. In total, 13 of the 19 DCEs who led the 12 urban districts of Greater Accra over the course of the NDC's administration (2009–2016) were Ga. The overrepresentation of the Ga also occurred under the NPP government prior to the 2008 election and appears set to continue after the NPP won the 2016 elections, even though the NPP receives far less electoral support from Ga voters (see Chapter 7). Four of the eight DCEs serving in these same districts in the second term (2005–2009) of NPP president John Kufuor were Ga.[41] Eight of the 12 DCEs initially nominated in 2017 by the new NPP government to lead the city's 12 districts were also Ga, including the NPP's new mayor of Accra. Ga control over the district assemblies helps force presidents from either party to nominate Ga party leaders as DCE. In most of Greater Accra, DCEs face a confirmation vote from a majority Ga assembly. These confirmation votes are not always rubber stamps. Ga elites see DCE positions in Greater Accra as rightfully belonging to their group and place significant pressure on the national government to only appoint Gas into these positions, threatening protests if "outsiders" are nominated instead.[42]

8.5.3 Who Assembly Members Help

Ga overrepresentation in the district assemblies comes at the expense of popular approval of local government performance, especially in wards where Gas are residentially segregated from other ethnic groups. By contrast, popular approval of local government officials is much higher in ELAs where turnout remains high and these local election results are more demographically representative.

The survey of residents of Greater Accra analyzed in the previous chapters did not include a question about turnout in the 2010 assembly election, but it did measure perceptions of assembly members' performance. Respondents were asked, "In your opinion, is your local assembly member in this area able to help community members when they have problems?" Because the main role of district assembly members is to provide basic constituent services, this serves as a performance evaluation

---

[41] The number of districts increased from 8 to 12 between 2009 and 2012. The other four DCEs in Kufuor's second term were Akans, the ethnic group more closely affiliated with the NPP. By contrast, only one of the NDC's 19 DCEs in the metropolitan area since 2009 has been an Akan, even though Akans are the plurality group in the city.
[42] For example, Washington (2017); "Only Ga-Dangmes should be MCEs, DCEs in Greater Accra" (2017).

of the assembly members. Overall, only 19% answered that their assembly member was either always or sometimes helpful. Six percent said that their assembly member only helped other people, never the respondent, and the remainder either said that the assembly member was never helpful to anyone (30%) or that they did not even know who their assembly member was (45%).

There is significant variation in these responses across respondents and across neighborhoods. I estimate a series of multilevel logistic regressions in which the outcome is a binary indicator for each respondent reporting that her assembly member is at least sometimes helpful. As in the previous chapters, the intercepts are partially pooled by the 48 sampling locations in the survey to account for the clustered nature of the sample and include district fixed effects to control for differences across separate municipal governments.[43] At the individual level, I include similar controls as in the models for vote choice in Chapter 7. At the neighborhood level, I include NDC vote share in the respondent's ELA in the 2008 presidential election, the neighborhood wealth index for the immediate area around each respondent, and population density.

The results are presented in Table 8.2. Column 1 shows that Ga respondents are significantly more likely to approve of their assembly member than other residents. Simulating from column 1, Ga respondents are 7.3 percentage points (95% CI: 0.6, 14.0) more likely to report their assembly member as helpful compared to other respondents. In addition, active members in local political party organizations have better performance evaluations of assembly members, especially respondents who are members of the ruling NDC, as shown in column 2. This is consistent with the argument that ruling party members and core supporters may be particularly likely to benefit from any goods their assembly member provides. I simulate that respondents who are NDC members are 11 percentage points (95% CI: 2.8, 20.4) more likely to approve of their assembly member than respondents who are not members of a party. By contrast, opposition NPP members are no more likely to find assembly members helpful than those who are not in a party.

Moreover, other respondents find Ga assembly members to be particularly unhelpful. This is seen in column 3, which includes an indicator

---

[43] I define the fixed effects at the level of the submetropolitan assemblies (subdistricts) within the AMA. Results are also robust to using clustered standard errors by sampling cluster instead of the multilevel model.

8.5 Analysis

TABLE 8.2: *Reported helpfulness of assembly members*

	1	2	3	4	5	6
Ga Assemblyman (by ELA)			−0.808† (0.439)	−1.927* (0.954)	1.715 (1.363)	
Ga % in ELA			−7.814* (3.814)	−7.293** (2.770)	−4.828 (3.479)	
Ga Assemblyman *Ga %				5.127 (3.476)		
Ga Segregation in ELA					−2.173 (2.098)	
Ga Assemblyman * Ga Seg.					−9.708† (5.203)	
Party Member	0.720** (0.228)		0.621* (0.251)	0.629* (0.250)	0.551* (0.252)	0.698* (0.272)
NDC Member		0.751* (0.295)				
NPP Member		0.423 (0.360)				
Turnout in 2010 (by ELA)						18.570* (8.982)
Ga	0.551* (0.250)	0.617* (0.282)	0.547* (0.275)	0.580* (0.275)	0.596* (0.283)	0.734* (0.322)
Ewe	−0.636* (0.307)	−0.452 (0.333)	−0.565† (0.326)	−0.605† (0.326)	−0.522 (0.329)	−0.642† (0.381)
Northerner	−0.259 (0.384)	−0.307 (0.428)	−0.285 (0.404)	−0.327 (0.406)	−0.249 (0.413)	−0.231 (0.433)
Full Individual-level Controls	Y	Y	Y	Y	Y	Y
Neighborhood-level Controls	Y	Y	Y	Y	Y	Y
District FEs	Y	Y	Y	Y	Y	Y
N	995	804	793	793	752	584

***$p < 0.001$, **$p < 0.01$, *$p < 0.05$, †$p < 0.1$. The outcome is a binary indicator for whether respondents report that their assembly member is at least "sometimes" helpful. All models are multilevel logistic regressions with intercepts partially pooled by sampling cluster, following Gelman and Hill (2007), and include district-level fixed effects (including for the submetropolitan assemblies within the AMA). Missingness in column 2 is for respondents who did not identify the party they belong to. Missingness in columns 3–5 is because the RAs could not agree on ethnicity codings for all assembly members. Respondents from Ga South and Ledzokuku-Krowor districts are dropped in column 6 because turnout data was not available.

for whether the current assemblyman is Ga.[44] In column 4, I interact the indicator for Ga assembly member with the Ga population percentage in each ELA. Although the interaction is not statistically significant ($p = 0.14$), it is signed in a direction suggesting that respondents believe Ga assembly members are most unhelpful in ELAs with few Gas. In these areas, Ga assembly members likely won their seat with support from only a small minority of registered voters and may target benefits narrowly to the few Gas living in the area. From column 4, I estimate that in an ELA with the 10th percentile in Ga population for Greater Accra (9.8% of the population is Ga), respondents are 21.0 percentage points (95% CI: 2.2, 38.7) less likely to see Ga assembly members as helpful than assembly members of other ethnicities. But in an ELA at the 90th percentile in Ga population for Greater Accra (51% of the population is Ga), respondents see Ga assembly members as no more or less helpful than others (95% CI: −18.0, 12.6).

Ga assembly members may be most unhelpful where the Ga community is segregated from surrounding neighborhoods. In an ELA that contains a segregated Ga enclave, the interviews suggest that a Ga assembly member may primarily target service provision to that enclave, at the expense of everyone else in the ELA. I examine the residential segregation of Gas within each ELA using a "dissimilarity" index of spatial segregation, based on comparing the Ga population percentage in each census enumeration area within an ELA to the overall Ga population percentage in the full ELA.[45] The index ranges from 0.02 to 0.59 in Greater Accra, with higher values indicating greater segregation. The index is calculated as a direct extension of the approach used to measure neighborhood characteristics around survey respondents in the previous chapters.[46] Figure 8.1 provides a visual example of how the spatial segregation of Gas within each ELA is calculated, comparing two ELAs with high and low values on the segregation index.

---

[44] A total of 202 observations are dropped in columns 3–5 because the ethnicity of an assembly member is unknown.

[45] Reardon and O'Sullivan (2004). This cannot be calculated in two ELAs in the survey data that correspond to only a single polygon in the enumeration area data. An additional 41 respondents are dropped.

[46] The spatial "dissimilarity" measure calculates the spatially weighted population shares of each ethnic group in a radius around the centroid of each enumeration area in an ELA – in the same manner described in Chapter 6 – and compares the population shares of groups around each enumeration area to the overall population shares in the full ELA. When the population shares for each enumeration area are more dissimilar from the ELA overall, there is more spatial segregation, and the index takes on a higher value.

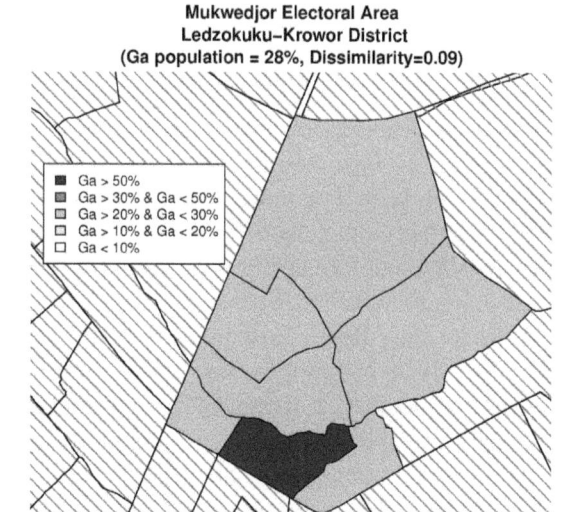

FIGURE 8.1: *Example of spatial segregation of Ga residents by electoral area*: The figure displays two ELAs with high and low scores on the dissimilarity index of spatial segregation of Ga residents (Reardon and O'Sullivan 2004). The polygons are census enumeration areas shaded by Ga population percentage. The key applies to both panels. In the top panel, Ga residents are heavily clustered in the southwestern corner of the ELA and largely absent in the north of the ELA, indicative of significant segregation. In the bottom panel, Ga residents are evenly distributed across the ELA, indicative of little segregation, except for a smaller cluster in one enumeration area.

In column 5 of Table 8.2, I find that survey respondents are significantly less likely to approve of Ga assembly members when living in ELAs where Gas are more segregated from other residents. As the Ga segregation index in the ELA increases by one standard deviation (0.12), I estimate that respondents become 9.5 percentage points less likely to see Ga assembly members as helpful (95%: 1.5, 14.3). But in areas where Ga residents are spatially intermixed with the rest of the community, respondents do not find Ga assembly members to be unhelpful compared to those of other ethnicities. Extrapolating to a difference in segregation at the same scale as pictured in Figure 8.1, this suggests that respondents are 36 percentage points less likely to find a Ga assembly member helpful when living in a highly segregated ELA such as Nmenmeette in central Accra (left panel of Figure 8.1) than in an ELA like Mukwedjor in Krowor constituency (right panel of Figure 8.1), which has a more uniform population distribution of Gas.

Finally, I find that turnout in 2010 is positively correlated with the perceived helpfulness of assembly members. I include turnout in each respondent's ELA in the 2010 assembly election as an explanatory variable in column 6 of Table 8.2.[47] As turnout in each respondent's ELA increases by 10 percentage points, respondents are 15.2 percentage points more likely to approve of their local assembly member (95% CI: 0.8, 29.4). This is consistent with assembly members providing better constituent services where they must maintain support of a larger group of voters to remain in office and face electoral pressure to address the needs of more constituents. It would also be consistent with more turnout from voters in ELAs where they believe assembly members are more likely to be able to address their preferences. But where turnout is very low, approval of assembly members is dramatically lower. It is in the low-turnout areas that local government seats are at greatest risk of capture by a local ethnic minority that narrowly targets benefits.

8.5.4 Impacts on Club Goods Distribution

The previous section examines individual residents' experiences with their district assembly members, providing suggestive evidence both that ruling-party control over each assembly means that core ruling-party supporters receive better service from assembly members than other voters

---

[47] Because assembly election results are not available for two districts included in the survey sample, an additional 168 respondents are dropped.

8.5 Analysis

and that Ga overrepresentation in the assemblies has negative consequences for the quality of representation experienced by most other residents. In this section, I scale up from individual-level evaluations to examine the distributive impacts of ruling party control and Ga overrepresentation on investments in club goods.

I focus on the distribution of three specific club goods – streetlights, roads, and schools – primarily under the purview of the district government. I find no favoritism in the allocation of streetlights, but favoritism in the allocation of roads and schools, with roads more likely to benefit Ga neighborhoods and school construction more likely to benefit all NDC-affiliated neighborhoods.

This difference can be explained by the different cost of streetlights compared to the latter two goods. Streetlights are relatively inexpensive to deliver; all assembly members can fund them through their discretionary Electoral Area Fund (see Section 8.1) without support or approval from the DCE. Aggregate patterns of favoritism may be difficult to observe if all assembly members, regardless of ethnicity or party affiliation, have the ability to provide a resource in each ELA.[48] By contrast, roads and schools are both more capital intensive projects that require approval from the DCE and the rest of the assembly, which can deny funding in NPP neighborhoods or in non-Ga areas.

These results must be interpreted with caution, however. The analysis relies on survey reports of where goods were distributed; systematic administrative data is not available on goods distribution by local governments in Greater Accra. Survey respondents cannot always reliably attribute responsibility for each good. Some goods could have been delivered separately by MPs through their discretionary funds or by private actors. Survey reports are also subject to potential biases from respondent recall that are difficult to control for in the analysis.

With these caveats noted, I combine two sources of survey data to produce a rough measure for local club goods distribution in the metropolitan area. First, research assistants were sent out to locate a representative, random sample of 238 polling stations across the city.[49] They interviewed three residents in the immediate vicinity of each polling

---

[48] Most assembly members interviewed reported providing streetlights to their communities from this discretionary fund, including the NPP-affiliated assembly members who complained about being blocked from delivering larger projects to their ELAs.

[49] Details on the polling station sample are in the Appendix. More than 95% of the sampled polling stations were successfully located, representing 37% of polling stations used in the 2012 elections.

station, selected via a random walk procedure beginning at the polling station.[50] Respondents were then asked a series of factual questions about whether several club goods had been built in the last five years – the period in which the NDC had been in power – in the immediate vicinity of their home: roads, schools, and streetlights.[51] Second, these same questions were repeated on the main survey to a randomly selected third (seven) of the respondents interviewed in each of the 48 sampling clusters.[52] Because there is inconsistency among respondents within locations on both surveys in answers to these questions, I collapse all of the responses to a binary indicator per location, in which survey locations are coded as having had a good delivered during the past five years if more than half of respondents in that location reported it.[53] Combining the surveys, I have data on goods distribution at 286 randomly selected locations throughout the metropolitan area.

Table 8.3 reports results of a series of logistic regressions where the outcomes are indicators for whether respondents at each location reported a road, school, or streetlight being constructed in the previous five years (since the NDC came to power).[54] All models control for neighborhood wealth and population density, as well as indicators for which of the two surveys each observation comes from and whether the survey enumerators noted that the location was in a commercial or residential area. I also include a measure of the population growth in the surrounding ELA for each location between the 2000 and 2010 censuses, which provides a measure of need for new club goods. Each model also includes

---

[50] Residents who reported living in that area for less than five years were replaced with a new respondent selected via the same procedure.
[51] Respondents were asked to point out these goods to the research assistant, if possible, so the research assistant could visually confirm their existence. Question wordings were: "In the last five years, have any roads been tarred or constructed in this neighborhood?"; "In the last five years, have any new streetlights gone up in this area?" ; "In the last five years, have any government schools been built or renovated in this area?"; and "In the last five years, have any new public toilets opened in this neighborhood?" In cases where one respondent answered "don't know" multiple times, the research assistant was prompted to resample an additional respondent and the uninformed respondent's responses were dropped.
[52] Respondents who reported living in their home for less than five years were also skipped.
[53] If a respondent in either survey reported that a good was delivered, she was asked a follow-up question about who she believed was responsible. Attribution for the same project was often inconsistent and I do not attempt to separate out responses based on the attributed actors.
[54] For roads, this includes reports of road maintenance (such as repaving). For schools this includes new government schools and renovation of existing schools.

8.5 Analysis

TABLE 8.3: *Distribution of roads, schools, and streetlights in Greater Accra*

Good:	1 Road	2 School	3 Streetlight	4 Road	5 School	6 Streetlight
NDC 2008 Vote Share (ELA)	−2.04 (1.73)	4.97* (1.96)	1.31 (1.89)	−1.70 (1.69)	4.97* (1.99)	1.05 (1.90)
Ga % (ELA)	2.61* (1.29)	1.37 (1.59)	−0.79 (1.38)			
Ga % (500m)				2.00† (1.16)	1.45 (1.42)	−0.21 (1.29)
Development Index (ELA)	0.55* (0.24)	−0.02 (0.24)	0.10 (0.24)			
Development Index (500m)				0.82*** (0.24)	−0.28 (0.25)	0.27 (0.24)
Commercial Area (0,1)	0.48 (0.35)	0.04 (0.38)	−0.27 (0.39)	0.77* (0.36)	−0.10 (0.39)	−0.21 (0.40)
Population Density (ELA)	0.01 (0.02)	0.00 (0.02)	−0.00 (0.02)	0.01 (0.01)	−0.01 (0.02)	0.00 (0.02)
%age Growth 2000–2010 (ELA)	−0.06 (0.09)	−0.08 (0.09)	−0.03 (0.05)	−0.10 (0.11)	−0.10 (0.09)	−0.02 (0.05)
From Voter Survey (0,1)	0.88* (0.40)	−2.58*** (0.47)	18.17 (909.24)	1.02* (0.40)	−2.67*** (0.48)	18.22 (913.00)
District FEs	Y	Y	Y	Y	Y	Y
N	246	225	224	243	222	221

***$p < 0.001$, **$p < 0.01$, *$p < 0.05$, †$p < 0.1$. Outcomes are binary indicators for whether each good listed above was delivered to the immediate area around the polling station or survey sampling cluster. All models are logistic regressions, with district-level fixed effects to control for baseline differences across local governments. Data is from a combination of two sources: a survey of a random sample of polling station locations in Greater Accra, and a representative survey of voters in Greater Accra, as described in the text. All but one location in the voter survey reported streetlights being delivered (columns 3 and 6), accounting for the large standard errors on the survey indicator variable in these columns.

district fixed effects to control for baseline differences in delivery of these goods across the 12 district governments.

Controlling for variables that measure baseline needs for new roads in each location, I find in column 1 that survey locations in ELAs with larger Ga populations are significantly more likely to have reported road construction and maintenance in the previous five years than locations in ELAs with smaller Ga populations.[55] A location in an ELA with the 90th percentile in Ga population share in Greater Accra (51%) is 19.6 percentage points (95% CI: 0.1, 24.7) more likely to have road construction or maintenance than an otherwise similar location in an ELA with the 10th percentile in Ga population share (9.8%).[56] In column 4, I repeat the model from column 1 but replace the Ga population percentage in the survey location's ELA with the Ga population percentage in the 500-meter radius immediately surrounding the sampled location, an area much smaller than the full ELA. Again, I find that survey locations in local neighborhoods within ELAs with larger Ga populations are more likely to have reported road construction, consistent with favoritism toward Ga areas.

In columns 2 and 4, I change the outcome to an indicator for school construction and renovations. Unlike for roads, I do not find evidence of favoritism to Ga ELAs or Ga neighborhoods in school construction. Instead, there is evidence of partisan targeting to NDC areas. Controlling for differences in poverty, population growth, and population density that should predict underlying needs for public schools, survey locations in ELAs with higher NDC presidential vote share in the 2008 presidential election are more likely to have reported school construction. As NDC vote share in the 2008 presidential election in the ELA increases by 10 percentage points, survey locations are 8.1 percentage points (95% CI: 0.02, 11.8) more likely to report school construction. Finally, in columns 3 and 6 I repeat these models for the construction of new streetlights. I find no favoritism in the distribution of streetlights, likely for the reasons given earlier.

---

[55] I also repeat column 1 of Table 8.3 subsetting only to the reports of road maintenance and find identical results.

[56] Conditional on being in the same place, Ga respondents are not more likely to know about road construction than other respondents. In a robustness test, I regress an indicator for whether each respondent in the larger survey of residents reported road, streetlight, or school construction on indicators for their ethnicity, controlling for survey location with survey location fixed effects. While responses vary across locations, there are no differences in reporting any of these club goods by ethnic group, except that Ewe respondents are slightly less likely to report knowledge of road construction.

While the results in Table 8.3 have limitations, they provide suggestive quantitative evidence of significant favoritism in the allocation of local government resources in line with the interview evidence. The data in Table 8.3 does not cover all goods distribution in the city. Under the Mills and Mahama NDC governments, for example, national-level ministries carried out some large-scale public infrastructure provision in Accra, such as construction of new highways. Such major projects are often funded (in part) by international donors on a case-by-case basis. Table 8.3 suggests that the delivery of more mundane, everyday resources – such as which residential streets to pave – are subject to favoritism, rather than targeted to address the city's most pressing needs.

8.6 SUMMARY

This chapter examined Greater Accra's local government system, documenting how low turnout and the exit of the urban middle class allows for capture by a minority group, perpetuating favoritism in the allocation of municipal resources. The chapter begins by developing an argument about which types of urban residents are more or less likely to vote in local-level elections and finds support for the argument in results from Ghana's 2010 and 2015 district assembly elections. Low turnout helps Ga candidates win assembly seats. Residents disapprove of the performance of Ga assembly members, especially in ethnically segregated wards where the Ga live apart from other residents. The chapter ends by examining the favoritism in the distribution of club goods by municipal governments that results both from this ethnic capture and from national ruling-party appointment of local government leaders.

Although the chapter shifts focus from national to local elections, it helps provide evidence for the final steps of the trap in Chapter 1. The capture examined here grows directly out of local-level analogs of the two processes examined in Parts II and III: abstention based on the inability of politicians to address many types of voter preferences, and ethnic voting rooted in expectations that most politicians will favor co-ethnics. The results of this capture, in turn, feed back into these dynamics. Local governments in African cities lack the resources and bureaucratic capacity necessary to confront all of the developmental challenges created by urban growth. But these shortcomings are exacerbated when turnout is low and local governments are captured by minority ethnic interests that steer already limited local government resources toward themselves.

Not only does this increase scarcity, feeding future demand for particularistic goods that can be targeted as patronage, but it helps reduce the credibility of broader national government efforts to address voters' universalistic preferences. In Ghana's deconcentrated political system, the local district-level officials studied here are often those tasked with implementing national-level policies. When district leaders are personally accountable primarily to only a small minority of the urban electorate, they may underinvest in following through on national policy priorities, or distort those policies to serve more parochial interests. In this way, the dynamics documented in this chapter may even reinforce the parallel credibility problem in national elections explored in Chapter 4.

Finally, and separately from the main argument of the book, the chapter also provides an in-depth illustration of the more general risks of capture in local elections in developing countries. District governments in Greater Accra were created through a decentralization process in the late 1980s similar to the widespread decentralization reforms seen elsewhere in Africa and the developing world in recent decades.[57] While proponents view decentralization as a means to improve local accountability by "bringing government closer to the people," the capture of local governments by local elites who siphon off resources (either as private rents or as selective benefits for a subset of residents) has been a persistent problem stymying these reforms.[58] Allowing for competitive local elections is often viewed as a means to prevent this capture.[59] But I highlight how low turnout, especially when combined with the abstention of higher-socioeconomic-status voters, can allow minority interest groups to continue to capture disproportionate local power despite the introduction of competitive local elections. Ultimately, local elections can only produce greater accountability if voters believe that turning out is worthwhile because local politicians have the capacity to supply policies that actually address voters' demands.

---

[57] Bardhan (2002), Grossman and Lewis (2014), and Hassan (2016).
[58] Olowu and Wunsch (2004), Reinikka and Svensson (2004), and Bardhan and Mookherjee (2006).
[59] Olowu and Wunsch (2004), Ferraz and Finan (2011), Martinez-Bravo et al. (2012), and Beath et al. (2013).

9

Paths out of the Trap?

The previous chapters suggest that Greater Accra is stuck in a trap. Despite a large middle class and high levels of ethnic diversity, politicians have strong incentives to persist with nonprogrammatic appeals and ethnic favoritism. Because voters continue to expect ethnicity to determine access to valuable state resources, ethnic voting remains common in many neighborhoods. The voters who form the most natural constituency for programmatic politics differentially abstain from electoral participation. Their exit only aids the ethnic capture of urban governments, allowing for inefficient distribution of already limited government resources. In turn, the inability of captured local governments to address voter demands for basic services may help to sustain the viability of nonprogrammatic appeals into the future and further undermine confidence in the government's ability to commit to programmatic policies.

Exploring the roots of this trap contributes to several lines of inquiry. First, it advances understanding of electoral politics in sub-Saharan Africa by focusing on urban areas, where elections have received relatively little explicit study despite rapid rates of urbanization. Second, it helps expand theories of political behavior, especially theories about neighborhood effects on voters and the origins of class-based differences in political participation. Third, it offers insights into how societies are able to – or can fail to – move toward programmatic political competition as they undergo socioeconomic development.

This final chapter focuses on the third contribution. Explaining the origins of programmatic competition has been a fundamental question of interest for decades to scholars of both new and advanced democracies. Dating at least to Shefter (1977), scholars have theorized politicians' choices over linkage strategies as akin to decisions made by firms competing in a competitive marketplace. In this framework, different electoral appeals emerge either from *demand-side* pressures – the socioeconomic characteristics and attitudes of voters – or *supply-side* factors – the resource endowments and institutional constraints of politicians.[1]

A central claim of this book has been that while two major demand-side changes to the electorate that many expect to transform urban politics in Africa – the growth of the middle class and high levels of ethnic diversity – have helped create considerable intra-urban variation in political behavior, they are not causing the wholesale political transformation that is often predicted. Despite Shefter's (1977) warning that patronage practices often persist "in the face of social changes of the sort – modernization, industrialization, assimilation, acculturation – that according to sociological theories ... lead to the rise or decline of patronage politics" (404), the existing literature often takes demand-side assumptions about the political effects of demographic change at face value, assuming that differences in the socioeconomic composition of the electorate will lead directly to differences in electoral competition. I show instead that politicians in many neighborhoods of Greater Accra do not face strong enough incentives to change the appeals they supply despite these two socioeconomic developments. In turn, what politicians supply shapes how voters behave – in terms of both participation and vote choice.

Are supply-side incentives really more binding in determining how politicians and voters interact in new democracies? Chapter 2 already details scope conditions for specific elements of the book's argument, focusing in particular on the comparison of Ghana to other African cases. But it is also instructive to look more broadly and consider whether this general claim about the centrality of supply-side factors extends further. If supply-side incentives are binding in the choice of electoral appeals, similar traps or lags in which nonprogrammatic modes of competition persist long after underlying demographic changes should be common in many contexts outside of Africa. And in cases where societies do transition into more programmatic competition, changes in politicians' supply-side incentives should appear as the more proximate cause.

The first half of the chapter examines whether this is the case. I examine existing literature on two sets of cases that are in many respects quite different from urban Ghana, but where there have also been long

---

[1] Also see definitions in Kitschelt and Wilkinson (2007) and Hicken (2011).

lags between demographic change and the evolution of political appeals. Unlike Ghana, both sets of cases include examples where transitions to programmatic politics ultimately did occur, at least partially. The external cases provide an opportunity to explore whether supply-side factors similarly explain why political change was often so delayed and to examine how political appeals changed once these supply-side constraints were removed.

I focus first on the persistence of clientelistic machine parties in many cities in the early-to-mid twentieth-century United States. Despite significant contextual differences, the success of machine parties echoes many of the dynamics in urban Ghana. Some US cities remained bastions of clientelism and ethnic competition well after many scholars expected socioeconomic transformations to have ended these practices. Second, I discuss changes over time in the prevalence of programmatic politics in new democracies in Latin America. Latin America provides examples of similar traps to that found in urban Ghana, with scholars such as Kitschelt et al. (2010) also observing lags between demographic development and the erosion of clientelism. But it also provides examples of "dual" or "mixed" programmatic and clientelistic appeals, in which parties are better able to overcome the same challenges I describe Ghanaian politicians as facing in addressing the divergent demands of poor and wealthier voters in unequal societies. In each set of cases, I show that existing literature has more convincingly tied the (lack of) emergence of programmatic competition to supply-side rather than demand-side influences on politicians. Considered together, these cases lend "out of sample" support for the book's broader argument, suggesting that we cannot take the oft-assumed political effects of demographic change for granted in the developing world.

The second half of the chapter pivots to considering the lessons these cases provide about the prospects for political change in urban Ghana. I engage in a thought experiment: what realistic shifts would undermine urban Ghana's trap? I identify four developments that occurred in the US and Latin American cases – two on the demand side, two on the supply side – that could plausibly happen in urban Ghana in the near future. None are panaceas. But by evaluating each against existing literature on the US and Latin American cases as well as the evidence in the previous chapters, it becomes clear that the two examples of supply-side changes are more likely than the two demand-side examples to alter patterns of electoral competition. This suggests that rather than simply waiting for more urbanization and economic growth to play out in

Ghana, institutional reforms that alter politicians' incentives to provide patronage and exhibit favoritism to co-ethnics may have more immediate effects on clientelism and ethnic politics.

9.1 EXTERNAL CASES: THE US AND LATIN AMERICA

If supply-side incentives are really more binding on politicians than changes to the characteristics of voters, variants of urban Ghana's trap are possible in a much broader set of cases. Chapter 2 details scope conditions for the main argument: I expect traps to operate similarly in urban areas in other new democracies where low state capacity creates similar credibility problems for programmatic campaigns, cities are internally heterogeneous in their demographic characteristics, elections are competitive, and the main parties are similarly polarized along ethnic lines. But even when the same mechanisms examined in Ghana may not be at play – for example, in higher capacity states or polities with less salient ethnic cleavages – other forces may similarly intervene to incentivize politicians to continue with nonprogrammatic appeals even as societies develop and populations become wealthier and more ethnically heterogeneous.

In an historical example that bears surprising resemblance to the Ghanaian case, albeit in a very different political context, some US cities were caught in their own self-reinforcing, clientelistic traps for decades. Eventually, they all escaped. Similar lags between demographic change and political appeals have also been observed in Latin America. But more recently, some Latin American parties have managed to diversify their appeals. Rather than differentially ignoring middle-class voters and doubling-down on patronage appeals to the poor, these parties are successfully reaching both types of voters. How did these two sets of cases end up on different paths than urban Ghana? A common theme running through the existing literature is that supply-side incentives were generally more proximate causes of politicians' decisions to eschew nonprogrammatic politics than demographic changes that altered voters' demands.

9.1.1 The Demise of America's Clientelistic Machines

Clientelism, ethnic favoritism, and ethnic voting all were common in some US cities deep into the twentieth century in the form of "machine" politics. The US was much wealthier throughout this period than Ghana

9.1 External Cases: The US and Latin America

is today and had considerably higher state capacity. But in patterns that match those of Greater Accra, local party organizations captured municipal governments for decades at a time, served the interests of narrow ethnic constituencies, and distributed municipal resources as patronage.

The most well-known machine-party organizations were in New York City under Tammany Hall and Chicago under the first Mayor Daley, but clientelistic machines also controlled smaller cities such as Albany and Memphis for extended periods. The stereotypical urban machine emerged by consolidating the support of particular European immigrant ethnic groups, such as the Irish or Italians.[2] In their late-nineteenth-century configurations, machines explicitly bought the votes of poor immigrants with gifts of cash, food, and other basic necessities. But explicit vote buying became rare throughout most of the US by the early twentieth century.[3] In later periods, machines transitioned instead into sustained forms of relational clientelism similar to those common in contemporary urban Ghana. The most important particularistic benefit provided by machines to supporters became patronage jobs in municipal or state governments.[4] Machines also specialized in providing various favors to voters and local businesses, usually targeted at core supporters.[5] Local party bosses would help supporters obtain special public services in times of need or allow them to skip local taxes or administrative fees.[6] Much as described in Chapter 6, party leaders would also give small businessmen favored access to city contracts in return for loyalty. Loyalty could be demonstrated through campaign donations or by providing additional jobs in private-sector firms to machine supporters.[7] Moreover, as in urban Ghana, machine parties often took advantage of low turnout in off-cycle municipal elections to win political power despite only representing minority interests. Much like the argument in Chapter 8, Wolfinger (1972) suggests that low turnout by issue-oriented voters was a key piece of machine survival, especially in ward-level primaries that served as the de facto selection points for many city leaders.

---

[2] Erie (1988).
[3] Stokes et al. (2013).
[4] Most famously, Mayor Daley in Chicago in the 1960s was said to control 35,000 patronage positions to be allocated to supporters of the Democratic Party. He was reported to personally decide on who received each job (Wolfinger 1972, 373).
[5] Cox and McCubbins (1986).
[6] Wolfinger (1972, 368) writes that "in these and numerous other categories of citizen relations with government, machine politicians were prepared to be obligingly flexible about the laws, but a *quid pro quo* was implicit in such requests."
[7] Wolfinger (1972) and Boulay and DiGaetano (1985).

But the most important parallel between contemporary urban Ghana and historical US machines is that clientelism and other patronage-based forms of political competition persisted in many US cities *for decades* despite changes in the same underlying socioeconomic characteristics that scholars, policymakers, and journalists are now expecting to produce much more immediate political transformations in African cities. US machines took power in cities undergoing similar demographic transitions, both in wealth – with the emergence of a broad middle class in the US over the course of the twentieth century – and in ethnic composition – with large influxes of European immigrants at the beginning of the twentieth century and African-Americans in later decades.

Just as for African cities, some scholars have pointed to both demographic developments to explain the eventual demise of urban clientelism in the US. But each fails as an adequate explanation for similar reasons that they fail to explain the Ghanaian case: these arguments do not adequately consider the supply-side incentives for politicians to change their behavior in response to demographic change. Writing at a time when political machines still controlled several major cities, Wolfinger (1972) pointed to the weakness of socioeconomic explanations for machine collapse in the US by wryly noting that "machine politics is always said to be on the point of disappearing, but nevertheless seems to endure" (365).[8]

It is instructive to lay out why these parallel arguments about US cities struggle to explain political change. Banfield and Wilson (1963) most famously tie the gradual collapse of machine parties to the rising power of middle-class voters, who they believe hold cultural values inimical to clientelism and ethnic politics. More recently, Stokes et al. (2013) suggest that the "belated demise of American clientelism" (237) occurred after middle-class voters became the large majority of the electorate in the years after World War II. But many other scholars cast doubt on any simple connection between the growth of the middle class and the end of urban clientelism. Machine parties remained dominant in many cities throughout much of the first half of the twentieth century despite there being large middle-class populations – especially by Ghanaian standards – during the entire period.[9] Others question the notion that urban middle

---

[8] Also see Ansell and Burris (1997) on the limits of common sociological explanations for machine politics in the US.
[9] Wolfinger (1972), Dutton and Northrop (1978), and Boulay and DiGaetano (1985).

class voters in the USA were necessarily opposed to machine parties in the first place.[10] In addition, Trounstine (2008) finds little statistical evidence that changes in a city's middle-class population predict the electoral defeat of machine parties. Moreover, the post-WWII expansion of the US middle class also coincided with the mass departure of middle-class residents out of cities to booming suburbs, especially with the construction of the federal interstate-highway system beginning in the 1950s.[11] Wolfinger (1972) argues that, paradoxically, the last major wave of machines finally collapsed in the 1960s and 1970s just as urban electorates became *poorer* in the face of "white flight" and other forms of middle class out-migration from cities. This is the opposite of what would be expected if the different demands of middle-class voters had forced the end of urban clientelism.

In another parallel to arguments commonly advanced about African cities, Banfield and Wilson (1963) also tie the demise of clientelism in the urban US to rising ethnic diversity, and in particular, to cross-ethnic assimilation.[12] Banfield and Wilson (1963) suggest that as second- and third-generation immigrants became more assimilated into white American culture, the parochial ethnic appeals of machine parties lost salience. Moreover, Erie (1988) and Boulay and DiGaetano (1985) describe at least some ethnic-based machines being weakened by the influx of African-Americans into northern US cities in the mid-twentieth century. The Great Migration challenged machines to appeal to a new ethnic group with whom their existing networks of party agents had few social ties that could facilitate clientelism. The out-migration of second- and third-generation European immigrants into suburbs after WWII may also have contributed to machine collapse by shrinking many machines' original ethnic bases.[13]

But many scholars also have doubts about the importance of changes in ethnic demographics in explaining the demise of American clientelism. Despite the stereotypical image of machines as immigrant-based, some machines did not draw primarily on the support of immigrant

---

[10] Wolfinger (1972) argues that there was a "sizable subcategory of the middle class" – including many small business owners – who benefited financially from patronage relationships with machine politicians and may have served as a "*stronger* [sic] constituency for machine politics than the working classes" (390).
[11] Baum-Snow (2007) and Nall (2015).
[12] Also see Cornwell (1976).
[13] Stokes et al. (2013).

constituencies, yet lost power at the same time and in similar fashion as their immigrant-based counterparts.[14] Moreover, some machines, such as the Daley organization in Chicago, were able to successfully incorporate African-American voters, surviving despite the challenges posed by the Great Migration.[15] Overall, Trounstine (2008) finds no support for hypotheses that changes in the size of the African-American or Latino population predict machine collapse in US cities throughout the twentieth century, suggesting that the challenge of incorporating new ethnic groups into existing patronage coalitions was usually not insurmountable for machine parties.

Yet, by the early 1980s, America's remaining major machines had collapsed, or had at least abandoned most remaining vestiges of clientelism. Clientelistic machines died off at various times throughout the twentieth century such that there is clearly no uniform cause of the end of urban clientelism in the US.[16] But the existing literature suggests that three supply-side factors appear to have been particularly influential: civil service reform, the creation of the federal welfare state, and structural changes to the nature of urban economies that resulted in declining business funding for clientelistic party organizations. Together, these developments appear to have forced an evolution in modes of political competition in US cities that demographic changes could not.

The first common supply-side culprit identified in the literature is civil service reform. Historians have long seen at least part of the explanation for machine collapse in the introduction of merit-based, nonpartisan civil service hiring that cut off supply of valuable patronage jobs.[17] While civil service reform occurred at the federal level in the 1880s with passage of the Pendleton Act, the creation of a merit-based civil service at the local and state levels was more gradual. Some states introduced civil service reforms that prevented patronage hiring as early as 1905 in response to Progressive Era activism. But others, such as Mississippi and Montana, only did so in the 1970s.[18] As of the mid-1960s, a sizable minority of major cities still did not have merit-based civil service rules; their supply of patronage jobs remained plentiful.[19] But civil service reforms appear to have undermined patronage-based parties whenever they were finally

[14] Wolfinger (1972) and Boulay and DiGaetano (1985).
[15] Erie (1988).
[16] Trounstine (2008).
[17] For example, Greenstein (1964) and DiGaetano (1991).
[18] Folke et al. (2011). Also see Grindle (2012).
[19] Wolfinger and Field (1966).

adopted. Folke et al. (2011) find that the probability that state legislatures were captured by a single party for many elections in a row decreased dramatically once civil service reforms were introduced. The adoption of civil service reforms is also one of the main predictors of machine collapse in Trounstine (2008).

The second common supply-side culprit was the creation of a large-scale national welfare state, beginning with the New Deal in the 1930s and continuing through the Great Society programs of the 1960s. These programs placed the supply of many particularistic resources the urban poor demanded under control of nonpartisan federal bureaucrats.[20] As voters who had relied on machines gained viable exit options from clientelistic relationships, access to governments benefits became increasingly determined by rational need-based criteria rather than by ties to party bosses. The introduction of a new supplier of particularistic benefits who did not ask for political loyalty in return helped undercut the market for patronage.

Neither of these first two culprits provide a perfect explanation for the end of clientelism in the urban US. Some machine parties were able to pervert or sidestep these constraints. The allocation of public employment as patronage persisted despite civil service reform in some cities, most famously under the first Daley organization in Chicago.[21] Some machines were able to partly substitute away from jobs and other welfare benefits to continue patronage relationships by distributing different benefits for which there was less competition and fewer constraints on supply.[22] Other machines were – at least initially – able to capture the new stream of welfare benefits flowing from New Deal programs by infiltrating the local offices of the new federal bureaucracies.[23] But for the most part, civil service reforms and the introduction of federal welfare programs seem to have shifted the types of benefits that machines could offer. Direct exchanges of patronage were replaced with preferential help navigating bureaucracies, forcing local politicians into providing

---

[20] Greenstein (1964), Erie (1988). Importantly, the federal bureaucracies that began distributing these benefits were already subject to civil service reforms, as described earlier, even in states and cities that had not themselves yet introduced protections against partisan hiring into government positions.

[21] Wolfinger and Field (1966).

[22] Wolfinger (1972). DiGaetano (1991) argues, for example, that some machines "proved to be much more resilient than good-government reformers had anticipated" (52), such that civil service reforms on their own were not enough to end clientelism.

[23] For example, see Boulay and DiGaetano (1985), Trounstine (2008), and Stokes et al. (2013).

relatively more benign forms of constituent service.[24] Erie (1988) argues that the machines that did survive past the New Deal were forced to employ considerably more programmatic appeals.

A third culprit in the demise of machines came via transformations to the underlying structure of the urban economy, which had supply-side implications for the machines' ability to fund clientelism. Urban businesses were a key source of funding for machine parties, trading government contracts, favors, and protection from city leaders for campaign financing.[25] Local businesses also provided "an auxiliary source of jobs for machine loyalists" (Boulay and DiGaetano, 1985, 45) to supplement patronage jobs in local governments.[26] But after WWII, economic power became increasingly concentrated in large, professionalized corporations with operations that spanned many cities. As firms developed increasing "locational mobility", becoming able to shift operations from city to city in search of more favorable conditions, local politicians' bargaining power to extract campaign funding from businesses was undermined.[27] Relatedly, Kuo (2018) shows that the emergence of large corporations that no longer depended on ad-hoc personal relationships with individual politicians encouraged major business-lobbying associations to play a large role in pushing for the civil service reforms that restricted machines' supply of patronage. Ultimately, this combination of increasing restrictions on external funding for machines and changes to urban politicians' ability to selectively allocate public jobs and other government benefits appear to have choked off the supply of patronage politics in the urban US.

9.1.2 Programmatic Transitions in Latin America

Latin American cases also demonstrate the importance of supply-side shifts in the emergence (or disappearance) of programmatic politics. As

---

[24] Wolfinger (1972, 385) describes the new forms of exchange that emerged after the New Deal, quoting from Whyte's (1955) description of what a Boston state senator offered a voter: "If you're qualified, you can get on [the WPA] without going to a politician. But it will be four weeks before you get certified, and I can push things through so that you get on in a week." Helping party supporters jump an administrative queue is still a form of patronage. But with federal welfare programs in place, politicians could no longer deny benefits to nonsupporters who were eligible, as in more pernicious forms of clientelism. The resulting patronage exchanges were significantly less binding on voter behavior.

[25] Wolfinger (1972), Boulay and DiGaetano (1985).

[26] This also closely mirrors urban Ghana, where local businesses seeking contracts with the state are a major source of local party financing (Brierley 2016).

[27] Boulay and DiGaetano (1985).

with the example of US cities, new democracies in Latin America differ from those in Africa along many dimensions. They are usually much more urbanized, have relatively larger middle classes and higher capacity states, and often have more meaningful fiscal and political decentralization, a particularly important difference that I highlight in Section 9.2.4. For these reasons, the same mechanisms sustaining nonprogrammatic appeals in Ghana are not always at play in these cases. But like in the Ghanaian case, politicians' supply-side incentives appear to have a strong role in explaining choices over electoral appeals.

In some Latin American cases, there also have been long lags between demographic change and the prevalence of clientelism.[28] For example, similar to US cities, but on a much grander scale, Mexican politics was dominated for decades by a clientelistic machine party, the *Partido Revolucionario Institucional* (PRI), in the face of steady urbanization and rising wealth. When political competition ultimately did change, some scholars have pointed, at least in part, to demand-side explanations. Magaloni (2006) explains the collapse of the PRI's single-party dominance in the 1990s and the emergence of a more programmatic party system by highlighting, among other factors, demographic shifts that altered the outlook of Mexican voters and increased support for programmatic opposition parties. She suggests that gradual urbanization helped undermine clientelism, arguing in similar fashion as Koter (2016) for African cities that clientelism was inherently less viable in urban areas. Magaloni (2006, 261–263) explicitly connects this element of her argument to modernization theory. She also ties the collapse of the PRI to generational shifts in the Mexican electorate, arguing that younger voters who came of age during a period of economic crisis in the 1980s developed different expectations than older voters about the PRI's likely economic performance that made them more susceptible to the programmatic appeals of opposition parties.

But others have placed much more emphasis on the supply-side incentives behind these shifts. Greene (2007) rejects demand-side explanations for the Mexican case, noting that the PRI dominated for decades despite urbanization and economic growth that modernization theories would expect to undermine clientelism, and then lost support abruptly after structural adjustment reforms implemented in the aftermath of an economic crisis dramatically shrank the PRI's available supply of patronage, especially public sector jobs. Greene (2007; 212) describes how the number of public sector jobs controlled by the PRI government shrank

---

[28] For a more general discussion, see Kitschelt et al. (2010).

by nearly 80% over the course of the 1990s, from 2.71 million state jobs to just 570,000, and links this decline to the increased viability of programmatic opposition parties.

Others similarly tie shifts over time between programmatic and non-programmatic political competition in Latin America – in both directions – to changes in what politicians have incentives to supply. For example, Hagopian et al. (2009) tie the emergence of more programmatically oriented legislative candidates in Brazil in the 1990s not to rising wealth in the electorate, but to abrupt restrictions in available patronage resources after structural adjustment reforms similar to those in Mexico. Most clearly at odds with a demand-side theory, Levitsky (2003) suggests that structural adjustment reforms in Argentina pushed electoral competition in the opposite direction in the 1990s – with a shift back into clientelism and away from programmatic politics. Neoliberal economic policies pursued as part of structural adjustment constrained the Peronists' (the *Partido Justicialistia*, PJ) ability to continue supplying left-wing appeals to their base in the labor movement. Unlike most African countries, Argentina already had a prominent programmatic cleavage in its politics. But after being forced to adopt free market economic policies by a combination of economic circumstance and international pressure, the Peronists' programmatic credibility with voters collapsed.[29] With their supply of leftist policy appeals constrained by this credibility problem, Levitsky (2003) argues that the Peronists turned increasingly to clientelism to maintain support among lower-class voters. The example of Argentina in the 1990s is particularly important because it demonstrates that the choice of appeals has not always been a narrative of a teleological progression toward greater programmatic competition as societies modernize, as most demand-side theories imply, but instead fluctuates in multiple directions with changes to politicians' incentives.

More recently, smaller-scale policy interventions in Latin America have shocked the supply of patronage and created space for programmatic appeals to the poor. Similar to New Deal-era welfare state programs in the US that centralized the distribution of particularistic goods that had previously been distributed by local party agents, new universalistic social welfare programs targeted at the Latin American poor – most famously, *Bolsa Familia* in Brazil and *Progresa* in Mexico – have received considerable attention for their perceived ability to break patronage-based modes of distribution. These conditional cash transfer

---

[29] Also see Lupu (2016).

9.1 External Cases: The US and Latin America 289

(CCT) programs have been pushed heavily by international donors and offer guaranteed welfare benefits to the very poor as long as they meet several basic conditions, such as ensuring their children are vaccinated and attend school. Unlike many other forms of private goods distribution in developing countries, CCTs by design have clear, widely publicized rules about program eligibility, aiming to reduce the chances that information about how to access program benefits is distributed selectively by party agents.[30] Moreover, in the Mexican case, *Progresa* is controlled by a newly created bureaucratic agency set up from scratch to administer the program with the goal of reducing the risks of bureaucratic capture, which often plagues attempts to programmatically distribute private benefits in poor countries.[31] Much like in the US case, these programs have by no means fully eliminated the ability of local politicians in Brazil and Mexico to engage in nonprogrammatic appeals; local politicians can still substitute into providing other types of patronage benefits to poor voters. But to the extent that CCT programs have been successfully implemented as designed, they appear to be constraining the full range of clientelistic activities available.

Moreover, there are cases from Latin America in which single parties are able to persist in dual programmatic and nonprogrammatic equilibria in which they simultaneously employ different strategies aimed at different categories of voters over extended periods of time. The existence of a significant proportion of middle-class voters alongside very poor voters in the same elections means that politicians in Latin America, especially in many cities, often confront a fundamentally similar choice to the one described in Chapter 4 for politicians in urban Ghana: make costly investments in programmatic policies to attract more middle- and upper-class support, or instead concentrate on clientelism and try to win power with primarily poor support only. Unlike in Ghana, however, some Latin American parties choose the first option rather than the second.

Perhaps the clearest evidence of what makes the first choice possible comes from Chile, where the *Unión Demócrata Independiente* (UDI) has combined support of wealthy and middle-class voters, attracted to the party's conservative policy program, with the support of poor voters, attracted via clientelism. Luna (2014) identifies several structural

---

[30] For example, see Auyero's (2000) description of the manipulation of information provision regarding an Argentinian food assistance program, also studied in Weitz-Shapiro (2014).
[31] De La O (2013) and Weitz-Shapiro (2014).

conditions that create incentives under which politicians are able to effectively supply both types of appeal at once. First is the segregation of socioeconomic classes into distinct electoral and administrative districts and municipalities. This allows parties such as the UDI to engage in dual appeals overall even as each individual politician only has to specialize in one type of linkage strategy.[32] Second, there must be a sufficient degree of party institutionalization, and party leaders must be sufficiently strong, to be able to coordinate the actions of local politicians across these different types of districts. Third, parties need access to resources to supply patronage benefits, especially if they are not in power. Luna (2010) describes the UDI drawing on a network of wealthy conservative donors who raise the private funds necessary to support nonprogrammatic distribution in poor areas.[33] A fourth key feature implicit in Luna's argument is the degree of decentralization. Where local municipal-level officials have the political and fiscal autonomy necessary to implement separate local policy agendas, it becomes easier for a party to separate its appeals across districts. Luna's (2014) argument raises the possibility that under different incentives, created by different structural conditions, Ghanaian politicians would similarly diversify their electoral appeals, even without further demographic change.

9.2 WHAT COULD BREAK THE TRAP IN URBAN GHANA? THE CASES APPLIED

Despite their differences, looking across the Atlantic to the US and Latin America provides insights about Ghana's trajectory, suggesting possible paths out of urban Ghana's trap. At the extremes, an easy case could be made that changes to either the demand-side characteristics of voters or the supply-side incentives of politicians would move urban Ghana out of the trap outlined in Chapter 1. On the demand side, if the middle class moved from being a potentially pivotal demographic minority to the large majority of the population, a threshold would eventually be crossed after which it becomes impossible for urban politicians to assemble

---

[32] For example, local politicians can engage in clientelism in poor areas without inviting electoral retaliation from wealthier voters, as examined in Weitz-Shapiro (2014).
[33] Similarly, Thachil (2014) describes how fundraising among wealthy, upper-caste, ideologically driven Hindu nationalists in India funds social service delivery targeted at poorer, lower-caste voters. This allows the Bharatiya Janata Party (BJP) to fuse ideological and nonprogrammatic appeals.

9.2 What Could Break the Trap in Urban Ghana? 291

any winning coalition without attracting support from many middle-class voters who demand universalistic policies. On the supply side, if there were major improvements in state capacity alongside large shifts in bureaucratic autonomy that allowed for the development of an expansive national welfare state free from political interference, the central credibility problem deterring investments in programmatic competition described in Chapter 4 would disappear. Ghanaian politicians would also lose much of their leverage to selectively allocate state resources as favoritism, reducing clientelism and incentives for ethnic voting.

But neither of these shifts is happening any time soon in Ghana, or in most other new democracies. While Ghana has been near the forefront of a group of African countries experiencing impressive economic growth over the last two decades, there is little evidence that these countries are new "Asian Tigers" – at the precipice of rapid economic transformations that will pull the large majority of their population into the middle class. Moreover, high state capacity is usually only gradually built over decades (or even centuries)[34] and widespread bureaucratic autonomy is also very slow to develop.[35] Other elements of transitions to programmatic politics in the cases above are unlikely to be replicable in Ghana, such as the civil service reforms that were influential in the US. Ghana already has a "reformed" civil service, at least de jure, but these rules are not fully binding because they have been implemented in a much weaker, lower capacity state.

The search for paths out of the trap must focus instead on more marginal changes that can plausibly happen in the near or medium term. The US and Latin American examples both offer several plausible candidates. I focus on four dynamics from these cases that parallel shifts that either are already underway in Ghana or are at least under active consideration. The first two are on the demand side, rooted in the characteristics of voters, and appear unlikely to fundamentally alter electoral competition in urban Ghana: (a) greater economic segregation across urban electoral and administrative districts; and (b) generational shifts in the electorate that place more electoral weight on the preferences of younger

---

[34] Tilly (1990) and Herbst (2000).
[35] Grindle (2012) shows that the successful depoliticization of bureaucracies in some Latin American countries only occurred after decades of piecemeal reforms. Parties who benefit from clientelism under the status quo often stymie the implementation of reforms that would increase autonomy in order to protect their electoral position (Cruz and Keefer 2015). Politicians are usually unwilling to voluntarily restrict their own supply of patronage (Shefter 1977).

voters who are not first-generation rural–urban migrants. Both could have effects even without substantial additional growth in the urban middle class or changes to overall levels of ethnic diversity.

The two other changes highlighted by the external cases operate on the supply side and offer a more promising path to shifting Ghana's politics: (c) the adoption of nonpartisan CCT programs administered by politically insulated agencies; and (d) greater fiscal and political decentralization to urban municipal governments. Both of these supply-side changes could have effects even without major changes in state capacity or the emergence of full bureaucratic autonomy. The limits to these third and fourth changes are not nearly as severe as the limits to the first two changes.

9.2.1 Demand Side: Economic Segregation

Perhaps the reason Greater Accra's middle class may not be inducing the political change that many expect is that middle-class voters are too spatially dispersed across the city's electoral and administrative districts. While many neighborhoods *within districts* are clearly delineated by socioeconomic class, Table 2.1 shows that most parliamentary constituencies (and, by extension, administrative districts) have middle- and upper-class populations close to the citywide average. Only a few are overwhelmingly poor, with tiny middle-class populations, and only one constituency – Ayawaso West, discussed in Chapter 4 – has a majority middle- and upper-class population. While the relatively low levels of economic segregation at the district and constituency levels in Ghana are common in West African cities, these patterns are beginning to change. Greater Accra is one of many African cities experiencing a boom in the construction of higher-end housing. While still only representing a small share of the city's current population, these developments often take the form of gated communities that separate middle- and upper-class residents from the poor in new self-contained neighborhoods.[36] If these trends continue, Greater Accra will become increasingly segregated by class *across districts*.

Class-based segregation across districts within Chilean cities allows politicians to specialize in programmatic appeals in some districts while concentrating on clientelism in others.[37] Under Greater Accra's current

---

[36] Grant (2009) and Pitcher (2017).
[37] Luna (2014).

patterns of economic segregation *within but not across* parliamentary constituencies, I show that while politicians forego direct clientelistic relationships in wealthier neighborhoods, they do not forego clientelism entirely – they instead concentrate clientelistic activity in the poorer neighborhoods of their constituencies, while differentially ignoring wealthier neighborhoods. But if whole parliamentary constituencies became homogeneously middle- and upper-class, with more cross-district segregation, perhaps politicians in wealthier districts will face greater pressure to give up on clientelism entirely and invest in more programmatic appeals to win local elections. Arguments about the impacts of post-WWII suburbanization on machine parties in US cities imply a similar prediction, with programmatic competition replacing clientelism in the more economically homogenous suburbs that the middle class moved into in the mid-twentieth century.

But the earlier chapters cast doubt on whether increased cross-district economic segregation would truly push politicians to develop more programmatic appeals. State capacity and bureaucratic autonomy would still be low and the credibility problems described in Chapter 4 would still bind. Politicians campaigning in wealthier constituencies – whether in national or district elections – would still face the same difficulties convincing middle-class voters that promises to address their universalistic preferences are credible.

Greater spatial concentration of wealthier voters may instead encourage increased abstention. Moving into the new gated communities described earlier is often bundled up in the process of exiting the social contract with the government for services and paying to privately provide them to yourself. These housing developments are often advertised as private, self-contained neighborhoods that achieve economies of scale in self-provision of basic public services. By facilitating residents' ability to forego demands on local governments for basic services, the same housing developments that increase economic segregation may also ease the decision of middle-class voters to abstain from electoral participation.[38] Indeed, Chapter 8 shows that in the wealthiest Electoral Areas (wards within districts) in Greater Accra, turnout is already commonly in the single digits in local government elections. Moreover, even as Luna (2014) suggests that greater economic segregation might allow programmatic politics to prevail in wealthier urban districts, his argument

---

[38] Hopkins and Williamson (2012) show that similar types of private housing developments can also be politically demobilizing in US elections.

also implies that clientelism would become even more entrenched in the poorer districts, further exacerbating the trap in slums.

Chapter 4 argues that credibility constraints are less binding on politicians' decisions where there has been a long history of ideological competition. Chilean elections have featured a clear left–right cleavage since at least the early twentieth century. Signaling credibility in its commitment to conservative policy proposals is a much less serious concern for a party like Chile's UDI, which grew directly out of the conservative Pinochet dictatorship. Voters can draw on past experience to differentiate the UDI's universalistic policy orientation from other parties' brands in a way that is simply not possible in much of Africa. Similarly, in Argentina, where Weitz-Shapiro (2014) also finds diversification among politicians within the same party in their appeals across municipalities with different levels of wealth, more programmatic parties already exist as an option on the ballot for voters who do not support clientelistic politicians. Wealthier voters in Argentina do not face as stark a choice as middle-class voters in Ghana between either abstaining or overcoming the organizational hurdles described in Chapter 4 of creating a new party to better represent their preferences.[39] Where every viable party is expected to engage in nonprogrammatic politics, middle-class voters who demand universalistic policies have a harder time finding *any* credible option to address their preferences.

In addition, many Latin American countries, including Argentina and Chile (until 2009), have compulsory voting laws. Even when not fully enforced, mandatory turnout laws constrain the extent to which the class-based turnout inequality that Kasara and Suryanarayan (2015) document across much of the developing world (including Ghana) can emerge.[40] If middle-class voters legally cannot abstain from voting, there will be less abstention and politicians will have stronger incentives to invest in better representing their interests.

---

[39] Studies of clientelism in Argentina typically assume that just one party is primarily engaged in clientelism (Calvo and Murillo 2004). As discussed in Chapter 4, the existence of a real choice between programmatic and nonprogrammatic options in Argentina is what allows the "audience costs" of clientelism among wealthier voters theorized by Weitz-Shapiro (2014) to become meaningful.

[40] Jaitman (2013) demonstrates that these laws significantly increase turnout despite limited enforcement. Unlike in other developing world regions, there is little evidence of significant class-based differences in turnout (in either direction) in Latin America (Fornos et al. 2004). Compulsory voting laws are common throughout Latin America, but rare elsewhere in the developing world, especially in Africa.

9.2.2 Demand Side: Generational Change

Generational change is a second demand-side development highlighted by the US and Latin American cases. Like much of the developing world, Ghana is experiencing a "youth bulge," with young people making up a disproportionate share of the population.[41] The majority of residents in Greater Accra are no longer first-generation rural–urban migrants. Most recent population growth in the city has been driven by natural increase rather than new migration from rural areas. Most of Greater Accra's youth have now always lived in the city. As this youth bulge continues to age, second- and third-generation urban residents are comprising an increasingly large share of the urban electorate. These voters may be increasingly disconnected from rural ethnic homelands and more incorporated into interethnic social networks, with higher levels of assimilation.

The similar assimilation of second- and third-generation European immigrants is a common (albeit contested) explanation for the collapse of ethnic-based machines in the urban US. Generational shifts in the Mexican electorate may also have helped lead to the collapse of the PRI's long-dominant patronage-based regime. Younger voters who came of age in a period of economic crisis may not have developed strong expectations that they would benefit from patronage distributed by the PRI.[42] If younger voters in urban Ghana are also more likely to discount ethnicity because they are more assimilated and less likely to expect to benefit from patronage based on parties' ethnic alignment, could similar generational shifts soon help undermine ethnic politics and clientelism in urban Ghana?

Much as interethnic assimilation does not appear to account for machine collapse in the US, the previous chapters suggest that the answer is also likely to be no for urban Ghana. In Chapter 7 I show that the best available measures of interethnic assimilation, including personal identification with other social identities over ethnicity and cohabitation with members of politically opposed ethnic groups, do not predict differences in ethnic voting. Nor does whether voters are first-generation rural–urban migrants or have always lived in the city. Moreover, I find no significant differences by age in preferences or behavior in any analyses in Chapters 3 and 7. Qualitative evidence on urban youth in Africa

[41] For example, see Acquah (2015).
[42] Magaloni (2006).

is consistent with these findings. Burbidge (2014) tracks a group of young middle-class voters in Nairobi through the campaign period before Kenya's 2013 presidential election. Despite disapproving of explicit ethnic appeals in campaigns and downplaying ethnicity in daily life, these youth ultimately still voted overwhelmingly for their co-ethnic presidential candidate, succumbing to the broader pressures in Kenya that incentivize support for ethnically aligned politicians.

This does not support an expectation that ethnic voting – and the incentives for ethnic favoritism that go along with it – will fade away as younger, more ethnically assimilated voters gain electoral strength. Instead, instrumental incentives to support ethnically aligned parties can still sustain patterns of ethnic voting in poor or ethnically segregated neighborhoods regardless of whether urban youth are more ethnically assimilated. High youth unemployment is an endemic problem in African cities. Younger urban voters are often those in the most precarious economic positions, most susceptible to clientelistic appeals that provide a leg up in the urban economy. As long as young voters continue to expect that access to highly valued economic resources depends on the ethnic affiliations of candidates or parties, they may not defect from ethnic voting – *even if* they personally decry the influence of ethnicity in politics.

9.2.3 Supply Side: Cash Transfers and the Proto-welfare State

A third possible change operates instead on the supply side. Even if Ghana does not develop a full-fledged welfare state, the adoption of specific large-scale welfare programs similar to Brazil's *Bolsa Familia* and Mexico's *Progresa* is plausible in the near future. These programs are increasingly common in developing countries, including in Africa. After taking power in 2009, the NDC began slowly rolling out a similar social welfare program, known as LEAP ("Livelihood Empowerment Against Poverty"). LEAP was originally introduced by the NPP government in 2008. Although the number of beneficiaries remains limited and the program's future trajectory under the new NPP government after the 2016 election is uncertain, LEAP was introduced with the intention of ultimately being scaled-up into a *Bolsa Familia*-type program.

While there is evidence that CCTs have positive impacts on poverty,[43] programs such as LEAP are unlikely to lead to such significant changes

---

[43] For example, see Rawlings and Rubio (2005).

in wealth that large numbers of poor voters in urban Ghana begin demanding universalistic policies over particularistic goods at levels akin to middle-class voters. But guaranteed access to cash assistance from a well-publicized, nonpartisan government program may help change very poor voters' expectations about how they can satisfy their particularistic demands. These programs could have similar effects as the New Deal programs had on urban machines in the US, crowding out at least some patronage exchanges that currently are common in poor urban neighborhoods. If fewer voters believe access to private goods from the state depends on the ethnic profile of the party in power, the incentives for ethnic voting in poor urban neighborhoods explained in Chapters 5 and 7 will be undermined. Along these lines, a growing body of evidence suggests that programmatic social welfare programs can help poor voters in developing countries break free of clientelistic relationships with local party agents, with sizable effects on vote choice, even in the absence of broader changes in the political environment or to levels of state capacity.[44]

Capture and manipulation of the bureaucracy administering a program like LEAP would prevent these political effects from being realized. Despite the success of New Deal programs at limiting some political machines, others were at least initially able to influence the agencies delivering the new benefits, allowing revised forms of clientelism to persist. CCT programs face similar risks of capture. Even in Brazil – the archetypical case of programmatic CCT success – Brollo et al. (2017) find suggestive evidence that some local mayors relax enforcement of the school attendance conditions for *Bolsa Familia* benefits before elections as a form of patronage.[45] Manipulation of program access will be a serious concern in Ghana. Past Ghanaian governments introduced other nominally universalistic social welfare programs, to provide jobs, job training, microfinance loans, and subsidized health insurance. But

---

[44] For example, see Hite-Rubin (2015) on microcredit in the Philippines, Blattman et al. (2017) on cash grants in Uganda, and Bobonis et al. (2017) on providing more consistent water access to rural farmers in Brazil.

[45] Subtle selective enforcement of the conditions on cash grants on the margins is likely far more benign than the out-and-out vote buying and other forms of direct clientelism that *Bolsa Familia* may be crowding out, however. Even with the manipulation shown by Brollo et al. (2017), for example, program beneficiaries who follow the official *Bolsa Familia* rules will still receive their benefits even if they publicly oppose the mayor, in contrast to what would happen under more pernicious forms of clientelism.

Chapters 4 and 6 explain that these programs have been dogged by corruption and implementation failures and that access to benefits is often distributed as patronage. Part of why many existing programs in Ghana have been so easily manipulated is that decisions about program access are usually made by local officials working at the district level who can be influenced and pressured by the ruling party leaders who control district governments.

Yet these hurdles are not insurmountable. Weitz-Shapiro (2014) argues that centralizing control over welfare benefits into new insulated national bureaucracies can help prevent capture by local politicians, pointing to the programmatic implementation of *Progresa* in Mexico as a model. Rather than reforming the existing bureaucracy, Mexico sidestepped it, setting up a new independent agency run by technocratic elites without strong partisan ties to distribute *Progresa* benefits and enacting a series of laws to protect the agency from subsequent political interference. This included a hard cap on the amount of benefits that can be distributed in election years. Creating a single new national-level agency is a significantly more plausible task for a developing country such as Ghana to replicate than reforming the entire state bureaucracy. This would allow social transfer programs like LEAP to at least begin partially breaking clientelistic ties with the poor through universalistic distribution of some benefits even if the remainder of the bureaucracy remains politicized. Similar to the earlier job and loan programs in Ghana, LEAP is currently being administered by a pre-existing bureaucracy, not an independent, insulated agency, and faces allegations that benefits are currently distributed as patronage in some districts. But this could be changed, especially with a stronger commitment of donor support that could fund a new administrating agency.

Shefter (1977, 1994) suggests that such an independent agency would only remain apolitical over time if a "constituency for bureaucratic autonomy" develops – a group of politicians who see it as in their interest to protect the agency. The potential electoral benefits of a scaled-up CCT program may help such a constituency develop – if only in regard to this specific program. Even as CCT programs break some clientelistic ties between voters and ruling parties, governments that have successfully implemented these policies do not appear to suffer at the polls. Instead, Zucco (2013) and Labonne (2013) find increased support for incumbent parties that implemented these programs in Brazil and the Philippines, respectively, even though recipients are under no obligation to support the ruling party.[46] If the electoral rewards to scaling-up such a program in a country like Ghana are similar, allowing at least some benefits to be distributed more programmatically via a CCT program may be cheaper to the ruling party than maintaining the full clientelistic status quo. At least in their initial stages, CCT programs are often heavily subsidized by international donors interested in poverty reduction, allowing governments to credit claim and reap electoral rewards for initiatives to which they do not have to contribute the party's own scarce resources.[47] As ruling parties come to learn that such a program will allow them to benefit at the polls, they may see an opportunity to avoid some of the organizational costs described in Chapter 5 of maintaining the dense networks of local party agents that they currently use to engage in individual-level clientelism in poor urban neighborhoods.[48] Reducing clientelism in this way may change some voters' expectations of benefiting from parties with different ethnic affiliations. Ethnic voting could then begin to decline and Greater Accra's trap may begin to unravel.

9.2.4 Supply Side: Fiscal and Political Decentralization

A second supply-side change with potential to disrupt current patterns of electoral competition is greater political and fiscal decentralization to Ghana's district governments. Ghana is administratively decentralized, with implementation of many national-level programs carried out by district-level officials, but only minimally politically and fiscally decentralized.[49] The main political decision-makers at the local level – the DCEs, or mayors – are appointed by the president. Chapter 8 shows that the powers of locally elected District Assembly members are limited relative to DCEs. DCEs and District Assemblies mostly lack the authority to introduce independent policies. Fiscally, district governments are heavily dependent on national government transfers, without latitude to pursue

---

[46] De La O (2013) also finds evidence that incumbents in Mexico are rewarded for *Progresa*, but see Imai et al. (2016).
[47] Cruz and Schneider (2017) suggest that the electoral rewards to credit-claiming for donor-funded projects in new democracies can be large.
[48] Stokes et al. (2013) suggest that party leaders will jump at opportunities like this to "slough off" inefficient party agents.
[49] Falleti (2010) defines these three forms of decentralization. As noted in Chapter 2, administrative decentralization without significant political and fiscal decentralization is the norm in most of sub-Saharan Africa (Olowu and Wunsch 2004, Grossman and Lewis 2014). Notable exceptions are Nigeria, South Africa, and Kenya after its new 2010 constitution.

their own agendas. While there is some local tax collection, local tax capacity remains very low and districts are limited in the types of levies they can impose. Unlike local governments in wealthier democracies, districts cannot float bonds to finance their own infrastructure spending or other local policy priorities.[50]

These constraints feed several elements of the trap. Fiscal and policymaking constraints limit what district assembly members can supply to voters, encouraging middle-class withdrawal in district elections. This facilitates the capture of local governments by narrow ethnic interests, with implications for the local implementation of national government policies that help reinforce the credibility problem in national elections as well. Centralization also incentivizes ethnic voting in presidential elections by creating a "winner-take-all" system in which control of the presidency determines access to state resources even within local urban neighborhoods.

There has been serious recent discussion in Ghana about allowing for more decentralization, however. A constitutional review commission created by the NDC after the 2008 election officially proposed allowing for the local election of DCEs.[51] The NPP endorsed this call in its 2008 and 2016 campaigns, and after taking office in 2017 the new NPP president repeated his intention to allow for the election of DCEs.[52] Separately, in recent years the national government has placed growing pressure on district governments to increase their internally generated revenues so that the District Assemblies can self-finance a greater share of their activities. Could these steps encourage greater participation by middle-class voters and ultimately reduce ethnic voting?

At first blush, this seems to run counter to the lessons of the US and Latin American cases. Good governance reforms meant to curb the power of clientelistic machines in the US often involved movement in the other direction, with state governments reducing the powers of urban politicians to constrain the supply of patronage. The civil service reforms discussed earlier were one such measure. The difference between the

---

[50] Bond financing is extremely rare in African cities. A notable recent exception is Lagos (Adams 2016). Dakar, Senegal attempted to float a municipal bond in 2015 and 2016, but was ultimately blocked by the central government (Paice 2016).
[51] "Moves to Elect DCEs – Government to Submit Proposals to Constitutional Review Commission" (2010).
[52] Given the parties' record of neglecting to follow through on these types of promises (see Chapter 4), however, whether this actually happens remains to be seen. The NDC never acted on these decentralization proposals in eight years in power, for example. "MMDCEs will be elected from 2018 – Akufo-Addo" (2016).

9.2 What Could Break the Trap in Urban Ghana? 301

successful nonpartisan implementation of antipoverty programs in Mexico versus clientelism in similar programs in Argentina highlighted by Weitz-Shapiro (2014) also appears to be that nationalized control over distribution helps avoid capture by local politicians.

However, this is not a question of decentralization versus no decentralization, but rather of whether greater political and fiscal decentralization can have an impact given that significant administrative decentralization has already occurred. Many of the problems reformers in the US sought to solve already exist in Ghana. Local politicians already have considerable discretion in the allocation of national government resources, but face little direct electoral accountability compared to those in the US. Political manipulation of antipoverty programs, as in Weitz-Shapiro (2014), is also already widespread. In general, the biggest risk of decentralization in the developing world is thought to be the risk of partisan or elite capture.[53] Urban Ghana already has capture, enabled in part by the abstention of middle-class voters from district-level elections. Greater political and fiscal decentralization will not necessarily make any of these problems worse.

Instead, other evidence from Latin America suggests that greater political and fiscal decentralization could increase the range of what local politicians can supply, potentially changing the credibility problem they face in building support among middle-class voters. In particular, Luna (2014) shows that the political and fiscal latitude that powerful locally elected mayors in Chile have to carry out separate policy agendas in their own jurisdictions is a key contextual feature that makes dual programmatic–clientelistic appeals possible. Unlike in Ghana, mayors in wealthier districts have the political autonomy and capacity to address some of the more programmatic preferences of wealthier voters.[54] Similar diversification is much less possible where policymaking is concentrated in the center. More broadly, a large literature has described Latin American mayors as "policy entrepreneurs," documenting how major decentralization reforms in the 1980s and 1990s have given them the authority to shape local policy independently and "produce myriad innovations in governance" (Campbell 2003, 7), some of which are then

---

[53] For example, Bardhan (2002) and Bardhan and Mookherjee (2006).
[54] Despite their relatively limited powers, local governments still have the latitude to address programmatic policy issues within their jurisdictions, such as property taxes, funding for local schools, and policies concerning the local administration of national government programs.

adopted by national governments. *Bolsa Familia* was one such local innovation, beginning in Brasilia before spreading nationwide.

Along similar lines, greater political and fiscal decentralization could give urban Ghana's DCEs and district assembly members a wider policy toolkit at their disposal, expanding the range of voter preferences they can promise to address in their campaigns. Low state capacity will persist, so local politicians will still not be able to address all of the middle-class preferences in Chapter 3. But local governments could address some of these universalistic preferences – including the collection of property taxes and the administration and regulation of utilities. If, on the margins, more middle-class voters come to believe that local politicians can do more than provide small particularistic benefits, they should be relatively less likely to abstain from district-level elections. If fewer middle-class voters abstain, Chapter 8 demonstrates that capture of District Assembly seats by minority interest groups becomes less likely. Less capture, in turn, could translate into less favoritism in the allocation of local government resources and better implementation of national government policies.

In the poorest urban districts, further decentralization will likely just make it even easier for local party machines to dominate local elections through clientelistic appeals. But local policy entrepreneurs could begin to emerge in at least some districts, similar to Latin America's mayors, trying out new policy ideas that better address middle-class preferences.[55] Over time, more local politicians may begin engaging with the middle class, allowing the parties to develop better reputations of responsiveness to middle-class preferences. As more policy-demanding voters experience good representation of their interests at the local government level, there may be gradual carry-over effects on participation in parliamentary and presidential elections.

Such a path out of the trap would echo elements of the Mexican case. In addition to the factors noted above, Magaloni (2006) also suggests that the ability of more programmatic opposition parties – especially the conservative *Partido Acción Nacional* (PAN) – to win local elections in the early 1990s and implement independent policies at the local level

---

[55] In another African example, dramatic recent gains in tax collection and local public goods provision by the Lagos State government in Nigeria suggest that real political and fiscal decentralization can empower local governments in African democracies to significantly alter their behavior even in the context of a very low capacity state. See Kaplan (2014) and de Gramont (2015).

helped these parties develop policy reputations with voters and make more credible commitments to address voters' preferences that allowed them to chip into support for the PRI. This was only possible because of decentralization reforms adopted in the 1980s and early 1990s.

Empowering and electing DCEs may also help undermine ethnic voting in national elections. If significant power is truly devolved to the district level, local elections should become more important than national elections for determining who gains access to the key particularistic resources that poor urban voters demand. Posner's (2005) argument about institutional shifts in the relative importance of presidential versus parliamentary elections in Zambia suggests that this will not eliminate the importance of ethnicity in electoral politics, but could make localized ethnic divisions much more salient relative to national ones. Differences may emerge from district to district within Greater Accra in the particular dimensions of ethnicity that are most relevant for political competition, as politicians seek to build winning coalitions given the particular demographics of their local jurisdictions. Though ethnicity would then remain a relevant feature in the politics of Greater Accra, this could significantly scramble the overall correlation between partisanship and ethnicity, helping to reduce voters' aggregate expectations of favoritism based on the outcomes of national elections.

Despite promises to the contrary, it may seem implausible that a ruling party would ever agree to such reforms. National governments are usually assumed to prefer to maintain their current powers.[56] Some Latin American governments have even recently sought to recentralize power to reduce threats from opposition control of local governments.[57] But O'Neill (2005) argues that ruling parties in Latin American have supported political and fiscal decentralization when they have long time horizons and expect to be in opposition in the near future. Devolving authority to lower tiers of government allows a party to smooth its consumption of political power – giving up some power in the present to ensure that it can maintain local power, at least in stronghold areas, in the future. With two institutionalized parties that rotate in power, Ghana may be the African case in which this argument best applies. The NDC

---

[56] Falleti (2010).

[57] Eaton (2014). There are similar examples in Africa. The Ugandan government recently undid fiscal and political decentralization in its capital city, Kampala, after opposition politicians took over the local city council and began implementing an independent policy agenda (Lambright 2014).

and NPP would be able to maintain control in their core regions even if they lost nationally. After Ghana's third peaceful democratic transition between these parties in two decades, decentralization may be an increasingly appealing means for the ruling party to ensure that it stays in power at the local level regardless of the uncertain outcome of future national elections.

9.3 CONCLUSION

This chapter draws on examples from the US and Latin America to identify nearer-term changes that could pull urban Ghana out of the trap outlined in Chapter 1. While each of the specific changes discussed here has limits, the two on the supply side – the expansion of CCT programs and greater political and fiscal decentralization – offer more promising prospects than the two on the demand side – greater economic segregation and generational change. The empirical evidence presented in the earlier chapters provides clear reasons to doubt whether these demand-side changes will alter politicians' incentives to supply new types of appeals and, in turn, allow voters to deviate from current patterns of political behavior. By contrast, while both supply-side changes have limitations, they have greater potential to incentivize politicians to change their electoral approach. Donor-backed, nonpartisan provision of cash to the very poor may crowd out some opportunities for clientelism. More substantive decentralization provides local politicians with more credible tools with which to engage with the urban middle class.

Understanding the power of supply-side factors is important for explaining the emergence (or lack thereof) of programmatic political competition in new democracies. It is also important for thinking about the future trajectory of electoral politics in sub-Saharan Africa, which is in the midst of a massive wave of urbanization. The United Nations (2014) projects that sub-Saharan Africa will become majority urban by 2040, adding nearly 500 million additional urban residents to the 250 million who have already joined the urban population since 1990. Almost all African countries will join Ghana as predominately urban societies. It is impossible to anticipate the myriad ways in which further urbanization will disrupt contemporary political dynamics on the continent. But it is clear that we must stop assuming that demand-side theories that directly link demographic and political change are correct. While this book shows that the emergence of the African middle class, high levels of ethnic diversity, and other demographic shifts common to

African cities can alter electoral competition, their impacts are not nearly as straightforward as is often assumed. Further urbanization and demographic change will likely produce a multiplicity of forms of competition within African cities, with variation across neighborhoods in clientelism and ethnic voting, not uniform shifts into programmatic politics.

Decades ago, Bates (1974, 1983) pushed back on similar demand-side narratives about African politics – rooted at that time in classical modernization theories – by shifting the analytic focus away from the social implications of demographic change to the strategic actions of politicians. He explained the salience of ethnic politics in post-independence Africa by pointing to politicians' incentives to foment ethnic conflict and construct new ethnic identities to aid their competition for control of scarce state resources, casting doubt on modernization theories that expected demographic shifts to undermine ethnicity. Despite the wide influence of his argument in political science, similar demand-side narratives remain quite prevalent. This book suggests the need to push back again. If future urbanization is to have a significant effect on electoral politics in Africa, it will come as much through how urban contexts alter what politicians can do as from urbanization's changes to who voters are and what they want from their governments. Without changes to what can be supplied, other cities will likely find themselves stuck in traps similar to Greater Accra's.

Data Appendix

A.1 URBAN SURVEY SAMPLING PROCEDURE

The main survey interviewed a representative, stratified random sample of residents in metropolitan Greater Accra. All parliamentary constituencies in urban Greater Accra were stratified by wealth (top or bottom half of the distribution on the same wealth index used throughout the book), ethnic diversity (top or bottom half of the distribution on ethnic fractionalization), and 2012 presidential vote share (as NDC or NPP stronghold, or as competitive) using census data. Ten constituencies were randomly selected, with the number selected per stratum determined by the proportion of the city's total population in each stratum and the selection probabilities within each stratum weighted by each constituency's population. The selected parliamentary constituencies were Ayawaso East, Ayawaso North, Ablekuma North, Ablekuma Central, and Okaikwei Central, within the official city of Accra (AMA), and Weija/Gbawe, Bortianor-Ngleshie Amanfro, La Dadekotopon, Ledzokuku, and Krowor, in the surrounding metropolitan area.

Within each constituency, five census enumeration areas were sampled with replacement, again stratifying by ethnic diversity and wealth using census data, with the number chosen per stratum proportional to the stratum's share of the constituency population and the selection probability of enumeration areas within strata weighted by population. Only four enumeration areas were selected in two constituencies that are significantly smaller than the others (Awayaso East and Ayawaso North), to make 48 total enumeration areas. Random geocoded starting points for enumerators were chosen within each tract.

Interviews were conducted in four languages (English, Akan/Twi, Ga, and Ewe). To select 21 respondents around each start point, the smartphone gave each enumerator a new random direction and number of houses to count off to recruit each respondent. The first walk began at the start point and then the enumerators continued each new walk from the previous respondent's home. Within households, the phone assigned a gender to be selected (alternating by interview) and randomly selected a specific person of that gender after ranking household members by age. Enumerators conducted "call backs" for respondents who were initially unavailable and otherwise sampled replacements (from new households) via the same walk procedure. All interviews were conducted in November and December 2013.

A.2 RURAL SURVEY SAMPLING PROCEDURE

A companion survey was conducted in five rural parliamentary constituencies of Ghana. The sampling frame was all rural constituencies in five regions of southern Ghana (excluding Greater Accra Region). The sampling frame was limited to southern Ghana because of budgetary constraints. Constituencies were randomly selected after stratifying on ethnic diversity and political competitiveness in a similar fashion as for the urban survey. The sample contains two very homogeneous, stronghold constituencies (Kpando, Volta Region, 89% NDC in the 2012 presidential election; Manso Nkwanta, Ashanti Region, 82% NPP), two less homogenous constituencies that leaned to each party (Lower Manya Krobo, Eastern Region, 67% NDC; Offinso South, Ashanti Region, 65% NPP), and a highly diverse, competitive constituency (Offinso North, Ashanti Region, 50% NPP, 47% NDC). This is in line with the actual distribution in southern Ghana, where there are relatively fewer diverse or politically competitive constituencies in comparison to urban areas.

Five villages or towns were randomly selected within each of the five constituencies after stratifying enumeration areas by ethnic diversity and wealth using census data. Random geocoded start points were selected within each enumeration area, as in the urban survey. The enumerators interviewed 21 randomly selected respondents, alternating by gender, in each village or town, selected via the same random walk procedure as in the urban survey. These interviews were also conducted in November and December 2013.

A.3 CALCULATION OF NEIGHBORHOOD CHARACTERISTICS

I measure the "neighborhood" around survey respondents in the individual-level analyses using a procedure that takes spatially weighted averages of the census characteristics in a given radius around each respondent. Information closer to the respondent is weighted higher and all data outside a given radius is weighted as 0. This smooths the census data over enumeration areas, following Reardon and O'Sullivan (2004), Lee et al. (2008), and Ichino and Nathan (2013a).

In this approach, the spatially weighted population share of group m around a respondent at point p is $\tilde{\pi}_{pm} = \frac{\int_{q \in R} \tau_{qm} \phi(p,q) dq}{\int_{q \in R} \tau_q \phi(p,q) dq}$, where τ_q is the population density at point q, τ_{qm} is the population density of group m at point q, $dist(p, q)$ is the distance in kilometers from the respondent at point p to the centroid of a surrounding census enumeration area (EA) at point q, and EAs are weighted by the function $\phi(p, q) = (dist(p, q) + 0.5)^{-1}$, as in Reardon and O'Sullivan (2004), up to a maximum distance, after which all EAs are weighted as 0. This is calculated via the seg package in R. I set the maximum radius to 500 meters for the reasons discussed in the text. This also accounts for population density, with the weights a function of both distance and population density around the respondent. The median census enumeration area is 0.03 sq. km in area, smaller than the 0.79 sq. km of each radius around respondents. Because the weights approach 0 further away from the respondent, minor changes in the size of the maximum radius (e.g., to 400m or 600m) do not significantly affect these measures for most respondents.

A.4 CALCULATION OF THE NEIGHBORHOOD WEALTH INDEX

The wealth of neighborhoods is calculated as the first dimension in a factor analysis of census data on assets, education, and employment, mirroring the individual-level indices that measure assets and socioeconomic class in the survey (Chapter 2). Variables that only measure public service provision are purposefully excluded, such that the index is primarily capturing differences in private wealth, not past distributive spending by the government. The index includes: % in the radius around each respondent with running water, which can be privately provided by wealthier residents via tanker or borehole; % with a flush toilet; % with electricity, which is available to all who can afford it; % in a single-family home, excluding informal structures; % with a computer; % adults with more than a middle school education; and % adults employed in the formal or public sectors.

A.5 Summary Statistics for the Urban Survey

For the main analysis of individual-level survey data, the neighborhood wealth index is calculated for the 500-meter radius around each enumeration area in Greater Accra, following the procedure described earlier. The index is scaled in standard deviations from the city-wide mean of 0. Higher values indicate greater local wealth in the radius around each respondent. For other analyses in the text, the same index is instead recalculated at the Electoral Area level, constituency level, or district level.

A.5 SUMMARY STATISTICS FOR THE URBAN SURVEY

TABLE A.1: *Summary statistics for the urban survey*

	mean	min.	max.	sd	N
NDC Vote in 2012 Presidential Elec. (0,1)	0.53	0.00	1.00	0.50	804
NPP Vote in 2012 Presidential Elec. (0,1)	0.45	0.00	1.00	0.50	804
Self-Reported Turnout in 2012 (0,1)	0.84	0.00	1.00	0.36	995
Co-Ethnic Party Vote (0,1)	0.76	0.00	1.00	0.43	797
Neighborhood Wealth Index (500m)	−0.10	−1.40	3.02	0.80	995
Ethnic Fractionalization (500m)	0.69	0.39	0.86	0.11	995
Ga % (500m)	0.25	0.05	0.76	0.19	995
Akan % (500m)	0.37	0.13	0.67	0.15	995
Ewe % (500m)	0.16	0.05	0.35	0.07	995
Northern % (500m)	0.12	0.01	0.53	0.13	995
Population Density per sq. km (by cluster)	28710	1650	95120	27050	48
Party Member (0,1)	0.16	0.00	1.00	0.37	995
Education/Employment Index	0.00	−1.04	1.74	1.00	995
More Than Middle School Education (0,1)	0.51	0.00	1.00	0.50	995
Formal Sector Employment (0,1)	0.16	0.00	1.00	0.36	995
Fluent in English (0,1)	0.45	0.00	1.00	0.50	995
Assets/Wealth Index	0.00	−1.10	2.30	1.00	995

(continued)

TABLE A.1: *(Continued)*

	mean	min.	max.	sd	N
Ethnicity Most "Salient" Social Identity (0,1)	0.49	0.00	1.00	0.50	995
Moved for Family/Ethnicity (0,1)	0.75	0.00	1.00	0.44	995
Age	35.54	18.00	93.00	13.07	995
Muslim (0,1)	0.20	0.00	1.00	0.40	995
Male (0,1)	0.50	0.00	1.00	0.50	995
Akan (0,1)	0.42	0.00	1.00	0.49	995
Ewe (0,1)	0.18	0.00	1.00	0.38	995
Northerner (0,1)	0.18	0.00	1.00	0.38	995
Ga-Dangme (0,1)	0.30	0.00	1.00	0.46	995
Years in Neighborhood (0,1)	15.34	0.00	80.00	14.28	995
Percent Life in Greater Accra	0.69	0.00	1.00	0.33	995
Met Chief in Last Year (0,1)	0.14	0.00	1.00	0.35	995

Ethnic categories do not add to 1 because some respondents are from multiple groups. Chapter 7 discusses how this is addressed when measuring ethnic voting.

A.6 INTERVIEWS AND FOCUS GROUPS IN GREATER ACCRA

Preliminary interviews were conducted during three months of field research between June and August 2012, in the campaign period before the 2012 elections. The remaining interviews were conducted over ten months of field research between June 2013 and April 2014.

Thirteen focus groups were conducted in summer and fall 2013, in advance of the survey. Each focus group interviewed 4–7 people, and attempted for an even mix of men and women. Neighborhoods were selected nonrandomly to represent a balanced cross-section of the city in terms of ethnic diversity and levels of wealth. Participants were selected via a random walk sampling procedure within each neighborhood, similar to the procedure used for the survey. Participants were compensated a small amount for their time. All focus groups were conducted in Twi or Ga, translated in real time by a research assistant.

A.7 CODING RULES FOR MANIFESTOS

I hand-coded 2,299 individual promises from the NDC and NPP manifestos from 1996 through 2012 on several dimensions. The full coded manifesto data is available on request. The following definitions were used:

- *Valence:* See Bleck and van de Walle (2012). *Valence* promises are those which refer to delivering universally "good things" – economic growth, jobs, higher cocoa yields – about which no mainstream (nonradical, nonanarchist) party would disagree. Providing basic public services that are core functions of any state are included as valence promises (e.g., building hospitals, public schools, or highways, expanding electricity-generating capacity, etc.). All promises not coded as valence were coded instead as *positions*.
- *Ideological Content*: Ideological content was coded on a left–right dimension defined by a distinction between calls for intervention into the economy, expansion of the welfare state, redistribution, and/or trade protectionism (*left*) versus calls for deregulation and tax cuts, retrenchment of the welfare state, free trade, and/or commitments of support to the private sector (*right*). Nonideological statements were any promises about providing basic public infrastructure, support for good governance and human rights, or other commitments to valence issues.
- *Overlaps Other Party*: Overlap was only calculated between manifestos from the same election year. *Identical* promises were those that appeared exactly in the other party's manifesto. *Similar* promises were those that shared the same goal, but proposed different policy interventions to reach that goal. *Unique* promises were those that did not appear at all in the other party's manifesto in the same year.
- *Clear Disagreement*: Promises were only coded as *clear disagreements* if the other party's manifesto contained an explicitly contradictory statement.
- *Targets Specific Class Group*: Promises were coded as targeting *no specific class* if benefits would apply to all Ghanaians or if there was not enough content to deduce who would benefit in particular. The remaining coding categories are not mutually exclusive and were applied to any promise for which one or two, but not all three, class groups would benefit. Promises were coded as benefiting *business* (upper-class) interests if they would increase the profitability of major private sector enterprises (e.g., proposed subsidies for manufacturers) or affected services primarily used by the elite (e.g., expansions of airports). Promises were coded as benefiting the *middle class* if they would particularly benefit people with secondary education, English literacy, and formal sector employment

(e.g., changes to university admissions policies; changes to civil service wages). Promises were coded as benefitting the *poor* if they involved an expansion of the welfare state or would improve the financial circumstances of the unskilled workforce.

A.8 SURVEY EXPERIMENT PROMPTS AND CONDITIONS

A.8.1 Survey Experiment in Chapter 4

Respondents were read two pairs of vignettes about two hypothetical candidates. The respondents were then asked about the credibility of one of the two candidates in each pair: "Do you think a politician like [NAME] will actually deliver on a promise like [PROMISE]?" (with the treatments inserted). The candidate that this follow-up question was asked about was randomly chosen from each pair. Each respondent thus answered this question on credibility twice, with two different conditions for NAME and PROMISE.

The vignettes about candidates varied on three dimensions: the name (and thus ethnicity) of the candidate, the good he promised to deliver, and his background. Table A.2 lists the possible values of each treatment. Inserting example treatments, the vignettes took the form: (in translation)

TABLE A.2: *Treatment permutations in the survey experiment in Chapter 4*

Treatment:	Value 1	Value 2	Value 3	Value 4
Ethnicity:				
AKAN	James Prempeh	Emmanuel Owusu Ansah	–	–
EWE	Joseph Dzorkpe	John Dodzi	–	–
GA	Alfred Nii Tawiah	Richard Laryea	–	–
NORTHERN	Isaac Yakubu	Amadu Muntari	–	–
Promise:				
PUBLIC	Water and fuel prices	National water production	–	–
CLUB	Roads in the constituency	Classrooms in the constituency	–	–
PRIVATE	Jobs for youth	Scholarships to families	–	–
Background Text:	Doctor	Lecturer	Lawyer	Businessman

A.8 Survey Experiment Prompts and Conditions

[AKAN 1, PUBLIC GOOD 1, LECTURER]: "Candidate A is named JAMES PREMPEH. He is a lecturer and teacher who graduated from KNUST [note: Kwame Nkrumah University of Science and Technology]. He lives in the constituency here. If elected, he is promising TO LOBBY FOR KEEPING THE PRICE OF FUEL AND UTILITIES LOW so that everyone IN GHANA can continue to afford fuel and electricity. With your support, JAMES PREMPEH believes he can bring about a transformation in the development of this community."[1]

[EWE 1, PRIVATE 1, DOCTOR]: "Candidate B is named JOSEPH DZORKPE. He is a doctor who lives in this constituency and is running for parliament. He received his medical training at the University of Ghana Medical School. In return for your support, he is promising TO FIND JOBS FOR SOME OF THE YOUTH in the constituency. JOSEPH DZORKPE wants you to vote for him so he can improve the lives of people in this community."

In each pair, respondents always received one candidate from their own ethnic group, and the other candidate's ethnicity was selected at random. For respondents who were not members of any of these four major ethnic categories, all names were assigned at random, with equal probability. The specific names within these ethnicities were also selected at random. In the second pair of vignettes, respondents received the other name from their own ethnic group and a name from one of the two ethnic groups that they had not received in the first vignette, again selected at random. The four backgrounds were randomly allocated to the four candidates, without replacement, such that each background treatment occurred once. In all pairs the candidates promised the same category of good, with one promising the first example and the other promising the second example, again assigned at random. The category of the first pair was selected at random with equal probability from the three categories (PUBLIC/UNIVERSALISTIC, CLUB, PRIVATE), and then the category of the second pair was selected at random from the remaining two. The order of each specific example within these categories (PRIVATE GOOD 1 vs. PRIVATE GOOD 2) was also randomized with equal probability, as was the order of all the other treatments within the pairs (names, backgrounds).

For example, a single Akan respondent would receive treatments such as: PAIR 1: [AKAN NAME 1, PUBLIC GOOD 1, LAWYER] vs.

---

[1] The "background" treatment also includes the filler text of the vignette. For doctors, the final sentence was always "[NAME] wants you to wants you to vote for him so he can improve the lives of people in this community." For lecturers it was: "With your support, [NAME] believes he can bring about a transformation in the development of this community," etc.

[NORTHERN NAME 2, PUBLIC GOOD 2, BUSINESSMAN]; PAIR 2: [AKAN NAME 2, CLUB GOOD 1, DOCTOR] vs. [EWE NAME 2, CLUB GOOD 2, LECTURER]. And the follow-up question about credibility could have been: [NORTHERN NAME 2, PUBLIC GOOD 2, BUSINESSMAN] for the first pair, and [AKAN NAME 2, CLUB GOOD 1, DOCTOR] for the second pair. The questions on credibility would then take the form:

"Do you think a politician like AMADU MUNTARI will actually deliver on a promise like CONSTRUCTING NEW WATER PRODUCTION FACILITIES IN GHANA?"

"Do you think a politician like EMMANUEL OWUSU ANSAH will actually deliver on a promise like CONSTRUCTING AND TARRING MORE OF THE ROADS IN THE CONSTITUENCY?"

Table A.3 provides balance statistics for differences in means for key covariates between the respondents receiving the credibility question in the experiment about a co-ethnic or about a non-co-ethnic. These statistics are listed separately by the type of good referenced in the question. Balance remains imperfect after the randomization, especially for the club goods promises. Because of this, all analyses of the survey experiment in Chapter 4 include co-variates as controls to adjust for remaining imbalance across these conditions.

A.8.2 Survey experiment in Chapter 7

Six specific examples of goods were used: three for private goods and three for club goods. These were randomly inserted into one of two texts (one text each for private and for club goods). The goods were then either to be delivered by the NDC or the NPP. Each respondent received one randomly assigned permutation of the prompt (e.g., NDC, private goods example #1 or NPP, club goods example #3). The good examples were: "giving out loans to people," "creating training programs for unemployed youth," or "giving financial assistance to people to help pay their bills and buy food" for private goods; "school construction," "laying new water pipes," or "constructing more drains and public toilets" were given for club goods. Each represents a common good actually delivered by politicians in Greater Accra. The examples were selected because they were the most common responses to open-ended questions asking about politicians' activities during a pilot version of the survey.

A.8 Survey Experiment Prompts and Conditions

TABLE A.3: *Differences in means, co-ethnic name treatment*

Variable:	difference in means	p-value
Promise: Universalistic/Public		
Universalistic preference (0,1)	0.037	0.235
Male (0,1)	−0.009	0.778
Some Secondary Education (0,1)	0.003	0.926
Formal Sector Employment (0,1)	0.016	0.493
English Literacy	−0.023	0.466
Education/Employment Index	−0.004	0.944
Assets Index	−0.056	0.373
Moved for Club Goods (0,1)	0.014	0.467
Age	0.281	0.731
Neigh. Wealth Index	0.033	0.527
Eth. Fractionalization	−0.017	0.016
Population Density	−1.773	0.318
Promise: Club Good		
Universalistic Preference (0,1)	0.086	0.007
Male (0,1)	−0.009	0.780
Some Secondary Education (0,1)	0.086	0.007
Formal Sector Employment (0,1)	0.063	0.007
English Literacy	0.094	0.003
Education/Employment Index	0.226	0.000
Assets Index	0.046	0.476
Moved for Club Goods (0,1)	0.039	0.041
Age	−0.119	0.887
Neigh. Wealth Index	0.101	0.042
Ethnic Fractionalization	−0.002	0.747
Population Density	−1.211	0.485
Promise: Private Good		
Universalistic Preference (0,1)	0.063	0.047
Male (0,1)	−0.087	0.006
Some Secondary Education (0,1)	−0.090	0.005
Formal Sector Employment (0,1)	−0.017	0.460
English Literacy	−0.057	0.070
Education/Employment Index	−0.152	0.016
Assets Index	0.024	0.707
Moved for Club Goods (0,1)	−0.009	0.629
Age	1.034	0.217
Neigh. Wealth Index	−0.007	0.885
Eth. Fractionalization	−0.008	0.216
Population Density	−0.415	0.806

TABLE A.4: *Balance after treatment assignment for survey experiment (from Chapter 7)*

	Co-Ethnic Party Treatment		NDC Treatment	
Variable	Diff. Means (T v. C)	p-value	Diff. Means (T v. C)	p-value
Male	−0.013	0.679	−0.007	0.827
More Than Middle School Education	0.031	0.323	0.013	0.691
Formal Sector Employment	−0.020	0.390	−0.007	0.770
Fluent English	0.022	0.478	−0.002	0.962
Party Member	0.003	0.902	−0.059	0.028
Ethnicity Salient	−0.035	0.116	0.080	0.000
Moved for Family or Ethnic Group	−0.058	0.004	−0.014	0.461

The full prompts were as follows. For the private goods examples (in this case when cued as NPP): "The national government has limited resources, so when they do something like [EXAMPLE], they can't do it for everyone. They have to do it for some people first, before giving it to other people. If the NPP had won the 2012 election, and the NPP government was [EXAMPLE], do you think that people like you and your family would get it or would they do it more for other people? I'm asking for your personal opinion." For the club goods examples (in this case when cued as NDC): "The national government has limited resources, so when they do something like [EXAMPLE], they can't do it everywhere. They have to do it in some places first before going to other places. If the NDC government was [EXAMPLE], do you think that neighborhoods like this would get it or would they do it more in other places? I'm asking for your personal opinion."

I report univariate balance statistics after randomization for the survey experiment here for the difference between respondents receiving treatment and control conditions when these are defined either as: (a) receiving the cue from your co-ethnic party vs. non-co-ethnic party, or (b) receiving the cue for the NDC versus the NPP. Because balance remains imperfect due to the limited sample sizes, I control for all of these covariates in all analysis of the survey experiment in Chapter 7.

In Table A.4 I provide differences in means for the main binary covariates, along with p-values, and show that the only variable with a significant difference between treatment and control groups for the co-ethnic party treatment is having moved to join family or co-ethnics. For the NDC treatment there is a significant difference between treatment conditions for the ethnicity salience variable. I control for both of these (and the other covariates) in regression models for all analysis of this data. In Figure A.1 I give quantile–quantile-plots of the balance between the same treatment and control groups for the continuous covariates. The weakest balance is for the individual assets index for the NDC treatment, which is also controlled for in all analysis.

A.9 CODING ETHNICITY OF ASSEMBLY CANDIDATES

Most names in Ghana are clearly associated with different major ethnic groups. The names of candidates in the district assembly elections were coded by a group of 5 Ghanaian research assistants. These research assistants were university students in Accra and each came from a different ethnic background. Each name was given to 3 of the 5 research assistants to code, who were asked to code a first, second, and third guess for each name. They were instructed to fill out only the first guess in cases where they were confident of the exact ethnicity and fill out the second and third guesses in cases where they were less confident. These guesses were aggregated using the following rules to successfully identify the major ethnic category (Akan, Ga, Ewe, Northern) for 91% of the candidates' names: (1) if two of three, or three of three, agreed on a single ethnicity coding, the name was assigned that ethnicity; (2) if all three put different ethnicities for the first guess, but two put the same ethnicity for their second guess that the third RA put for his first guess, the name was assigned to that ethnicity. In all other cases, the name was coded as missing.

A.10 POLLING STATION SURVEY SAMPLE

In Chapter 8 I analyze a randomly selected sample of polling stations from Greater Accra. Polling stations were sampled from all urban districts in Greater Accra, after collapsing the list of polling stations by location to account for polling stations that share the same location. The number sampled per district was proportional to the number of registered voters in 2012 and the probability of selecting each polling station within districts was weighted again by the number of registered voters

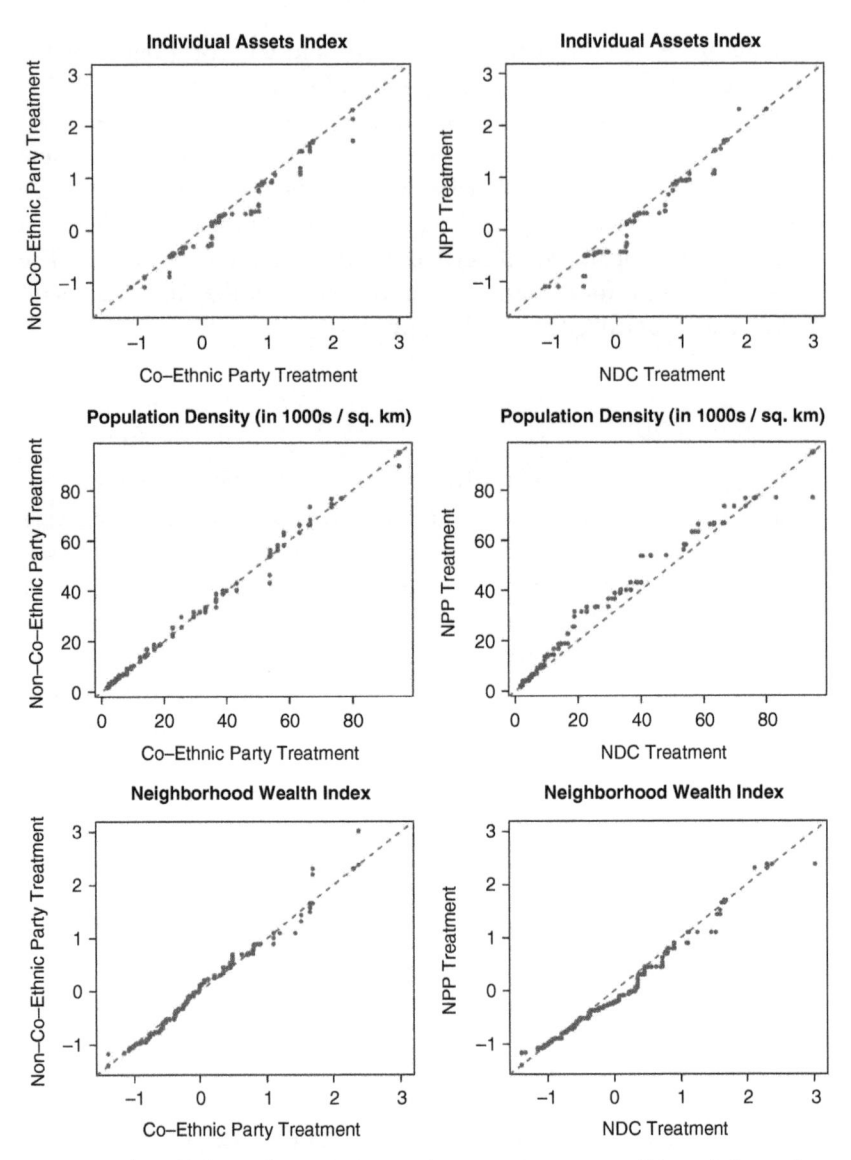

FIGURE A.1: *Balance for survey experiment treatment conditions*: balance for continuous covariates when the main treatment in the survey experiment analyzed in Chapter 7 is defined either as receiving the cue for your co-ethnic party or receiving the cue for the NDC.

A.10 Polling Station Survey Sample

at each polling station. A minimum of 1 polling station was selected per Electoral Area. More than 95% of the sampled polling stations were successfully located by the team of research assistants. In addition to the data on club goods delivery in Chapter 8, these polling station locations were also used to create the hand-drawn map of Electoral Areas used for all maps throughout the book.

Bibliography

"35,000 Nurses, Midwives Declare Strike," *Peace FM Online*, July 2.

Acemoglu, Daron, Tristan Reed, and James A. Robinson. 2014. "Chiefs: Economic Development and Elite Control of Civil Society in Sierra Leone." *Journal of Political Economy* 122(2):319–368.

"Accra Floods: More Than 100 Feared Dead after Explosion," *The Daily Guide*, June 4, 2015.

Acquah, Raymond. 2015. "Ghana's Youth Population to Hit 5.3 Million by the End of 2015," *Citi FM Online*, November 27.

Adams, Paul. 2016. "State(s) of Crisis: Sub-national Government in Nigeria." *African Research Institute*, Briefing Note.

Ades, Alberto F. and Edward L. Glaeser. 1995. "Trade and Circuses: Explaining Urban Giants." *Quarterly Journal of Economics* 110(1):195–227.

Adida, Claire L., Karen E. Ferree, Daniel N. Posner, and Amanda Lea Robinson. 2016. "Who's Asking? Interviewer Coethnicity Effects in African Survey Data." *Comparative Political Studies* 49:1630–1660. 12.

Akinyele, Rufus T. 2009. Contesting for Space in an Urban Centre: The Omo Onile Syndrome in Lagos. In *African Cities: Competing Claims on Urban Spaces*. Boston: Brill Publishers, pp. 109–134.

Albertus, Michael. 2013. "Vote Buying with Multiple Distributive Goods." *Comparative Political Studies* 46(9):1082–1111.

Allotey, Godwin A. 2016. "Mahama's Progressive Free SHS Has Failed – Karbo," *Citi FM*, September 6.

Allport, Gordon. 1954. *The Nature of Prejudice*. Reading, MA: Addison Wesley.

Amat, Francesc and Pablo Beramendi. 2016. "Economic and Political Inequality: The Role of Political Mobilization." Working Paper.

Ansah, Marian. 2016. "Mahama Beats Hasty Retreat on Another 'Dumsor' Promise," *Citi FM*, January 12.

Ansell, Christopher K. and Arthur L. Burris. 1997. "Bosses of the City Unite! Labor Politics and Political Machine Consolidation, 1870–1910." *Studies in American Political Development* 11(1):1–43.

Ansolabehere, Stephen and Eitan Hersh. 2012. "Validation: What Big Data Reveal about Survey Misreporting and the Real Electorate." *Political Analysis* 20(4):437–549.
Anzia, Sarah F. 2014. *Timing and Turnout: How Off-Cycle Elections Favor Organized Groups*. Chicago, IL: University of Chicago Press.
Ardayfio-Schandorf, Elizabeth, Paul W. K. Yankson, and Monique Bertrand. 2012. *The Mobile City of Accra: Urban Families, Housing, and Residential Practices*. Dakar: CODESRIA.
Arku, Godwin. 2009. "Housing Policy Changes in Ghana in the 1990s." *Housing Studies* 24(4):261–272.
Arku, Godwin, Isaac Luginaah, and Paul Mkwandawire. 2012. "'You Either Pay More Advance Rent or You Move Out': Landlord/Ladies' and Tenants' Dilemmas in the Low-Income Housing Market in Accra, Ghana." *Urban Studies* 49(14):3177–3193.
Arriola, Leonardo R. 2012. *Multi-Ethnic Coalitions in Africa: Business Financing of Opposition Election Campaigns*. New York: Cambridge University Press.
Aryeetey, Ernest. 1996. *Structural Adjustment and Aid in Ghana*. Accra: Friedrich Ebert Stiftung.
Auerbach, Adam M. 2015. "India's Urban Constituencies Revisited." *Contemporary South Asia* 23(2):136–150.
Auerbach, Adam M. 2016. "Clients and Communities." *World Politics* 68(1):111–148.
Auerbach, Adam and Thariq Thachil. 2016. "Capability, Connectivity, and Co-Ethnicity: The Origins of Political Brokerage in India's Urban Slums." Working Paper.
Auyero, Javier. 2000. "The Logic of Clientelism in Argentina: An Ethnographic Account." *Latin American Research Review* 35(3):55–81.
Ayee, Joseph R. A. 1996. "The Measurement of Decentralization: The Ghanaian Experience." *African Affairs* 95(378):31–50.
Baker, Pauline H. 1974. *Urbanization and Political Change: The Politics of Lagos, 1917–1967*. Berkeley, CA: University of California Press.
Balaton-Chrimes, Samantha. 2013. "Indigeneity and Kenya's Nubians: Seeking Equality in Difference or Sameness?" *Journal of Modern African Studies* 51(2):331–354.
Baldwin, Kate. 2015. *The Paradox of Traditional Chiefs in Democratic Africa*. New York: Cambridge University Press.
Banerjee, Abhijit and Esther Duflo. 2008. "What Is Middle Class about the Middle Classes around the World?" *Journal of Economic Perspectives* 22(2):3–28.
Banfield, Edward C. and James Q. Wilson. 1963. *City Politics*. Cambridge, MA: Harvard University Press.
Banful, Afua. 2011. "Do Formula-Based Intergovernmental Transfer Mechanisms Eliminate Politically Motivated Targeting? Evidence from Ghana." *Journal of Development Economics* 96(2):380–390.
Bardhan, Pranab. 2002. "Decentralization of Governance and Development." *Journal of Economic Perspectives* 16(4):185–205.

Bardhan, Pranab and Dilip Mookherjee. 2006. "Decentralisation and Accountability in Infrastructure Delivery in Developing Countries." *The Economic Journal* 116(508):101–127.

Barkan, Joel D. 2008. "Legislatures on the Rise?" *Journal of Democracy* 19(2):124–137.

Bates, Robert H. 1974. "Ethnic Competition and Modernization in Contemporary Africa." *Comparative Political Studies* 6(2):457–484.

Bates, Robert H. 1983. Modernization, Ethnic Competition, and the Rationality of Politics in Contemporary Africa. In *State versus Ethnic Claims: African Policy Dilemmas*, ed. Donald Rothchild and Victor A. Olorunsola. Boulder, CO: Westview Press, pp. 152–171.

Baum-Snow, Nathaniel. 2007. "Did Highways Cause Suburbanization?" *Quarterly Journal of Economics* 122(2):775–805.

Beath, Andrew, Fotini Christia, and Ruben Enikolopov. 2013. "Do Elected Councils Improve Governance? Experimental Evidence on Local Institutions in Afghanistan." Working Paper.

Birdsall, Nancy. 2010. "The (Indispensable) Middle Class in Developing Countries; or, The Rich and the Rest, Not the Poor and the Rest." Center for Global Development Working Paper #207.

Blattman, Christopher, Mathilde Emeriau and, Nathan Fiala. 2017. "Do Anti-Poverty Programs Sway Voters? Experiment Evidence from Uganda." Forthcoming, *Review of Economics and Statistics*.

Bleck, Jaimie and Nicolas van de Walle. 2012. "Valence Issues in African Elections: Navigating Uncertainty and the Weight of the Past." *Comparative Political Studies* 46(11):1394–1421.

Bob-Milliar, George M. 2012. "Political Party Activism in Ghana: Factors Influencing the Decision of the Politically Active to Join a Political Party." *Democratization* 19(4):668–689.

Bobo, Lawrence and Vincent L. Hutchings. 1996. "Perceptions of Racial Group Competition: Extending Blumer's Theory of Group Position to a Multiracial Social Context." *American Sociological Review* 61(6):951–972.

Bobonis, Gustavo, Paul Gertler, Marco Gonzalez-Navarro, and Simeon Nichter. 2017. "Vulnerability and Clientelism." NBER Working Paper No. 23589.

Bodea, Cristina and Adrienne LeBas. 2016. "The Origins of Voluntary Compliance: Attitudes toward Taxation in Urban Nigeria." *British Journal of Political Science* 46(1):215–238.

Boone, Catherine. 2014. *Property and Political Order in Africa: Land Rights and the Structure of Politics*. New York: Cambridge University Press.

Boone, Catherine and Michael Wahman. 2015. "Rural Bias in African Electoral Systems: Legacies of Unequal Representation in African Democracies." *Electoral Studies* 40:335–346.

Boulay, Harvey and Alan DiGaetano. 1985. "Why Did Political Machines Disappear?" *Journal of Urban History* 12(1):25–49.

Bratton, Michael. 2008. "Vote Buying and Violence in Nigerian Election Campaigns." *Electoral Studies* 27:621–632.

Bratton, Michael, Ravi Bhavani, and Tse-Hsin Chen. 2011. "Voting Intentions in Africa: Ethnic, Economic or Partisan?" Afrobarometer Working Paper No. 127.

Brierley, Sarah. 2016. "Unprincipled Principles: Co-opted Bureaucrats and Corruption in Local Governments in Ghana." Working Paper.

Brierley, Sarah. 2017. "Managing Transitions to Meritocracy in Clientelistic Democracies." Working Paper.

Brierley, Sarah and Eric Kramon. 2015. "Political Party Campaign Strategies and Incumbency Advantages in an African Election." Working Paper.

Brollo, Fernanda, Katja Kaufmann and Eliana La Ferrara. 2017. "The Political Economy of Enforcing Conditional Welfare Programs: Evidence from Brazil." Working Paper.

Brooks, David. 2014. "The Real Africa," *The New York Times*, May 8.

Brusco, Valeria, Marcelo Nazareno and Susan C. Stokes. 2004. "Vote Buying in Argentina." *Latin American Research Review* 39:66–88.

Burbidge, Dominic. 2014. "'Can Someone Get Me Outta This Middle Class Zone?!' Pressures on Middle Class Kikuyu in Kenya's 2013 Election." *Journal of Modern African Studies* 52(2):205–225.

Burgess, Robin, Rémi Jedwab, Edward Miguel, Ameet Morjaria, and Gerard Padro i Miquel. 2015. "The Value of Democracy: Evidence from Road Building in Kenya." *American Economic Review* 105(6):1817–1851.

Calvo, Ernesto and M. Victoria Murillo. 2004. "Who Delivers? Partisan Clients in the Argentine Electoral Market." *American Journal of Political Science* 48:742–757.

Camp, Edwin. 2017. "Cultivating Effective Brokers: A Party Leader's Dilemma." *British Journal of Political Science* 47(3):521–543.

Campbell, Tim. 2003. *The Quiet Revolution: Decentralization and the Rise of Political Participation in Latin American Cities*. Pittsburgh, PA: University of Pittsburgh Press.

Carlson, Elizabeth. 2014. "Social Desirability Bias and Reported Vote Preferences in African Surveys." Afrobarometer Working Paper No. 144.

Carlson, Elizabeth. 2015. "Ethnic Voting and Accountability in Africa: A Choice Experiment in Uganda." *World Politics* 67(2):353–385.

Carlson, Elizabeth. 2016. "Finding Partisanship Where We Least Expect It: Evidence of Partisan Bias in a New Democracy." *Political Behavior* 38(1):129–154.

Casey, Katherine. 2015. "Crossing Party Lines: The Effects of Information on Redistributive Politics." *American Economic Review* 105(8):2410–2448.

Chabal, Patrick and Jean-Pascal Daloz. 1999. *Africa Works: Disorder as Political Instrument*. Bloomington, IN: Indiana University Press.

Chandra, Kanchan. 2004. *Why Ethnic Parties Succeed: Patronage and Head Counts in India*. New York: Cambridge University Press.

Chandra, Kanchan. 2011. "What Is an Ethnic Party?" *Party Politics* 17(2):151–169.

Chatterjee, Partha. 2004. *Politics of the Governed: Popular Politics in Most of the World*. New York: Columbia University Press.

Cheeseman, Nic. 2015. "'No Bourgeoisie, No Democracy?' The Political Attitudes of the Kenyan Middle Class." *Journal of International Development* 27:647–664.

Chhibber, Pradeep and Irfan Nooruddin. 2004. "Do Party Systems Count? The Number of Parties and Government Performance in the Indian States." *Comparative Political Studies* 37(2):152–187.

Cho, Wendy K. Tam and Thomas J. Rudolph. 2008. "Emanating Political Participation: Untangling the Spatial Structure behind Participation." *British Journal of Political Science* 38:273–289.

Chong, Alberto, Ana L. De La O, Dean Karlan, and Leonard Wantchekon. 2015. "Does Corruption Information Inspire the Fight or Quash the Hope? A Field Experiment in Mexico on Voter Turnout, Choice, and Party Identification." *Journal of Politics* 77(1):55–71.

Chubb, Judith. 1982. *Patronage, Power, and Poverty in Southern Italy: A Tale of Two Cities*. New York: Cambridge University Press.

Cohen, Abner. 1969. *Custom and Politics in Urban Africa: A Study of Hausa Migrants in Yoruba Towns*. Berkeley, CA: University of California Press.

Conroy-Krutz, Jeffrey. 2009. "Who Are Africa's (Non) Ethnic Voters? Evaluating Theories on the Salience of Ethnicity in African Electoral Politics." Working Paper, Michigan State University.

Conroy-Krutz, Jeffrey. 2013. "Information and Ethnic Politics in Africa." *British Journal of Political Science* 43(2):345–373.

Conroy-Krutz, Jeffrey. 2017. "Individual Autonomy and Local-Level Solidarity in Africa." *Political Behavior* 40(3):593–627.

Conroy-Krutz, Jeffrey and Devra C. Moehler. 2015. "Moderation from Bias: A Field Experiment on Partisan Media in a New Democracy." *Journal of Politics* 77(2):575–587.

Cornwell, Elmer C. 1976. Bosses, Machines, and Ethnic Groups. In *The City Boss in America*, ed. Alexander B. Callow. New York: Oxford University Press.

Cox, Gary W. and Matthew D. McCubbins. 1986. "Electoral Politics as a Redistributive Game." *Journal of Politics* 48:370–389.

Croke, Kevin, Guy Grossman, Horacio A. Larreguy, and John Marshall. 2016. "Deliberate Disengagement: How Education Can Decrease Political Participation in Electoral Authoritarian Regimes." *American Political Science Review* 110(3):579–600.

Crook, Richard C. 1999. "'No Party' Politics and Local Democracy in Africa: Rawlings' Ghana in the 1990s and the Ugandan Model." *Democratization* 6(4):114–138.

Cruz, Cesi and Christina J. Schneider. 2017. "Foreign Aid and Undeserved Credit Claiming." *American Journal of Political Science* 61(2):396–408.

Cruz, Cesi and Philip Keefer. 2015. "Political Parties, Clientelism, and Bureaucratic Reform." *Comparative Political Studies* 48(14):1942–1973.

Dalinjong, Philip Ayizem and Alexander Suuk Laar. 2012. "The National Health Insurance Scheme: Perceptions and Experiences of Health Care Providers and Clients in Two Districts in Ghana." *Health Economics Review* 2(1):1–13.

Davis, Charles L., Roderic Ai Camp, and Kenneth M. Coleman. 2004. "The Influence of Party Systems on Citizens' Perceptions of Corruption and Electoral Response in Latin America." *Comparative Political Studies* 37(6):677–703.

de Gramont, Diane. 2015. "Governing Lagos: Unlocking the Politics of Reform." Technical Report: Carnegie Endowment for International Peace.

de Kadt, Daniel and Horacio Larreguy. 2018. "Agents of the Regime? Traditional Leaders and Electoral Behavior in South Africa." *Journal of Politics* 80(2):382–399.

de Kadt, Daniel and Melissa Sands. 2017. "Segregation Drives Racial Voting: New Evidence from South Africa." Working Paper.

De La O, Ana L. 2013. "Do Conditional Cash Transfers Affect Electoral Behavior? Evidence from a Randomized Experiment in Mexico." *American Journal of Political Science* 57(1):1–14.

Deaton, Angus. 2010. "Price Indexes, Inequality, and the Measurement of World Poverty." *American Economic Review* 100(1):5–34.

Dery, Severious Kale. 2014. "Cholera Outbreak Worsening in Gt. Accra; Over 6000 Cases Recorded," *The Daily Graphic*, August 26.

Deutsch, Karl. 1961. "Social Mobilization and Political Development." *American Political Science Review* 55(3):493–514.

Diaz-Cayeros, Alberto, Federico Estévez, and Beatriz Magaloni. 2016. *The Political Logic of Poverty Relief: Electoral Strategies and Social Policy in Mexico*. Cambridge University Press.

DiGaetano, Alan. 1991. "Urban Political Reform: Did It Kill the Machine?" *Journal of Urban History* 18:37–67.

Dickinson, Elizabeth. 2011. "Middle Class Africa," *Foreign Policy: Passport Blog*, May 6.

Dixit, Avinash and John Londregan. 1996. "The Determinants of Success of Special Interests in Redistributive Politics." *Journal of Politics* 58:1132–1155.

Djabanor, Fred and Edwin Kwakofi. 2017. "NDC Scraps Biometric Register, Will Register Members Manually," *Citi FM Online*, October 17.

"Doctors in Ghana Continue to Strike over Salary Dispute," *BBC News*, April 12, 2013.

Downs, Anthony. 1957. *An Economic Theory of Democracy*. New York: Harper and Row.

Dunning, Thad and Lauren Harrison. 2010. "Cross-cutting Cleavages and Ethnic Voting: An Experimental Study of Cousinage in Mali." *American Political Science Review* 104(1):1–19.

Dutton, William H. and Alana Northrop. 1978. "Municipal Reform and the Changing Pattern of Urban Party Politics." *American Politics Quarterly* 6(4):429–452.

Eaton, Kent. 2014. "Recentralization and the Left Turn in Latin America: Diverging Outcomes in Bolivia, Ecuador, and Venezuela." *Comparative Political Studies* 47(8):1130–1157.

Eifert, Benn, Edward Miguel, and Daniel N. Posner. 2010. "Political Competition and Ethnic Identification in Africa." *American Journal of Political Science* 54(2):494–510.

Ejdemyr, Simon, Eric Kramon and Amanda Robinson. 2017. "Segregation, Ethnic Favoritism and the Strategic Targeting of Local Public Goods." *Comparative Political Studies* 50(9): 1111–1143.

Ekeh, Peter P. 1975. "Colonialism and the Two Publics in Africa: A Theoretical Statement." *Comparative Studies in Society and History* 17(1):91–112.

Elischer, Sebastian. 2013. *Political Parties in Africa: Ethnicity and Party Formation*. New York: Cambridge University Press.

Enos, Ryan D. 2017. *The Space between Us: Social Geography and Politics*. New York: Cambridge University Press.

Epstein, A. L. 1958. *Politics in an Urban African Community*. Manchester: Manchester University Press.

Erie, Steven P. 1988. *Rainbow's End: Irish Americans and the Dilemmas of Urban Machine Politics*. Berkeley, CA: University of California Press.

Essuman, Collins. 2016. "Manifestos Are Just Intents, Not Binding on Parties," *TV3 News*, June 24.

Evans, Geoffrey and Robert Andersen. 2006. "The Political Conditioning of Economic Perceptions." *Journal of Politics* 68(1):194–207.

Evans, Peter B., Dietrich Rueschemeyer and Theda Skocpol, eds. 1985. *Bringing the State Back In*. New York: Cambridge University Press.

Faller, Julie. 2013. "The Importance of Timing: Elections, Partisan Targeting and the Ghana Education Trust Fund." Working Paper.

Falleti, Tulia G. 2010. *Decentralization and Subnational Politics in Latin America*. New York: Cambridge University Press.

Fedderson, Timothy J. 2004. "Rational Choice Theory and the Paradox of Not Voting." *Journal of Economic Perspectives* 18(1):99–112.

Ferraz, Claudio and Frederico Finan. 2011. "Electoral Accountability and Corruption: Evidence from Audits of Local Governments." *American Economic Review* 101(4):1274–1311.

Ferree, Karen. 2006. "Explaining South Africa's Racial Census." *Journal of Politics* 68(4):803–815.

Ferree, Karen E. 2010. "The Social Origins of Electoral Volatility in Africa." *British Journal of Political Science* 40(3):759–779.

Ferree, Karen E. and James D. Long. 2016. "Gifts, Threats, and Perceptions of Ballot Secrecy in African Elections." *African Affairs* 115(461):621–645.

Fletcher, Pascal. 2013. "Africa's Emerging Middle Class Drives Growth and Democracy," *Reuters*, May 10.

Filmer, Deon and Lant H. Pritchett. 2001. "Estimating Wealth Effects without Expenditure Data – Or Tears: An Application to Educational Enrollments in States of India." *Demography* 38(1):115–132.

Firmin-Sellers, Kathryn. 1996. *The Transformation of Property Rights in the Gold Coast: An Empirical Analysis Applying Rational Choice Theory*. New York: Cambridge University Press.

Fobih, Nick. 2010. "Dynamics of Political Parties' Administration in Ghana." *Africa Today* 57:25–41.

Folke, Olle, Shigeo Hirano, and James M. Snyder Jr. 2011. "Patronage and Elections in US States." *American Political Science Review* 105(3):567–585.

Fornos, Carolina A., Timothy J. Power, and James C. Garand. 2004. "Explaining Voter Turnout in Latin America, 1980 to 2000." *Comparative Political Studies* 37(8):909–940.

Franck, Raphael and Ilia Rainer. 2012. "Does the Leader's Ethnicity Matter? Ethnic Favoritism, Education, and Health in Sub-Saharan Africa." *American Political Science Review* 106(2):294–325.

French, Howard W. 2013. "How Africa's New Urban Centers Are Shifting Its Old Colonial Boundaries," *The Atlantic*, July 1.

Fridy, Kevin S. 2007. "The Elephant, Umbrella, and Quarrelling Cocks: Disaggregating Partisanship in Ghana's Fourth Republic." *African Affairs* 106(423):281–305.

Gadugah, Nathan. 2016. "Peerless Mahama Solves 'Dumsor' in 1 Year – Ayariga Claims," *My Joy Online*, March 2.

Gay, Claudine. 2004. "Putting Race in Context: Identifying the Environmental Determinants of Black Racial Attitudes." *American Political Science Review* 98:547–562.

Gelman, Andrew and Jennifer Hill. 2007. *Data Analysis Using Regression and Multilevel/Hierarchical Models*. New York: Cambridge University Press.

Gerber, Alan S. and Donald P. Green. 2000. "The Effects of Canvassing, Telephone Calls, and Direct Mail on Voter Turnout: A Field Experiment." *American Political Science Review* 94(3):653–663.

Ghana Living Standards Survey: Report of the Fifth Round (GLSS 5). 2008. Ghana Statistical Service.

Gilens, Martin. 2012. *Affluence and Influence: Economic Inequality and Political Power in America*. Princeton, NJ: Princeton University Press.

Golden, Miriam and Brian Min. 2013. "Distributive Politics around the World." *Annual Review of Political Science* 16:73–99.

Goldstein, Markus and Christopher Udry. 2008. "The Profits of Power: Land Rights and Agricultural Investment in Ghana." *Journal of Political Economy* 116(6):981–1022.

Gonzalez-Ocantos, Ezequiel, Chad Kiewiet de Jonge, Carlos Melendez, Javier Osorio and David W. Nickerson. 2012. "Vote Buying and Social Desirability Bias: Experiment Evidence from Nicaragua." *American Journal of Political Science* 56(1):202–217.

Gottlieb, Jessica, Guy Grossman, and Amanda Lea Robinson. 2018. "Do Men and Women Have Different Policy Preferences in Africa? Determinants and Implications of Gender Gaps in Policy Prioritization." *British Journal of Political Science* 48(3): 611–636.

Gottlieb, Jessica and Horacio Larreguy. 2015. "An Informational Theory of Electoral Targeting: Evidence from Senegal." Working Paper.

Gough, Katherine and Paul Yankson. 2006. Conflict and Cooperation: Environmental Management in Peri-Urban Accra, Ghana. In *The Peri-Urban Interface: Approaches to Sustainable Natural and Human Resource Use*, ed. Duncan McGregor, David Simon and Donald Thompson. London: Earthscan, pp. 196–210.

Gough, Katherine V. and Paul Yankson. 2011. "A Neglected Aspect of the Housing Market: The Caretakers of Peri-Urban Ghana." *Urban Studies* 48:793–810.

Grant, Richard. 2009. *Globalizing City: The Urban and Economic Transformation of Accra, Ghana*. Syracuse, NY: Syracuse University Press.

Green, Elliot. 2014. "The Political Economy of Urbanization in Botswana." Working Paper, London School of Economics.

Greene, Kenneth F. 2007. *Why Dominant Parties Lose: Mexico's Democratization in Comparative Perspective*. New York: Cambridge University Press.

Greenstein, Fred I. 1964. "The Changing Patterns of Urban Party Politics." *Annals of the American Academy of Political and Social Science* 353(1):1–13.

Grindle, Merilee S. 2012. *Jobs for the Boys: Patronage and the State in Comparative Perspective*. Cambridge, MA: Harvard University Press.

Grossman, Guy and Janet I. Lewis. 2014. "Administrative Unit Proliferation." *American Political Science Review* 108(1):196–217.

Grossman, Shelby. 2016. "The Politics of Order in Informal Markets: Evidence from Lagos." PhD Thesis, Harvard University.

Guardado, Jenny and Leonard Wantchekon. 2017. "Do Electoral Handouts Affect Voting Behavior?" Afrobarometer Working Paper No. 171.

Gugler, Josef. 2002. "The Son of the Hawk Does Not Remain Abroad: The Urban-Rural Connection in Africa." *African Studies Review* 45(1):21–41.

Gugler, Josef and William G. Flanagan. 1978. *Urbanization and Social Change in West Africa*. New York: Cambridge University Press.

Hagopian, Frances, Carlos Gervasoni, and Juan Andres Moraes. 2009. "From Patronage to Program: The Emergence of Party-Oriented Legislators in Brazil." *Comparative Political Studies* 42:360–391.

Hainmueller, Jens, Daniel J. Hopkins, and Teppei Yamamoto. 2013. "Causal Inference in Conjoint Analysis: Understanding Multi-Dimensional Choices via Stated Preference Experiments." *Political Analysis* 22(1):1–30.

Hajnal, Zoltan and Jessica Trounstine. 2005. "Where Turnout Matters: The Consequences of Turnout in City Politics." *Journal of Politics* 67(2):515–535.

Hanmer, Michael J. and Kerem Ozan Kalkan. 2013. "Behind the Curve: Clarifying the Best Approach to Calculating Predicted Probabilities and Marginal Effects from Limited Dependent Variable Models." *American Journal of Political Science* 57(1):263–277.

Harding, Robin. 2010. "Urban-Rural Differences in Support for Incumbents Across Africa." Afrobarometer Working Paper No. 120.

Harding, Robin. 2015. "Attribution and Accountability: Voting for Roads in Ghana." *World Politics* 67(4):656–689.

Harriss, John. 2006. "Middle-Class Activism and the Politics of the Informal Working Class." *Critical Asian Studies* 38(4):445–465.

Hassan, Mai. 2016. "A State of Change: District Creation in Kenya after Multi-Party Elections." *Political Research Quarterly* 69(3):510–521.

Hendrix, Cullen S. 2010. "Measuring State Capacity: Theoretical and Empirical Implications for the Study of Civil Conflict." *Journal of Peace Research* 47(3):273–285.

Herbst, Jeffrey. 1993. *The Politics of Reform in Ghana, 1982–1991*. Berkeley, CA: University of California Press.
Herbst, Jeffrey. 2000. *States and Power in Africa: Comparative Lessons in Authority and Control*. Princeton, NJ: Princeton University Press.
Hicken, Allen. 2011. "Clientelism." *Annual Review of Political Science* 14(1):289–310.
Hite-Rubin, Nancy. 2015. "Including the Other Half: How Financial Modernization Disrupts Patronage Politics." Working Paper.
Hoffman, Barak D. and James D. Long. 2013. "Parties, Ethnicity, and Voting in African Elections." *Comparative Politics* 45(2):127–146.
Hopkins, Daniel J. 2010. "Politicized Places: Explaining Where and When Immigrants Provoke Local Opposition." *American Political Science Review* 104(1):40–60.
Hopkins, Daniel J. and Thad Williamson. 2012. "Inactive by Design? Neighborhood Design and Political Participation." *Political Behavior* 34(1):79–101.
Horowitz, Donald. 1985. *Ethnic Groups in Conflict*. Berkeley, CA: University of California Press.
Horowitz, Jeremy. 2016. "The Ethnic Logic of Campaign Strategy in Diverse Societies: Theory and Evidence from Kenya." *Comparative Political Studies* 49(3):324–356.
Ichino, Nahomi and Noah L. Nathan. 2012. "Primaries on Demand? Intra-Party Politics and Nominations in Ghana." *British Journal of Political Science* 42(4):769–791.
Ichino, Nahomi and Noah L. Nathan. 2013a. "Crossing the Line: Local Ethnic Geography and Voting in Ghana." *American Political Science Review* 107(2):344–361.
Ichino, Nahomi and Noah L. Nathan. 2013b. "Do Primaries Improve Electoral Performance? Clientelism and Intra-Party Conflict in Ghana." *American Journal of Political Science* 57(2):428–441.
Imai, Kosuke, Gary King, and Carlos Velasco Rivera. 2016. "Do Nonpartisan Programmatic Policies Have Partisan Electoral Effects? Evidence from Two Large Scale Randomized Experiments." Working Paper.
Inglehart, Ronald. 1997. *Modernization and Postmodernization: Cultural, Economic, and Political Change in 43 Societies*. Princeton, NJ: Princeton University Press.
Inkeles, Alex. 1966. The Modernization of Man. In *Modernization: The Dynamics of Growth*, ed. Myron Weiner. New York: Basic Books, pp. 138–150.
Jaitman, Laura. 2013. "The Causal Effect of Compulsory Voting Laws on Turnout: Does Skill Matter?" *Journal of Economic Behavior and Organization* 92:79–93.
"Junior Doctors on Strike over Unpaid Salaries," *The Daily Guide*, June 3, 2015.
Kaplan, Seth. 2014. "Africa's City on a Hill: Lessons from Lagos." *Foreign Affairs*. www.foreignaffairs.com/articles/africa/2014-08-20/africas-city-hill
Karp, Jeffrey A. and David Brockington. 2005. "Social Desirability Bias and Response Validity: A Comparative Analysis of Overreporting Voter Turnout in Five Countries." *Journal of Politics* 67(3):825–840.

Kasara, Kimuli. 2007. "Tax Me If You Can: Ethnic Geography, Democracy, and the Taxation of Agriculture in Africa." *American Political Science Review* 101(1):159–172.

Kasara, Kimuli. 2013. "Separate and Suspicious: Local Social and Political Context and Ethnic Tolerance in Kenya." *Journal of Politics* 75(4):921–936.

Kasara, Kimuli and Pavithra Suryanarayan. 2015. "When Do the Rich Vote Less Than the Poor and Why? Explaining Turnout Inequality across the World." *American Journal of Political Science* 59(3):613–627.

Keefer, Philip. 2007. "Clientelism, Credibility, and the Policy Choices of Young Democracies." *American Journal of Political Science* 51(4):804–821.

Keefer, Philip and Razvan Vlaicu. 2008. "Democracy, Credibility, and Clientelism." *Journal of Economics, Law, and Organization* 24(2):371–406.

Kessides, Christine. 2006. *The Urban Transition in Sub-Saharan Africa: Implications for Economic Growth and Poverty Reduction*. Washington, DC: The Cities Alliance/The World Bank.

Key, Valdimer Orlando. 1949. *Southern Politics in State and Nation*. A. A. Knopf.

Kimenyi, Mwangi S. 2006. "Ethnicity, Governance and the Provision of Public Goods." *Journal of African Economies* 15:62–99.

Kitschelt, Herbert. 2000. "Linkages between Citizens and Politicians in Democratic Polities." *Comparative Political Studies* 333(3):845–879.

Kitschelt, Herbert. 2007. The Demise of Clientelism in Affluent Capitalist Democracies. In *Patrons, Clients, and Policies: Patterns of Democratic Accountability and Political Competition*, ed. Herbert Kitschelt and Steven I. Wilkinson. New York: Cambridge University Press, pp. 298–321.

Kitschelt, Herbert and Daniel M. Kselman. 2013. "Economic Development, Democratic Experience, and Political Parties' Linkage Strategies." *Comparative Political Studies* 46(11):1453–1484.

Kitschelt, Herbert, Kirk A. Hawkins, Juan Pablo Luna, Guillermo Rosas, and Elizabeth J. Zechmeister. 2010. *Latin American Party Systems*. New York: Cambridge University Press.

Kitschelt, Herbert and Steven I. Wilkinson. 2007. Citizen-Politician Linkages: An Introduction. In *Patrons, Clients, and Policies: Patterns of Democratic Accountability and Political Competition*, ed. Herbert Kitschelt and Steven I. Wilkinson. Cambridge University Press, pp. 1–49.

Kobo, Ousman. 2010. "'We Are Citizens Too': The Politics of Citizenship in Independent Ghana." *Journal of Modern African Studies* 48(1):67–94.

Koter, Dominika. 2013. "King Makers: Local Leaders and Ethnic Politics in Africa." *World Politics* 65(2):187–232.

Koter, Dominika. 2016. *Beyond Ethnic Politics in Africa*. New York: Cambridge University Press.

Kramon, Eric. 2016. "Electoral Handouts as Information: Explaining Unmonitored Vote Buying." *World Politics* 68(3):454–498.

Kramon, Eric and Daniel N. Posner. 2013. "Who Benefits from Distributive Politics? How the Outcome One Studies Affects the Answer One Gets." *Perspectives on Politics* 11(2):461–472.

Kropp Dakubu, M.E. 1997. *Korle Meets the Sea: A Sociolinguistic History of Accra*. New York: Oxford University Press.

Kuo, Joanna Didi. 2018. *Clientelism, Capitalism, and Democracy: The Rise of Programmatic Politics in the United States and Britain*. New York: Cambridge University Press.

Labonne, Julien. 2013. "The Local Electoral Impacts of Conditional Cash Transfers: Evidence from a Field Experiment." *Journal of Development Economics* 104(1):73–88.

Lambright, Gina M. S. 2014. "Opposition Politics and Urban Service Delivery in Kampala, Uganda." *Development Policy Review* 32(1):39–60.

LeBas, Adrienne. 2013. "Violence and Urban Order in Nairobi, Kenya and Lagos, Nigeria." *Studies in Comparative International Development* 48:240–262.

Lee, Barrett A., Glenn Firebaugh, Stephen A. Matthews, Sean F. Readon, Chad R. Farrell, and David O'Sullivan. 2008. "Beyond the Census Tract: Patterns and Determinants of Racial Segregation at Multiple Scales." *American Sociological Review* 73(5):766–791.

Lerner, Daniel. 1958. *The Passing of Traditional Society: Modernizing the Middle East*. New York: The Free Press.

Levitsky, Steven. 2003. *Transforming Labor-Based Parties in Latin America: Argentine Peronism in Comparative Perspective*. New York: Cambridge University Press.

Levitsky, Steven and Lucan Way. 2010. *Competitive Authoritarianism: Hybrid Regimes after the Cold War*. New York: Cambridge University Press.

Lieberman, Evan and Gwyneth McClendon. 2013. "The Ethnicity-Policy Preferences Link in Sub-Saharan Africa." *Comparative Political Studies* 46(5):574–602.

Lieberman, Evan S. 2003. *Race and Regionalism in the Politics of Taxation in Brazil and South Africa*. New York: Cambridge University Press.

Lindbeck, Assar and Jorgen W. Weibull. 1987. "Balanced-Budget Redistribution as the Outcome of Political Competition." *Public Choice* 52(3):273–297.

Lindberg, Staffan I. 2010. "What accountability pressures do MPs in Africa face and how do they respond? Evidence from Ghana." *Journal of Modern African Studies* 48(1):117–142.

Lindberg, Staffan I. and Yongmei Zhou. 2009. Co-optation Despite Democratization in Ghana. In *Legislative Power in Emerging African Democracies*, ed. Joel Barkan. Boulder, CO: Lynne Rienner Publishers.

Lipset, Seymour Martin. 1960. *Political Man: The Social Bases of Politics*. Garden City, NY: Doubleday.

Little, Kenneth. 1964. *West African Urbanization: A Study of Voluntary Associations in Social Change*. Cambridge University Press.

Lofchie, Michael. 2015. The Political Economy of the African Middle Class. In *The Emerging Middle Class in Africa*, ed. Mthuli Ncube and Charles Lufumba. Routledge Publishers, pp. 34–58.

Luna, Joseph. 2016. "Political Finance in Developing States." PhD thesis, Harvard University.

Luna, Juan Pablo. 2014. *Segmented Representation: Political Party Strategies in Unequal Democracies*. New York: Oxford University Press.

Lupu, Noah. 2016. *Party Brands in Crisis: Partisanship, Brand Dilution, and the Breakdown of Parties in Latin America*. New York: Cambridge University Press.

MacGaffey, Wyatt. 2006. "Death of a King, Death of a Kingdom? Social Pluralism and Succession to High Office in Dagbon, Northern Ghana." *Journal of Modern African Studies* 44(1):79–99.

Magaloni, Beatriz. 2006. *Voting for Autocracy: Hegemonic Party Survival and Its Demise in Mexico*. New York: Cambridge University Press.

Magaloni, Beatriz, Alberto Diaz-Cayeros, and Federico Estévez. 2007. Clientelism and Portfolio Diversification: A Model of Electoral Investment with Applications to Mexico. In *Patrons, Clients, and Policies: Patterns of Democratic Accountability and Political Competition*, ed. Herbert Kitschelt and Steven I. Wilkinson. New York: Cambridge University Press, pp. 182–205.

"Mahama's 200 Day Schools in Limbo," *Daily Guide*, June 28.

Mares, Isabela. 2015. *From Open Secrets to Secret Voting: Democratic Electoral Reforms and Voter Autonomy*. New York: Cambridge University Press.

Martinez-Bravo, Monica, Gerard Padro i Miquel, Nancy Qian and Yang Yao. 2012. "Elections in China." NBER Working Paper 18101.

Mattes, Robert. 2015. "South Africa's Emerging Black Middle Class: A Harbinger of Political Change?" *Journal of International Development* 27:665–692.

McCann, James A. and Jorge I. Dominguez. 1998. "Mexicans React to Electoral Fraud and Political Corruption: As Assessment of Public Opinion and Voting Behavior." *Electoral Studies* 17(4):483–503.

Melson, Robert. 1971. "Ideology and Inconsistency: The 'Cross-Pressured' Nigerian Worker." *American Political Science Review* 65(1):161–171.

Meltzer, Allan H. and Scott F. Richard. 1981. "A Rational Theory of the Size of Government." *The Journal of Political Economy* 89(5):914–927.

Mensah, Frank. 2009. "NDC Supporters Scramble for Public Toilets," *Ghanaian Chronicle*, January 22.

Mensah, Kent. 2014. "Ghana's Successful but Unpopular Healthcare," *Al Jazeera*, August 6.

Mitlin, Diana and David Satterthwaite. 2013. *Urban Poverty in the Global South: Scale and Nature*. London: Routledge.

"MMDCEs will be elected from 2018 – Akufo-Addo," *Ultimate FM Online*, December 27, 2016.

"Moves to Elect DCEs – Government to Submit Proposals to Constitutional Review Commission," *The Daily Graphic*, January 22, 2010.

Mummolo, Jonathan and Clayton Nall. 2016. "Why Partisans Do Not Sort: The Constraints on Political Segregation." *Journal of Politics* 79(1):45–59.

Munoz, Paula. 2014. "An Informational Theory of Campaign Clientelism." *Comparative Politics* 47(1):79–98.

Nall, Clayton. 2015. "The Political Consequences of Spatial Policies: How the Interstate Highways Facilitated Geographic Polarization." *Journal of Politics* 77(2):394–406.

National Democratic Congress, the. 2012. "Advancing the Better Ghana Agenda: Jobs, Stability, Development." Manifesto of the National Democratic Congress.
Ncube, Mthuli. 2015. Introduction. In *The Emerging Middle Class in Africa*, ed. Mthuli Ncube and Charles Leyeka Lufumpa. New York: Routledge, pp. 1–8.
"NDC foot soldiers join NPP," *Ghana Web*, July 11, 2016.
"NDC foot-soldiers reject GHC10,000," *Daily Guide*, April 21, 2016.
"NDC Supporters Scramble for Public Toilets," *Ghanaian Chronicle*, January 22, 2009.
New Patriotic Party, the. 2008. "Moving Ghana Forward – Building a Modern Ghana." Manifesto of the New Patriotic Party.
New Patriotic Party, the. 2012. "Transforming Lives, Transforming Ghana: Building a Free, Fair and Prosperous Society." Manifesto of the New Patriotic Party.
"NHIS must Promptly Pay Claims – Healthcare Providers," *Citi FM*, August 23, 2013.
Nichter, Simeon. 2008. "Vote Buying or Turnout Buying? Machine Politics and the Secret Ballot." *American Political Science Review* 102:19–31.
Nichter, Simeon and Michael Peress. 2017. "Request Fulfilling: When Citizens Demand Clientelist Benefits." *Comparative Political Studies* 50(8):1086–1117.
"NPP Could Declare 2016 Election Results," *My Joy Online*, June 7, 2016.
Ntewusu, Samuel. 2012. "Settling In and Holding On, A Socio-Historical Study of Northern Traders and Transporters in Accra's Tudu: 1908–2008." PhD Thesis, Leiden University.
Ntsebeza, Lungisile. 2005. *Democracy Compromised: Chiefs and the Politics of Land in South Africa*. Boston: Brill Publishers.
Öhman, Magnus. 2004. "The Heart and Soul of the Party: Candidate selection in Ghana and Africa." PhD Thesis, Uppsala Universitet (Sweden).
Oliver, J. Eric and Janelle Wong. 2003. "Intergroup Prejudice in Multiethnic Settings." *American Journal of Political Science* 47(4):567–582.
Olowu, Dele and James S. Wunsch, eds. 2004. *Local Governance in Africa: The Challenges of Democratic Decentralization*. Boulder, CO: Lynne Rienner Publishers.
O'Neill, Kathleen. 2005. *Decentralizing the State: Elections, Parties, and Local Power in the Andes*. New York: Cambridge University Press.
"Only Ga-Dangmes should be MCEs, DCEs in Greater Accra," *Class FM Online*, January 17, 2017.
Onoma, Ato Kwamena. 2010. *The Politics of Property Rights Institutions in Africa*. New York: Cambridge University Press.
Openshaw, Stan. 1983. *The Modifiable Areal Unit Problem*. Norwich, UK: Geo Books.
Osei, Anja. 2016. "Formal Party Organisation and Informal Relations in African Parties: Evidence from Ghana." *Journal of Modern African Studies* 54(1):37–66.
Padro i Miquel, Gerard. 2007. "The Control of Politicians in Divided Societies: The Politics of Fear." *Review of Economic Studies* 74(4):1259–74.

Paice, Edward. 2016. "Dakar's Municipal Bond Issue: A Tale of Two Cities." *African Research Institute* Briefing Note.

Paller, Jeffrey W. 2014. "Informal Institutions and Personal Rule in Urban Ghana." *African Studies Review* 57(3):123–142.

Paller, Jeffrey W. 2015. "Whose City Is It Anyway? Evidence from a Survey Experiment in Urban Ghana." Working Paper.

Paller, Jeffrey W. 2018. *Democracy in Ghana: Everyday Politics in Urban Africa*. New York: Cambridge University Press.

Parker, John. 2000. *Making the Town: Ga State and Society in Early Colonial Accra*. Oxford: James Currey Press.

Peil, Margaret. 1991. *Lagos: The City Is the People*. Boston, MA: G. K. Hall.

Pellow, Deborah. 2002. *Landlords and Lodgers: Socio-Spatial Organization in an Accra Community*. Praeger Publishers.

Persson, Anna, Bo Rothstein, and Jan Teorell. 2012. "Why Anticorruption Reforms Fail – Systemic Corruption as a Collective Action Problem." *Governance* 26(3):449–471.

Pitcher, M. Anne. 2017. "Varieties of Residential Capitalism in Africa: Urban Housing Provision in Luanda and Nairobi." *African Affairs* 116(464):365–390.

Political Risk Services Group, The. 2014. "International Country Risk Guide (IRCG) Research Dataset."

Posner, Daniel N. 2004. "Measuring Ethnic Fractionalization in Africa." *American Journal of Political Science* 48(4):849–863.

Posner, Daniel N. 2005. *Institutions and Ethnic Politics in Africa*. New York: Cambridge University Press.

Posner, Daniel N. and David Simon. 2002. "Economic Conditions and Incumbent Support in Africa's New Democracies: Evidence from Zambia." *Comparative Political Studies* 35(3):313–336.

Prempeh, H. Kwasi. 2008. "Presidents Untamed." *Journal of Democracy* 19(2):109–123.

Radelet, Steven. 2010. *Emerging Africa: How 17 Countries Are Leading the Way*. Washington, DC: Brookings Institution Press.

Rathbone, Richard. 2000. *Nkrumah and the Chiefs: Politics of Chieftaincy in Ghana, 1951–1960*. Athens, OH: Ohio University Press.

Ravallion, Martin. 2009. "The Developing World's Bulging (but Vulnerable) 'Middle Class'." World Bank Policy Research Working Paper #4816.

Rawlings, Laura B. and Gloria M. Rubio. 2005. "Evaluating the Impact of Conditional Cash Transfer Programs." *The World Bank Research Observer* 20(1):29–55.

Reardon, Sean F. and David O'Sullivan. 2004. "Measures of Spatial Segregation." *Sociological Methodology* 34:121–162.

Reinikka, Ritva and Jakob Svensson. 2004. "Local Capture: Evidence from a Central Government Transfer Program in Uganda." *Quarterly Journal of Economics* 119(2):679–705.

"Rejection of NHIS Cards at Hospitals," *The Ghanaian Chronicle*, January 25, 2013.

Resnick, Danielle. 2011. "In the Shadow of the City: Africa's Urban Poor in Opposition Strongholds." *Journal of Modern African Studies* 49(1):141–166.
Resnick, Danielle. 2014. *Urban Poverty and Party Populism in African Democracies*. New York: Cambridge University Press.
Resnick, Danielle. 2015a. "The Middle Class and Democratic Consolidation in Zambia." *Journal of International Development* 27:693–715.
Resnick, Danielle. 2015b. "The Political Economy of Africa's Emergent Middle Class: Retrospect and Prospects." *Journal of International Development* 27:573–587.
Riedl, Rachel Beatty. 2014. *Authoritarian Origins of Democratic Party Systems in Africa*. New York: Cambridge University Press.
Robinson, Amanda Lea. 2014. "National Versus Ethnic Identification: Modernization, Colonial Legacy, and the Origins of Territorial Nationalism." *World Politics* 66:709–746.
Rosenstone, Steven J. and John Mark Hansen. 1993. *Mobilization, Participation, and Democracy in America*. New York: MacMillan.
Rueda, Miguel R. 2015. "Buying Votes with Imperfect Local Knowledge and a Secret Ballot." *Journal of Theoretical Politics* 27(3):428–456.
Sampson, Robert J. 2012. *Great American City: Chicago and the Enduring Neighborhood Effect*. Chicago, IL: University of Chicago Press.
Scheiner, Ethan. 2006. *Democracy without Competition in Japan: Opposition Failure in a One-Party Dominant State*. New York: Cambridge University Press.
Scheiner, Ethan. 2007. Clientelism in Japan: The Importance and Limits of Institutional Explanations. In *Patrons, Clients, and Policies: Patterns of Democratic Accountability and Political Competition*, ed. Herbert Kitschelt and Steven I. Wilkinson. New York: Cambridge University Press, pp. 276–297.
Schelling, Thomas C. 1971. "Dynamic Models of Segregation." *The Journal of Mathematical Sociology* 1(2):143–86.
Schildkrout, Enid. 1976. *People of the Zongo: The Transformation of Ethnic Identities in Ghana*. New York: Cambridge University Press.
Schneider, Mark A. 2017. "Do Brokers Know Their Voters? A Test of Guessability in India." Working Paper.
Scott, James C. 1969. "Corruption, Machine Politics, and Political Change." *American Political Science Review* 63:1142–1158.
Severino, Jean-Michel and Olivier Ray. 2011. *Africa's Moment*. Cambridge, MA: Polity Press.
Shefter, Martin. 1977. "Party and Patronage: Germany, England, and Italy." *Politics and Society* 7:403–451.
Shefter, Martin. 1994. *Political Parties and the State: the American Historical Experience*. Princeton, NJ: Princeton University Press.
Smith, David and Lucy Lamble. 2011. "Africa's Burgeoning Middle Class Brings Hope to a Continent," *The Guardian*, December 25.
Snyder, Richard. 2001. "Scaling Down: The Subnational Comparative Method." *Studies in Comparative International Development* 36(1):93–110.

Southall, Roger. 2014. "The Black Middle Class and Democracy in South Africa." *Journal of Modern African Studies* 52(4):647–670.

Stokes, Susan C. 2005. "Perverse Accountability: A Formal Model of Machine Politics with Evidence from Argentina." *American Political Science Review* 99(3):315–325.

Stokes, Susan C., Thad Dunning, Marcelo Nazareno, and Valeria Brusco. 2013. *Brokers, Voters, and Clientelism: The Puzzle of Distributive Politics*. New York: Cambridge University Press.

"Target Floating Voters – Amissah-Arthur Charges Campaign Team," *Ghana Web*, October 12, 2016.

"Teach the Foot Soldiers How to Fish," *Ghanaian Chronicle*, August 3, 2010.

Thachil, Tariq. 2014. *Elite Parties, Poor Voters: How Social Services Win Votes in India*. New York: Cambridge University Press.

African Development Bank. 2011. *The Middle of the Pyramid: Dynamics of the Middle Class in Africa*. www.afdb.org/fileadmin/uploads/afdb/Documents/Publications/The%20Middle%20of%20the%20Pyramid_The%20Middle%20of%20the%20Pyramid.pdf.

Thurlow, James, Danielle Resnick, and Dumebi Ubogu. 2015. "Matching Concepts with Measurement: Who Belongs to Africa's Middle Class?" *Journal of International Development* 27:588–608.

Tiebout, Charles M. 1956. "A Pure Theory of Local Expenditures." *Journal of Political Economy* 64(5):416–424.

Tilly, Charles. 1990. *Coercion, Capital, and European States: AD 990–1992*. Cambridge, MA: Wiley-Blackwell Publishers.

Trounstine, Jessica. 2008. *Political Monopolies in American Cities: The Rise and Fall of Bosses and Reformers*. Chicago, IL: University of Chicago Press.

UN-Habitat. 2010. "The State of African Cities 2010: Governance, Inequality, and Urban Land Markets." http://mirror.unhabitat.org/pmss/getElectronicVersion.aspx?nr=3034&alt=1.

UN-Habitat. 2014. "The State of African Cities 2014: Re-Imagining Sustainable Urban Transitions." http://unhabitat.org/books/state-of-african-cities-2014-re-imagining-sustainable-urban-transitions/.

United-Nations. 2014. "World Urbanization Prospects: The 2014 Revisions." Department of Economic and Social Affairs.

van de Walle, Nicolas. 2001. *African Economies and the Politics of the Permanent Crisis, 1979–1999*. New York: Cambridge University Press.

van de Walle, Nicolas. 2003. "Presidentialism and Clientelism in Africa's Emerging Party Systems." *Journal of Modern African Studies* 41(2):297–321.

van de Walle, Nicolas. 2007. Meet the New Boss, Same as the Old Boss? The Evolution of Political Clientelism in Africa. In *Patrons, Clients, and Policies: Patterns of Democratic Accountability and Political Competition*, ed. Herbert Kitschelt and Steven I. Wilkinson. Cambridge University Press, pp. 50–67.

Verba, Sidney, Kay Schlozman and Henry Brady. 1995. *Voice and Equality: Civic Voluntarism in American Politics*. Cambridge, MA: Harvard University Press.

Wahman, Michael and Catherine Boone. 2018. "Captured Countryside? Stability and Change in Sub-National Support for African Incumbent Parties." *Comparative Politics* 50(2):189–208.

Wallerstein, Immanuel. 1964. Voluntary Associations. In *Political Parties and National Integration in Tropical Africa*, ed. James Coleman and Carl G. Rosberg. Berkeley, CA: University of California Press, pp. 318–339.
Wantchekon, Leonard. 2003. "Clientelism and Voting Behavior: Evidence from a Field Experiment in Benin." *World Politics* 55(3):399–422.
Washington, Elvis. 2017. "We Won't Respect Non-Ga MCE – Tema Chiefs," *Citi FM Online*, March 27.
Weeks, John R., Allan G. Hill, Arthur Getis, and Douglas Stow. 2006. "Ethnic Residential Patterns as Predictors of Intra-Urban Child Mortality Inequality in Accra, Ghana." *Urban Geography* 27(6):526–548.
Weghorst, Keith R. and Staffan I. Lindberg. 2013. "What Drives the Swing Voter in Africa?" *American Journal of Political Science* 57(3):717–734.
Weiner, Myron. 1978. *Sons of the Soil: Migration and Ethnic Conflict in India*. Princeton, NJ: Princeton University Press.
Weitz-Shapiro, Rebecca. 2012. "What Wins Votes: Why Some Politicians Opt Out of Clientelism." *American Journal of Political Science* 56(3):568–583.
Weitz-Shapiro, Rebecca. 2014. *Curbing Clientelism in Argentina: Politics, Poverty, and Social Policy*. New York: Cambridge University Press.
Whyte, William F. 1955. *Street Corner Society: The Social Structure of an Italian Slum*. 2nd edn. Chicago, IL: University of Chicago Press.
Williams, Martin J. 2017. "The Political Economy of Unfinished Development Projects: Corruption, Clientelism, or Collective Choice?" *American Political Science Review* 111(4):705–723.
Wolfinger, Raymond E. and John Osgood Field. 1966. "Political Ethos and the Structure of City Government." *American Political Science Review* 60(2):306–326.
Wolfinger, Rayomnd E. 1972. "Why Political Machines Have Not Withered Away and Other Revisionist Thoughts." *Journal of Politics* 34(2):365–398.
Wolpe, Howard. 1974. *Urban Politics in Nigeria: A Study of Port Harcourt*. Berkeley, CA: University of California Press.
Wong, Cara, Jake Bowers, Tarah Williams, and Katherine Drake Simmons. 2012. "Bringing the Person Back In: Boundaries, Perceptions, and the Measurement of Racial Context." *Journal of Politics* 74(4):1153–1170.
World Bank, The. 2015. "Rising through Cities in Ghana: Ghana Urbanization Review Overview Report." The World Bank Group.
Wunsch, James S. 2001. "Decentralization, Local Governance, and 'Recentralization' in Africa." *Public Administration and Development* 21(1):277–288.
Yeboah, Ian E. A. 2008. "Ethnic Emancipation and Urban Land Claims: Disenfranchisement of the Ga of Accra, Ghana." *Geographic Research* 46(4):435–445.
Zakaria, Mahama. 2009. "NHIS Challenges Can Cripple Health Delivery – GMA Prez," *Public Agenda*, November 19.
Zucco Jr., Cesar. 2013. "When Payouts Pay Off: Conditional Cash Transfers and Voting Behavior in Brazil 2002–10." *American Journal of Political Science* 57(4):810–822.

Index

Accra, see Greater Accra
Accra Metropolitan Assembly, see AMA
administrative regions, 42
affective theories, see expressive theories
Africa, see Ghana; sub-Saharan Africa
Afrobarometer survey, 214, 217
Agbogbloshie (slum), 51, 59, 63
Akan (ethnic group), 41, 50, 65, 77–79, 192, 211, 220
Akuapem (Akan ethnic subgroup), 78
Akyem (Akan ethnic subgroup), 78
AMA (Accra Metropolitan Assembly), 43, 50, 54, 247, 264
Argentina, 116, 288
Ashaiman (slum), 63
  land rights, 59
Ashanti (Akan ethnic subgroup), 43
Ashanti Region, 78–79
autocracy
  transition from, 73–75
Ayawaso West, 63, 134, 292

basic services
  challenges to delivery, 5, 20, 52–54
  funding for, 53
  neighborhood-level variation, 20–21, 52–54, 65, 102–103
Brazil, 288, 289, 296
brokers
  distributive politics and, 15–16, 18–21, 32, 83, 176–177, 190–192

Bureaucratic Quality index, 72

campaign pledges, see also NDC; NPP
  credibility, 119–127, 129, 144
capture, see ethnic capture
CCT (conditional cash transfer), 288, 296, 298
chieftaincy/chiefs
  in rural areas, 16, 51, 176–177, 203–208
Chile
  dual appeals, 289, 301
  political credibility, 294
Chorkor, 51
civil service reform(s) (US), 29, 284
clientelism, see also nonprogrammatic politics; particularistic goods/preferences, 8, 11, 18
  as election strategy, 25–26, 182–187, 193–198, 203–206, 209
  clientelist brokers, 83, 176, 190–192
  club goods as, 22, 25, 164
  core ethnic groups and, 156–159, 181, 185–190, 198–199
  in slums, 21, 24, 162–164
  in the US, 279–286
  Latin America, 286–289
  local government, 248–251, 271–275
  neighborhood-level variation, 201–203
  political cost, 201–202
  relational, 160–163, 174, 190–192, 197
  role of chiefs, 16, 51, 176–177, 203–208

338

Index

club goods, *see also* distributive politics;
    voter behavior, 91–93, 98
  clientelism and, 22, 25, 164
  distribution of, 270–275
  study methodology for, 271
  vs. private goods, 167–168, 177,
    205–206, 208
conditional cash transfer, *see* CCT
contact theory/hypothesis, *see* social
    contact theory
core ethnic groups
  clientelism and, 156–159, 181, 185–190,
    198–199
core voter model, *see* voter models
credibility, 5, 6, 23, 107–111
  in distributive politics, 116–117,
    125–131, 144
  of campaign pledges, 119–127, 129, 144
  of MPs (Members of Parliament),
    133–135
  perceptions of, 128–130
  study methodology, 106, 128–129
cross-ethnic voting, 152, 221–225

Dangme (ethnic group), *see* Ga-Dangme
data sources
  2010 census, 48–50
  Afrobarometer survey, 214, 217
  Bureaucratic Quality index, 72
  DHS (Demographic Health Surveys), 9,
    48–49, 68–72
  district assembly election results,
    258–259
  embedded vignette experiment, 118,
    129–133
  focus groups, 35, 118
  interviews, 35, 106, 118
  party manifesto content analysis, 106,
    118
  representative survey data (urban, rural),
    35, 94–101, 117
  survey experiment, 35, 128
  wealth index, 198–200, 202
DCE, *see* District Chief Executive
decentralization, 110, 276
  impact of on Ghana, 292–304
  in Latin America, 287, 290, 301
demand-side factors, *see also*
    modernization theories, 89, 93, 178
  impact of, 293–296
  in new democracies, 33–35, 278

Demographic and Health Surveys, *see* DHS
demographics
  role of in urban African politics, 3–5,
    9–11, 21, 30
developing countries
  challenges to, 19–28
  programmatic politics, 3–6
DHS (Demographic and Health Surveys),
    9, 48–49, 68–70
differential abstention, 5, 24, 111–114,
    245
distributive politics, *see also*
    nonprogrammatic politics
  clientelist brokers, 83, 176, 190–192
  ethnic favoritism, 24–27, 32, 149–152,
    160, 164–168, 180–181, 255–258
  ethnic overrepresentation, 192–193,
    247, 253–254, 257, 264–265
  institutionalization of, 76, 81, 83,
    116–117
  neighborhood-level variation, 17–18, 26,
    94, 152–153, 193
  political cost of, 201–202
  programmatic, 4–7, 92, 119–120,
    134–135
  rural–urban differences, 203–208
district assemblies (local), 55, 74, 76,
    247–251, 255–258, 299
  voter approval of members, 265–268,
    270
District Chief Executive (DCE), 54, 74, 75,
    247–248, 299
dual appeals, 12, 63, 108, 111, 115–116,
    139
  Latin American success with, 279, 290,
    301

Eastern Region, 78–79, 204
education, *see* secondary education
ELAs (Electoral Areas), 54–60, 247
  spatial segregation by, 270
electoral competition, 24–26, 92, 182–190,
    193–197, 203–206, 208
  distributive politics, 79–84, 111,
    180–188
  ethnicity and, 8–9, 149–152
  programmatic vs. nonprogrammatic,
    4–7, 89–90, 104
electoral intermediaries, *see* brokers
electoral strategies, 92

clientelism as, 24–26, 164, 182–187, 193–200, 203–206
private goods as, 174, 182–188, 193–199, 205, 208–209
employment (Greater Accra)
as measure of socioeconomic class, 9–11, 47, 95
private vs. public, 49
English literacy
as measure of socioeconomic class, 9–11, 47, 95
Enumeration Areas (EA), 14–15, 56, 154
episodic "gift-giving", 174
ethnic affiliations, 76–79, 240–241, 297
voter behavior and, 211–213, 241–242
ethnic alignment, *see* ethnic affiliations
ethnic capture
of local government, 27, 254, 263–265, 276, 277
ethnic competition, 8–9, 149–152, 178
ethnic composition (Greater Accra), 50–52, 60
neighborhood-level variation, 64–65
ethnic favoritism
in distributive politics, 25–28, 32, 151, 160, 255–258
neighborhood-level variation, 22, 157, 164–168
study methodology, 225–227
voter expectations of, 161–164, 169, 174, 185–190, 208, 211–213
ethnic land rights/land use, 51, 59
ethnic migrant associations, 52
ethnic politics, *see also* distributive politics; voter behavior
capture (of local government), 27, 254, 263–265, 276, 277
expressive theories of, 13, 149, 157–159, 172, 242
fractionalization, 14–15, 152, 216, 219
instrumental theories, 15, 26–27, 31, 150, 156–158, 172
NDC (National Democratic Congress), 224, 226
neighborhood-level variation, 17–18, 26, 152, 153
relational clientelism and, 160, 164–168, 168
threat hypothesis, 154, 232, 253–254
ethnic voting, 76–80, 213, 226–230
in parliamentary elections, 225

neighborhood-level variation, 150–152, 214–224
study methodology for, 213–216
ethnically aligned voters, *see* ethnic voting
ethnicity
electoral competition and, 8–9, 149–152
party affiliations and, 76–79, 81, 220, 222–224, 226
party favoritism for core, 157–159, 185–190, 199–200, 201
voter behavior and, 26, 79–80, 152–153
Ewe (ethnic group), 50, 78, 220
expressive theories
of ethnic politics, 13, 149, 157–159, 172, 242
vs. instrumental theories, 15, 26–27, 31, 150, 156–158, 172
expressive voting, 242

Fanti (ethnic group), 79
favoritism, *see* ethnic favoritism
fractionalization, 14–15, 64, 152, 216, 219

Ga (ethnic group), 40, 50, 51, 64, 78
characteristics unique to, 236–240
political overrepresentation by, 247, 253–258, 264–265, 271–275
Ga Mashie, 51, 239
Ga-Dangme (ethno-linguistic group), 42, 50, 78
Gbawe
socioeconomic growth of, 40–42
GDP growth rates (sub-Saharan Africa), 66
generational change
in voting behavior, 295
Ghana, 4, 41–43
interethnic assimilation, 15, 149
interethnic assimilation vs. US, 29, 283, 295
political system, 73–76
size of middle class, 68
supply-side factors, 296–302
vs. US and Latin America, 290
Great Migration (US), 283
Greater Accra, *see also* middle class; urbanization, 4
administrative districts, 43, 54
demographic changes, 40
ethnic composition, 50–52, 64–65
history of, 40, 43
infrastructure, 52–54

political structure, 54–56, 247–251
socioeconomic growth of, 40–43

housing
  expansion of middle class, 41
  neighborhood-level variation, 21, 54, 59–60, 163–164, 202
  voter behavior and, 235–236

identity-based voting, 157–158
industrialization
  Ghana vs. Western democracies, 49
infrastructure
  government provision of, 52–54
instrumental benefits
  voters' expectations of, 242
instrumental theories
  ethnic politics and, 15, 26–27, 31, 150–158, 172
  vs. expressive theories, 13, 149, 157–159, 172, 242
interethnic assimilation
  Ghana, 15, 149
  Ghana vs. US, 29, 283, 295
intra-urban variation, see neighborhood-level variation

Jamestown (slum), 63
  land rights of, 59

Kenya
  co-ethnic voting, 77, 296
Konkomba (ethnic group), 79
Kufuor, John, 265
Kumasi, 78

Lagos (Nigeria), 254
land rights/land use, see ethnic land rights/land use
Latin America
  clientelism, 286–289
  programmatic transitions, 279, 286–290
LEAP (Livelihood Empowerment Against Poverty program), 296
linkages, see dual appeals
Livelihood Empowerment Against Poverty program, see LEAP
local agents/party agents, 75, 83, 162, 163, 190–193
local elections
  voter behavior in, 246–247

local government
  clientelism, 248–251, 271–275
  ethnic capture of, 27, 254, 263–265, 276, 277
  turnout inequality, 246–247, 251–254, 260–265, 275–276

machine era/machine politics (US), 29, 280–286
Madina Zongo, 51
Mahama, John Dramani, 78, 125, 127
MCE (Metropolitan Chief Executive), see District Chief Executive
media
  political reporting of, 13, 16, 184, 187, 188
  voter behavior and, 232
median voter theory, 12, 114–115
Members of Parliament, see MPs
methodology, see study methodology
Metropolitan Chief Executive (MCE), see District Chief Executive
Mexico, 288, 289, 298
middle class, see also ethnicity; Greater Accra; urban politics
  demographics, 3–4, 9–11, 21
  distribution, 48–49, 58
  ethnic composition, 63–65
  forms of employment, 49
  housing-based definitions, 46
  income-based definitions, 45–46
  size of, 68
  socioeconomic-based definition, 9–11, 47
  voter mobilization, 135–137
Mills, John Evans Atta, 79
mixed appeals, see dual appeals
mobilization, see voter mobilization
modernization theories, 12–14, 16–18, 33, 149, 153, 212, 216, 305
  of programmatic politics, 3–7, 89, 105
MPs (Members of Parliament), 73–74, 76, 133
  patronage benefits by, 187–188
municipal government, see local government
Muslims, 50, 78

National Democratic Congress, see NDC
national elections
  "winner-take-all", 74, 82, 300

National Youth Employment Programme, *see* NYEP
NDC (National Democratic Congress), *see also* clientelism; distributive politics; electoral strategies
  campaign pledges, 119–127, 129
  ethnic affiliations, 78–82, 192, 210, 213, 220
  ethnic politics and, 75–82, 224, 226
  manifesto analysis, 119–126
neighborhood wealth, 216–220
  voter mobilization by, 134–137
neighborhood wealth index
  goods distribution by, 193–199
neighborhood-level variation, *see also* distributive politics
  clientelism, 201–203
  ethnic favoritism, 157, 164–168
  ethnic politics, 17–18, 26, 152–153
  ethnic voting, 150–152, 214–224
  ethnicity, 63–65
  housing, 21, 54, 59–60, 163–164
  in basic services, 20–21, 52–54, 65
  in socioeconomic class(es), 58–64, 201–203
  in urban politics, 17–18
  preferences, 90
  private goods distribution, 193–199
  within Electoral Areas, 59
neighborhoods
  defining, 54–57
  variation, 59–63, 134–137
New Deal (US), 29, 285, 288, 297
new democracies
  challenges to, 19–28, 107–109
  characteristics of, 20–22, 36
  demand-side vs. supply-side factors, 33–35, 278
  growth of middle class, 3, 11
  programmatic politics, 3–6
New Patriotic Party, *see* NPP
Nima (slum), 51, 63, 190
  land rights of, 59
nonprogrammatic politics, *see also* clientelism; distributive politics, 242
  dominance of, 106–107, 144–145, 245
  vs. programmatic politics, 4–7, 89–90, 104
Northern ethnic groups, 50, 52, 78

NPP (New Patriotic Party), *see also* clientelism; distributive politics; electoral strategies, 75–77
  campaign pledges, 119–127
  ethnic affiliations, 78–82, 192, 210, 213, 220
  manifesto analysis, 119–126
NYEP (National Youth Employment Programme), 128

Odododiodioo, 63, 239
Old Fadama (Agbogbloshie), 51
organizational capacity (parties), 75–78, 83, 113, 163, 190–193

parliamentary constituencies, 43
  ethnic composition, 60–63
  ethnic voting, 225
  middle class size, 63
particularistic goods/preferences, 22
  distribution of, 167–168, 174, 181–188, 193–197
  private vs. club, 167–168, 177, 205–206, 208
  vs. universalistic, 89–93
patronage-based politics, *see also* clientelism; distributive politics; nonprogrammatic politics, 187–190
pledges, *see* campaign pledges
PNDC (Provisional National Defense Council), 75
policy rhetoric, 24, 114, 119
policy-based competition, 111
policy-based politics, *see* programmatic politics
political change
  demand-side vs. supply-side theories of, 33–35, 278, 304
political competition, 84
  programmatic vs. nonprogrammatic, 7
political credibility, *see* credibility
political participation, 5, 33, 104
  class-based differences, 24, 112–114, 139–143
  differential abstention, 24, 111–114, 245
  local turnout inequality, 245–246, 251–254, 260–265, 275–276
political parties, *see also* clientelism; nonprogrammatic politics, distributive politics, 78, 180–188, 192–197
  campaign pledges of, 119–127, 129, 144

credibility of, 116–117, 125–131, 144
electoral competition, 80, 84, 111
ethnic alignment of, 78–82
in rural areas, 177, 203–209
institutionalization, 75–76, 83, 116–117
relational clientelism and, 159–163, 174, 190–193, 197
structure, 75–76, 83, 113, 163, 190–193
voter expectations of, 26–27, 110–111, 158, 174, 185–190, 208, 211–213, 226–230
voter mobilization by, 134–138
political structure (Accra), 54–56
political system (Ghana), 73–76, 76
"winner-take-all", 82
preferences
effect of socioeconomic class on, 89–91, 100–104
neighbor-hood level variation, 90
universalistic vs. particularistic, 89–93, 104
private goods, 97–100
as election strategy, 174, 181–188, 193–199, 205–209
neighborhood-level variation, 193, 199
relational clientelism vs. episodic "gift-giving", 160–161, 193, 197
programmatic politics, *see also* universalistic preferences
electoral competition and, 4–7, 7, 92–94, 119–120, 134–135
Ghana vs. Latin America, 287
Ghana vs. the US, 280–282
in developing countries, 3–6
policy rhetoric, 24, 114, 119
policy-based competition, 111
vs. nonprogrammatic politics, 4–7, 89–90, 91, 104
weakness of, 23–25, 105
Provisional National Defense Council, *see* PNDC

Rawlings, Jerry John, 75, 78, 80
relational clientelism
ethnic politics and, 160, 164–168
political parties and, 159–161, 163, 174, 190–193, 197
US transition to, 281
vs. episodic "gift-giving", 160–161, 193, 197
resource allocation

favoritism in, 74, 275
rhetoric, *see* policy rhetoric
rural areas
club vs. private goods distribution, 177
distributive politics, 175–177, 203–209
role of chiefs, 16, 51, 176–177, 203–208
voter behavior and, 233–234
vs. urban areas, 9, 203
rural–urban migration, 30, 43, 50, 233–234

Sabon Zongo, 51
scarcity of services, 20–21, 65, 111
secondary education
as measure of socioeconomic class, 9–11, 47, 95
segregation
benefits of socioeconomic, 293–294
neighborhood ethnic, 21
services, *see* basic services
slums, *see also* distributive politics; middle class; preferences
clientelism in, 21, 24, 162–164
urban population growth and, 59–63
social contact theory, 4, 15–16, 154
voter behavior and, 231–232
social welfare programs
Bolsa Família (Brazil), 288, 296
Progresa (Mexico), 288, 298
implementing in Ghana, 296–298
LEAP (Ghana), 298
socioeconomic class, *see also* middle class; neighborhoods; slums
effect of on preferences, 89–91, 100–104
measures of, 9–11, 47
neighborhood-level variation, 59–64, 201–203
voter mobilization by, 134–137
spatial models/spatial segregation, 114, 268–270, 293
state capacity, 20, 109, 125–127, 291
state presence, 21, 54, 90
study methodology, 35–38, 40
campaign mobilization, 133–135, 138
defining "neighborhood", 54–59
defining middle class, 9–10
ethnic voting, 213–216
favoritism expectations, 226–227
Ga voting behavior, 236–241
local club goods distribution, 271, 274
manifesto content analysis, 106, 118

particularistic vs. universalistic preferences, 94–97, 100–104
party credibility, 106, 128–130
private goods distribution, 193, 197–200
turnout inequality, 141–143, 258–259, 264
voter approval, 265–270
sub-Saharan Africa
rural vs. urban areas, 9, 203
urban growth across, 3–7, 65–73, 304
supply-side factors, *see also* modernization theories, 33–35, 104, 107–108, 151, 178
impact of, 296–304
in new democracies, 278, 287
swing voter model, *see* voter models

tax redistribution
impact of, 33, 142–143
threat hypothesis
in ethnic politics, 154, 232, 253–254
traditional elites, *see* chieftaincy/chiefs
Tudu, 51
turnout inequality, 24, 112–114, 139–143
in local government elections, 245–247, 251–254, 260–265, 275–276
study methodology, 139, 143, 258–259, 264

United States (US)
demise of clientelism, 282–286
explicit vote-buying, 281
interethnic assimilation, 29, 283, 295
machine era/machine politics, 29, 279–286
New Deal, 29, 285, 288, 297
transition to relational clientelism, 281
universalistic preferences, 97–103, 108–109, 288
vs. particularistic, 89–93
urban growth (sub-Saharan Africa), 3–7, 65–73, 304
urban middle class, *see* middle class
urban planning
extent of, 60, 65
urban politics, *see also* expressive theories; instrumental theories, 4–6, 22–28, 30
expected transformation of, 3–4
neighbor-hood level variation, 17–18

role of demographics, 3–5, 9–11, 21, 30
role of scarcity, 20–21, 111
state capacity and, 19, 109, 125–128
urbanization, 4, 20, 49, 179
slums as outcome of, 59–60
Ushertown, 51

valence issues
campaign pledges on, 120–124
voter behavior
"blackmail" of parties, 189
by ethnic party affiliations, 211–213, 241–242
ethnicity and, 26, 79–80, 152–153
Ga-specific, 236–241
generational change, 295
Ghana vs. US, 154
housing constraints and, 235–236
in local elections, 245–247
media impact on, 232
politicians' impressions of, 133–135
predictions for, 169–175, 216–221
resource allocation and, 74
rural ties and, 233–234
social contact theory and, 231–232
urban slums vs. rural areas, 175–178, 208
voter expectations
of ethnic favoritism, 161–164, 169, 174, 185–190, 208, 211
of instrumental benefits, 242
of political parties, 26–27, 110–111, 158, 174, 185–190, 208, 211–213, 226–230
voter mobilization
by socioeconomic class, 134–138
political cost of, 28, 108, 111–114, 162–163
voter models, 157–158, 173–174

wealth index, 154, 197, 202
wealthy elites, 48, 89, 93, 94
welfare state (US), 284–286

youth associations, *see* ethnic migrant associations

Zongo neighborhoods ("foreigner's quarters"), 50, 64, 79

Other Books in the Series (continued from page ii)

Laia Balcells, *Rivalry and Revenge: The Politics of Violence during Civil War*
Lisa Baldez, *Why Women Protest? Women's Movements in Chile*
Kate Baldwin, *The Paradox of Traditional Chiefs in Democratic Africa*
Stefano Bartolini, *The Political Mobilization of the European Left, 1860–1980: The Class Cleavage*
Robert Bates, *When Things Fell Apart: State Failure in Late-Century Africa*
Mark Beissinger, *Nationalist Mobilization and the Collapse of the Soviet State*
Pablo Beramendi, *The Political Geography of Inequality: Regions and Redistribution*
Nancy Bermeo, ed., *Unemployment in the New Europe*
Carles Boix, *Democracy and Redistribution*
Carles Boix, *Political Order and Inequality: Their Foundations and Their Consequences for Human Welfare*
Carles Boix, *Political Parties, Growth, and Equality: Conservative and Social Democratic Economic Strategies in the World Economy*
Catherine Boone, *Merchant Capital and the Roots of State Power in Senegal, 1930–1985*
Catherine Boone, *Political Topographies of the African State: Territorial Authority and Institutional Change*
Catherine Boone, *Property and Political Order in Africa: Land Rights and the Structure of Politics*
Michael Bratton and Nicolas van de Walle, *Democratic Experiments in Africa: Regime Transitions in Comparative Perspective*
Michael Bratton, Robert Mattes, and E. Gyimah-Boadi, *Public Opinion, Democracy, and Market Reform in Africa*
Valerie Bunce, *Leaving Socialism and Leaving the State: The End of Yugoslavia, the Soviet Union, and Czechoslovakia*
Daniele Caramani, *The Nationalization of Politics: The Formation of National Electorates and Party Systems in Europe*
John M. Carey, *Legislative Voting and Accountability*
Kanchan Chandra, *Why Ethnic Parties Succeed: Patronage and Ethnic Headcounts in India*
Eric C. C. Chang, Mark Andreas Kayser, Drew A. Linzer, and Ronald Rogowski, *Electoral Systems and the Balance of Consumer-Producer Power*
José Antonio Cheibub, *Presidentialism, Parliamentarism, and Democracy*
Ruth Berins Collier, *Paths toward Democracy: The Working Class and Elites in Western Europe and South America*
Daniel Corstange, *The Price of a Vote in the Middle East: Clientelism and Communal Politics in Lebanon and Yemen*
Pepper D. Culpepper, *Quiet Politics and Business Power: Corporate Control in Europe and Japan*
Sarah Zukerman Daly, *Organized Violence after Civil War: The Geography of Recruitment in Latin America*
Christian Davenport, *State Repression and the Domestic Democratic Peace*

Donatella della Porta, *Social Movements, Political Violence, and the State*
Alberto Diaz-Cayeros, *Federalism, Fiscal Authority, and Centralization in Latin America*
Alberto Diaz-Cayeros, Federico Estévez, and Beatriz Magaloni, *The Political Logic of Poverty Relief: Electoral Strategies and Social Policy in Mexico*
Jesse Driscoll, *Warlords and Coalition Politics in Post-Soviet States*
Thad Dunning, *Crude Democracy: Natural Resource Wealth and Political Regimes*
Thad Dunning et al., *Information, Accountability, and Cumulative Learning: Lessons from Metaketa I*
Gerald Easter, *Reconstructing the State: Personal Networks and Elite Identity*
Margarita Estevez-Abe, *Welfare and Capitalism in Postwar Japan: Party, Bureaucracy, and Business*
Henry Farrell, *The Political Economy of Trust: Institutions, Interests, and Inter-Firm Cooperation in Italy and Germany*
Karen E. Ferree, *Framing the Race in South Africa: The Political Origins of Racial Census Elections*
M. Steven Fish, *Democracy Derailed in Russia: The Failure of Open Politics*
Robert F. Franzese, *Macroeconomic Policies of Developed Democracies*
Roberto Franzosi, *The Puzzle of Strikes: Class and State Strategies in Postwar Italy*
Timothy Frye, *Building States and Markets after Communism: The Perils of Polarized Democracy*
Geoffrey Garrett, *Partisan Politics in the Global Economy*
Scott Gehlbach, *Representation through Taxation: Revenue, Politics, and Development in Postcommunist States*
Edward L. Gibson, *Boundary Control: Subnational Authoritarianism in Federal Democracies*
Jane R. Gingrich, *Making Markets in the Welfare State: The Politics of Varying Market Reforms*
Miriam Golden, *Heroic Defeats: The Politics of Job Loss*
Jeff Goodwin, *No Other Way Out: States and Revolutionary Movements*
Merilee Serrill Grindle, *Changing the State*
Anna Grzymala-Busse, *Rebuilding Leviathan: Party Competition and State Exploitation in Post-Communist Democracies*
Anna Grzymala-Busse, *Redeeming the Communist Past: The Regeneration of Communist Parties in East Central Europe*
Frances Hagopian, *Traditional Politics and Regime Change in Brazil*
Mark Hallerberg and Rolf Ranier Strauch, Jürgen von Hagen, *Fiscal Governance in Europe*
Henry E. Hale, *The Foundations of Ethnic Politics: Separatism of States and Nations in Eurasia and the World*
Stephen E. Hanson, *Post-Imperial Democracies: Ideology and Party Formation in Third Republic France, Weimar Germany, and Post-Soviet Russia*
Michael Hechter, *Alien Rule*
Timothy Hellwig, *Globalization and Mass Politics: Retaining the Room to Maneuver*

Gretchen Helmke, *Courts under Constraints: Judges, Generals, and Presidents in Argentina*
Gretchen Helmke, *Institutions on the Edge: The Origins and Consequences of Inter-Branch Crises in Latin America*
Yoshiko Herrera, *Imagined Economies: The Sources of Russian Regionalism*
Alisha C. Holland, *Forbearance as Redistribution: The Politics of Informal Welfare in Latin America*
J. Rogers Hollingsworth and Robert Boyer, eds., *Contemporary Capitalism: The Embeddedness of Institutions*
John D. Huber, *Exclusion by Elections: Inequality, Ethnic Identity, and Democracy*
John D. Huber and Charles R. Shipan, *Deliberate Discretion? The Institutional Foundations of Bureaucratic Autonomy*
Ellen Immergut, *Health Politics: Interests and Institutions in Western Europe*
Torben Iversen, *Capitalism, Democracy, and Welfare*
Torben Iversen, *Contested Economic Institutions*
Torben Iversen, Jonas Pontussen, and David Soskice, eds., *Unions, Employers, and Central Banks: Macroeconomic Coordination and Institutional Change in Social Market Economics*
Thomas Janoski and Alexander M. Hicks, eds., *The Comparative Political Economy of the Welfare State*
Joseph Jupille, *Procedural Politics: Issues, Influence, and Institutional Choice in the European Union*
Karen Jusko, *Who Speaks for the Poor? Electoral Geography, Party Entry, and Representation*
Stathis Kalyvas, *The Logic of Violence in Civil War*
Stephen B. Kaplan, *Globalization and Austerity Politics in Latin America*
David C. Kang, *Crony Capitalism: Corruption and Capitalism in South Korea and the Philippines*
Junko Kato, *Regressive Taxation and the Welfare State*
Orit Kedar, *Voting for Policy, Not Parties: How Voters Compensate for Power Sharing*
Robert O. Keohane and Helen B. Milner, eds., *Internationalization and Domestic Politics*
Herbert Kitschelt, *The Transformation of European Social Democracy*
Herbert Kitschelt, Kirk A. Hawkins, Juan Pablo Luna, Guillermo Rosas, and Elizabeth J. Zechmeister, *Latin American Party Systems*
Herbert Kitschelt, Peter Lange, Gary Marks, and John D. Stephens, eds., *Continuity and Change in Contemporary Capitalism*
Herbert Kitschelt, Zdenka Mansfeldova, Radek Markowski, and Gabor Toka, *Post-Communist Party Systems*
David Knoke, Franz Urban Pappi, Jeffrey Broadbent, and Yutaka Tsujinaka, eds., *Comparing Policy Networks*
Ken Kollman, *Perils of Centralization: Lessons from Church, State, and Corporation*
Allan Kornberg and Harold D. Clarke, *Citizens and Community: Political Support in a Representative Democracy*

Amie Kreppel, *The European Parliament and the Supranational Party System*
David D. Laitin, *Language Repertoires and State Construction in Africa*
Fabrice E. Lehoucq and Ivan Molina, *Stuffing the Ballot Box: Fraud, Electoral Reform, and Democratization in Costa Rica*
Benjamin Lessing *Making Peace in Drug Wars: Crackdowns and Cartels in Latin America*
Mark Irving Lichbach and Alan S. Zuckerman, eds., *Comparative Politics: Rationality, Culture, and Structure*, 2nd edition
Evan Lieberman, *Race and Regionalism in the Politics of Taxation in Brazil and South Africa*
Richard M. Locke, *The Promise and Limits of Private Power: Promoting Labor Standards in a Global Economy*
Julia Lynch, *Age in the Welfare State: The Origins of Social Spending on Pensioners, Workers, and Children*
Pauline Jones Luong, *Institutional Change and Political Continuity in Post-Soviet Central Asia*
Pauline Jones Luong and Erika Weinthal, *Oil Is Not a Curse: Ownership Structure and Institutions in Soviet Successor States*
Doug McAdam, John McCarthy, and Mayer Zald, eds., *Comparative Perspectives on Social Movements*
Lauren M. MacLean, *Informal Institutions and Citizenship in Rural Africa: Risk and Reciprocity in Ghana and Côte d'Ivoire*
Beatriz Magaloni, *Voting for Autocracy: Hegemonic Party Survival and Its Demise in Mexico*
James Mahoney, *Colonialism and Postcolonial Development: Spanish America in Comparative Perspective*
James Mahoney and Dietrich Rueschemeyer, eds., *Historical Analysis and the Social Sciences*
Scott Mainwaring and Matthew Soberg Shugart, eds., *Presidentialism and Democracy in Latin America*
Melanie Manion, *Information for Autocrats: Representation in Chinese Local Congresses*
Isabela Mares, *From Open Secrets to Secret Voting: Democratic Electoral Reforms and Voter Autonomy*
Isabela Mares, *The Politics of Social Risk: Business and Welfare State Development*
Isabela Mares, *Taxation, Wage Bargaining, and Unemployment*
Cathie Jo Martin and Duane Swank, *The Political Construction of Business Interests: Coordination, Growth, and Equality*
Anthony W. Marx, *Making Race, Making Nations: A Comparison of South Africa, the United States, and Brazil*
Bonnie M. Meguid, *Party Competition between Unequals: Strategies and Electoral Fortunes in Western Europe*
Joel S. Migdal, *State in Society: Studying How States and Societies Constitute One Another*
Joel S. Migdal, Atul Kohli, and Vivienne Shue, eds., *State Power and Social Forces: Domination and Transformation in the Third World*

Scott Morgenstern and Benito Nacif, eds., *Legislative Politics in Latin America*
Kevin M. Morrison, *Nontaxation and Representation: The Fiscal Foundations of Political Stability*
Layna Mosley, *Global Capital and National Governments*
Layna Mosley, *Labor Rights and Multinational Production*
Wolfgang C. Müller and Kaare Strøm, *Policy, Office, or Votes?*
Maria Victoria Murillo, *Labor Unions, Partisan Coalitions, and Market Reforms in Latin America*
Maria Victoria Murillo, *Political Competition, Partisanship, and Policy Making in Latin American Public Utilities*
Monika Nalepa, *Skeletons in the Closet: Transitional Justice in Post-Communist Europe*
Noah L. Nathan, *Electoral Politics and Africa's Urban Transition: Class and Ethnicity in Ghana*
Ton Notermans, *Money, Markets, and the State: Social Democratic Economic Policies since 1918*
Simeon Nichter, *Votes for Survival: Relational Clientelism in Latin America*
Richard A. Nielsen, *Deadly Clerics: Blocked Ambition and the Paths to Jihad*
Aníbal Pérez-Liñán, *Presidential Impeachment and the New Political Instability in Latin America*
Roger D. Petersen, *Understanding Ethnic Violence: Fear, Hatred, and Resentment in 20th Century Eastern Europe*
Roger D. Petersen, *Western Intervention in the Balkans: The Strategic Use of Emotion in Conflict*
Simona Piattoni, ed., *Clientelism, Interests, and Democratic Representation*
Paul Pierson, *Dismantling the Welfare State? Reagan, Thatcher, and the Politics of Retrenchment*
Marino Regini, *Uncertain Boundaries: The Social and Political Construction of European Economies*
Kenneth M. Roberts, *Changing Course in Latin America: Party Systems in the Neoliberal Era*
Marc Howard Ross, *Cultural Contestation in Ethnic Conflict*
Roger Schoenman, *Networks and Institutions in Europe's Emerging Markets*
David Rueda and Daniel Stegmueller *Who Wants What? Redistribution Preferences in Comparative Perspective*
Ben Ross Schneider, *Hierarchical Capitalism in Latin America: Business, Labor, and the Challenges of Equitable Development*
Lyle Scruggs, *Sustaining Abundance: Environmental Performance in Industrial Democracies*
Jefferey M. Sellers, *Governing from Below: Urban Regions and the Global Economy*
Yossi Shain and Juan Linz, eds., *Interim Governments and Democratic Transitions*
Beverly Silver, *Forces of Labor: Workers' Movements and Globalization since 1870*
Prerna Singh, *How Solidarity Works for Welfare: Subnationalism and Social Development in India*

Theda Skocpol, *Social Revolutions in the Modern World*
Austin Smith et al, *Selected Works of Michael Wallerstein*
Regina Smyth, *Candidate Strategies and Electoral Competition in the Russian Federation: Democracy without Foundation*
Richard Snyder, *Politics after Neoliberalism: Reregulation in Mexico*
David Stark and László Bruszt, *Postsocialist Pathways: Transforming Politics and Property in East Central Europe*
Sven Steinmo, *The Evolution of Modern States: Sweden, Japan, and the United States*
Sven Steinmo, Kathleen Thelen, and Frank Longstreth, eds., *Structuring Politics: Historical Institutionalism in Comparative Analysis*
Susan C. Stokes, *Mandates and Democracy: Neoliberalism by Surprise in Latin America*
Susan C. Stokes, ed., *Public Support for Market Reforms in New Democracies*
Susan C. Stokes, Thad Dunning, Marcelo Nazareno, and Valeria Brusco, *Brokers, Voters, and Clientelism: The Puzzle of Distributive Politics*
Milan W. Svolik, *The Politics of Authoritarian Rule*
Duane Swank, *Global Capital, Political Institutions, and Policy Change in Developed Welfare States*
Sidney Tarrow, *Power in Movement: Social Movements and Contentious Politics*
Sidney Tarrow, *Power in Movement: Social Movements and Contentious Politics, Revised and Updated Third Edition*
Tariq Thachil, *Elite Parties, Poor Voters: How Social Services Win Votes in India*
Kathleen Thelen, *How Institutions Evolve: The Political Economy of Skills in Germany, Britain, the United States, and Japan*
Kathleen Thelen, *Varieties of Liberalization and the New Politics of Social Solidarity*
Charles Tilly, *Trust and Rule*
Daniel Treisman, *The Architecture of Government: Rethinking Political Decentralization*
Guillermo Trejo, *Popular Movements in Autocracies: Religion, Repression, and Indigenous Collective Action in Mexico*
Rory Truex, *Making Autocracy Work: Representation and Responsiveness in Modern China*
Lily Lee Tsai, *Accountability without Democracy: How Solidary Groups Provide Public Goods in Rural China*
Joshua Tucker, *Regional Economic Voting: Russia, Poland, Hungary, Slovakia and the Czech Republic, 1990–1999*
Ashutosh Varshney, *Democracy, Development, and the Countryside*
Yuhua Wang, *Tying the Autocrat's Hand: The Rise of the Rule of Law in China*
Jeremy M. Weinstein, *Inside Rebellion: The Politics of Insurgent Violence*
Stephen I. Wilkinson, *Votes and Violence: Electoral Competition and Ethnic Riots in India*
Andreas Wimmer, *Waves of War: Nationalism, State Formation, and Ethnic Exclusion in the Modern World*
Jason Wittenberg, *Crucibles of Political Loyalty: Church Institutions and Electoral Continuity in Hungary*

Elisabeth J. Wood, *Forging Democracy from Below: Insurgent Transitions in South Africa and El Salvador*
Elisabeth J. Wood, *Insurgent Collective Action and Civil War in El Salvador*
Deborah J. Yashar, *Homicidal Ecologies: Illicit Economies and Complicit States in Latin America*
Daniel Ziblatt, *Conservative Parties and the Birth of Democracy*

Lightning Source UK Ltd.
Milton Keynes UK
UKHW010639040720
365959UK00001B/8